AMERICA AFTER THE FALL

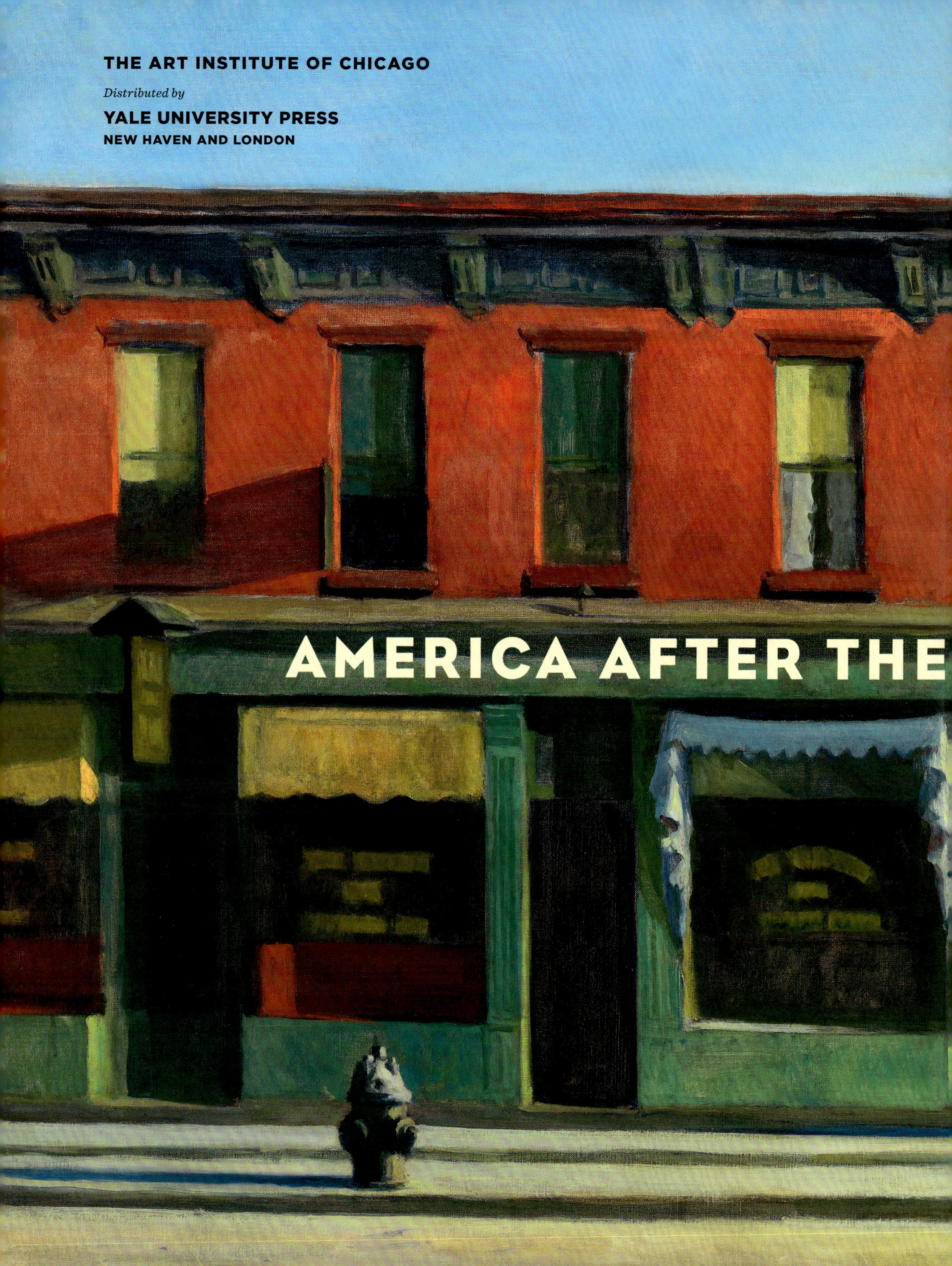

THE ART INSTITUTE OF CHICAGO
Distributed by
YALE UNIVERSITY PRESS
NEW HAVEN AND LONDON
AMERICA AFTER THE

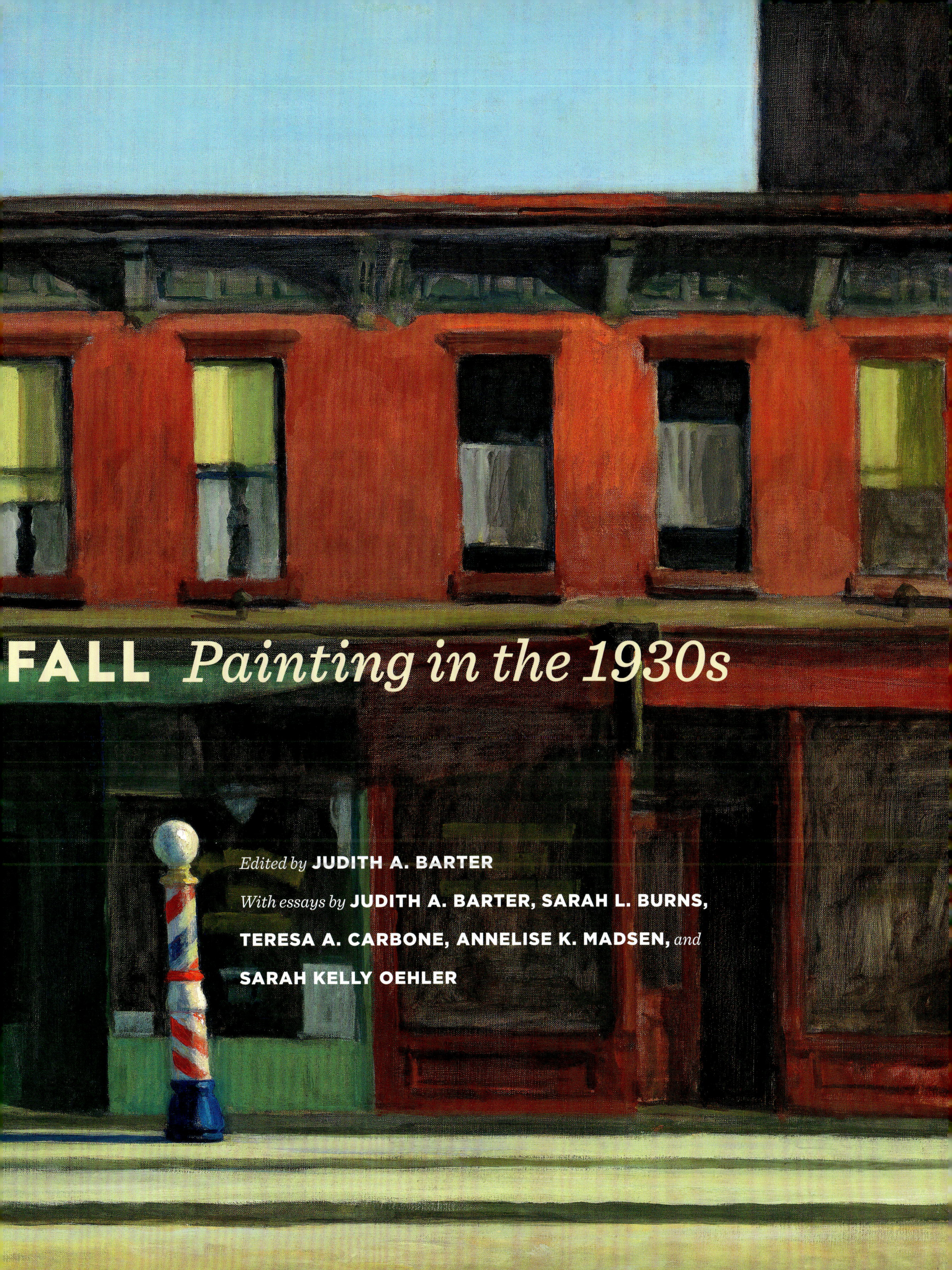

FALL Painting in the 1930s
Edited by JUDITH A. BARTER
With essays by JUDITH A. BARTER, SARAH L. BURNS,
TERESA A. CARBONE, ANNELISE K. MADSEN, and
SARAH KELLY OEHLER

*America after the Fall: Painting in the 1930s* was published in conjunction with an exhibition of the same title organized by the Art Institute of Chicago.

*Exhibition Dates*

The Art Institute of Chicago
June 5 to September 18, 2016

Musée de l'Orangerie, Paris
October 15, 2016, to January 30, 2017

Royal Academy of Arts, London
February 25 to June 4, 2017



First edition
Printed in Italy

Hardcover ISBN: 978-0-300-21485-7
UK softcover ISBN: 978-1-910350-59-1

Published by
The Art Institute of Chicago
111 South Michigan Avenue
Chicago, Illinois 60603-6404
www.artic.edu

Distributed by
Yale University Press
302 Temple Street
P.O. Box 209040
New Haven, Connecticut
   06520-9040
www.yalebooks.com/art

Produced by the Department of Publishing, the Art Institute of Chicago, Sarah E. Guernsey, Executive Director

Edited by Kate Steinmann and Greg Nosan

Production by Joseph Mohan and Lauren Makholm

Photography research by Katie Levi

Unless otherwise noted, photography of works of art is by Robert Lifson, Bob Hashimoto, and Chris Gallagher, with postproduction by Jonathan Mathias, Department of Imaging, the Art Institute of Chicago.

Indexing by Theresa Duran

Proofreading by Juliet Clark

Design and typesetting by Joan Sommers, Glue + Paper Workshop, Chicago

Printing, binding, and separations by Graphicom, Verona

This book was made using paper and materials certified by the Forest Stewardship Council, which ensures responsible forest management.

Library of Congress Cataloging-in-Publication Data

Names: Barter, Judith A., 1951– editor. | Art Institute of Chicago organizer, host institution. | Musée de l'Orangerie, host institution. | Royal Academy of Arts (Great Britain), host institution.

Title: America after the fall : painting in the 1930s / Edited by Judith A. Barter ; With essays by Judith A. Barter, Sarah L. Burns, Teresa A. Carbone, Annelise K. Madsen, and Sarah Kelly Oehler.

Description: First edition. | Chicago : The Art Institute of Chicago, 2016. |
   Includes bibliographical references.

Identifiers: LCCN 2016009063
ISBN 9780300214857 (hardback)
ISBN 9780865592827 (softcover)

Subjects: LCSH: Painting, American—20th century—Exhibitions. | National characteristics, American, in art—Exhibitions. | Art and society—United States—History—20th century—Exhibitions. | BISAC: ART / American / General. | ART / History / Modern (late 19th Century to 1945). | ART / Collections, Catalogs, Exhibitions / Group Shows.

Classification: LCC ND212 .A4478 2016 | DDC 759.13—dc23

LC record available at http://lccn.loc.gov/2016009063

Details: pp. 2–3: Edward Hopper, *Early Sunday Morning*, 1930 (cat. 22); pp. 12–13: Charles Sheeler, *Classic Landscape*, 1931 (cat. 44); pp. 26–27: Grant Wood, *Fall Plowing*, 1931 (cat. 48); pp. 54–55: Arthur Dove, *Swing Music*, 1938 (cat. 15); pp. 86–87: Grant Wood, *The Midnight Ride of Paul Revere*, 1931 (cat. 49); pp. 114–15: Federico Castellón, *The Dark Figure*, 1938 (cat. 8); pp. 144–45: Paul Cadmus, *The Fleet's In!*, 1934 (cat. 7); pp. 172–73: Jackson Pollock, *Untitled*, c. 1938/41 (cat. 39); pp. 182–83: Ilya Bolotowsky, *Study for the Hall of Medical Sciences Mural at the 1939 World's Fair in New York*, 1938/39 (cat. 6).

# CONTENTS

**2009–2017 SEASON SUPPORTED BY**

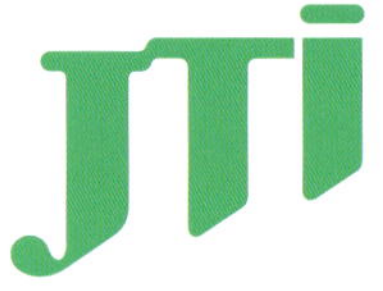

**SUPPORTED BY**

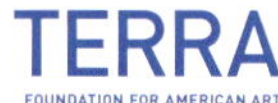

## SUPPORTER'S STATEMENT

As the Season Supporter of the Sackler Wing of Galleries since 2009, JTI is delighted to help bring *America after the Fall* to the Royal Academy of Arts.

Our long-term partnership with the Royal Academy of Arts is part of both our broader approach to supporting communities across the UK and our ambition to widen access to the arts, which we believe play such an important role in society.

The Sackler Galleries have been home to a wide range of exhibitions of historical and cultural significance. For today's generation, the themes of *America after the Fall*, encompassing the years of the Great Depression, the Wall Street Crash, and America's entry into the Second World War, will have particular resonance.

We do hope you enjoy this showcase of such an absorbing and thought-provoking artistic period.

*Daniel Sciamma*
MANAGING DIRECTOR UK, JTI

Europen travelers have long visited the Art Institute of Chicago expressly to see *American Gothic*, which has come to represent Americanness in a powerful way to viewers around the world. One of the most iconic works in the museum's collection, the painting has never left North America until now, and we look forward to its warm reception at the Musée de l'Orangerie, Paris, and the Royal Academy of Arts, London. That the Art Institute purchased the canvas from Grant Wood in 1930, just months after its creation, is a testament to the museum's persistent desire to acquire major works of contemporary art even during the lean years of the Great Depression.

During the 1930s, Regionalist pictures such as Wood's celebrated hard work, frugality, and other values recognized as particularly American and predominantly rural. At the same moment, photographer and modernist impresario Alfred Stieglitz—then the most important art dealer in the United States—was championing a markedly different set of American values. He promoted his wife, Georgia O'Keeffe, as well as Charles Demuth, Arthur Dove, and Marsden Hartley, all of whom eschewed the realism practiced by many artists of the time, choosing instead an abstraction that addressed themes including industrialization, popular culture, and urban life. The Art Institute gave O'Keeffe her first retrospective in 1943, and many of her works—and those of her colleagues—came to the museum as part of Stieglitz's estate. They now form the core of one of the most important collections of American modernism in the world.

Long overdue, this exhibition captures a turbulent economic and political moment and explores the dynamic process of rethinking modernism that took place within it. The idea to bring together fifty important—and at times startlingly different—canvases originated in the Art Institute's Department of American Art with Judith A. Barter, Field-McCormick Chair and Curator, and her colleagues Sarah Kelly Oehler and Annelise Madsen. We thank them for organizing this groundbreaking project with grace, enthusiasm, and rigor. We also acknowledge the early support and leadership of Douglas Druick, who recently retired from his position as president and director of the Art Institute. Art historians Sarah L. Burns and Teresa Carbone, whose scholarly expertise was essential to the success of the undertaking, made important contributions to the catalogue. The exhibition has also benefited from the deep interest and enthusiastic support of Laurence des Cars of the Musée de l'Orangerie and Adrian Locke at the Royal Academy of Arts. We are grateful to both of them.

A quarter of the works in *America after the Fall* is drawn from the Art Institute's collection, and the museum is delighted that many of its treasures—along with others from across the United States—will be enjoyed by new audiences in London and Paris. Enormous thanks are due to the many lenders whose generosity made this project possible.

We are also profoundly grateful for the financial support of key organizations and individuals in both the United States and Europe. In Chicago, lead funding for *America after the Fall* is provided by the Terra Foundation for American Art.

Generous support is also provided by Shawn M. Donnelley and Christopher M. Kelly. The Auxiliary Board of the Art Institute is the lead affiliate sponsor, with additional funding provided by the Suzanne and Wesley M. Dixon Exhibition Fund. Annual support for Art Institute exhibitions is provided by members of the Exhibitions Trust: Kenneth Griffin, Robert M. and Diane v.S. Levy, Thomas and Margot Pritzker, Betsy Bergman Rosenfield and Andrew M. Rosenfield, the Earl and Brenda Shapiro Foundation, and the Woman's Board.

In London we are indebted to the ongoing support JTI provides for the exhibitions programme in the Sackler Wing of Galleries. We also thank most sincerely the Terra Foundation for American Art for its generosity.

We are proud of the collaborative spirit that has enabled our institutions to present this exhibition in our three cities, showcasing works that help us see in a new way what was, aesthetically, perhaps the most fertile decade of the twentieth century.

*James Rondeau*
PRESIDENT AND ELOISE W. MARTIN DIRECTOR
THE ART INSTITUTE OF CHICAGO

*Guy Cogeval*
PRESIDENT
MUSÉE D'ORSAY AND MUSÉE DE L'ORANGERIE

*Christopher Le Brun* PRA
PRESIDENT
THE ROYAL ACADEMY OF ARTS, LONDON

**T**he definition of modern American art was an unsettled subject in the 1930s: artists and critics challenged its meanings and forms passionately, reaching no easy consensus. Some, for example, believed that Edward Hopper's paintings were not modern enough to justify a solo exhibition at the Museum of Modern Art in 1933. But the director, Alfred H. Barr, Jr., argued for modernism's expansiveness. "Ten years ago," he insisted, "critics found generalization easy: modern art was characterized by a concern with expression through distortion, by an interest in abstract design or by sympathy with the naïve and primitive. Today it is impossible to generalize." This exhibition explores how, during the 1930s, artists broadened their subject matter and changed the agenda of modern American painting. As we shall see, their search for a national aesthetic in particular created a new freedom of the brush that gave rise to styles and approaches ranging from abstraction to magic realism, surrealism to social protest, the utopic to the dystopian.

Remarkably, *America after the Fall: Painting in the 1930s* has benefited from the talents of three directors of the Art Institute of Chicago—while Daniel Catton Rich acquired many of its key works in the 1930s and 1940s, Douglas Druick and James Rondeau have lent their clarifying vision and steadfast support much more recently. I am grateful as well to our Parisian colleagues Guy Cogeval, President of the Musée d'Orsay and the Musée de l'Orangerie; Laurence des Cars, Director of the Musée de l'Orangerie; Pascale Desriac; and Hélène Flon. At the Royal Academy of Arts, London, acknowledgment goes to Charles Saumarez Smith, Secretary and CEO; Tim Marlow, Artistic Director; Kathlean Soriano, formerly Director of Exhibitions; Idoya Beitia; Adrian Locke; and Andrea Tarsia.

I am also deeply indebted to the following individuals and institutions who lent their important paintings: Andrew J. Walker, Amon Carter Museum of American Art; Simone Wicha, Blanton Museum of Art; Teresa A. Carbone, Arnold Lehman, and Anne Pasternak, Brooklyn Museum; the Cedar Rapids School District; Sean Ulmer, Cedar Rapids Museum of Art; Julie Aronson and Cameron Kitchin, Cincinnati Art Museum; Nannette V. Maciejunes, Columbus Museum of Art; Maxwell L. Anderson, Dallas Museum of Art; Heather R. Haskell, Michele and Donald D'Amour Museum of Fine Arts; Graham W. J. Beal and Salvador Salort-Pons, Detroit Institute of Arts; Colin B. Bailey and Richard Benefield, Fine Arts Museums of San Francisco; Barney A. Ebsworth; Gwendolyn Everett and Eileen Johnston, Howard University Gallery of Art; Nathan Augustine, John Deere Company; Thomas Campbell and Randall Griffey, Metropolitan Museum of Art; Gary Tinterow, Museum of Fine Arts, Houston; Glenn Lowry, Cora Rosevear, and Ann Tempkin, Museum of Modern Art; Earl A. Powell, National Gallery of Art; Timothy Rub, Philadelphia Museum of Art; Randall Suffolk, Philbrook Museum of Art; Dorothy Kosinski, Phillips Collection; Christin Mamiya and Wally Mason, Sheldon Museum of Art; Elizabeth Broun and Virginia Mecklenburg, Smithsonian American Art Museum; Brent R. Benjamin and Melissa Wolfe, Saint Louis Art Museum; Gayle Munro, U.S. Navy Art Collection; Kevin Murphy and Christina Olsen, Williams College Museum of Art; Adam Weinberg, Whitney Museum of American Art; and two private collectors who wish to remain anonymous.

Funding for *America after the Fall* is provided by the Terra Foundation for American Art; the Auxiliary Board of the Art Institute of Chicago; and the Suzanne and Wesley M. Dixon Exhibition Fund. Annual support for Art Institute exhibitions is provided by the Exhibitions Trust: Kenneth Griffin, Robert M. and Diane v.S. Levy, Thomas and Margot Pritzker, Betsy Bergman Rosenfield and Andrew M. Rosenfield, the Earl and Brenda Shapiro Foundation, and the Woman's Board. The Art Institute's development department, led by Eve Coffee Jeffers and including George Martin, Jennifer Moran, and Jennifer Oatess, was a key partner is raising funds for the project. Thanks are also due to all our authors. My colleagues in American Art, Sarah Kelly Oehler and Annelise Madsen, wrote insightful essays; as curators, they also helped shape the exhibition and publication in many important ways. I am deeply grateful to them and to the gifted art historians Sarah L. Burns and Teresa A. Carbone, whose essays offer exciting new ways of looking at the paintings of the 1930s.

Every Art Institute exhibition is a collaboration of many experts from across the museum, from editors to electricians, all too numerous to acknowledge individually. But I would like to attempt to call out those who were most supportive. I wish to thank Martha Tedeschi and David Thurm for their crucial encouragement from the start. Jennifer Sostaric in Legal and staff in Exhibitions and Registration including Jennifer Draffen, Susanna Hedblom, Jennifer Paoletti, Megan Rader, and formerly Dorothy Schroeder, managed the budget, organized contractual arrangements, assured safe handling and transit of the objects, and attended to myriad loan details. I also thank other invaluable members of my own department, including Denise Mahoney, who kept track of all exhibition correspondence and loan requirements, and Christopher Shepherd and Tim Roby, who led the installation team. In Conservation Frank Zuccari, Kelly Keegan, Allison Langley, and Kirk Vuillemot attended to the welfare of the objects with great care. The stunning Chicago installation was the creative work of Yau-mu M. Huang in Design and Construction, whose vision was realized by Bill Caddick, Joe Vatinno, and their talented colleagues in Museum Facilities, who include a team of master carpenters, painters, and electricians. Jeff Wonderland and his colleagues in Graphic Design provided the show's visual language and signage, and the skills of Nenette Luarca, Fawn Ring, and Robert Smith in Museum Education helped us engage our audiences in the most compelling ways possible.

Our research was supported by the staff of Ryerson and Burnham Libraries, including former colleagues Jack Perry Brown and Mary Woolever, new director Douglas Litts, and especially Autumn Mather. That scholarship took beautiful form in the hands of Publishing, led by Sarah Guernsey, Joseph Mohan, and our newly returned and beloved Greg Nosan, as well as Katie Levi, Lauren Makholm, and freelance editor Kate Steinmann. They expertly oversaw all aspects of the catalogue while Wilson McBee tackled the wall labels. Glue + Paper Workshop's Joan Sommers created yet another fabulous and energetic book design.

My final thanks go to the citizens of Chicago, America's great modernist city, who have supported the art of their time throughout the history of this great institution.

*Judith A. Barter*
FIELD-McCORMICK CHAIR AND CURATOR OF AMERICAN ART
THE ART INSTITUTE OF CHICAGO

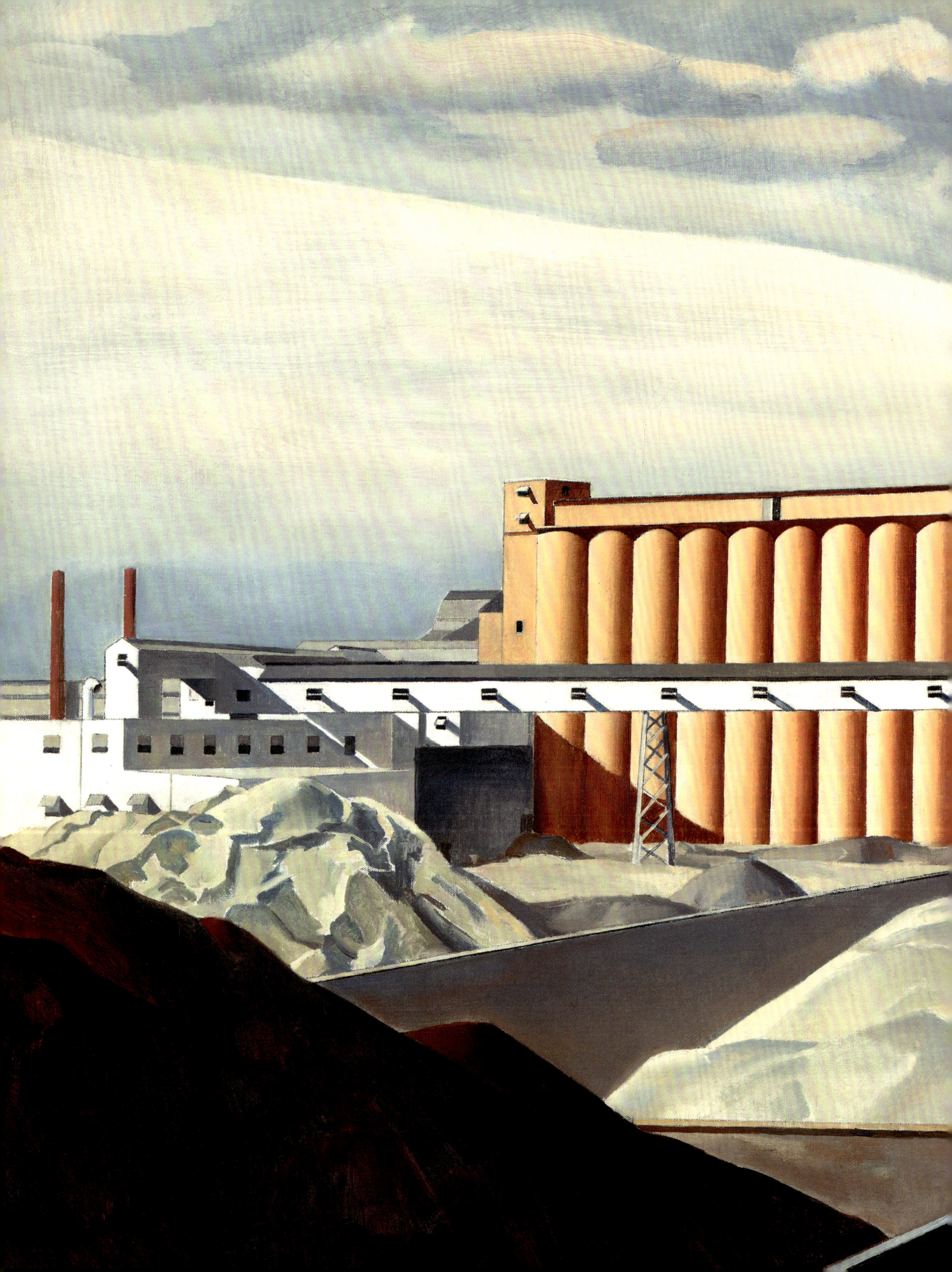

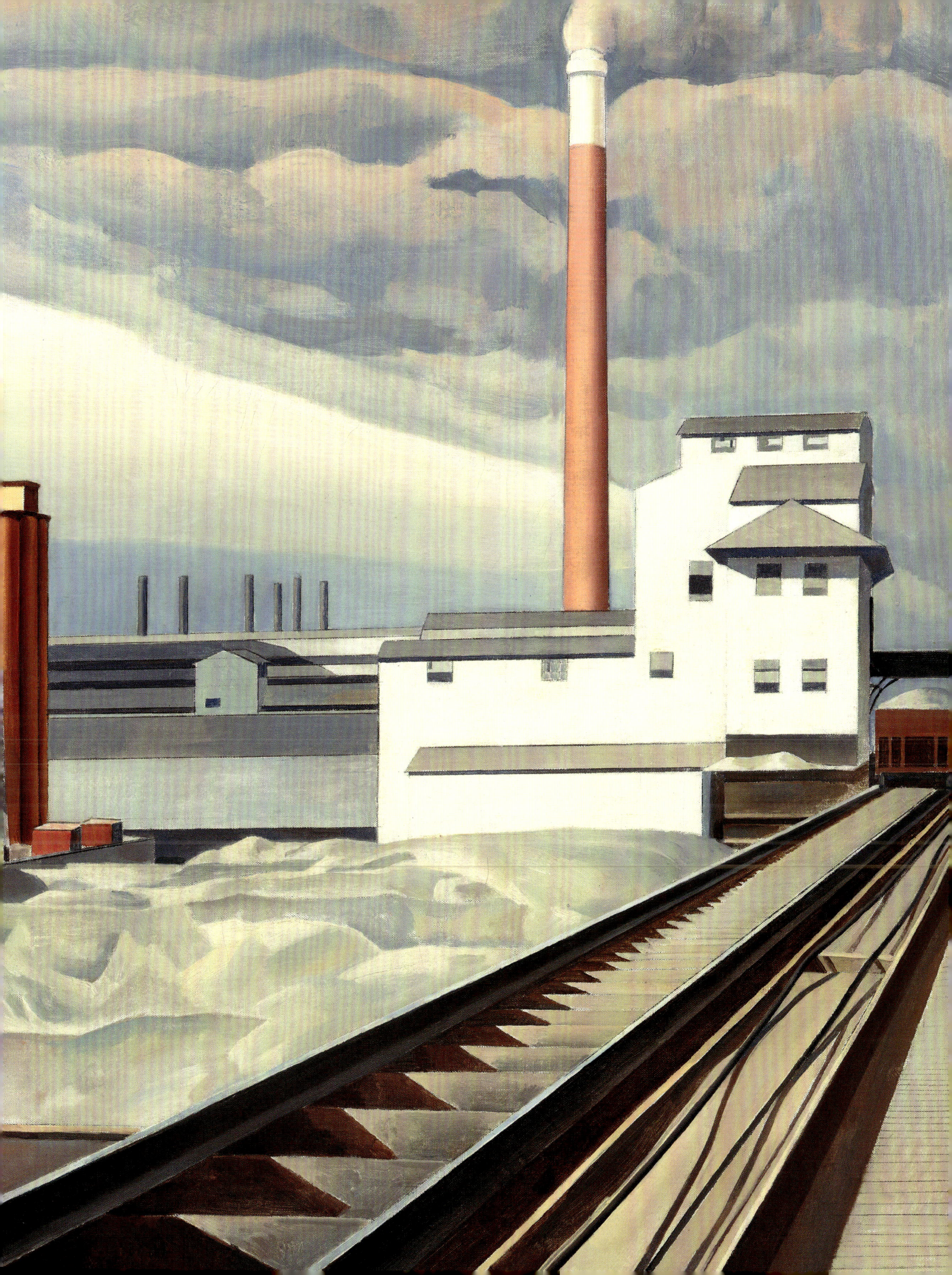

**JUDITH A. BARTER**

# INTRODUCTION

The "fall" in *America after the Fall* refers to what was more commonly called the stock market crash of October 29, 1929. It also aptly describes a fall from innocence: how an entire generation of people who lost their jobs, homes, savings, and dignity perceived their own expulsion from the American Garden of Eden. Never before had such disillusionment visited the nation, a proverbial "city upon a hill" built upon utopian notions of opportunity, progress, and hope. The 1930s called for a reexamination of American culture and values—a rethinking of the meaning of democracy—and prompted new forms of articulating this American dilemma.

What the Depression brought to the arts in the 1930s was a reassessment of what it was to be American and how to express that aesthetically. What form would a national art take, and what subjects would it explore? The 1930s was a decade of seeking for what was original to America itself, for native subjects and themes. This was not a monolithic effort; it took many aesthetic forms and was confused, partisan, and sometimes embittered. But artists pursued, and the government supported, a search for the "American Scene" in art and literature that addressed native culture. The result was artistic sparring throughout the 1930s between those who wanted an American art based on realism and those who felt that abstraction was a universal language that pushed beyond nationalism. Many artists sought a new realist aesthetic language aimed at the people; others tried to express the inner world of dreams and imagination. Some used their work for social protest and to address politics; still others tried to create new forms of art and politics that could repair a democracy damaged by economic chaos.

The exhibition covers the period from the late 1920s, just before the crash of 1929, to the United States' entry into World War II in December 1941. The crash serves as a symbol for the Depression, but more important factors leading to that debacle are found after the close of World War I in 1919. In that period of economic chaos, both Communism and Fascism took hold of European politics and had an impact on the art and politics of the United States.

John Maynard Keynes, in his clear-eyed book *The Economic Consequences of the Peace* (1920), pointed out that the economic disruptions of the Great War were continued in the untenable treaty of Versailles. Defeated Germany was stripped of overseas colonies, foreign investments, and control of tariffs and waterways, and was further saddled with thirty-three billion dollars in reparations to the victorious nations. There was little doubt that the country could not pay its bills, and when it defaulted on them in 1922, the French moved in and occupied the heart of its manufacturing region, the Ruhr, further crippling German industry. Unemployment rose to 30 percent by 1930, and the rise of Fascism began.[1]

Around the same time, the Russian Revolution of 1917 spurred the creation of a new form of government, Communism, which was devised to combat economic inequality and forge a new world order. By 1936 the Popular Front united Communists, Socialists, and intellectuals on the political left to oppose the rise of Fascism in Spain. The bitter economic hardships of the 1930s led some Americans to regard democracy as an inefficient form of government, and they supported the ideals of Communism or Fascism until their totalitarian nature became apparent, for both depended on dictatorship, anticonstitutional forces, and the suppression of human rights, dignity, and freedom of thought.[2]

All these ideas existed in the United States as well. In fact, the country's citizenship was a global one. America's population doubled between 1890 and 1930, and by the time of the 1929 crash, one in ten Americans either was foreign born or had a parent who was an immigrant.[3] These new arrivals were drawn mainly to urban areas and factory jobs; there they sought, alongside some native-born Americans, to increase their salaries by organizing into unions and workers' associations. Many European-born Americans were persecuted for their ideas as well as their national origins. The most famous example was that of Nicola Sacco and Bartolomeo Vanzetti, Italian American anarchists who were wrongfully accused of murdering two payroll employees at a Boston area shoe factory. Sacco and Vanzetti were first convicted in 1921 based on circumstantial evidence and conflicting witness reports. Their case was appealed and eventually went to the Massachusetts Supreme Judicial Court. In 1927, even after another man confessed to the killings, the presiding judge, Webster Thayer, upheld their sentences.

Distinguished jurist Felix Frankfurter was so incensed by the miscarriage of justice that he wrote an article in the *Atlantic* magazine outlining the reasons for declaring a mistrial.[4] Nonetheless, Sacco and Vanzetti were condemned to death, and they were executed on August 23, 1927. The case enraged leftist artists such as Ben Shahn, who created a series of gouache paintings about the pair. The most famous of these may well be *The Passion of Sacco and Vanzetti* (1931–32; fig. 1), which depicts the two men in their coffins with the architectural symbols of American justice behind and Judge Thayer to the side. The artist points out the injustices practiced against the poor, the foreign born, and those who embraced the politics of revolt. Shahn, along with painters Philip Evergood, Joe Jones, Reginald Marsh, Charles White, and many others on the left, continued to create figurative work throughout the 1930s. Some were later labeled Communists in the hearings orchestrated by Republican Senator Joseph McCarthy simply because they defended workers, were politically progressive, or flirted with new ideas about improving justice and democracy. Most American artists during the 1930s avidly supported President Franklin Roosevelt's New Deal programs.[5] In fact, the New Deal created hundreds of thousands of jobs for the unemployed—including writers and artists—and may well have saved democracy in the United States by making government the largest employer. This changed the relationship of the federal government to its citizens, helping them to stave off economic disaster. The very few artists who were actual members of the Communist Party became disillusioned and finally abandoned their sympathies after Joseph Stalin signed a nonaggression pact with Adolf Hitler in 1939. By then the rising tide of Fascism in Germany, Italy, and Spain became a larger cause. As historian Warren Susman notes, describing the 1930s as a "Red" decade was inaccurate and promoted by those on the right during the 1940s. Left-leaning American artists

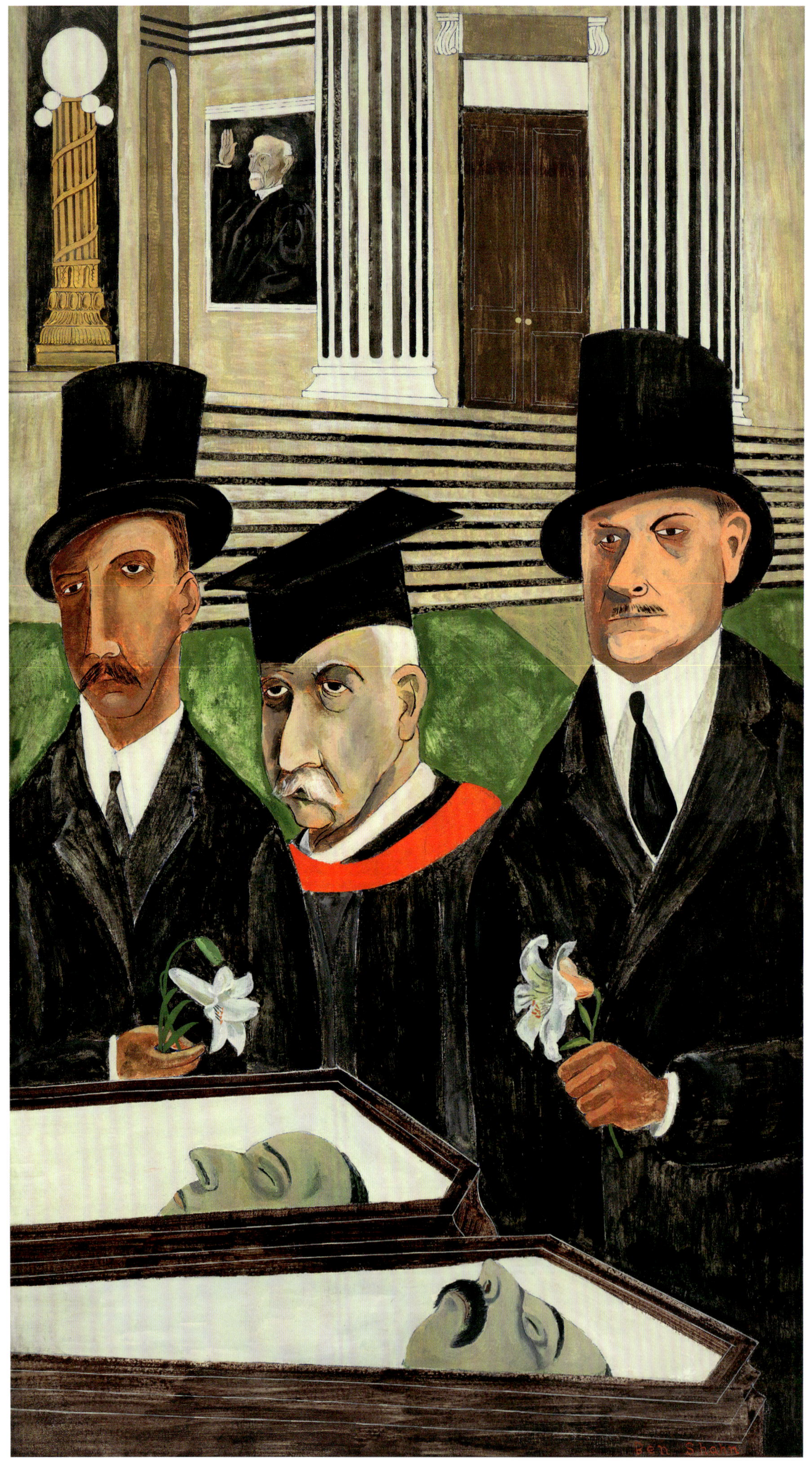

more often aligned themselves with social protest and popular culture than with radical political movements.[6]

Fascism appealed to some progressives and conservatives alike. Detroit's anti-Semitic, anti–Wall Street, antigovernment priest, Father Charles Coughlin, broadcast bombastic radio programs that attacked the New Deal as Communist, admired the rising dictators of Europe, and accused the government of not doing enough to punish rich Jewish bankers. Aviator-hero Charles Lindbergh loved the efficiency and technology of Hermann Goering's Luftwaffe and Hitler's Germany more generally; similarly, Henry Ford relished not only German engineering and material production, but also the racial attitudes of the Nazi Party. After all, Ford had created the Detroit suburbs of Inkster for his black workers and Dearborn for his white employees. Louisiana Senator Huey Long's "Share Our Wealth" philosophy called for the government to modify capitalism and redistribute large fortunes to address income inequality. He wanted each citizen to receive five thousand dollars to buy a home and a car. With essentially populist roots, he was a dictator in his home state, corruptly buying votes and influence until his assassination in 1935.[7]

A common ground for artists of the 1930s was an interest in the details of everyday lives, including those of the less fortunate. Residents of the nation's rural areas were particularly hard hit. Farmers had experienced economic depression since the end of World War I, as surpluses rose and prices dropped. They drowned in the debts incurred to mechanize their operations and plant their land during the war years. Living in marginal circumstances, many could not afford electricity or indoor plumbing. Some regions—especially the rural South—suffered more than others, and poverty prompted blacks to migrate to northern cities in search of factory jobs. This history of decay informed the work of writers such as William Faulkner, who exposed a seething cesspool of fallen planter aristocrats who still influenced the social realities of class and race.

Indeed, the attention paid to lower classes, the poor, and the struggling marked the arts of the 1930s. Previously, culture was the province of the rich and well born, but during the suffering caused by the Depression, its definition was broadened

to include the middle and working classes, the "lowbrows." One of the most popular books of the decade, Ruth Benedict's *Patterns of Culture* (1934), signaled a new interest in how the wider society shapes values and creates meaning.[8] Thornton Wilder's play *Our Town* (1938) explored average citizens, small-town life, and conformity. Composer Aaron Copland, who, like many American artists, had spent the 1920s in Paris, returned home and left European modernist experimentation behind. Friendly with artists of Alfred Stieglitz's circle, he came to believe that American art should reflect democratic values. In 1937 he composed *Prairie Journal* for radio broadcast, one of his first explorations of the American West. He continued his populist themes, using familiar ballads and stories in *Billy the Kid* (1938), *Ballad of John Henry* (1939), *Fanfare for the Common Man* (1942), and *Rodeo* (1942). During the 1930s, Virgil Thompson composed works based on Shaker songs and commonly known ballads, elevating popular music to serious cultural expression.

Counterparts to such themes were found in literature and visual art, too. Regionalist writing and painting covered all sections of the country. John Steinbeck's novel *The Grapes of Wrath* (1939) addressed the nomadic life of the impoverished. Joe Jones, Philip Guston, Alice Neel, and others painted the dispossessed and disaffected, chronicling the dystopic realities of the Depression. Grant Wood's famous *American Gothic* (1930; p. 40, fig. 9), a rendering of the independent yeoman Iowa farmer of the late nineteenth century, celebrated the family farm—which by this time was nearly an anachronism—addressing both the dystopic and the idealistic sides of this difficult decade. *American Gothic* is also a depiction of conservative, straitlaced farmers holding fast to long-dead ways.

Midwestern Regionalists such as Wood, Thomas Hart Benton, and John Steuart Curry opposed the urbanization of the country, the concentration of money on Wall Street, and what they regarded as the effete intellectualism of the East Coast. In the art world, they rejected the personalized, abstract works of European modernists and their followers. They proselytized for a "back to the land" movement and found in the American farmer the true pioneer character of the country.

Their pictures celebrated an earlier Jeffersonian ideal of small farms and merchants in a time when the nation's citizens lived mostly in urban areas and industry fed the country's economic growth. Because the nation had become predominantly urban, artists depicted the activities of city dwellers, too. Evergood, Marsh, and Paul Cadmus painted the entertainments enjoyed by sailors and moviegoers. Figures and gestures became large, and canvases were crowded with life.

Paintings of the "American Scene," with realistic and uplifting subjects that showed local places and common people, were preferred by the support programs of the New Deal administered through the Public Works of Art Project, active in 1933 and 1934, which provided art to ornament new housing projects, courthouses, post offices, and hospitals. Such was the quality and quantity of artistic output during the 1930s that the *Nation* magazine commented that the Depression was the best thing that ever happened to American artists.[9]

Farther west, New Mexico attracted modernists intrigued by the landscape. Tired of New York, Georgia O'Keeffe took an extended visit to the Southwest in 1929, shifting her aesthetic interest from skyscrapers to the natural environment. In 1931 she created a series of still lifes of bleached animal bones, including *Cow's Skull: Red, White, and Blue* (fig. 2). She maintained a quasi-abstract quality in her compositions of a cow's skull on a blue background. She highlighted the jagged edges and framed the death's head with red, white, and blue stripes, evoking the national spirit. Unlike the midwestern Regionalists, she took her inspiration not from farms but from the land itself.

To find the quintessential national character, if such a thing existed, artists looked backward, re-creating history through the lens of nostalgia. Novelists celebrated the country's heritage and myths, making Americans feel good about themselves. Renewed interest in the drama of the past led to bestselling novels such as Walter D. Edmonds's *Drums along the Mohawk* (1936), Kenneth Roberts's *Northwest Passage* (1937), and, most famously, Margaret Mitchell's *Gone with the Wind* (1936). Wood's paintings *The Midnight Ride of Paul Revere* (1931; p. 106, fig. 18) and *Parson Weems' Fable* (1939;

p. 108, fig. 19) traded on old stories to promote a sense of pride and recall a nation of small farmers. The Federal Art Project (1935–43), directed by folk art specialist Holger Cahill, commissioned artists to paint watercolors of furniture, glass, quilts, weathervanes, and objects of vernacular design from across the country, which were later gathered together in an archive known as the Index of American Design.[10]

Some artists saw connections between modern styles and early American decorative arts, noticing their shared geometry and undecorated simplicity of line and form. In *Home, Sweet Home* (1931; p. 99, fig. 10), for example, Charles Sheeler painted old, plain objects from his collection of Shaker chairs, tables, stoves, ceramics, and rag rugs, recalling the history of the country and celebrating these works' streamlined modernity. But his eye had been trained by the sleek contours of modern industrial architecture. For the first two decades of the twentieth century, the expansion of American manufacturing had continued unabated. More and cheaper goods required increased consumption. Companies such as Ford, General Motors, and US Steel—and the mass marketing and consumerism they promoted—flourished in the 1920s. By 1925, a new Ford rolled off the factory line every ten seconds; a decade earlier, it had taken fourteen hours to produce an automobile.[11] Even during the Depression, the streamlined aesthetic continued. Characterized by clean lines and uncluttered, unbroken surfaces, the designs created by Norman Bel Geddes (see fig. 3), Donald Deskey, Henry Dreyfuss, Raymond Lowey, Walter Dorwin Teague, and others were meant to epitomize modernity and stimulate consumer demand for new products. During the 1930s, they designed alarm clocks, kitchen appliances, lamps, radios, wastebaskets—anything that could be distinguished from its competitors in a sluggish marketplace.[12] The streamlined look suggested simplicity and efficiency, both ideas that appealed to business and the public during the Depression years.

In 1927 Sheeler was commissioned by the N. W. Ayer advertising agency and Edsel Bryant Ford, son of Henry Ford and the current president of Ford Motor Company, to photograph and paint the River Rouge plant, which had just opened and begun to manufacture the Model A. Sheeler produced oil

Fig. 2  Georgia O'Keeffe. *Cow's Skull: Red, White, and Blue*, 1931.
Metropolitan Museum of Art. Cat. 37.

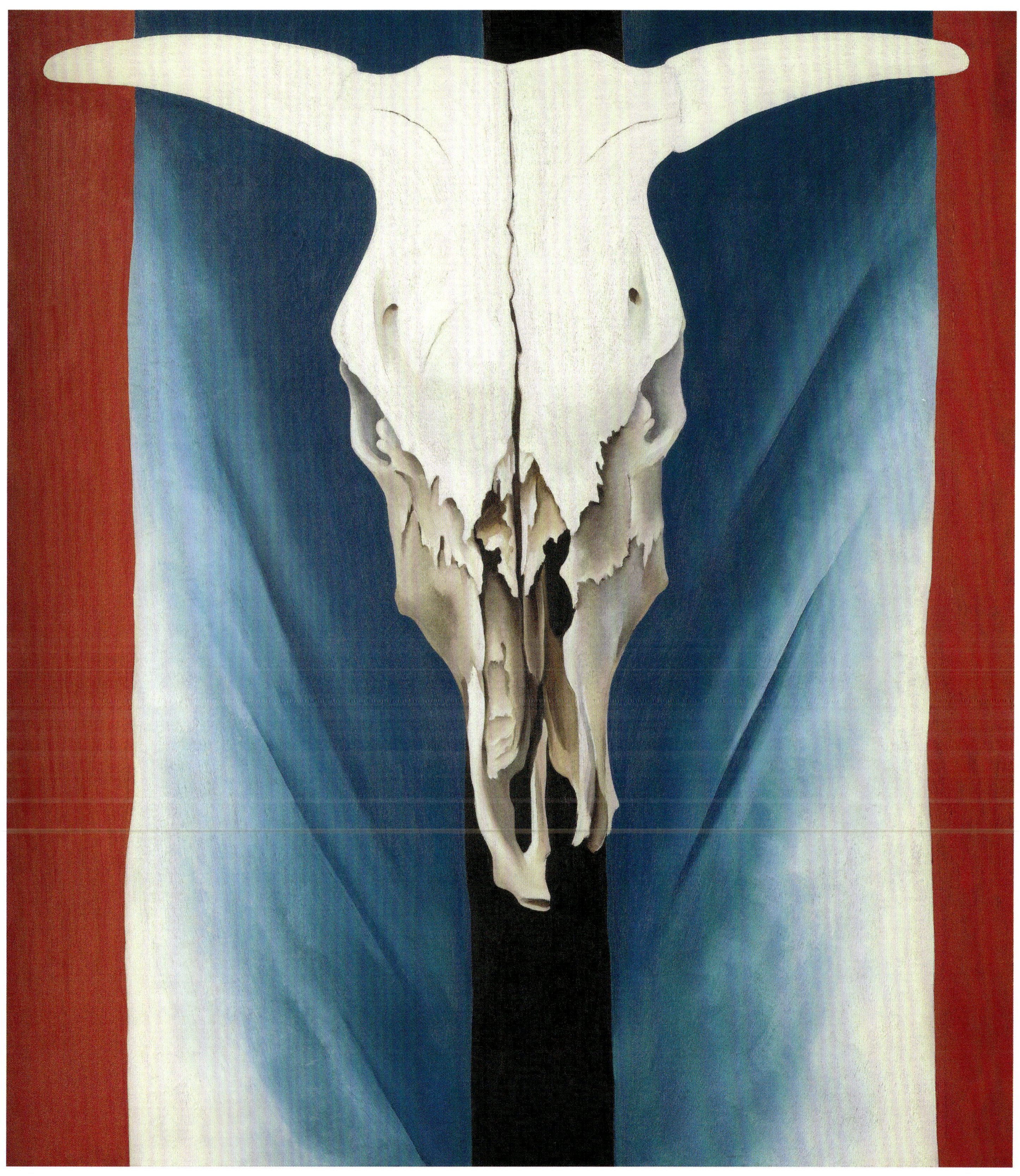

**Fig. 3**  Designed by Norman Bel Geddes (American, 1893–1958). Manufactured by Revere Copper and Brass Company, Rome, New York, 1801–present. *Manhattan Cocktail Set*, designed 1934/35; produced c. 1939–41. Chrome-plated brass; tray: 2.5 × 36.8 × 29.2 cm (1 × 14½ × 11½ in.); shaker: 33 × 8.9 cm (13 × 3½ in.); goblets: 11.4 × 7 cm (4½ × 2¾ in.) Each piece impressed on the bottom: Revere/Rome, NY. The Art Institute of Chicago, Restricted gift of Charles C. Haffner III, 2005.50.1-8.

**Fig. 4**  Charles Sheeler. *Classic Landscape*, 1931. National Gallery of Art. Cat. 44.

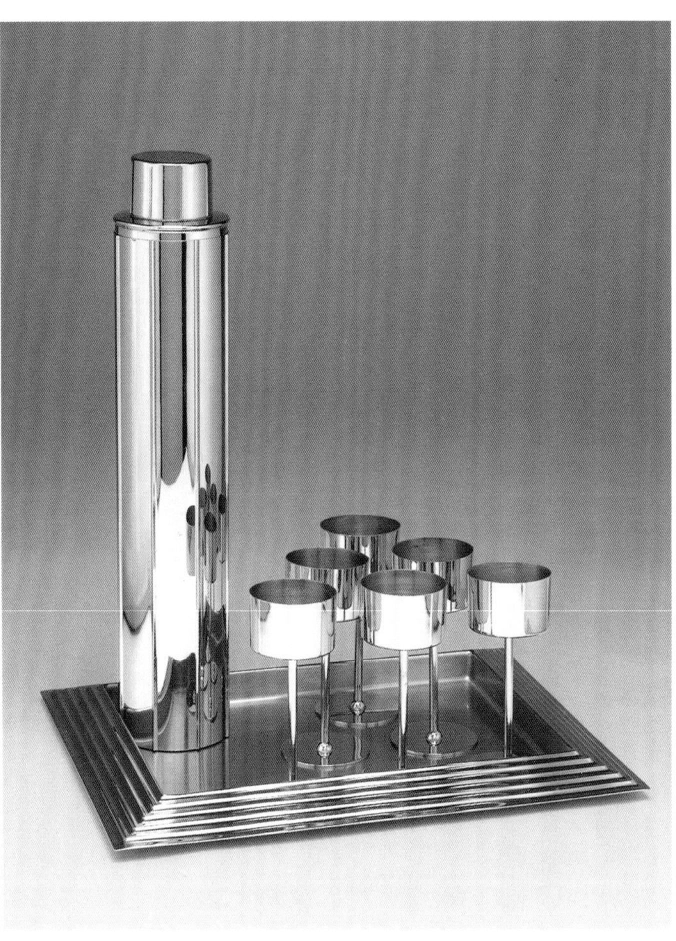

1930, just months after the crash, was America's first business journal. Its aim was to restore confidence, educating and uplifting the nation's businessmen in order to turn them into cultural leaders. To bridge the gulf between industry and the arts, Luce hired important photographers—Margaret Bourke-White, Walker Evans—and a team of writers including James Agee, Alfred Kazin, and Archibald MacLeish. His magazine published articles and pictures that sought to raise the social consciousness of readers about the struggles of the dispossessed and unemployed. Bourke-White's famous photograph *World's Highest Standard of Living* (1937; fig. 5) addressed racial and economic inequity, telling a story far different from that of the American dream. In front of a propaganda-filled billboard stand a line of people testifying to the reality of poverty. While Luce wanted his mainly urban, white, affluent readers to see what was happening, he also believed that business's responsibility was to provide a solution, especially in the face of increasing government programs. Around 1938 *Fortune* shifted from human interest features to probusiness stories, and a year later Luce commissioned Sheeler to paint a series of pictures to be used as illustrations on the theme of American power. As the country geared up for entry into World War II, pride in manufacturing became patriotic. One of Sheeler's canvases, aptly named *Suspended Power* (1939; fig. 6), pits a huge drill-like machine against tiny and insignificant human figures.

paintings from his photographic studies in 1930 and 1931. Erasing any sense of his own touch, clean, spare works such as *Classic Landscape* (1931; fig. 4) and *American Landscape* (1930; p. 64, fig. 5) are celebrations of linear design that salute American industry while ignoring any human presence save for an occasional tiny figure that magnifies the scale of technological forces.[13] While Sheeler's art seems to belong to the classicizing realism of the 1920s, he continued to create these objective, surreally silent landscapes throughout the 1930s. His compositions provided confidence in American industrial and commercial power during bleak years.

Sheeler's work was appealing to the commercial community. *Fortune* magazine, founded by Henry Luce in February

In contrast to Sheeler's antiseptic industrial landscapes are Edward Hopper's gritty street scenes of the early 1930s. Hopper chose to paint not the new urban vistas of skyscrapers but rather the human-scaled, older, tired-looking buildings of the city. In an interview with critic Katharine Kuh, he admitted to a documentary impulse in creating *Early Sunday Morning* (1930; p. 102, fig. 14), a close rendition of New York's Seventh Avenue not far from Washington Square. Such a realist attitude is rare for Hopper, who edited and combined the elements of his scenes extensively.[14] In *Early Sunday Morning* the street is austere, empty, and solitary, evoking an eerie lack of life and energy. Cropped at the edges like a photograph, the lateral extent of

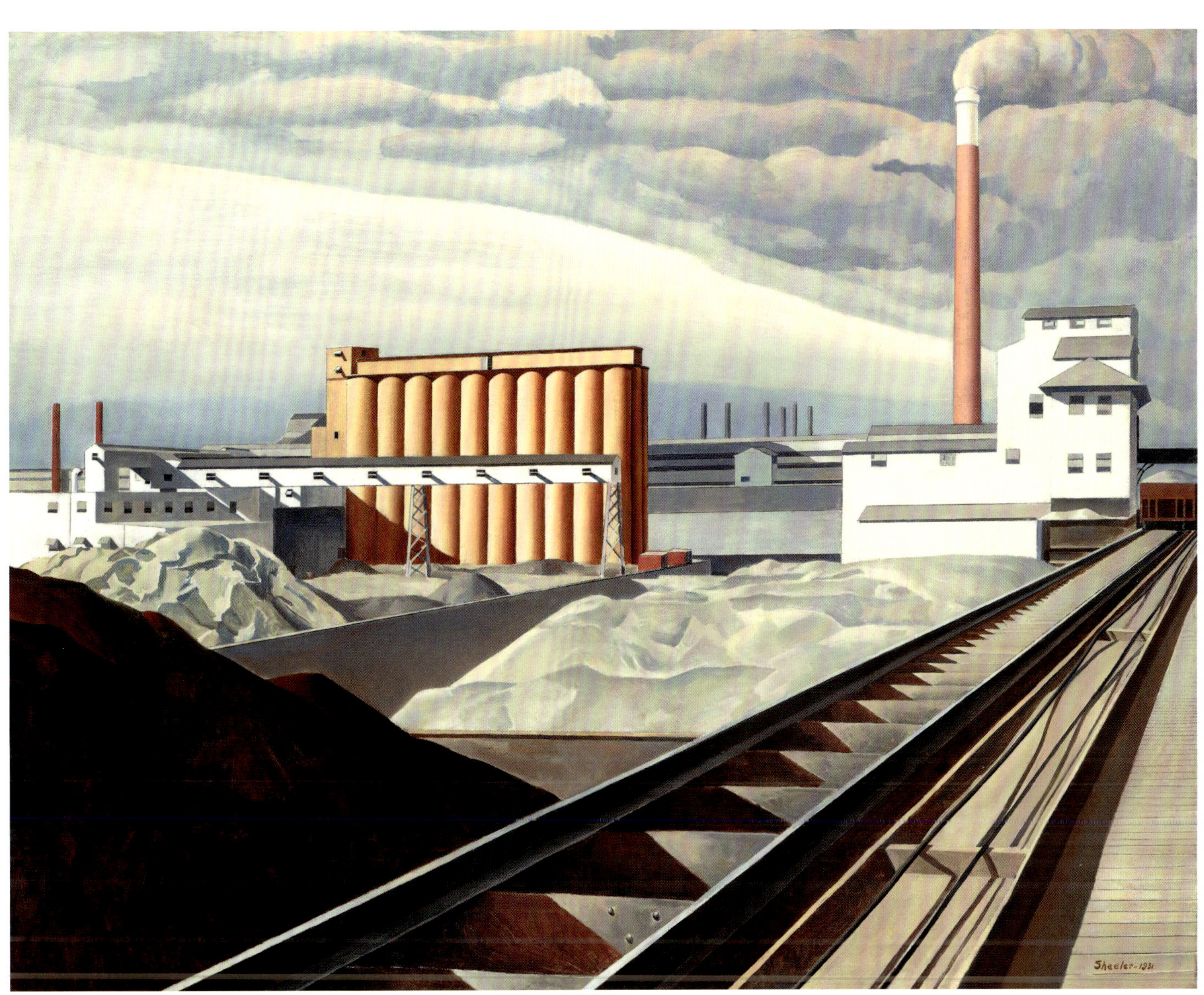

Sheeler-1931

 Margaret Bourke-White (American, 1904–1971). *World's Highest Standard of Living*, 1937. Gelatin silver print, printed later; 55.6 × 73.5 cm (21 $\frac{57}{64}$ × 28 $\frac{15}{16}$ in.). The Art Institute of Chicago, Gift of Boardroom, Inc., 1992.560.

Fig. 6 Charles Sheeler. *Suspended Power*, 1939. Dallas Museum of Art. Cat. 46

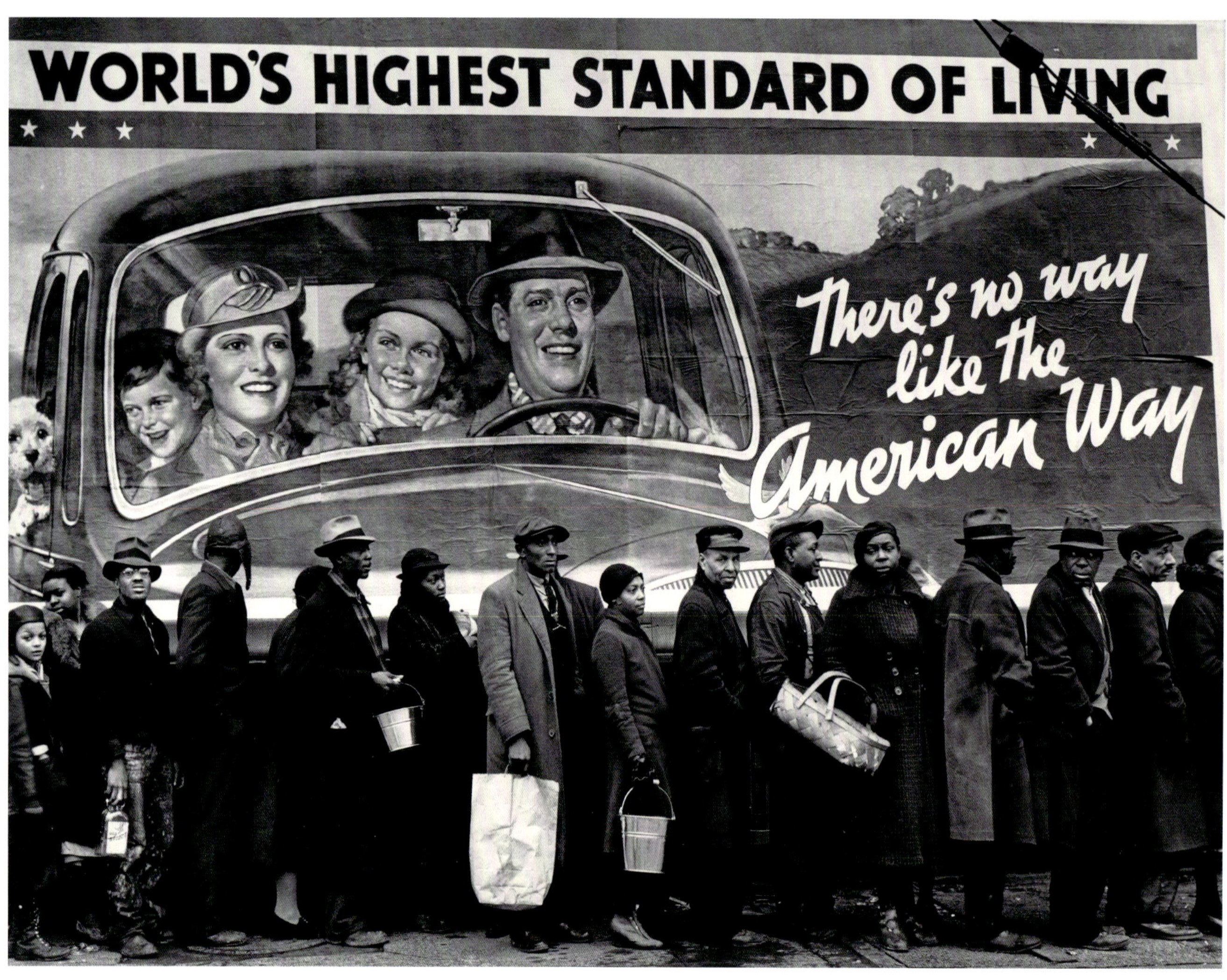


the composition seems limitless and without any focal point. The barbershop is closed; there are no strikers, office workers, movie theaters, or shop windows filled with goods. Hopper records a place and moment in time that would soon pass away. The artist always maintained that his pictures contained no political or social meanings and that he painted only light and form. More than Sheeler's industrial landscapes, however, Hopper's empty street speaks to the deflated mood of the Great Depression and the feelings of emptiness of those who experienced its devastation.

European-based movements such as Surrealism informed the Magic Realist works of O. Louis Guglielmi, Morris Kantor, and Helen Lundeberg. Although painted realistically, their compositions were subjective, imagined, dreamlike scenes that exist more as personal expressions than easily understandable narratives. So too, American abstract artists, maintaining the European modernist values of the 1920s, continued their explorations of color, shape, and composition. They rejected the figurative realism of the Regionalist painters and expressed themselves through purely formal means. The conflicts between modernists such as Stuart Davis and realists such as Benton were bitter. Neither could address the work of the other without invoking politics. The two sparred in the art magazines during April 1935. Benton, who viewed Davis's

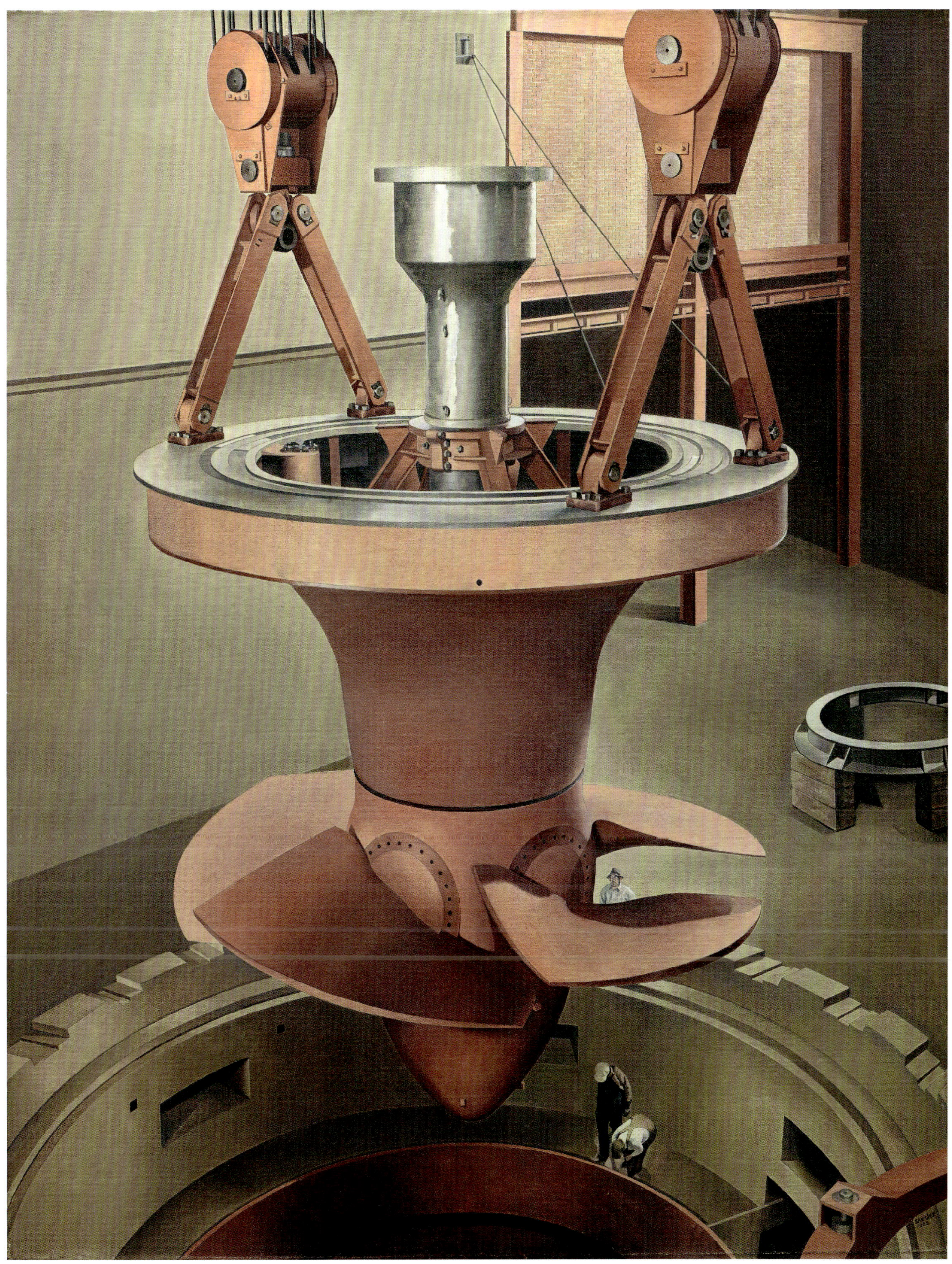

paintings as European-inspired and not sufficiently American in theme, associated them with a fey, unmasculine internationalism centered in New York. He also implied that Davis took a "Marxist slant."[15] Davis, for his part, found Benton's midwestern farm scenes parochial and provincial. But the work of both artists can be seen as a bridge between early modernism and the Abstract Expressionism that triumphed after the war. Davis's abstract shapes and Benton's twisting forms and brilliant color were incorporated into what came next. Indeed, Benton's most famous student was Jackson Pollock.

Struggles over artistic style and content lasted until the end of the decade. So, too, did the Depression, which lingered until America's entry into World War II in 1941. The twelve years since the crash were marked by both suffering and creativity, and by compelling literary and visual portraits of individual dignity and communal life. Both criticism and support of American cultural values existed side by side. For those who lived through the Great Depression, survival was most important, but there was also acknowledgment of the need for support, for belonging, for community—for sharing the national experience of anxiety that colored these years.

The role of the federal government in creating entitlements and supporting programs for the unemployed changed traditional ideas about laissez-faire economics and self-reliance, serving to reinforce the changing relationship among individuals, community, and government. Finally, there was the need to define and redefine the meaning of American culture. What was it, and how had it changed? Was it about progress and modernity, traditional history or myth, farm or factory? The 1930s began the process of defining America's way of life, documenting its artistic traditions and its values. But by the end of the decade, many European artists fled to the United States, and the advent of war ended forever the country's isolation as government, citizens, and artists alike adopted wider, more international attitudes and forms of expression.

America's rapid industrialization during World War II made the artistic explorations of national culture increasingly poignant. Then, the United States seemed innocent in its separation from the rest of the world. As this book shows, the enormous creativity of the decade produced widely different themes and types of artistic expression and helped define the nation's art, literature, and culture in new ways. This diversity represented a desire to remake American life, marking the 1930s as the most artistically creative and important period of the twentieth century.

**1** David M. Kennedy, *Freedom from Fear: The American People in Depression and War, 1929–1945* (Oxford University Press, 1999), pp. 7–8. German inability to pay war debts to France and England was hampered by the adherence of Western European allies and the United States to the gold standard. Cheaper money, based on paper and silver currencies, would have prompted inflation, always a friend to the debtor. But the United States would not denounce the gold standard until the first one hundred days of the Roosevelt Administration's New Deal, in 1932–33. The rigid adherence to gold-supported currency in part caused tightened lending throughout the global economy and helped to lead to the thousands of bank failures of the early 1930s.

**2** Kennedy, *Freedom from Fear*, pp. 14–15. In the United States, the decade of the 1920s was often called "the Roaring Twenties," primarily because the repressive laws of Prohibition made the illicit more fun. The Puritan strain of American thinking and social experimentation that prompted such legislation created a new market for bootleg liquor, speakeasies, and nightclubs, where marcelled hair, the Charleston, and easy sex predominated. These were city entertainments based on the affluence of urban areas. Banks had money to lend, in part because Germany borrowed heavily from the United States to pay reparations to England and France. Speculation in business stocks seemed a sure thing. Long before the great crash of 1929, however, the economy slowed; as more goods were produced and fewer customers were buying, corporate profits declined, layoffs began, and the resulting xenophobia was predictable. Blaming immigration for job competition, the Ku Klux Klan spurred Congress to practically close off immigration.

**3** See Campbell J. Gibson and Emily Lennon, "Historical Census Statistics on the Foreign-Born Population of the United States: 1850–1990" (Population Division, US Bureau of the Census, February 1999), table 1, http://www.census .gov/population/www/documenta tion/twps0029/twps0029.html.

**4** Felix Frankfurter, "The Case of Sacco and Vanzetti," *Atlantic*, March 1, 1927, pp. 409–32.

**5** David Eldridge, *American Culture in the 1930s* (Edinburgh University Press, 2008), p. 11. In 1932 fifty-two American writers joined together to support the Communist Party's presidential and vice-presidential candidates, William Foster and James Ford. Playwright Sherwood Anderson, poet John Dos Passos, novelist Waldo Frank, poet Langston Hughes, and critics Malcolm Cowley and Edmund Wilson all signed on to the idea of a new world. Believing that a new system of Socialism or Communism would prevent the spread of Fascism, they called for a new political transformation. They published their open letter about the decay of capitalism in a booklet entitled *Culture and the Crisis,* for, as they suggested, the cultural fate of the country was dependent upon new economic policies.

**6** Warren I. Susman, "The Culture of the 1930s," in *Culture as History: The Transformation of American Society in the Twentieth Century* (1974; repr., Smithsonian Institution Press, 2003), pp. 152–53.

**7** Long's politics were immortalized in Robert Penn Warren's novel *All the King's Men*, published in 1946.

**8** Susman, "Culture of the 1930s," p. 154.

**9** Jonathan Harris, *Federal Art and National Culture: The Politics of Identity in New Deal America* (Cambridge University Press, 1995), p. 42.

**10** Index of American Design, National Gallery of Art, Washington, DC, https://www .nga.gov/collection/iad/history /overview.shtm.

**11** Kennedy, *Freedom from Fear*, p. 21.

**12** Streamlined trains captured the public interest when the Burlington Line's Zephyr was unveiled at the Chicago Century of Progress Exposition in 1933.

**13** Charles Brock, *Charles Sheeler: Across Media*, exh. cat. (National Gallery of Art/University of California Press, 2006), pp. 86–87.

**14** Katharine Kuh, *The Artist's Voice: Talks with Seventeen Artists* (Harper and Row, 1962), p. 131.

**15** "Benton Goes Home," *Art Digest* 9 (April 15, 1935), p. 13.

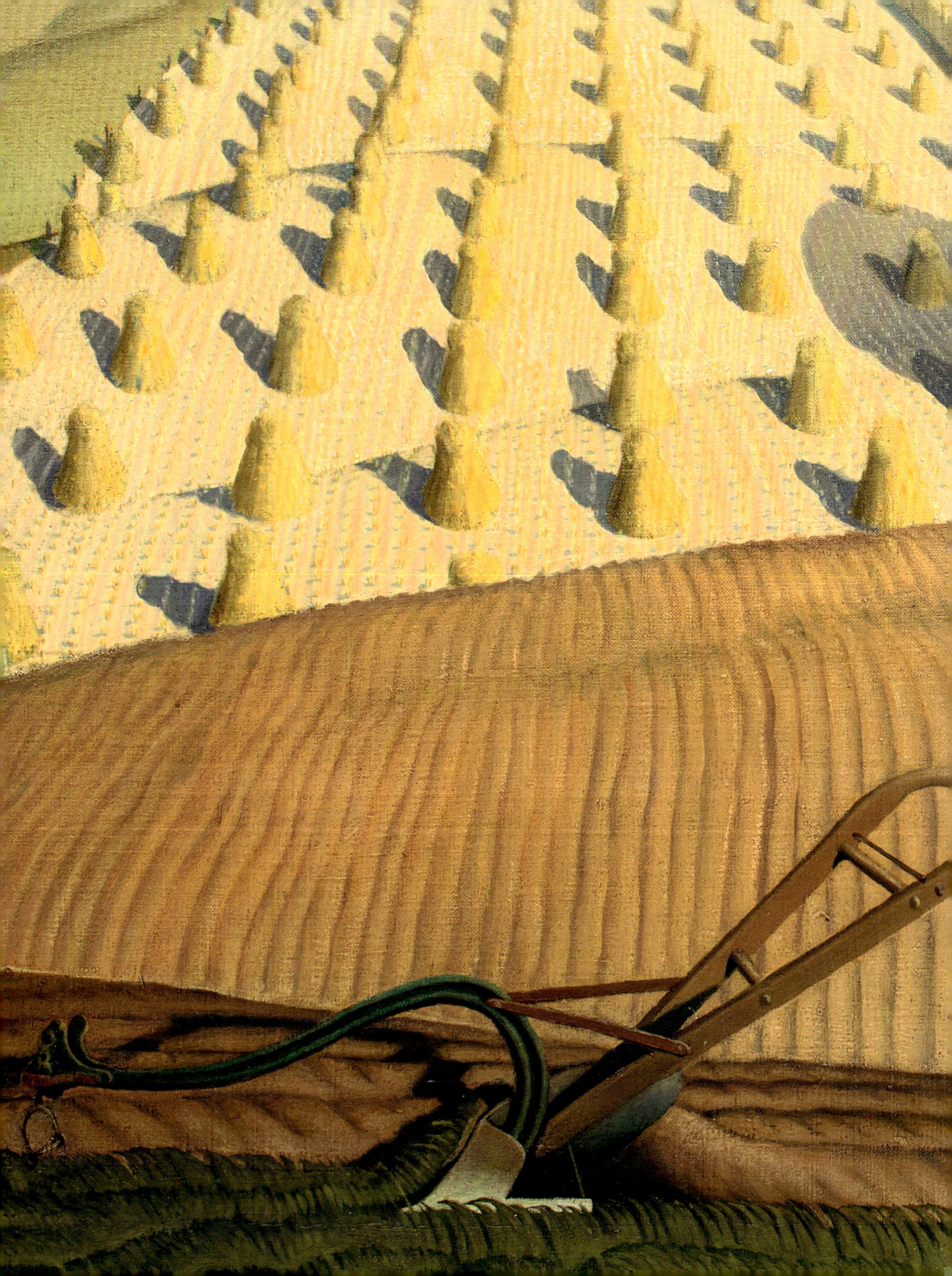

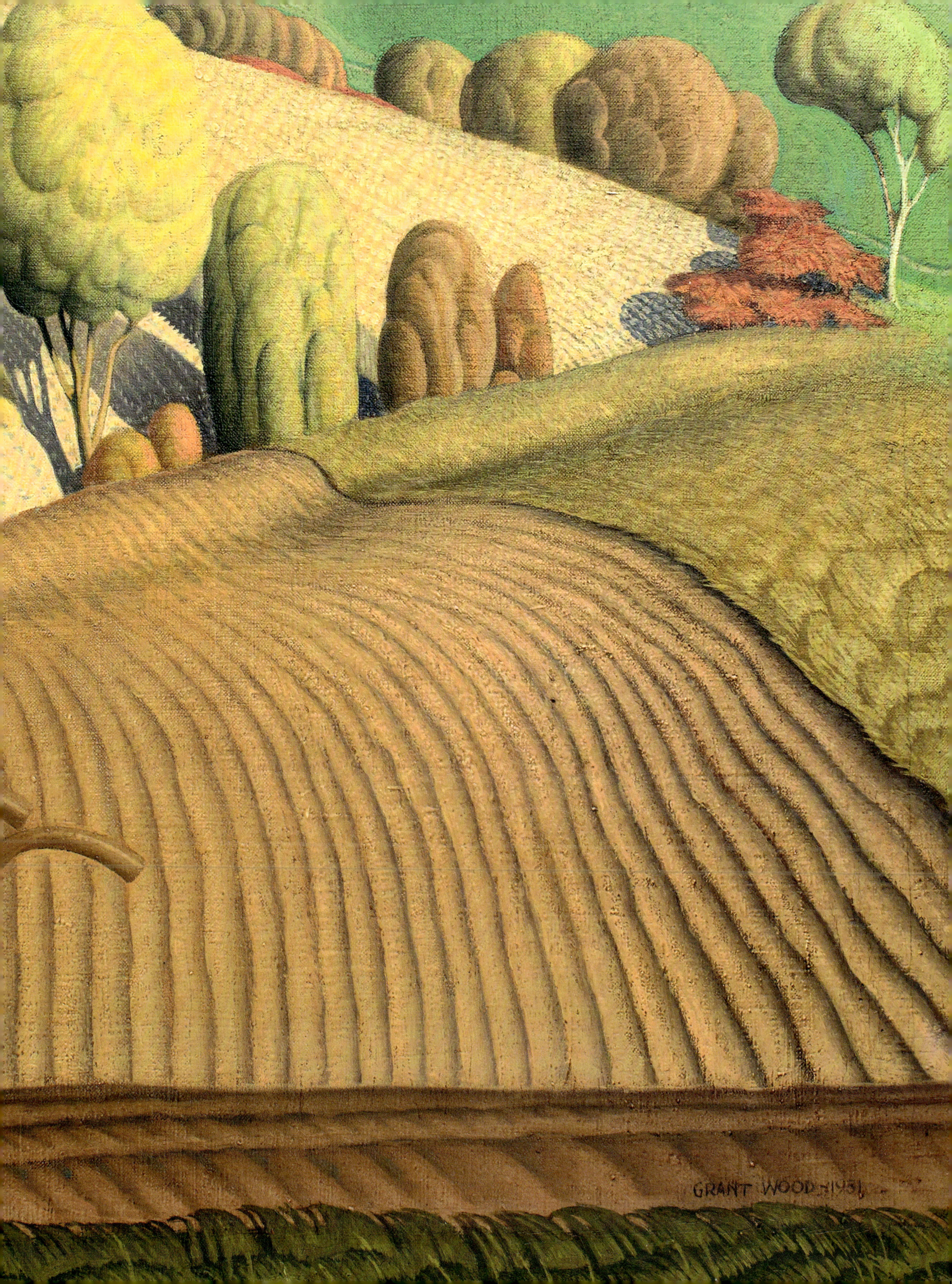

GRANT WOOD 1931

**JUDITH A. BARTER**

**I**n the Midwest, Regionalist authors created a picture of life on the land from the 1890s through the 1930s in works such as Hamlin Garland's *Main-Travelled Roads* (1891), Sinclair Lewis's *Main Street* (1920) and *Babbitt* (1922), Willa Cather's *O Pioneers!* (1913) and Pulitzer Prize–winning *One of Ours* (1922), Sherwood Anderson's *Winesburg, Ohio* (1919), Laura Ingalls Wilder's *Little House on the Prairie* (1935), and even L. Frank Baum's *Wonderful Wizard of Oz* (1900), which depicted Aunt Em, Uncle Henry, Dorothy, and Toto on a Kansas farm. In all these works, midwesterners are presented as people who are independent, egalitarian, hardworking, plainspoken, churchgoing; driven by education and self-betterment, they are stewards of a peaceful farm belt that was the most vital and productive region of the United States. As one contemporary

# ONE     *Prairie Pastoral*

author stated, "Iowa goes to bed early but not before it has read an improving book."[1] But within these novels there are also tensions between immigrant ethnic groups, farm and town dwellers, physical and mental occupations, isolation and culture, hardship and ease, progressive politics and conservative traditions. Within these conflicting value systems, the Midwest came to be seen as the arcadian ideal even as New England maintained its taciturn Puritan identity.[2]

In the Midwest, the pastoral myth of the yeoman farmer that existed from the first settlement days of the early republic persisted. The Midwest was a land of migration. As Cather showed so well, many languages were spoken and cultural customs maintained. Because the churches held communities together, strife was usually avoided, and accommodation prevailed. Unifying values were desires for opportunity, freedom, progress, public education, and material abundance.

The region was not a homogenous entity. Instead, it was a pluralist society where more than two-thirds of all farmers were foreign born at the turn of the twentieth century. African Americans, Germans, Irish, Slavs, and Swedes, to name only a few, lived in an area that had once been called the Northwest Territory and included Ohio, Michigan, Indiana, Illinois, Wisconsin, and a part of what is today Minnesota. These sections were all admitted as states by the mid-nineteenth century, and the region expanded. Missouri, Iowa, Minnesota, North and South Dakota, and the plains of Kansas, Oklahoma, and Nebraska were added to the regional identity, and the area was called the "West," as opposed to the "Great West." Around 1900 the name "Midwest" was coined to differentiate the area from the mountain states and deserts farther west.[3]

Until around 1920, prosperity reigned in the nation's heartland. But with the end of World War I, the region experienced a recessionary economy a decade ahead of the great Wall Street crash of 1929. Farms had been overproducing to provide for the war effort and feed European nations and troops; this all collapsed after the armistice was signed in November 1919. Wheat and corn prices plummeted, and so began the cycle of debt and foreclosure. Washington turned a deaf ear to the crisis, since the industrial and banking economy of the Eastern Seaboard was not yet affected.

Not only was the Midwest not ethnically homogenous, but it was not even predominantly rural by 1920, when the census showed that for the first time the majority of the nation's population lived in urban areas. Chicago, Cleveland, and Detroit formed the industrial hubs of the nation—manufacturing steel, trains, and automobiles—and states like Wisconsin and Minnesota supported timber and mining. Yet Regionalist painters of the 1930s continued to depict an idealized vision of rural life. Three of them—Thomas Hart Benton, John Steuart Curry, and Grant Wood—explored this theme, eventually painting scenes that were meant to call viewers back to the farms and villages of an earlier, arcadian land that had already disappeared.

Benton began his career as a modernist. He had studied in Paris and returned to live in New York with his friend Stanton Macdonald-Wright, an advocate of Synchromism, a technique in which abstract artists sought to render emotion through pure color. Benton flirted with this style, but he was always more comfortable with figuration. Modernism, learned in Europe, was about using abstract elements and flattening the picture plane. Benton, however, believed that modern art could still accommodate the figure and that modernism itself was too narrowly defined.[4]

The artist's love of twisting figural forms and energized landscapes boldly defined by saturated color eventually dominated his return to a realist style of modernism. In his first attempt at this approach, he depicted not midwestern themes but rather the landscape of the South. In 1928 Benton completed a series of sketches of African American workers picking, baling, and loading cotton. The South, poor since the days of Reconstruction, grew steadily poorer, and the contrast between its suffering and the strength of the North's urban industrial economy was stark.

*Cotton Pickers* (fig. 1) was painted in 1945 but is based closely on a sketch Benton made during a trip through Georgia in 1928.[5] He depicted hardworking African Americans too poor to leave the land and head north for factory jobs as others had done. These sharecroppers, who rented their farms and had insurmountable debt, watched the price of cotton fall 60 percent during the 1930s. Such poverty brought both illness and a lack of medical attention, and the skinny baby shown under the blanket at right had half as much a chance of survival as a white urban child. By 1937 two-thirds of the nation's tenant farmers lived in eight southern states.[6]

In their use of illusionism and rejection of complete abstraction, Benton's pictures tell a readable story even when they lack a sequential narrative. In *Cotton Pickers* we can sense the backbreaking labor, the dry Georgia clay, unforgiving heat, and intense thirst. As the group picks cotton to be delivered to the horse-drawn wagon in the background, a woman offers another worker a drink of water from a pail. A lean-to protects the sleeping child from the hot sun. Benton rendered all the bodies in his signature sinuous style and unified the composition through beautiful juxtapositions of blue, green, and red.

**Fig. 1** Thomas Hart Benton. *Cotton Pickers*, 1945. Art Institute of
Chicago. Cat. 4.

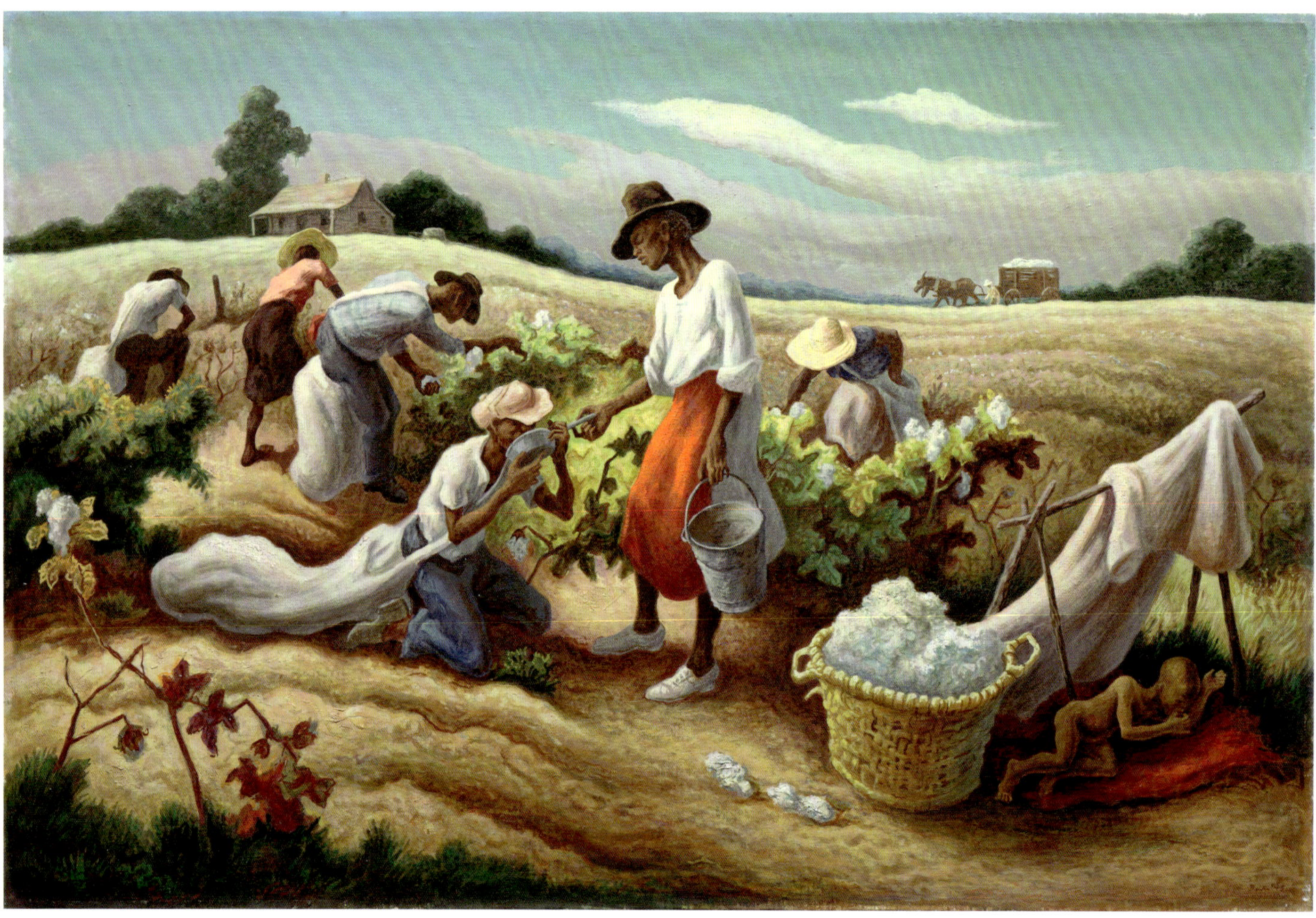

His inclusion of African and Native Americans in his murals
and paintings shows his desire to create an inclusive history
rather than erasing race from his narratives.[7] The artist exhibited his southern paintings at the Delphic Galleries in New York
in 1930, and the exhibition cemented his position as a painter of
American life.[8]

Benton's sympathy for the poor coincided with the
national debate on theories of eugenics. Some northerners and
southerners alike, considering themselves progressives, promoted the view that "poor white trash"—as well as some African
Americans, criminals, and other groups—were degenerate, rife
with disease and illiteracy. In order to improve the stock of the
nation, they encouraged sterilization of those considered less
desirable. Even East Coast journalists such as H. L. Mencken,

editor of the *American Mercury*, thought that eugenic thinking might solve the problem of poverty. He wrote, "Sterilize
the males of the present generation [of sharecroppers], and so
cut off the flow of their congenital and incurable inferiority."[9]
Books like Erskine Caldwell's *Tobacco Road* (1932), later made
into a popular Broadway play, encouraged such attitudes about
rural degeneracy. It is no accident that Benji, one of William
Faulkner's narrators in *The Sound and the Fury* (1929), is mentally challenged, his narrative, as in Shakespeare, "a tale told by
an idiot." So too, John Steinbeck included a mentally challenged
protagonist in *Of Mice and Men* (1937) to show the cruelty of
ignorance and prejudice.

Eugenic thinking was supposed to be rational, scientific,
and modern. Its appeal was that it projected a perception of

recovery, control, and stability as the Depression deepened. Powerless to remedy the present, eugenicists focused on defining the future of the country through the genetic improvement of its citizens, not unlike the idea of racial purification promoted by Nazis in Europe.

Benton's sympathy for the working class came from his roots. The artist was born into a prominent Missouri political family; his father, Maecenas Benton, served in the House of Representatives, and his great-uncle and namesake was the state's most famous senator and an opponent of slavery's spread in the first half of the nineteenth century. Benton favored a populist view of American history in which the story of the nation was not that of great leaders but rather that of workers. Populism based on erasing economic inequality, the promotion of opportunity, and the celebration of common people became highly important in the rural areas of the South, Midwest, and West. In the Midwest, it entailed a tentative alliance of immigrants, struggling farmers, factory workers, and labor unionists who all wanted cheap paper money to alleviate debt.[10] Not until 1932, in the depths of the Depression, did President Roosevelt finally take the United States off the gold standard in an effort to loosen the money supply. Within this workingman's coalition of farm and factory, Benton found his most compelling subject matter and a platform for his view of a classless American society. He, like other utopian thinkers in the 1930s, hoped for a newly refined capitalist system that maintained private ownership but measured success in terms of the commonweal instead of profit.[11]

During the 1930s Benton produced murals that would establish his reputation as a populist, a Regionalist, and a painter who concentrated on themes and locales. In the ten-panel *America Today* (1930–31; Metropolitan Museum of Art), painted for the New School for Social Research in New York, he retooled many of the sketches he made during trips he took in the late 1920s. The abrupt juxtapositions of his subjects along the walls give a frenetic, restless quality to his themes, allowing viewers to look at the murals outside of a narrative or sequential pattern. *America Today* emphasized the power of labor and industry. In the panel entitled *The South*, Benton repeated the

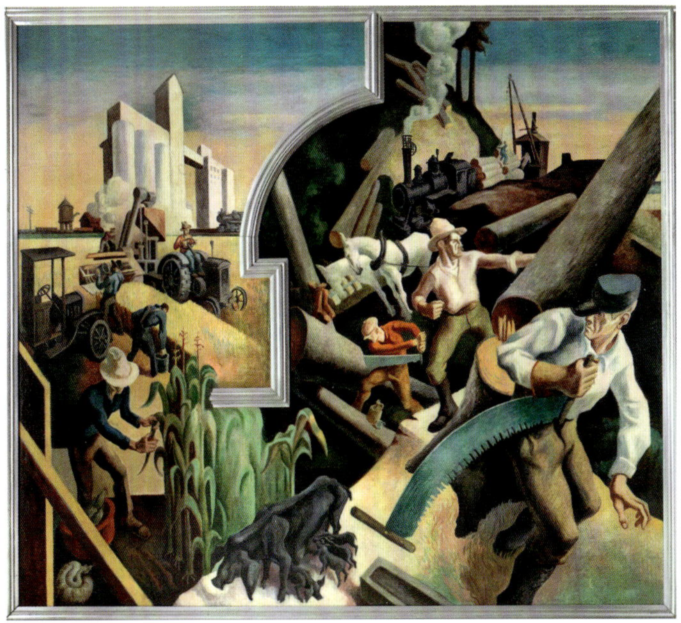



theme of cotton and contrasted white and black workers, hand labor and mechanization. In *Midwest* (fig. 2), one of eight panels representing life in different regions of the country, he depicted farmers in cornfields that were newly mechanized with tractors and automobiles. In the background stands a grain elevator the size of a skyscraper or factory, much like Ford's River Rouge plant, which Charles Sheeler painted around the same time (see *Classic Landscape*, 1931; p. 21, fig. 4). Muscular lumberjacks cut trees by hand like their farm counterparts, claiming a living from the land. Other panels included *Changing West*, which contrasts traditional cattle ranching with modern oil drilling, coal mining, steel production, and city life.

Benton went on to repeat his performance with *The Arts of Life in America*, executed for the Whitney Museum of American Art in 1932.[12] In particular, the panel he created for the library, *Arts of the West* (fig. 3), showed his focus on what was original to American rural life. At left, guitar and harmonica playing and fiddling are accompanied by a whiskey jug. Gaming, horseshoes, poker, and shooting, all games in which wagers were laid, occupy the middle. On the far right, cowboys attempt to break wild horses. Benton wrote that the subject of the mural was "what an individual has known and felt about things encountered in a real world of real people and actual doings."[13] These were American scenes.

The reaction to these murals was mixed. Some critics and artists were offended by Benton's critical depictions of East Coast highbrow magazines and the liberal intellectual establishment in a section entitled *Political Business and Political Ballyhoo*; others found the exaggerated execution of this grouping aesthetically displeasing. Opinions were divided even among his fellow artists. Because of the overstated quality of his figures, Benton ran the risk of stereotyping his subjects. While he sought the archetypal symbols of common events, his critics derided his paintings as racist because their African American figures possessed caricature-like qualities. Stuart Davis, then teaching at New York's Art Students League, led a group of students and faculty in signing a petition to destroy Benton's murals because they depicted African Americans in poverty and, the petitioners claimed, conveyed an antihuman quality. But Benton's view was that his murals "portray American life in the twentieth century realistically. It may be life that should be criticized; but not my painting of it."[14] "To the critical objections to my murals that they are too loud and too disturbing to be in good taste," he said, "there is only the answer that they represent the US which is also loud and not in 'good taste.'"[15] In fact, in Benton's murals, white and black figures alike have a caricatured quality.

Modernist advocates of abstraction such as Davis believed that Benton's muscular, chauvinistic realism was aesthetically backward-looking and pandered to plebeian tastes. Davis felt that for art to "have any cultural value it must be done in the light of the real discoveries of modern art."[16] Benton and Davis sparred for years. Critic Edward Alden Jewell, decrying the animosity of their debate, wrote the following in 1935:

**[W]hen we compare their respective styles, their divergent methods of dealing with a theme, Mr. Benton and Mr. Davis might, on first thought, be esteemed poles apart. But is the cleavage actually so formidable? Both men are fundamentally interested in the creation of works of art rather than in the mere exploitation of subject. . . . Their job is to say all that they have to say in the form of created art. And if they do this to the very best of their ability, they will have said enough. . . . As for the American Scene—with which both these artists, if we are to credit their titles, are concerned . . . that can be communicated only in terms of art that is rich in understanding. . . . Everything else is just skating about on the surface of life and of art alike.[17]**

Benton's notoriety landed him one the largest mural commissions ever—14 feet high and 230 feet long. The painting was to depict the history of Indiana and be displayed in Chicago at the Century of Progress exhibition in 1933–34. Again, the artist's compositions included workers on farms and in steel mills, oil refineries, railroads, and colleges, in addition to fur traders, pioneers, and hooded members of the Ku Klux Klan. The latter inclusion infuriated critics, who did not want to admit that the Klan was a part of Indiana's history (as it was in all border states). But in fact, several known members of the group had been elected to political office in 1924. Benton's reference to Klansmen may have been a nod to the practice of lynching. In 1930 the *Chicago Defender*, an African American newspaper, published a photograph of an Indiana lynching that was then widely reproduced.[18]

Benton painted this theme in 1934 in a composition (now lost) showing a young black man being hanged while a mob destroys his cabin. In 1932 fully half of all African Americans were out of work. Racial violence had again become more common because of economic competition, with many whites calling for blacks to be fired from jobs as long as there were whites who were unemployed. Documented lynchings increased fourfold between 1932 and 1933. While Congress repeatedly failed to pass federal antilynching laws, the Communist Party, of which Benton's fellow Missourian and artist Joe Jones was a member, attributed such violence to the economic and racial inequalities of capitalism and called for artists to protest this lawless practice through graphic portrayals. Jones also painted a lynching scene, ironically entitled *American Justice* (1933; fig. 4). Jones countered criticism of his subject by likening his picture to a Renaissance crucifixion scene, pointing out that while both depict mob violence, one is recognized as beautiful and sacred,

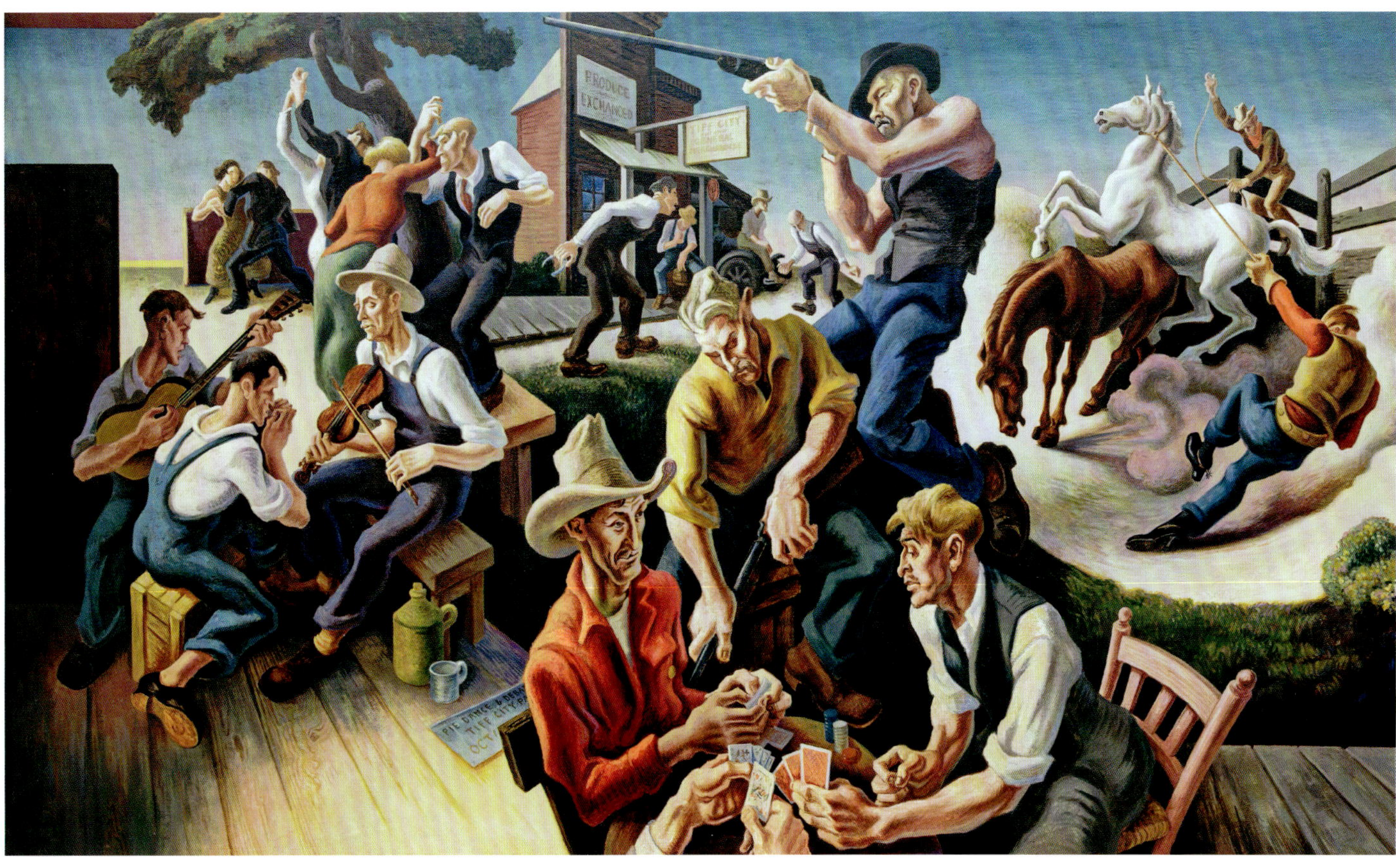

while the other is considered shocking.[19] In the early 1930s, Curry, like Jones and Benton, also addressed racial issues. His *Manhunt* (1931; Joslyn Art Museum, Omaha) depicts dogs and white men on foot and horseback entering the forest in search of their quarry. The scene is the prelude to the main event, the capture and lynching of the victim. The darkness and menacing faces of the pursuers bespeak evil. Curry was an early civil rights activist and a member of the National Urban League. *Manhunt* was acquired by the vice president of the National Association for the Advancement of Colored People.[20]

By the time Benton finished the Indiana commission and returned to New York in 1934, he was famous. That year his portrait graced the Christmas Eve cover of *Time* magazine, provoking criticism from many in the New York art world. The author of the *Time* article recalled the early French modernists featured in the 1913 New York Armory Show as practitioners of "arbitrary distortions and screaming colors."[21] He lambasted the "crazy parade" of Cubism, Futurism, Dadaism, and Surrealism, which were so "deliberately unintelligible that it was no longer news when a picture was hung upside down." The author's xenophobia prompted him to say that the opposition to "outlandish" art first took root in the Midwest, where representational art depicting fields, factories, shipyards, and streets, understood by all, replaced introspective abstractions.

The article featured Benton but went on to discuss other American Scene painters, presenting Benton, Curry, and Wood as a triumphant trio of midwestern Regionalist artists, even though Benton lived in New York and Curry (born in Kansas) lived in Westport, Connecticut. Only Wood, who had traveled in Europe like the other two, returned to the Midwest, residing

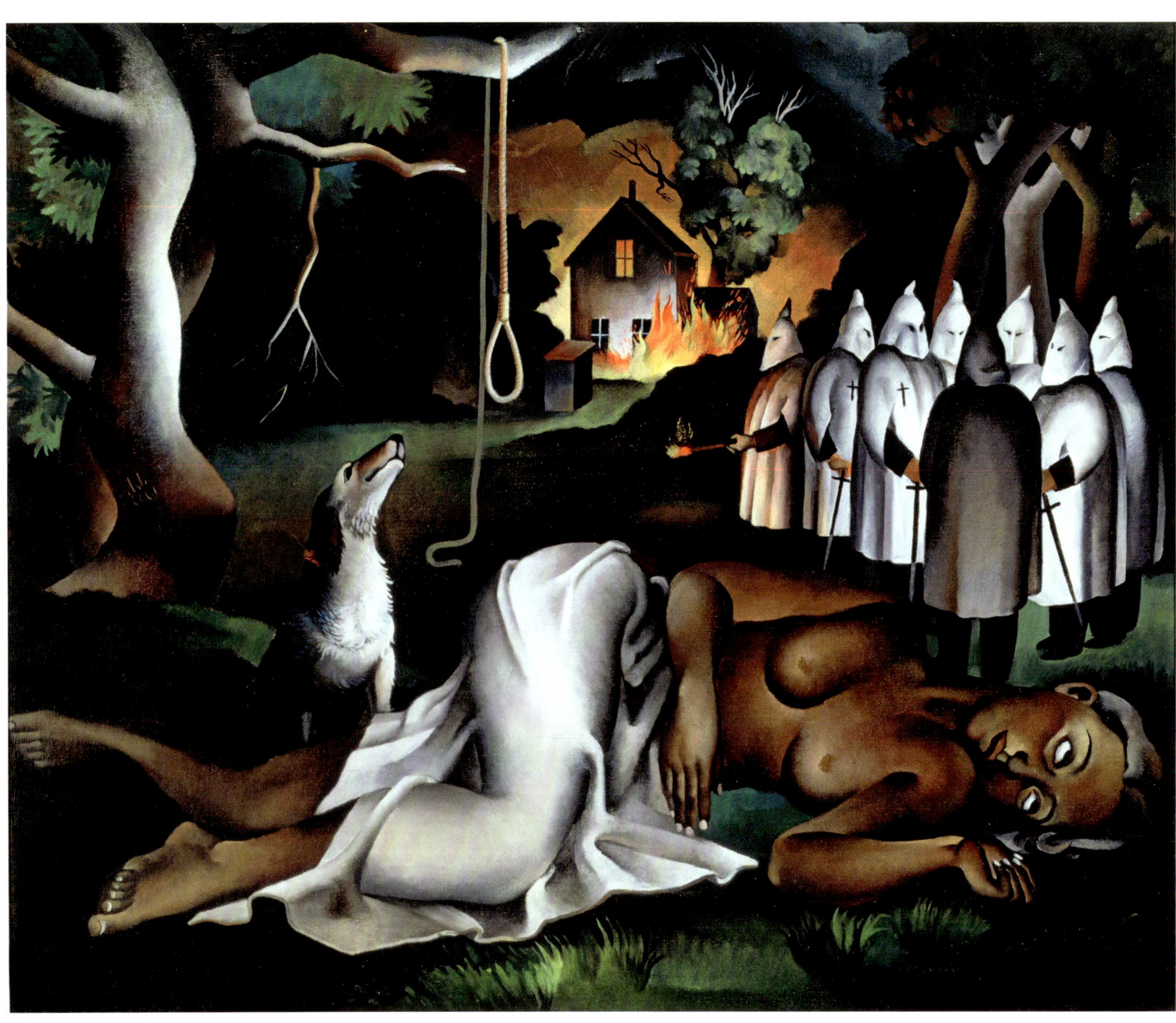

in his home state of Iowa. The three men had shown together in a 1933 exhibition at the Kansas City Art Institute. The organizer, Maynard Walker, said that their work represented a new direction in American art, one associated with the Midwest: "I mean an art which really springs from American soil and seeks to interpret American life. . . . [M]uch of the most vital modern art in America is coming out of our long backward Middle West."[22] The connections linking their subject matter made by Walker, and later by the *Time* article, gave the three painters national publicity upon which they would capitalize. And so, by 1934 midwestern Regionalism, considered by supporters to be a renaissance in the heartland and a celebration of American values, was born. By 1935 Walker was acting as the dealer for all three artists.[23]

To its critics, Regionalist painting seemed chauvinistic and parochial in its the content. As events in Europe escalated during the 1930s, it seemed to many that the emphasis on American and midwestern subjects resembled the intolerant and violent nationalism practiced in Nazi Germany.[24] To others it seemed "nostalgic and sentimental."[25] Urban modernists took exception to some of Benton's unfortunate rhetoric about "degenerate" modernism, especially after he left New York and returned to Missouri in 1934. Walker defended Regionalism as authentically American and "virile," describing European modernists Pablo Picasso, Henri Matisse, and their followers as "freaks," calling their paintings "rubbish" and their ideas effete.[26] To Regionalism's supporters, the movement seemed patriotic because of its reliance on American history subjects (see Annelise K. Madsen's essay in this volume) and pastoral scenes that were easy to understand, offering a positive, hopeful outlook in a time of economic chaos. When Wood's *American Gothic* was on view at the Art Institute of Chicago in 1930, Chicago critic C. J. Bulliet called the artist the American version of Henri Rousseau:

**Wood's big contribution to the joy of the moment is not that he is a mere imitator of Rousseau but that, working with American motifs, he gives an American something of the thrill that Rousseau, a follower of the little Dutchmen and the primitives of Flanders, gave with French motifs to twentieth century Frenchmen.[27]**

Bulliet ascribed a healthy naïveté to Wood's painting style that was both charming and modern. He attempted to describe a middle ground for Regionalism by calling it modern in style but uniquely nationalistic in vision. Despite its critics, Regionalism seemed popular with the public, and it received a boost from the vast government support of the arts under the new Roosevelt administration. Treasury Department official Edward Bruce and artist George Biddle created a temporary Public Works of Art Project that, in 1933 and 1934, employed artists and sculptors to ornament public buildings: courthouses, hospitals, schools, and more than 1,100 post offices. The project brought work to thousands of artists whose output was seen by many thousands more. While abstract modernists such as Ilya Bolotowsky and Davis were sometimes hired, in the main, these public commissions focused on history and specific locales and were realist in style. Wood wrote that in order to earn their weekly salary, artists were to depict "the contemporaneous American scene," while "experiments in abstraction and transcripts of still life" were outside the guidelines. Acceptable were landscapes, rural subjects, the field and the factory, and any work having "social significance."[28] The government's role in nurturing and defining a national culture meant that "official" art was further distanced from European modernism.[29]

Just before the Kansas Art Institute exhibition in 1933, Curry traveled to Iowa to meet Wood.[30] Curry was to teach at Wood's Stone City Art Colony and School, founded the previous year. Wood hoped that Stone City would become the center of midwestern painting, rivaling artists' colonies on the East Coast. Like Benton, Curry had started painting local subjects— in his case, his home state of Kansas—around 1928. Working as an illustrator for many years, he finished his first major canvas, *Baptism in Kansas* (fig. 5), that summer. Later that year it was displayed at the Corcoran Gallery of Art's biennial exhibition of contemporary art. Well reviewed, it was noticed by Gertrude Vanderbilt Whitney, who offered Curry a generous stipend for a

**Fig. 5**  John Steuart Curry (American, 1897–1946). *Baptism in Kansas*, 1928. Oil on canvas. 101.6 × 127 cm (40 × 50 in.). Whitney Museum of American Art, New York, Gift of Gertrude Vanderbilt Whitney. 31.159.

**Fig. 6**  John Steuart Curry. *Hogs Killing a Snake*, c. 1930. Art Institute of Chicago. Cat. 10.

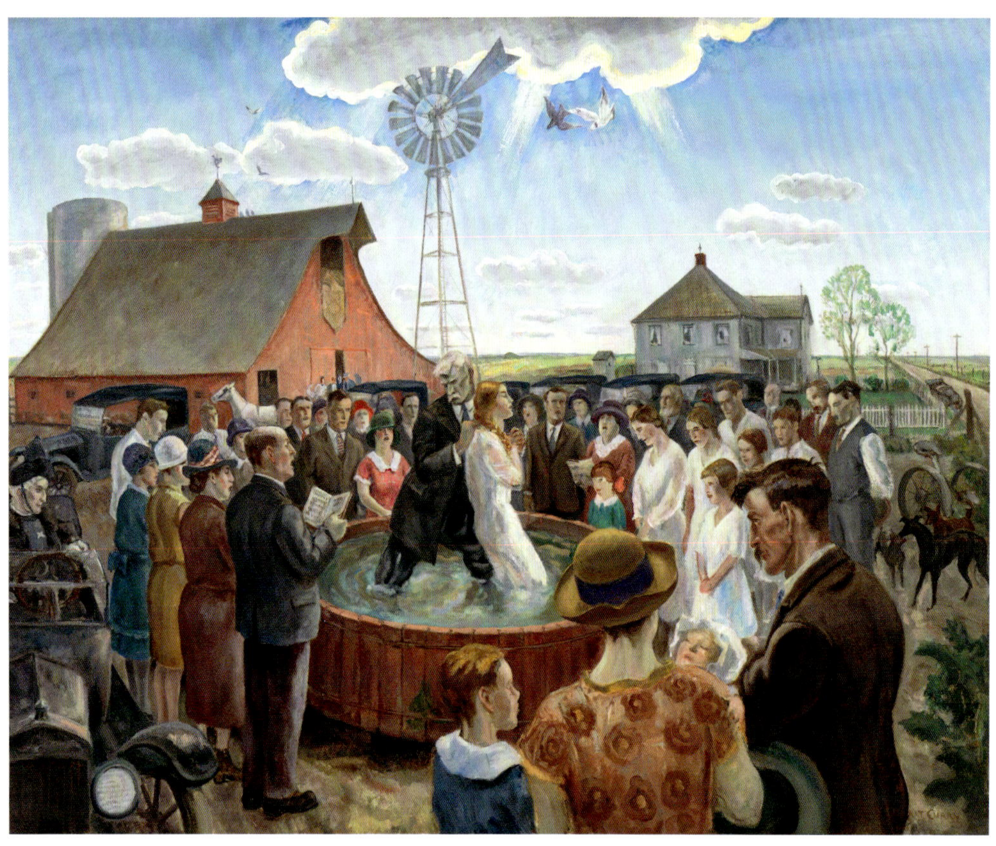

year in order to continue to paint.[31] His great success preceded the consequent fame of both Benton and Wood by two years. *Baptism in Kansas* reflects the artist's background as an illustrator and uses stereotypes of farm life: the red barn, the old house, the windmill, and the cattle trough, where the baptism takes place. The singing congregation draws us into its midst, while the horizon line of the endless prairie pulls us out again. Curry's composition was not unusual, but his contrast of the stark farm landscape, the somber faces of the onlookers, and the allusion to fundamentalist religion with the birds above, surrounded by rays of sun, made a very dramatic statement about an older culture, one particularly out of place on the urban East Coast. City dwellers could look on in fascination at this unfamiliar type of scene in an unknown world, an anecdotal picture with an understandable narrative.

Perhaps Curry's masterpiece is *Hogs Killing a Snake* (c. 1930; fig. 6), whose power resides in its departure from his usual formula. The canvas is devoid of human figures or sequential narrative, and its undercurrent of dark violence repeats the artist's ambivalent depictions of rural life. Wild boars converge upon a serpent, biting and trampling it to death before it strikes. Here color, movement, and composition are reminiscent of the work of the Flemish Baroque painter Peter Paul Rubens, one of Curry's favorite artists. The subject is filled with kinetic energy, and the close-up view eliminates the illustrative qualities of much of Curry's early work. Like many of his pictures, the scene draws from the artist's religious upbringing. Besides the snake, he includes an apple tree, recalling the Garden of Eden. In this garden, all is not well; there is danger, violence, and death. The painting offers an epic interpretation of the struggle of nature and the will to live.

Curry, like so many other artists, lived marginally during the early years of the Depression. The opportunity to teach at Stone City provided much-needed income and also an

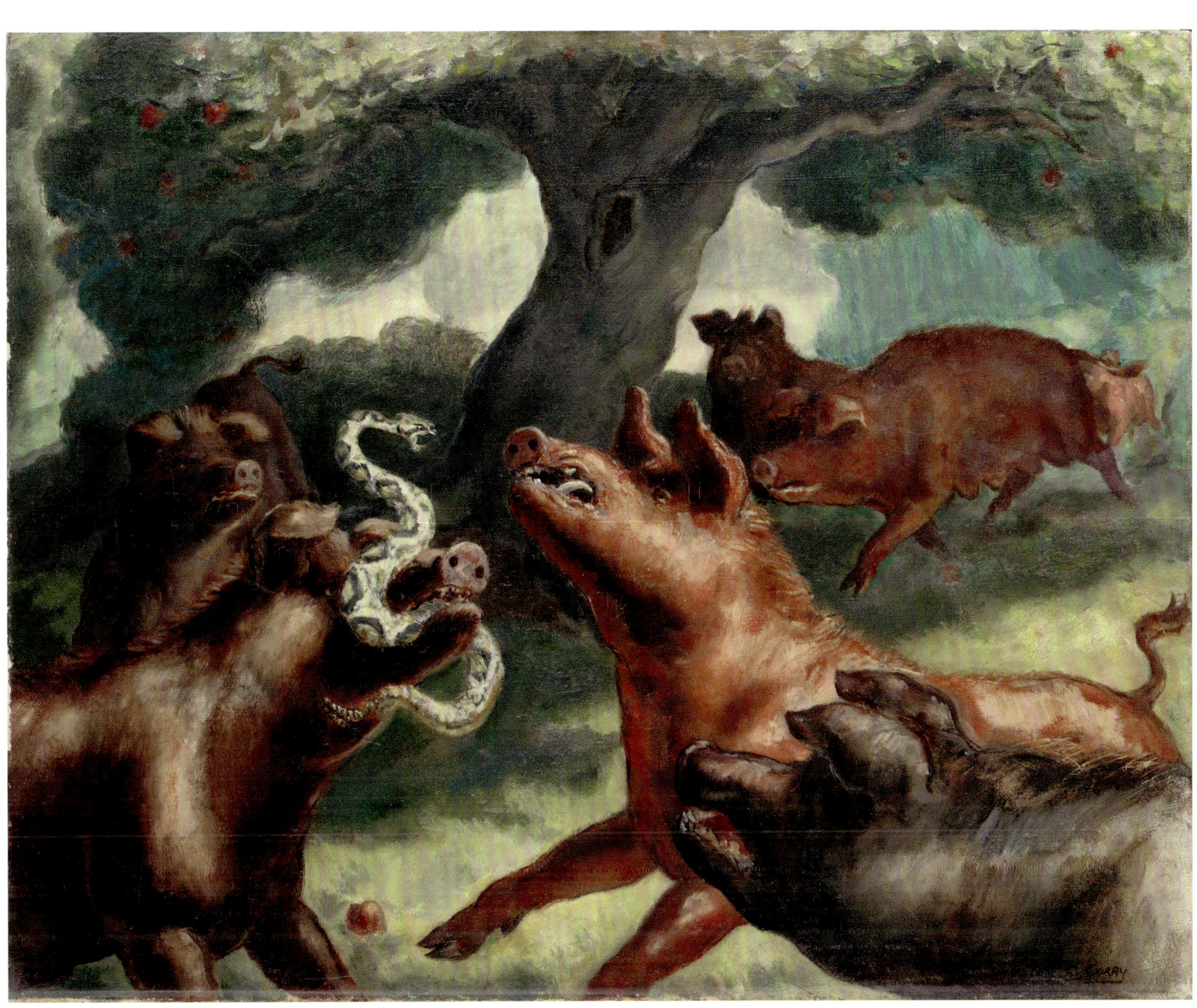

**Fig. 7** John Steuart Curry and Grant Wood wearing overalls in Stone City, Iowa. *Time*, December 24, 1934, p. 24. Photograph by John Barry, Jr., Cedar Rapids Museum of Art.

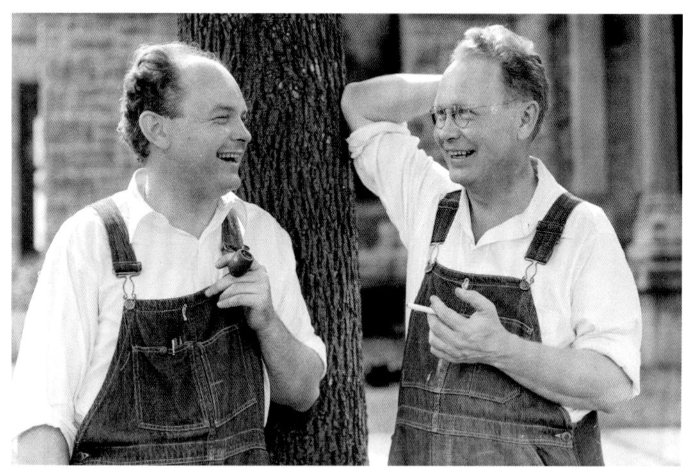

opportunity to wear the farmer's bib overalls Wood favored (see fig. 7). Wood also arranged for Curry to become an artist in residence at the University of Wisconsin in 1936, when Curry finally moved to the Midwest. Only now did the entire trio of famous Regionalists live in the area they chose to represent.

Wood lived the longest in the Midwest. A native of Cedar Rapids, he had traveled abroad four times before 1930. Despite his dress, he was never a farmer but was, like Benton and Curry, interested in American subject matter. He was not, as he said, advertising any particular locale but wanted a true and native "art expression to grow from the soil itself."[32] Wood chose for his subject matter the land and people of his native Iowa, painting them in a meticulously flat and stylized fashion derived from his study of early northern European painting during a 1928 trip to Munich. His hyperreal, highly detailed figures and landscapes have an immediacy that is also found in the portrait work of the German Renaissance artist Albrecht Dürer and the early Netherlandish painter Hans Memling (see fig. 8). Indeed, Lincoln Kirstein called Wood "the Iowa Memling" both for the ways he stylized his compositions and for the detailed nature that he presented.[33]

One of his earliest and most famous paintings is *American Gothic* (1930; fig. 9), shown at the Art Institute of Chicago the year it was painted and immediately purchased by the museum. Wood depicted a white Gothic Revival cottage he had seen while driving through Eldon, Iowa (see p. 98, fig. 7). He wrote,

"This gave me an idea. That idea was to find two people who by their severely straight-laced characters would fit into such a home."[34] Eventually, he settled on his sister and his dentist to depict the farm couple. The vertical pattern of the house's board-and-batten siding is repeated in the farmer's collarless shirt. The window curtains within the Gothic arch echo the woman's apron, under which she wears her good black dress with white collar, dressed up with her family cameo. He partially covers his bib overalls with what may be his only suit jacket. They pose in their Sunday best but still with the tools of their work. The couple is divided by their traditional gender roles. On the right is the barn, where presumably he is headed with the pitchfork; on the left, the house, with plants upon the porch. Wood's subject addressed Victorian things: home, pitchfork, apron, cameo. In their dourness, the couple does not look modern—they exist in an antique, insular world. The art that Wood drew from "native" soil was not without satiric content. He depicted the pair as neat, plain, quite literally straightforward and direct, but also as symbols of conformity and traditionalism. The artist reinforces this theme with the rigidity of his figures and the verticality of the composition. While offensive to some Iowans, who thought that Wood portrayed his subjects as provincial, *American Gothic* was a hit with audiences in Chicago because, like Curry's *Baptism in Kansas*, it represented an exotic, unknown world.

In 1930 the small, independent homestead of *American Gothic* was already an anachronism. One of Wood's acquaintances, Des Moines resident and Regionalist author Ruth Suckow, wrote a popular novel entitled *The Folks* in 1932. Focusing on ordinary Iowa lives, the book describes family farms as empty places for old people whose children have moved to the comfort of town. The grandchildren have left for both coasts—to California in search of material opportunity and New York for intellectual stimulation and personal freedom. Indeed, that was exactly what was happening demographically even earlier. Sinclair Lewis's 1920 novel *Main Street* differentiated between farm and small-town life, taking aim at the smug self-satisfaction of the latter. According to Lewis, the townies of Gopher Prairie enforced conformity "under a hundred

**Fig. 8** Hans Memling (Netherlandish, 1430/40–1494). *Young Man at Prayer with St. William of Maleval* (interior wing panel from the Triptych of Jan Crabbe), c. 1470. Tempera on panel; 83.5 × 26.99 cm (32 ⅞ × 10 ⅝ in.). The Pierpont Morgan Library, New York, Purchased by Pierpont Morgan, AZ012.2.

guises and pompous names, such as Polite Society, the Family, the Church, Sound Business, the Party, the Country, [and] the Superior White Race."[35]

Wood also made distinctions between what he saw as the forthrightness of the farmer's world and the intellectual and historical pretensions of the village aristocracy. His composition *Daughters of Revolution* (1932; p. 90, fig. 1) is an acid depiction of such self-satisfaction. The artist's trip to Munich had been to oversee the production of his design for a stained-glass window memorializing World War I veterans in Cedar Rapids. Patriotic groups in Iowa vigorously protested the manufacture of the window in the land of the enemy, even though the war had ended eleven years before. As Wood later wrote, "They could ladle it out. I thought I'd see if they could take it."[36] Beyond this tit for tat, Wood's subject was the exclusion of immigrants and the foreign-born from organizations founded to promote social and economic superiority.

At the height of immigration in the 1890s, white, primarily Protestant groups such as the Daughters of the American Revolution, the Mayflower Society, and the Colonial Dames of America were all formed to promote the study and importance of Anglo-Saxon family roots.[37] The three women in Wood's painting, seated under a reproduction of Emanuel Leutze's famous *Washington Crossing the Delaware* (1851; p. 92, fig. 3), are self-satisfied believers in their own genealogical superiority. While the painting reminds the viewer of the father of the country and his military daring, these genteel ladies would support nothing revolutionary. One of them holds a Victorian, Chinese-influenced blue willow teacup; in her ignorance, she is innocent of the origins of the design, remaining opposed to the foreign and the different. About to sip tea rather than sherry, she and friends belong to the right groups and are no doubt affiliated with the Women's Christian Temperance Union, which started in the Midwest and staunchly supported Prohibition as the law of the land. (Prohibition was repealed two years later.) They are, as Sinclair Lewis put it in *Main Street*, "casually cruel and proudly dull."[38]

Wood stopped painting such satiric pictures of midwestern life when he became the Iowa director of Public Works of

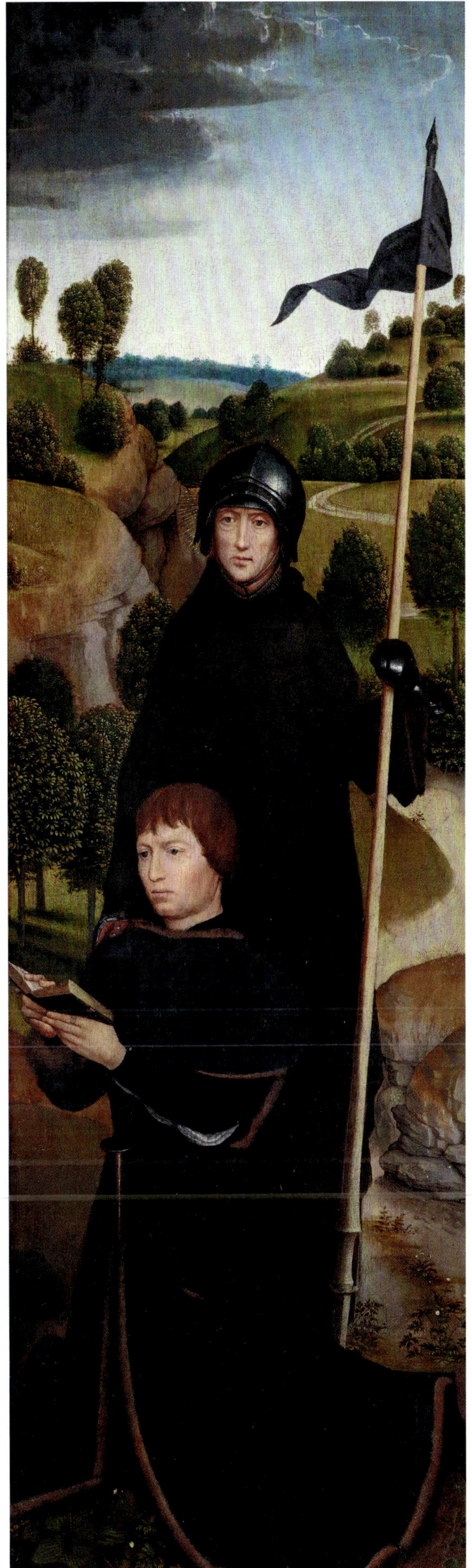

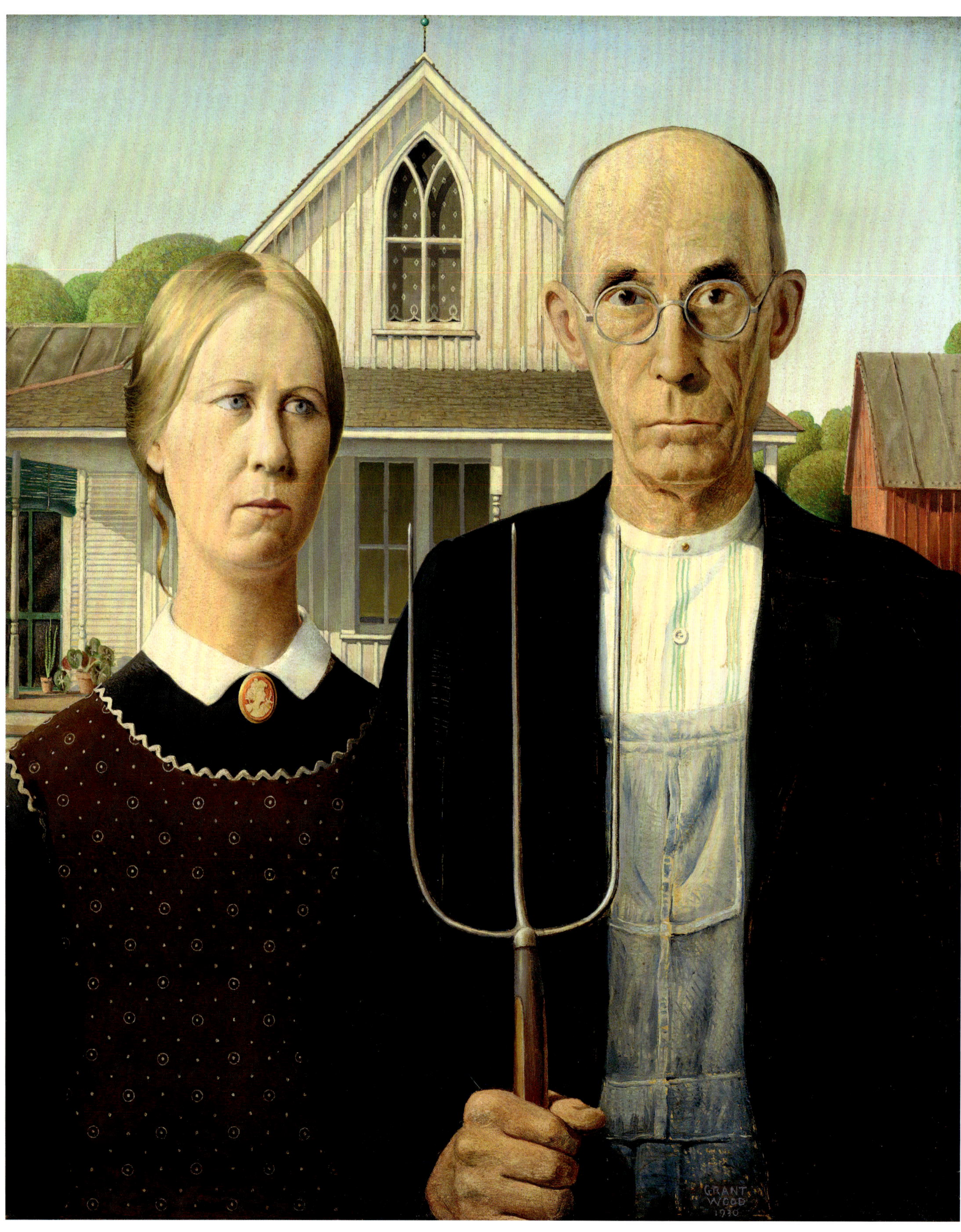

Art Projects in 1934. His later works feature commonplace subjects and beautiful landscapes depicting the state's rolling farmland. In fact, after 1936, he, Benton, and Curry mostly stopped painting acerbic social commentary, turning to more neutral, bucolic, and arcadian subjects. Indeed, the "back to the farm" movement of the 1930s peaked at about the same time. Contemporary writers estimated that millions of people left the cities hoping to find an easier, cheaper living in the country. The federal government encouraged this, financing around one hundred resettlement colonies. Even President Roosevelt supported this development, hoping it would lessen urban relief rolls.[39]

The American heartland was a place where utopianism had always thrived. Some religious and millennial groups had come to the area in the nineteenth century, and secular utopias were founded there as well. According to Horace Greeley, editor of the *New-York Tribune*, these were fellowships based on economic equality, where there were "no paupers and no surplus labor . . . [no] inefficiency in production and waste in consumption."[40] Such self-sufficient communities sought to eliminate the dehumanizing conditions of capitalism, financial distress, and factory work. Settlements such as Amana, Iowa; Bethel, Missouri; Bishop Hill, Illinois; New Harmony, Indiana; Zoar, Ohio; and numerous "phalanxes" started by followers of utopian socialist Charles Fourier were agriculturally based but also traded products with larger markets. From the late eighteenth century until the Depression, almost three hundred utopias had been founded in the old Northwest Territory.[41]

In his 1935 essay "Revolt against the City," Wood drew upon that utopian and pastoral tradition, seeking to enshrine it in contemporary times. Writing that the Midwest "always stood as the great conservative section of the country," he meant that such conservatism was a virtue and that it bespoke unchanging American values. Those values were associated with the farmer. Wood believed (like Thomas Jefferson) not only that farmers represented the basic economic foundation of the country, but also that each was "a little unit of his own . . . developing extraordinary independence." "The term 'rugged individualism' has been seized upon as a political catchword, but

it suits the farmer's character very well."[42] Benton wrote in his autobiography, *An Artist in America* (1937), that Regionalism represented an "escape" from "narrow metropolitan intellectualism."[43] Asked in an *Art Front* interview in 1935 if the future of American art lay in the Midwest, Benton replied, "Yes, because it is . . . the least provincial area in America. . . . Because, unlike the East, . . . it has never had a colonial psychology, that dependent attitude of mind which acts as a check on cultural experiments motivated in the environment." Benton associated himself with the idealism of earlier communal groups such as the Amana colonists, the Harmonists, and the Owenites.[44] But in opposing the Eastern art establishment, urban interests, and European-inspired modern art, the Regionalists became viewed as reactionaries.

These artists' subject matter was popularized by the media, particularly *Time* and *Life* magazines' illustrations of their works. *Life*, for example, featured the paintings of Wood's friend Doris Lee, who, while born in rural Aledo, Illinois, had studied with modernist painters in Italy and France. She attended the Kansas City Art Institute and at the California School of Fine Arts in San Francisco before moving to New York. She exhibited her painting *Thanksgiving* (c. 1935; p. 105, fig. 17) at the Art Institute of Chicago in 1935, where it won a medal and caused great controversy when a trustee, Josephine Logan, found it crudely painted and the subject disgusting. Logan wanted art to be "uplifting and beautiful," and discovered neither uplift nor beauty in Lee's picture or in "modern art."

Indeed, Lee chose to depict the common and the rural. In *Thanksgiving*, she chose a traditional American subject, the great American food fest. Deliberately choosing a naïve or primitive style of painting, the artist showed an old-fashioned farm kitchen complete with wood-burning stove and devoid of any plumbing or modern conveniences. The room is filled with women preparing the meal, and a well-dressed, younger, citified woman has just arrived and takes off her hat. Her clothing forms a contrast to the long flowered dresses and aprons of her older relatives. No men are present, reinforcing traditional gender roles and associating women with domesticity, much as Wood had done in *American Gothic*. Lee used rough, uneven

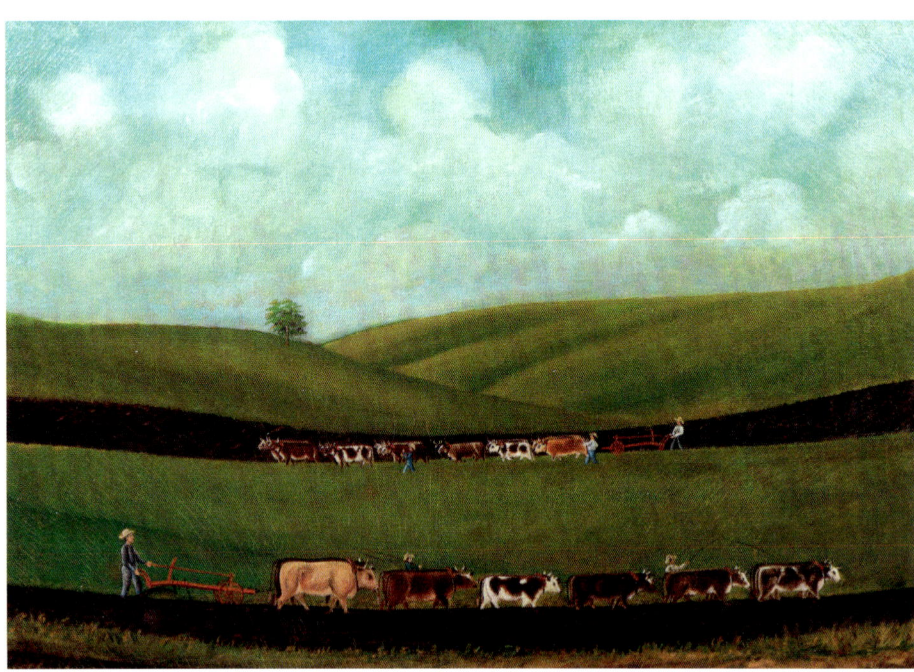

brushwork to make the picture surface seem primitive. Her seemingly untutored style fit well with modernist leanings. In fact, many American painters and sculptors of the late 1920s and 1930s favored primitive or folk objects because their bold areas of color and simplicity of line and proportion seemed modern.[45] Contrasted to this was the content of their pictures.

Wood's landscapes were characterized by their quaint view of a peaceful, mythic rural life. In *Fall Plowing* (1931; fig. 11), the artist painted an infinite expanse of tilled, virtually treeless cropland. Tiny sheaves of wheat create scale and a sense of the sublime. The plow stands alone, waiting for a team of horses; no machines exist in this world. The repetition of elements creates a calming effect. This is not a true rendition of a farm landscape of 1936, for by 1932 one in six farmers owned a tractor.[46] Instead it is an imagined landscape from the past, akin to primitive utopian views such as those painted by Olof Krans at Bishop Hill, Illinois, in the 1890s (see fig. 10). In the work of both Krans and Wood, flatness, repetition, linearity, and geometry express a pastoral view that appears timeless.

Wood seemed satisfied by such images. *Fall Plowing* presents the muted browns and golds of the fall, and *Young Corn* (fig. 12), of the same year, encapsulates the palette of early summer in small figures and neat rows. Wood was devoted to the cyclical patterns of farm life: his compositions recall the late medieval French illustrated manuscript *Les très riches heures du Duc de Berry* (1412/16), which describes the seasons and rhythms of nature and the toilers on the land (see fig. 13). As the artist put it, "The rhythms of the low hills, the patterns of crops upon them, the mystery of the seasons, and above all, a feeling for the integrity of the ground itself—these are my deep-rooted heritage."[47] In *Fall Plowing* he includes the old-fashioned, self-scouring steel plow invented by John Deere in the nineteenth century. The tool appears as a symbol of the heroic Cincinnatus, a Roman farmer turned soldier, just as Daniel Chester French had used it in his *Minute Man* sculpture (1875; Old North Bridge, Concord, Massachusetts) to represent the brave farmers who left their fields and took up arms at Concord and Lexington in 1775. *Young Corn* and *Fall Plowing* are works of true imagination, for the spring and summer of 1931 brought high temperatures and one of the most severe droughts the Midwest and Great Plains states had seen in decades. For those who were painting the land of the Dust Bowl,

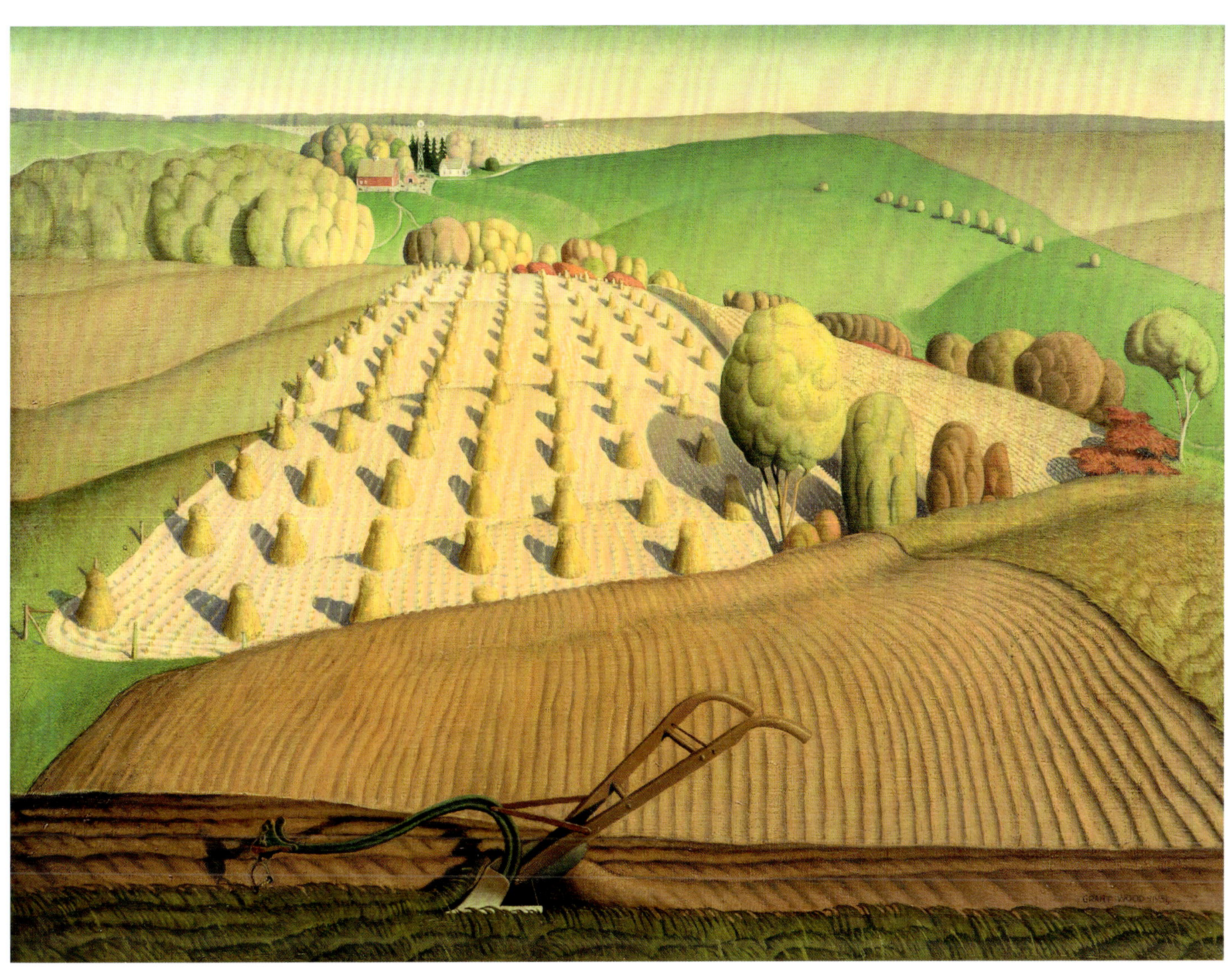

GRANT WOOD-1931

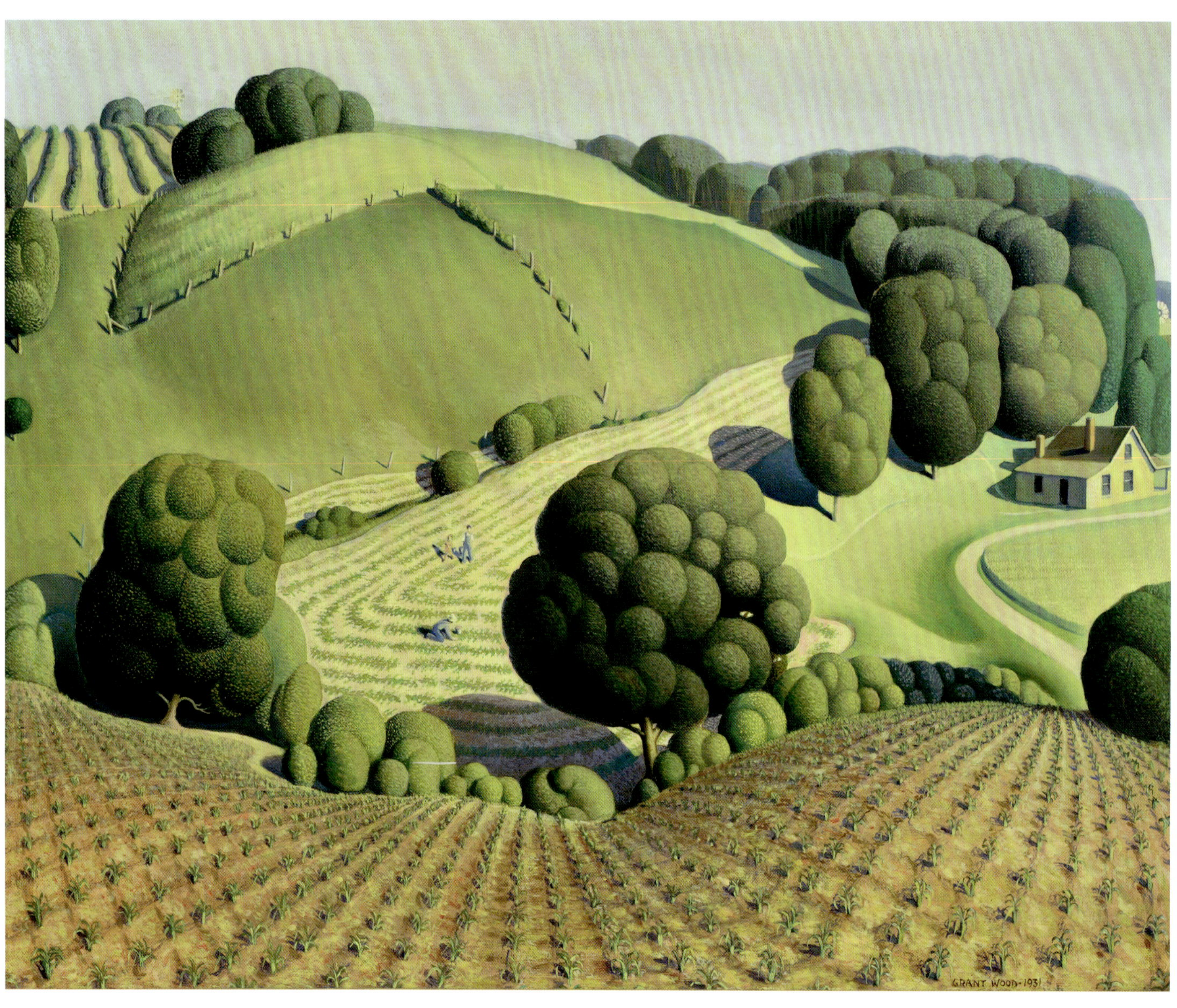

**Fig. 13** Herman, Paul, and Jean de Limbourg (Netherlandish; act. 1399–1416). *March,* from *Les très riches heures du Duc de Berry,* 1412/16. Pigments and gold on parchment; 30 × 21.5 cm (11 ¹³⁄₁₆ × 8 ½ in). Musée Condé, Chantilly.

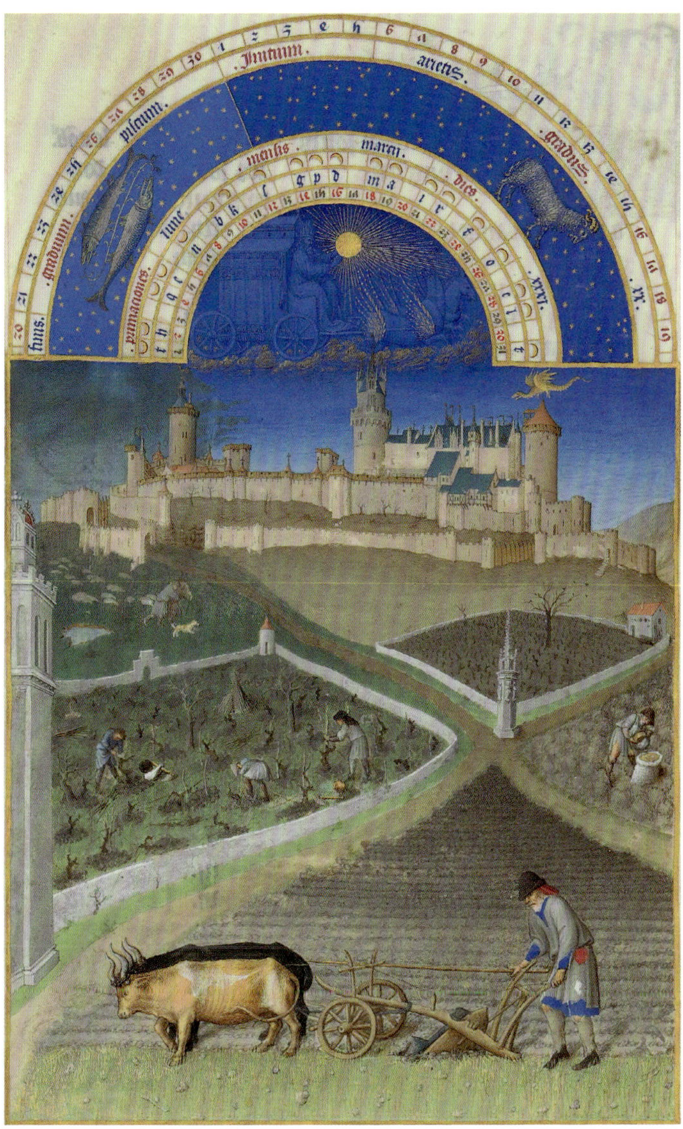

Wood's optimistic view of midwestern fecundity must have seemed escapist, nostalgic, and sentimental—a cultural rather than a realist landscape.

Even more arcadian were Marvin Cone's landscapes of rolling hills, rivers, and valleys. Between 1930 and 1938, the artist focused on the landscape of the Midwest. He befriended Wood years earlier; the two went on sketching trips together, and Cone was an instrumental teacher at the Stone City Art Colony. By 1936 Cone, who taught at Coe College in Cedar Rapids, was showing his work in competitive national

exhibitions at the Pennsylvania Academy of the Fine Arts, the Corcoran Gallery, and in Chicago and New York commercial galleries. Using Iowa scenery for inspiration, specifically the bluffs along the Cedar River, Cone executed a series of about fifteen pictures of the river's bend between 1935 and 1940. One of these, *River Bend No. 4* (1938; fig. 14), is a study of flattened patterns of pale blues and greens. In their serial nature and subtlety, such paintings recall the atmospheric abstractions of Monet's haystack compositions. Unlike Wood's landscapes, Cone's subjects are not hard-edged but are suffused with light and atmosphere. Cone did not consider himself part of the Regionalist milieu. Instead of describing specific places, his landscapes are individual responses to physical experiences. There is a sense of tranquility and mystery about them. One critic compared them to early Italian landscapes in their lyrical subtlety.[48] Devoid of human presence, Cone's series emphasizes elegiac mood rather than narrative. However, these are also history paintings of a sort, as they show the unchanging geography of the land. Friend to Cone and to Wood, poet Jay Sigmund penned verses akin to Cone's canvases. In "Stone City, Iowa" (before 1937), he wrote, "The world has folded up its crust/In giant wrinkles, and the rain/Falls gently on these fields of dust/As though to cool Earth's pain."

The Midwest's pastoral countryside was also the subject of Benton's paintings of the late 1930s. In *Haystack* (1938; fig. 15), rhythmic, swirling forms make farm life seem utopic, as humanity works in harmony with nature. Like Wood, Benton made the landscape one of idealized sustenance and plenitude; he was likewise influenced by early European art in his techniques. In the manner of Renaissance fresco painters, he worked in tempera, mixing his pigments with egg yolk and water, and laying the paint down on boards covered with gesso. He covered the pigments with layered glazes that made the surface rich and the colors vivid. This technique, along with the sensual motion of his forms, joined his compositions together. *Cradling Wheat* (1938; fig. 16) is devoid of machines and even work animals. The energy that Benton used in his earlier murals is present, although now the scene is not fractured with many subjects but instead presents a continuous narrative of

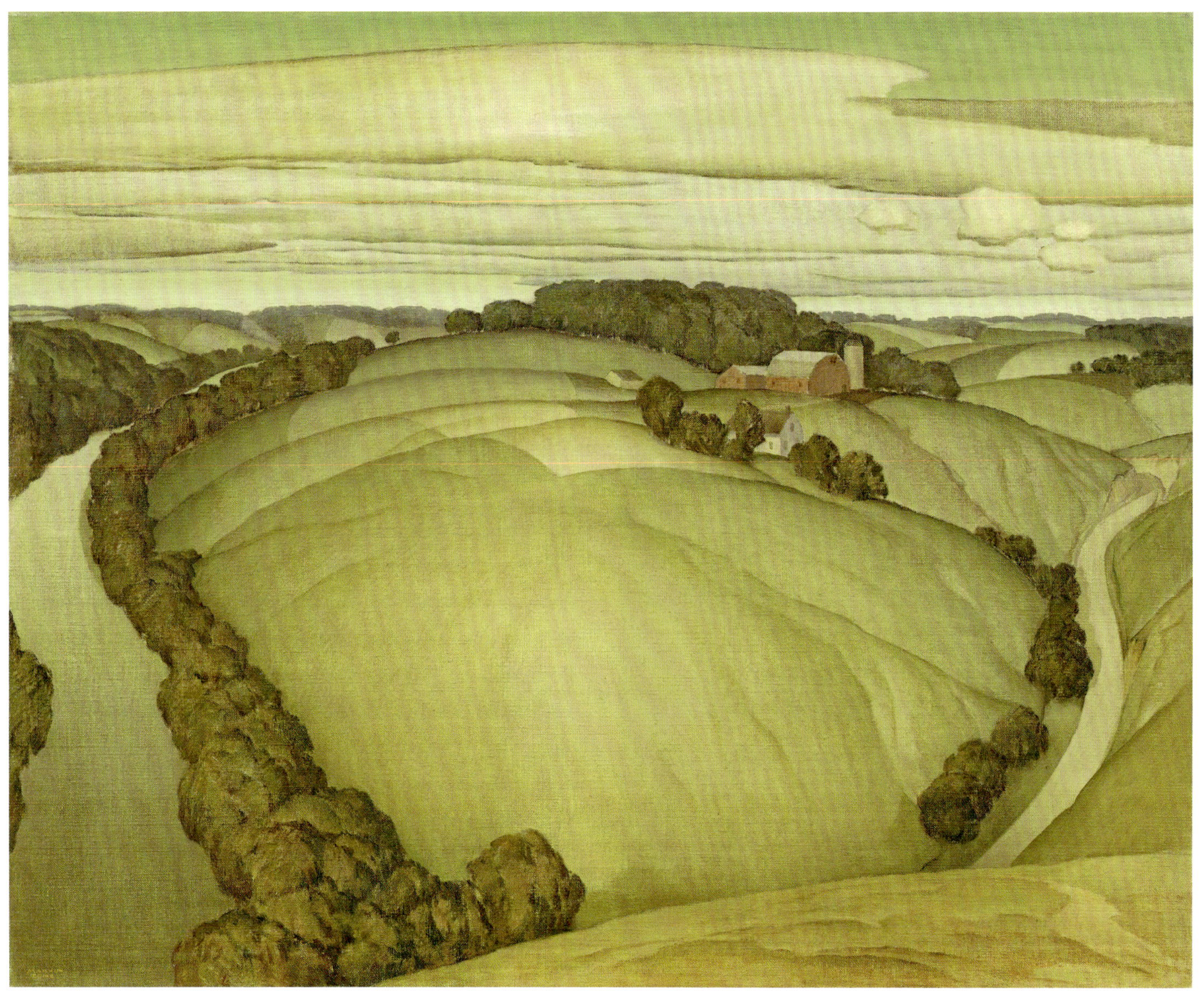

**Fig. 15** Thomas Hart Benton. *Haystack*, 1938. Museum of Fine Arts, Houston. Cat. 3.

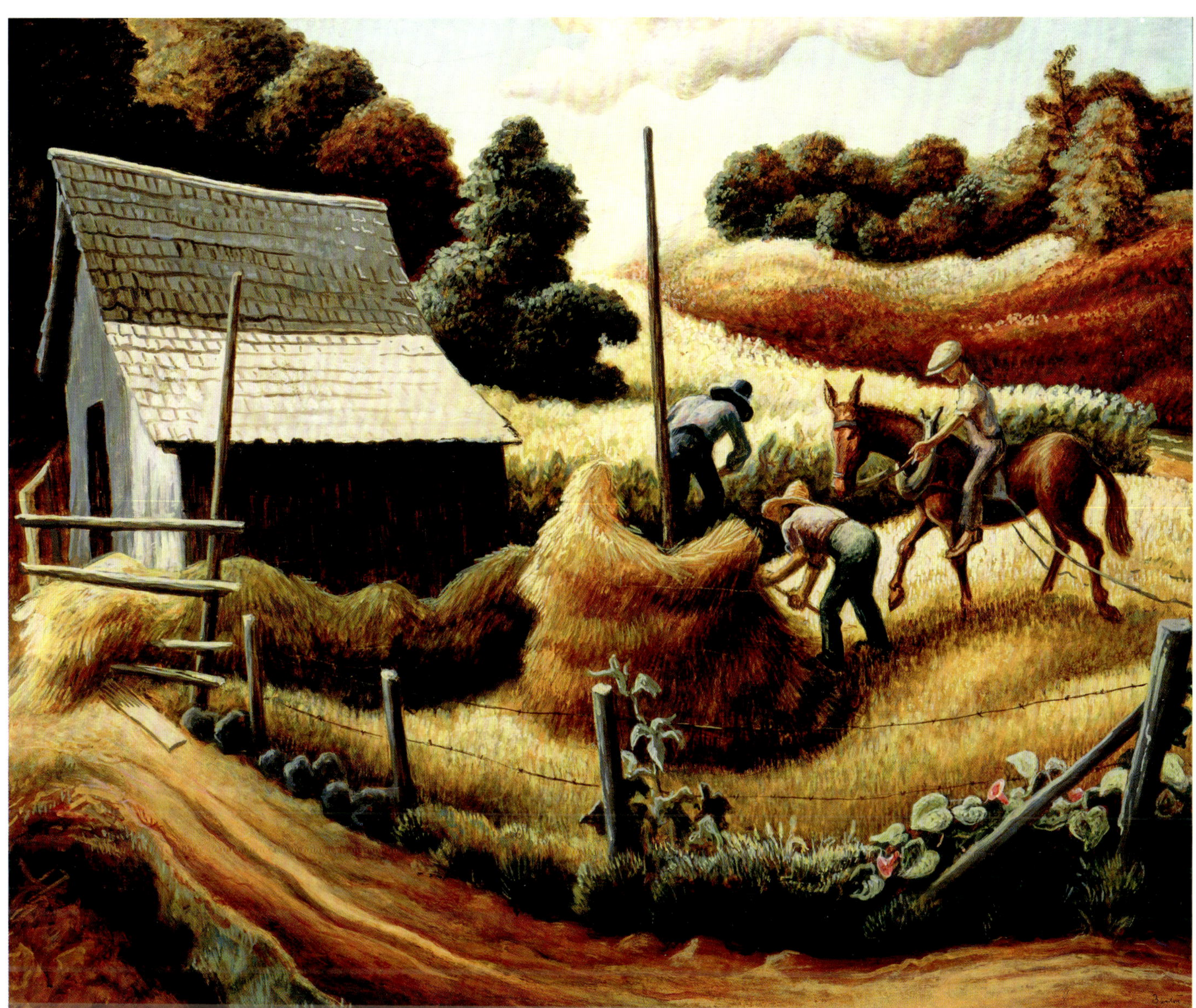

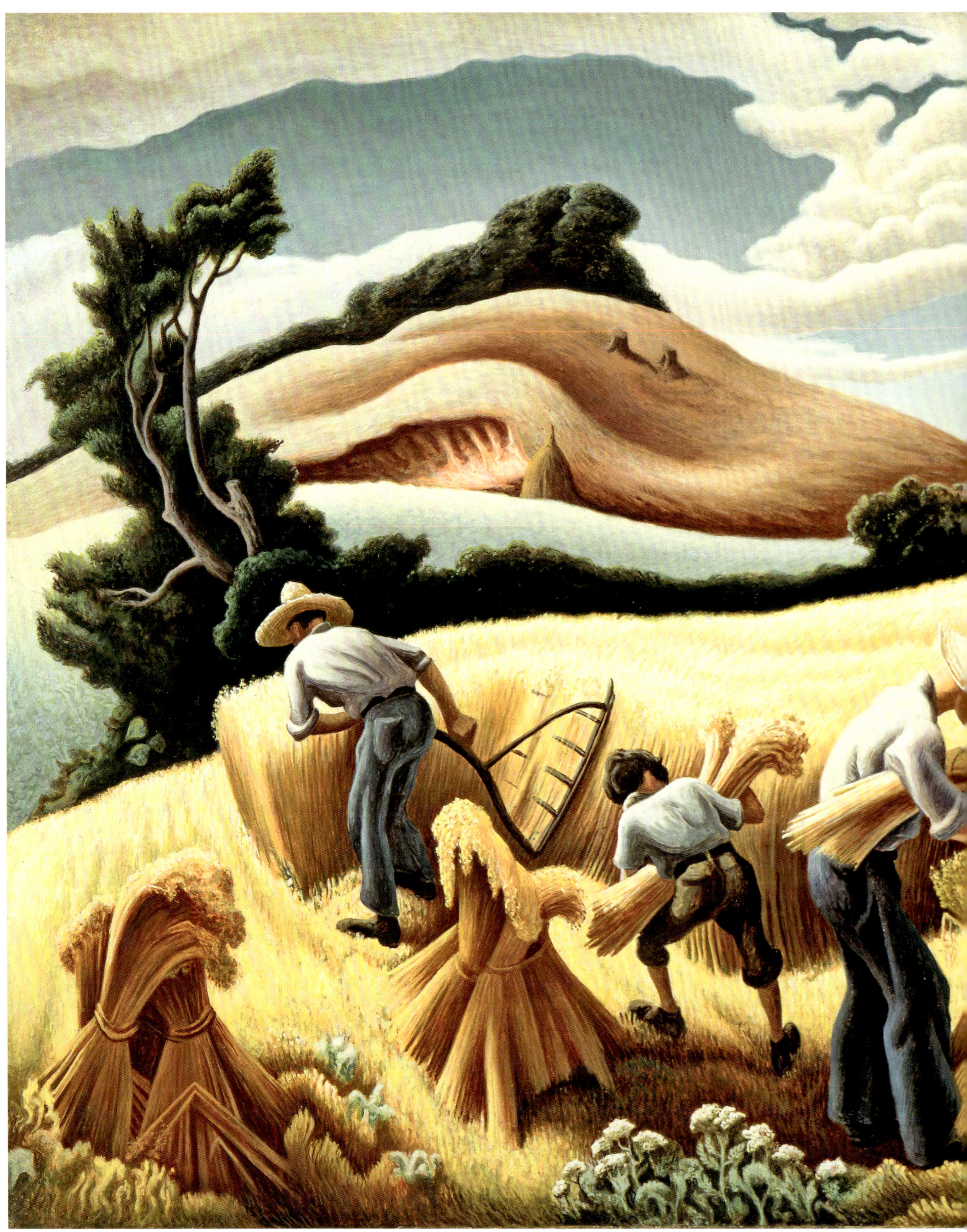

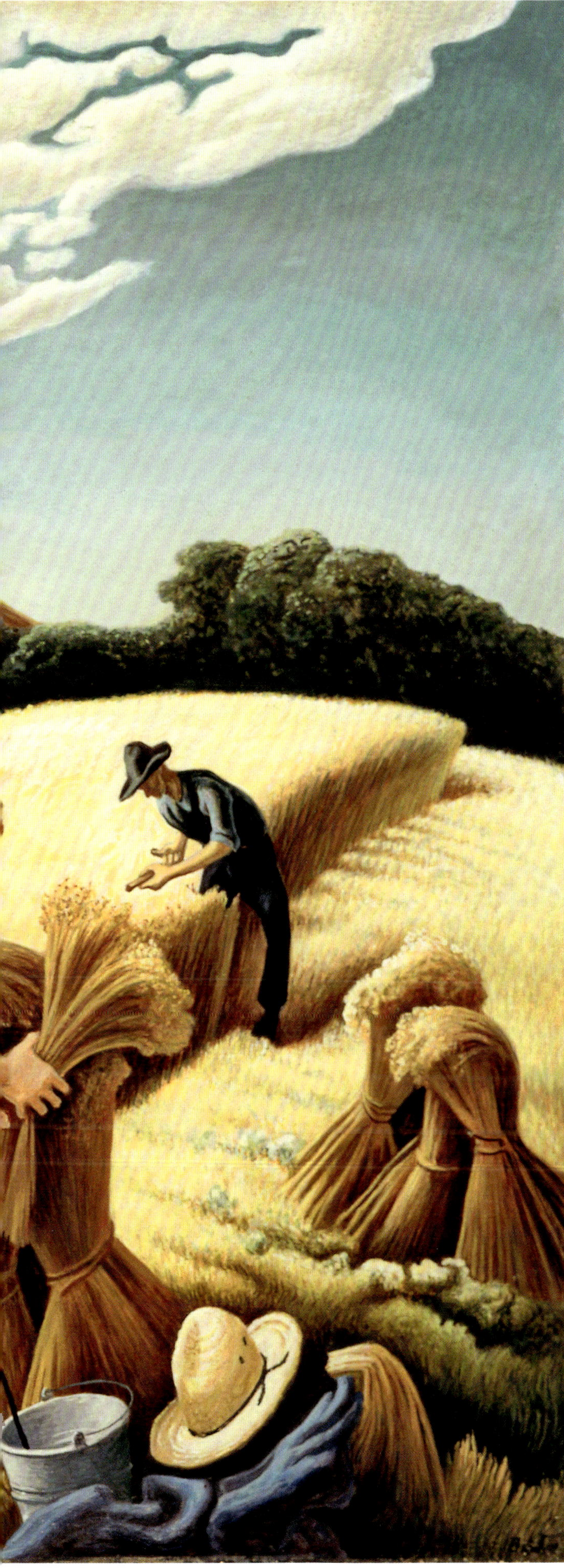



motion. A farmer cuts the wheat with an old-fashioned scythe in an era when steam-powered threshers were common. The rhythm of cutting and bundling grain matches that of the rolling fields: people and landscape are one. For Benton, looking back at farming traditions held more allure than depicting the modernization of the American farm. He bemoaned the changes taking place as the United States entered World War II, the economy recovered, and pastoral scenes became harder to find. Now he used his imagination to create restorative landscapes. At the end of the Depression decade, he recalled, "Ten years ago I'd start out with a pencil and notebook and a harmonica. I'd head for the country roads, cut across pastures and fallow fields, working along the way. Along about dark I'd stop at a farmhouse, ask for a meal and a night's lodging, and even pay for it sometimes with my harmonica playing. . . . You can't travel like that now. . . . [T]oo many persons are bitter and suspicious."[49]

Wood, Benton, Curry, and others put a nostalgic spin on an earlier rural life, railing against the materialism and industrialization that drove people from farms to towns and cities. It was a reaction to a hard reality. Others, such as Jones, faced change head on. His painting *Our American Farms* (1936; fig. 17), shown in the Whitney Museum's third biennial, depicts the Dust Bowl: the drought, erosion, misuse of land, and subsequent physical and emotional isolation of farmers during the Depression years. This picture shares its apocalyptic view with Alexandre Hogue's paintings *Drouth Stricken Area* (1934; Dallas Museum of Art) and *Erosion No. 2—Mother Earth Laid Bare* (1936; fig. 18). Hogue, also born in Missouri, became part of a Texas-based group of Regionalists called the Dallas Nine, and eventually taught in Tulsa. He learned about the sanctity of the earth from his mother, and the effects of the Dust Bowl had a profound influence on his work. *Erosion No. 2* suggests the rape of the landscape through the mindless spread of wheat farming, which led to erosion and drought.

Regionalism could not sustain the pastoral myth upon which it was based. The siege mentality that sought to protect rural culture from corrupting outside influences, whether aesthetic or moral, simply did not hold. After Japan's attack on the naval base at Pearl Harbor, the nation united against a threat

**Fig. 17** Joe Jones. (American, 1909–1963). *Our American Farms*, 1936. 76.2 × 101.6 cm (30 × 40 in.). Whitney Museum of American Art, New York, Purchase, 36.144.

**Fig. 18** Alexandre Hogue. *Erosion No. 2—Mother Earth Laid Bare*, 1936. Philbrook Museum of Art. Cat. 21.

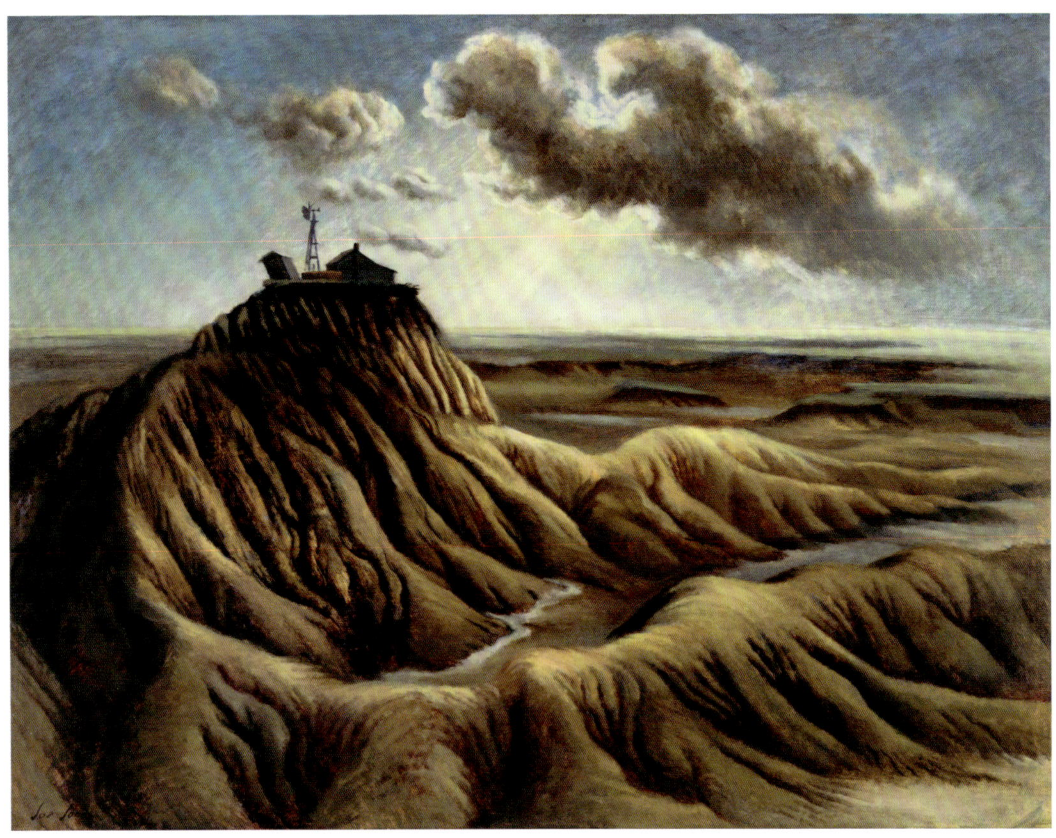

larger than regional lifestyles and economies, coming together in the war effort and committing itself to saving the European democracies. The run-up to full production of war materials by the American government from 1939 to 1941 meant that the country emerged from the Depression, and later from the war, as a fully industrialized urban economy, setting the stage for the enormous prosperity of the 1950s. Soldiers came home and went to college on the government's GI Bill rather than return to their family farms. And the art world changed, too. Wood died in 1942; Curry died in 1946. Benton lived until 1975, but the realism and sentimentality of his work fell from fashion during the 1940s and 50s. After the war, the center of the art world had shifted from Paris to New York, and it remained there, far from the Midwest. Radio and President Roosevelt's New Deal programs had enhanced national communication and enlarged the responsibility of the federal government in ways that undercut sectionalism. Old traditions and the rural myth of self-reliance proved ill-suited to a new, more globally connected world. In the end, Americans did not "revolt against the city" and return to the farms, as Wood had predicted. In fact, in the late 1940s and 1950s, Benton's most famous student, Jackson Pollock, at work in New York, turned his teacher's energetic, colorful designs into a vigorous personal Abstract Expressionism associated with urban intellectuals such as Clement Greenberg and Paul Rosenfeld.

Regionalism was an art that attempted to retain cultural history and be modern at the same time. For its advocates, preserving the past meant a brighter, renewed, more hopeful future. However, as a movement that looked backward to the rural, pioneer foundation of the United States, it was doomed to be short-lived as the nation's economy became based in the military-corporate-industrial complex of the postwar period.

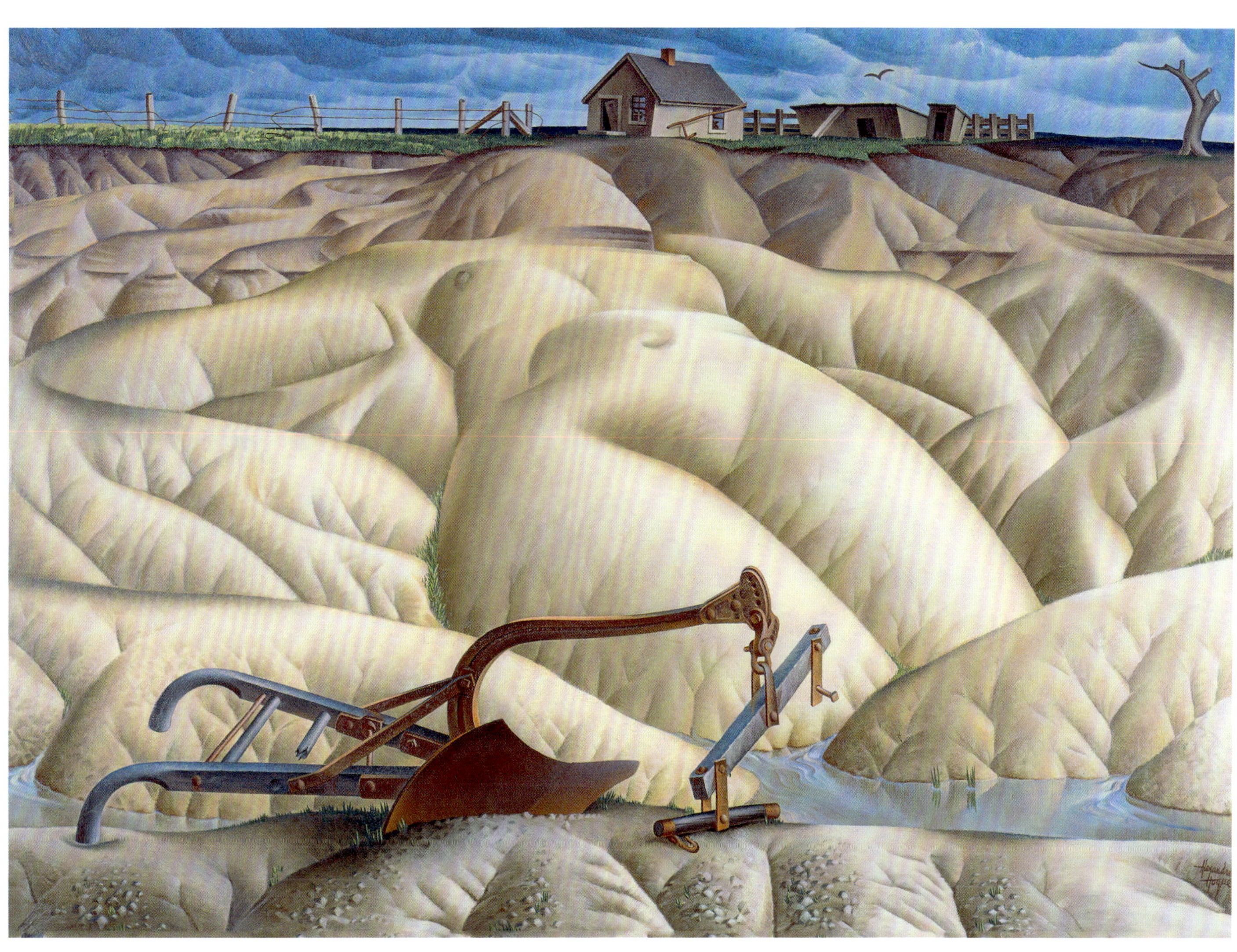

1 Meredith Nicholson, *Valley of Democracy* (Scribner, 1918), quoted in R. Douglas Hurt, "Midwestern Distinctiveness," in Andrew R. L. Cayton and Susan E. Gray, eds., *The American Midwest: Essays on Regional History* (Indiana University Press, 2001), p. 168.

2 James R. Shortridge, *The Middle West: Its Meaning in American Culture* (University Press of Kansas, 1989), p. 7.

3 Hurt, "Midwestern Distinctiveness," p. 163.

4 Debra Bricker Balken, *After Many Springs: Regionalism, Modernism, and the Midwest*, exh. cat. (Des Moines Art Center/Yale University Press, 2009), pp. 47–48.

5 Benton explored this theme in small-scale watercolors and tempera sketches, including *Cotton Pickers, Georgia* (1928–29; Metropolitan Museum of Art) and *Cotton Pickers* (1931; Los Angeles County Museum of Art). The latter composition was shown at the Art Institute of Chicago in the *Fourteenth International Exhibition of Water Colors, Pastels, Drawing and Monotypes*, 1934, cat. no 241.

6 Betsy L. Nies, "Defending Jeeter: Conservative Arguments against Eugenics in the Depression Era South," in Susan Currell and Christina Cogdell, eds., *Popular Eugenics: National Efficiency and American Mass Culture in the 1930s* (Ohio University Press, 2006), p. 122.

7 Austen Barron Bailly, "Art for America: Race in Thomas Hart Benton's Murals, 1919–36," *Indiana Magazine of History* 105, no. 2 (June 2009), pp. 150–66.

8 Henry Adams, *Thomas Hart Benton: An American Original* (Knopf, 1989), p. 151.

9 H. L. Mencken, "Utopia by Sterilization," *American Mercury* 41 (1937), p. 403; http://theamericanmercury.org/2010/09/utopia-by-sterilization/.

10 Jackson Lears, *Rebirth of a Nation: The Making of Modern America, 1877–1920* (Harper Collins, 2009), p. 185. Populism in the United States had earlier roots in the depression economy of the 1890s. Summed up in one word, the labor organizer Samuel Gompers said his philosophy was one of "more" for workers. As a political movement, populism was a tenuous association of struggling farmers and factory, railroad, and other industry workers. The organization of these workers by Eugene Debs, Samuel Gompers, Jacob Coxey, and other leaders laid bare the deep class divisions in American culture. Egalitarian visions were part of the Populist and Socialist movements that called for better working conditions, higher wages, the right to organize, and cheap money. This last goal would be achieved through removing the United States from the gold standard and placing the economy on a silver and paper money standard, which allowed inflation to ameliorate the crushing burden of debt, especially for farmers.

11 See James M. Dennis, *Renegade Regionalists: The Modern Independence of Grant Wood, Thomas Hart Benton, and John Steuart Curry* (University of Wisconsin Press, 1998), pp. 47–48.

12 When the small original Whitney Museum moved to a new location in 1954, the murals were sold to the New Britain Museum of American Art.

13 Thomas Hart Benton, "The Arts of Life in America," in *The Arts of Life in America: A Series of Murals* by Thomas Benton, exh. cat. (Whitney Museum of American Art, 1932), p. 5. Two years later Benton painted another composition, *The Ballad of the Jealous Lover of Lone Green Valley* (1934). That work included the themes of fiddle, harmonica playing, and whiskey with a trio of men but introduced violence in the background. The painting took its name from the eponymous ballad about jealousy and murder that Benton might have heard on earlier trips through the Ozark Mountains: "Down in the lone green valley/where the violets used to bloom/There sleeps one gentle Lemo/Now silent in the tomb." Benton connected foreground and background through the tipped perspective, rolling hills, angular fence, and the swirling swath of the path from lower left to upper right. Bands of color link the upper and lower halves of the composition together, creating the drama and emotional turmoil of the tragedy.

14 Arthur Le Duc, "Painters Deny Whitney Art Imperils Child," *New York Journal*, November 9, 1934, n. pag.

15 "Art: Benton," *Time* 17, no. 1 (January 5, 1931), p. 32.

16 Diane Kelder, ed., *Stuart Davis* (Praeger, 1971), p. 121.

17 Edward Alden Jewell, "When Cobblers Turn from the Last: Issues in the Debate between Leading Exponents of 'Abstract' and 'Nationalist' Tendencies," *New York Times*, April 7, 1935, p. X8.

18 Shawn Michelle Smith, "The Evidence of Lynching Photographs," in Dora Apel and Shawn Michelle Smith, *Lynching Photographs* (University of California Press, 2007), p. 20.

19 M. Melissa Wolfe, "Joe Jones: Worker-Artist," in Andrew Walker and Janeen Turk, *Joe Jones: Radical Painter of the American Scene*, exh. cat. (Saint Louis Art Museum/University of Washington Press, 2010), pp. 39–40.

20 Balken, *After Many Springs*, p. 87.

21 Allen Jackson, "Art: U.S. Scene," *Time* 24, no. 26 (December 24, 1934), pp. 26–31.

22 "Mid-West Is Producing an Indigenous Art," *Art Digest* 7, no. 20 (September 1, 1933), p. 10.

**23** The celebrity of its proponents was managed by Walker, who placed articles in *Time* and *Life* magazines, as well as the influential art critic Thomas Craven, who wrote for the *American Mercury* and *Scribner's*.

**24** Balken, *After Many Springs*, p. 185.

**25** Milton Brown, "From Salon to Saloon," *Parnassus* 13 (March 1941), p. 193.

**26** Balken, *After Many Springs*, pp. 78–80.

**27** C. J. Bulliet, "American Normalcy Displayed in Annual Show," *Chicago Evening Post Magazine of the Art World*, October 28, 1930, part 3, p. 1.

**28** James M. Dennis, *Grant Wood: A Study in American Art and Culture* (Viking, 1975), p. 193.

**29** David Eldridge, *American Culture in the 1930s* (Edinburgh University Press, 2008), pp. 158–59, 170.

**30** Balken, *After Many Springs*, p. 83.

**31** Patricia Junker, ed., *John Steuart Curry: Inventing the Middle West* (University of Wisconsin Press, 1998), p. 80.

**32** F. A. Whiting, Jr., "Stone, Steel and Fire: Stone City Comes to Life," *American Magazine of Art* 25, no. 6 (December 1932), p. 337.

**33** Lincoln Kirstein, "An Iowa Memling," *Art Front* 1 (July 1935), p. 8.

**34** "An Iowa Street," *Art Digest* 8, no. 1 (October 1, 1933), p. 6.

**35** Sinclair Lewis, *Main Street: The Story of Carol Kennicott* (Harcourt Brace, 1920), p. 430, quoted in Shortridge, *Middle West*, p. 45.

**36** Darrell Garwood, *Artist in Iowa: A Life of Grant Wood* (W. W. Norton, 1944), p. 138, quoted in Matthew Baigell, *Artist and Identity in Twentieth-Century America* (Cambridge University Press, 2001), p. 106.

**37** Judith A. Barter, ed., *Art and Appetite: American Painting, Culture, and Cuisine*, exh. cat. (Art Institute of Chicago/Yale University Press, 2013), p. 46.

**38** Sinclair Lewis, *Main Street and Babbitt* (Library of America, 1992), p. 6.

**39** Franklin Roosevelt, "Back to the Land," *Review of Reviews* 84 (October 1931), pp. 63–64. For the subsistence homestead movement, see Shortridge, *Middle West*, p. 59.

**40** Robert P. Sutton, *Heartland Utopias* (Northern Illinois University Press, 2009), p. 4.

**41** These are described in ibid.

**42** Grant Wood, *Revolt against the City* (Clio, 1935), pp. 29–31.

**43** Matthew Baigell, *Thomas Hart Benton* (Abrams, 1974), p. 139.

**44** "On the American Scene," *Art Front* 1, no. 4 (April 1935), p. 8.

**45** During the 1930s, New York dealer Edith Halpert of the Downtown Gallery showed folk art works alongside paintings by Yasuo Kuniyoshi and Stuart Davis.

**46** Kate Meyer, "Broken Ground: Plowing and America's Cultural Landscape in the 1930s," Ph.D. diss., University of Kansas, 2011, pp. 45–47.

**47** Park Rivard, "Return from Bohemia, A Painter's Story," M.A. thesis, University of Iowa, 1939, p. 4, quoted in Wanda M. Corn, *Grant Wood: The Regionalist Vision*, exh. cat. (Minneapolis Institute of Arts/Yale University Press, 1983), p. 90.

**48** Joseph S. Czestochowski, *Marvin D. Cone: Art as Self Portrait* (Cedar Rapids Art Association, 1990), pp. 28–29.

**49** Thomas Hart Benton (1940), quoted in H. Adams, *Thomas Hart Benton*, pp. 318–19.

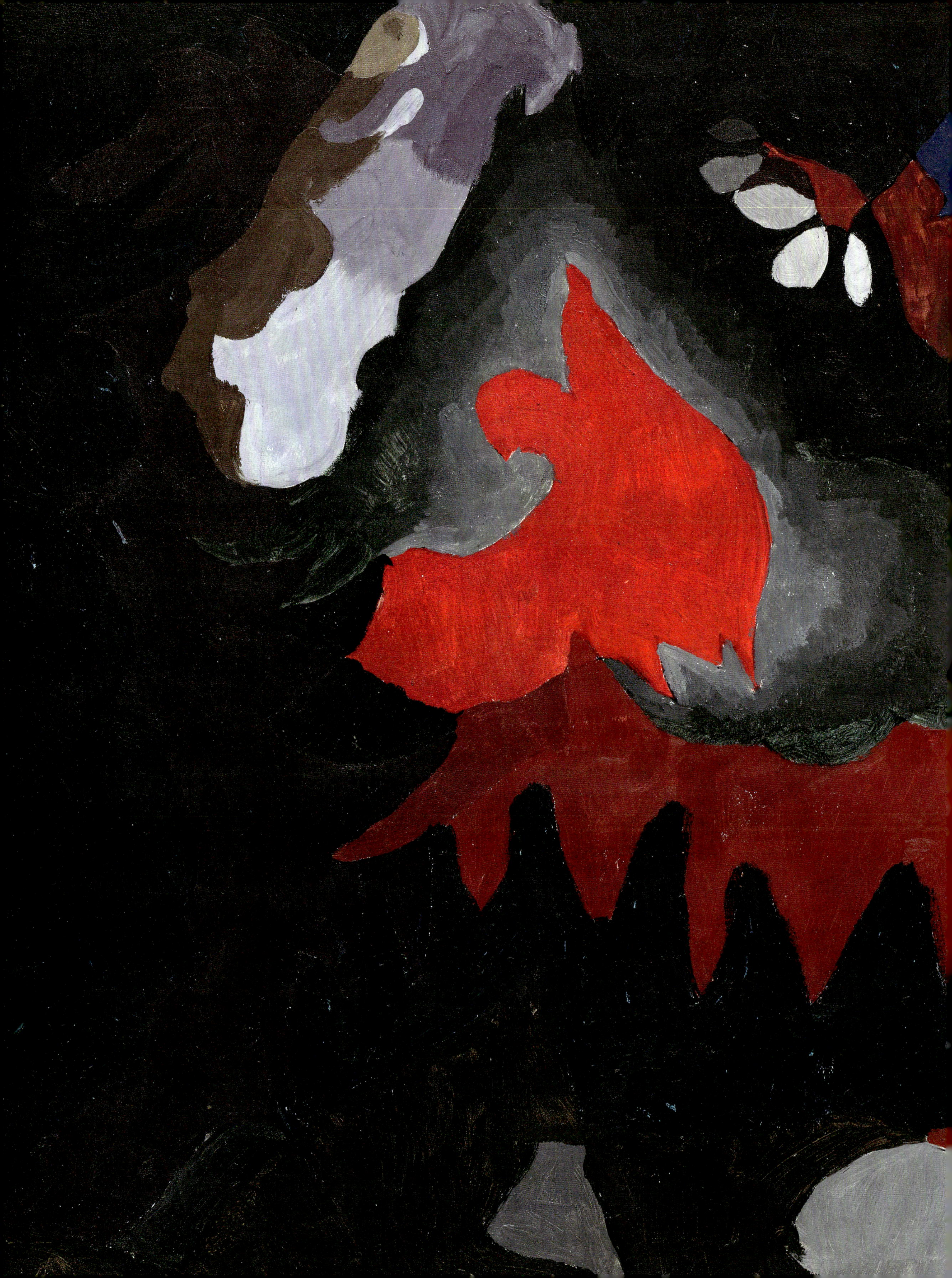

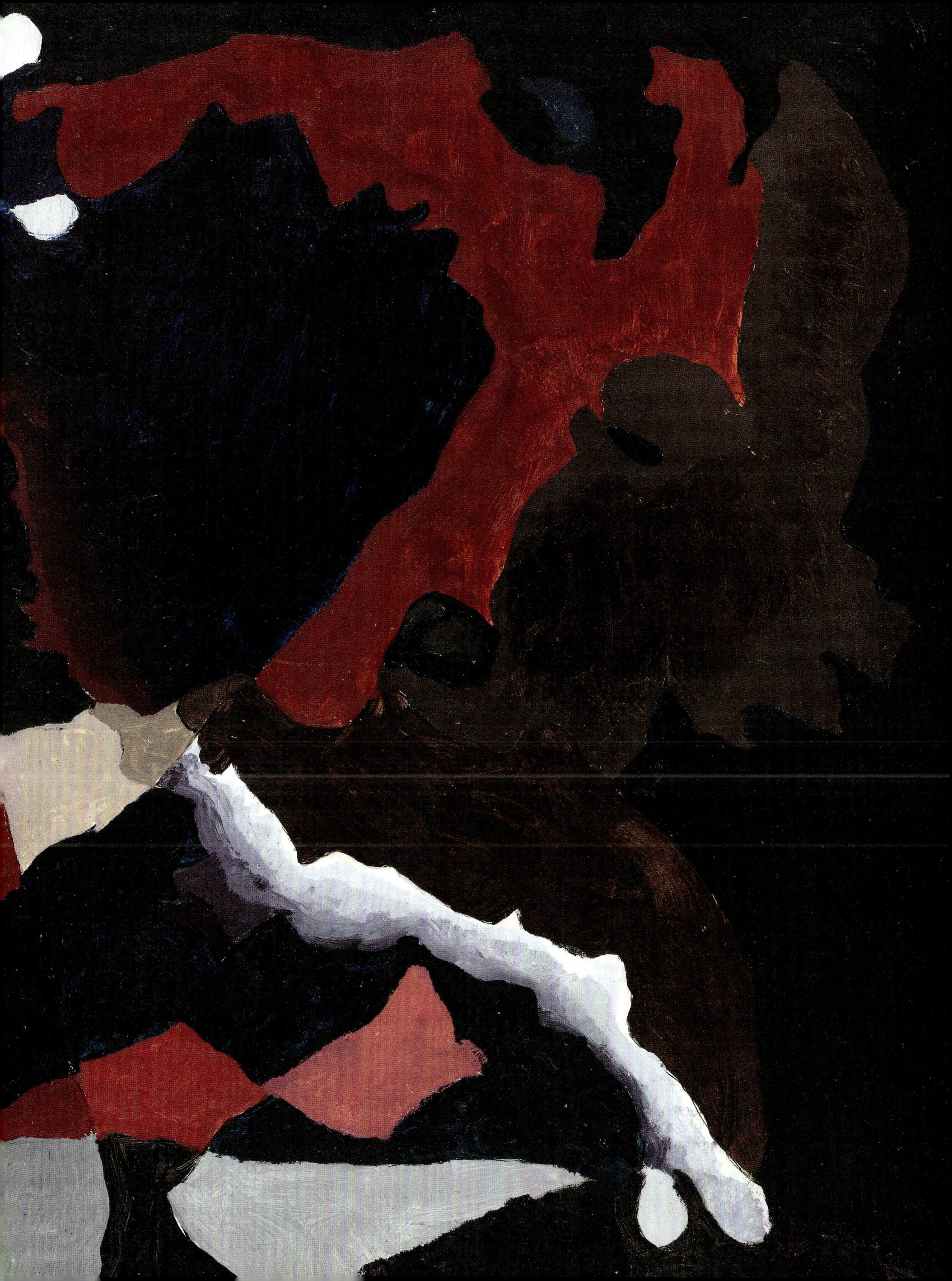

**SARAH KELLY OEHLER**

**Over here we are racially English-American, Irish-American, German-American, French, Italian, Russian or Jewish-American and artistically we are Rembrandt-American, Renoir-American and Picasso-American. But since we live here and paint here we are first of all, American.**

—Stuart Davis, "Letter to Henry McBride"[1]

**W**hen in 1930 the artist Stuart Davis voiced the opinion that American artists "are Rembrandt-American, Renoir-American and Picasso-American," he raised a point that would become one of the most debated of the 1930s: the nature of American art and the acceptability of foreign influence on the country's art scene. Building on a nationalistic rhetoric that had developed in the 1920s, cultural commentators

## TWO — *American Made? Transatlantic Expressions in the 1930s*

championed the development of an American art that was at times xenophobic, as artists were encouraged to rid themselves of European—that is to say, modernist—aesthetics. For Thomas Hart Benton and other Regionalists, American art depended on accessible stylistic and thematic choices, such as small-town or agrarian traditions, represented without modernist trickery (see the essay by Judith A. Barter in this volume).

Davis instead saw parallels between a multicultural American society built on immigration and a pluralistic, modernist approach to art. In his argument, foreign influences not only were acceptable but had been a historically significant aspect of artistic inspiration in the United States. Asking, "Has any American artist created a style which was unique in painting, completely divorced from European models?," Davis looked back at the history of American art, including such early masters as John Singleton Copley, to decry the folly of believing that American artists should or could excise any taint of foreign influence.[2] While Davis himself was clearly a "Picasso-American," he wanted to emphasize that his adaptation of Cubist techniques should be no more censured than another artist's reliance on the Old Masters: "But why one should be penalized for a Picasso influence and not for a Rembrandt or a Renoir influence I can't understand."[3] But in the end, he believed that, despite such a broad amalgamation of ethnicities and aesthetics, the specific context of life in the United States ultimately shaped a national artistic character.

The question was, how precisely should that be defined? Did Regionalist painters best speak to the nation's experiences, using easy-to-digest styles to paint rural locales far from the metropolitan center of New York, or did urban modernists such as Davis? Or perhaps the select group of modernists—Charles Demuth, Arthur Dove, Marsden Hartley, John Marin, and Georgia O'Keeffe—gathered around the photographer and gallery owner Alfred Stieglitz? Or, later in the decade, would it be the champions of nonobjectivity such as George L. K. Morris and the American Abstract Artists (AAA) group? For differing reasons, all of the latter believed that Regionalism was an artistic dead end and promoted modernist aesthetics instead.

Their varied approaches are key to understanding the persistence of modernist expression in the 1930s; instead of being strictly pigeonholed, modernism was a flexible concept that could be employed in numerous ways and by many artists. In some cases, such as those of Davis or the AAA, it was overtly European in its derivation. In others, such as that of O'Keeffe, modernism could be expressed without explicit reference to Europe but with a shared ideological belief in the primacy of formal concerns. This essay explores the continuation and evolution of modernist aesthetics throughout the decade, as numerous artists sought to refute the arguments of their so-called conservative counterparts by explicitly laying claim to a practice that was to varying degrees responsive to European modernism yet could be distinguished as distinctly American. Crucially, however, while modernist ideals and pictorial construction were of paramount importance, many progressive artists, from O'Keeffe to Charles Green Shaw, strategically employed nationalistic emblems to heighten the appeal of their art for resistant audiences. It was a negotiation necessitated by the pressures of the era, and some artists, including O'Keeffe, undertook it with ambivalence. Others, among them Morris, embraced the strategy as a means of further extending a dialogue with preexisting avant-garde approaches.

Davis clearly advocated for a progressive American art that was receptive to European precedent, setting himself in opposition to those who claimed a nationalistic ideological and aesthetic purity that he found galling (and impossible). In particular, the critic Thomas Craven argued for the antimodernist, anti-European side, championing "an art proceeding from strong native impulses, simple ideas, and popular tastes."[4] Due to this support, the Regionalists became associated with such hard-line beliefs, which Davis described as "vicious and windy chauvinistic ballyhoo."[5] Indeed, the artist would soon find himself in the middle of an art world contretemps with Benton, a battle played out in the pages of *Time*, *Art Front*, and other magazines, in which the pair sparred about the merits of European modernism versus American Regionalism. A 1934 article in *Time* on American Scene painting set the tone by condemning modernism: "U.S. painters . . . tried copying the French, turned out a profusion of spurious Matisses and Picassos, cheerfully joined the crazy parade of Cubism, Futurism, Dadaism, Surrealism. . . . In the U.S. opposition to such outlandish art first took root in the Midwest."[6] Davis sallied forth with a rebuttal, condemning the Regionalists as provincial in their mindset and technically inferior in their painting. In particular, he faulted them for their avoidance of modernism: "How can a man who paints as though no laboratory work had ever been done in painting, who willfully or through ignorance ignores the discoveries of Monet, Seurat, Cezanne and Picasso . . . how can a man with this mental attitude be considered an asset to the development of American painting?"[7] The Regionalists, in his argument, had ignored the artistic advances of the past fifty years in favor of unsophisticated, narrow-minded canvases that could not compete on an international level. Furthermore, he read their representational stylistic choices as evidence of conservative, isolationist, even Fascist politics, again linking their art with Craven's isolationism.

The extent of the divide between these two groups, however, should not be overemphasized. Regardless of their aesthetic interests, political affiliations, and physical locations, artists in the United States all felt pressed to negotiate between nationalism and modernism, even if to very different stylistic ends. Numerous Regionalists, including Benton, had spent time in Europe and continued to flirt with modernist techniques. Conversely, modernists such as Demuth, Hartley, and O'Keeffe conveyed a strong sense of American places in their art; they were just as regionally aligned as Benton or Wood.[8] Moreover, as Wanda M. Corn has most eloquently described, critics and artists on both sides of the Regionalist/modernist debate in the 1930s shared the belief that there was indeed a trait that could be called American about the nation's art, regardless of aesthetics.[9] Although the two camps surely believed they had little common ground in this struggle for dominance, they both lay claim to the inherent value of their approach as they sought authentic and independent voices that could speak for the nation.

Davis's dual attitude—both international and national—had been recently encouraged by the founding of several galleries and public institutions in New York devoted to modern art. In December 1927, the collector and later abstract artist Albert E. Gallatin founded the Gallery of Living Art (later the Museum of Living Art) at New York University, where he displayed avant-garde works from both sides of the Atlantic, from Pablo Picasso and Fernand Léger to Demuth and Alexander Calder (see fig. 1). Not a commercial endeavor but a permanent collection open daily to the public, the gallery quickly became a formative influence on numerous artists interested in transatlantic styles, among them Davis.[10] Two years later, in 1929, the Museum of Modern Art opened its doors with *Cézanne, Gauguin, Seurat, Van Gogh*, an exhibition that honored European precursors to modernism, but soon turned to programs that focused on an international array of contemporary artists. These included solo exhibitions for the Swiss Paul Klee, the German sculptor Wilhelm Lehmbruck, the French Aristide Maillol, and the Mexican muralist Diego Rivera, as well as Americans Charles Burchfield, Edward Hopper, and Max Weber.[11] Interest in the newest international trends was not confined to New York; the Art Institute of Chicago likewise committed to collecting and displaying modern European art beginning in the late 1920s. In particular, the museum's acceptance of the Helen Birch Bartlett and Joseph Winterbotham collections fostered the creation of one of the preeminent repositories of modern art in an encyclopedic museum.[12]

However, these European-oriented institutions prompted responses from supporters of American modernists. The patron Gertrude Vanderbilt Whitney had supported living American artists for many years, but after her collection was rejected by the Metropolitan Museum of Art, she opened the Whitney Museum of American Art in 1931 with a mandate to display and collect works by primarily contemporary practitioners.[13] Many of the Whitney's exhibitions in the 1930s were of realists such as Hopper, but in 1935, it mounted *Abstract Painting in America* to showcase modernists working in international styles, including Davis. He also wrote the catalogue introduction, in which he articulated a defense of abstraction.[14]

Stieglitz's efforts were significant as well. After championing a diverse array of international modernists at his gallery 291 (1905–17), he began promoting a smaller circle of American artists, headlined by O'Keeffe, at the Intimate Gallery (1925–29) before making his purpose explicitly clear with the opening of An American Place, his third and final gallery, in December 1929, two months after the stock market crash. He thus emphasized his allegiance to a specifically nationalistic program of supporting his preferred artists, who benefitted financially from the cooperative system he employed.[15]

Throughout the 1930s, therefore, modernist painting from both Europe and the United States was supported by important new collections and exhibitions despite the growing rhetoric against it from Regionalist artists and sympathetic critics. But the varied approaches of these institutions do indicate the extent of the debate over internationalism and nationalism in the period. Regardless, with all this emphasis on modern art, Davis was not out of line for thinking that, despite the economic pressures of the Great Depression, the American art world would still embrace a modernist approach

**Fig. 1** Opening installation of Albert Gallatin's Gallery of Living Art at New York University, December 1927. Philadelphia Museum of Art Archives.

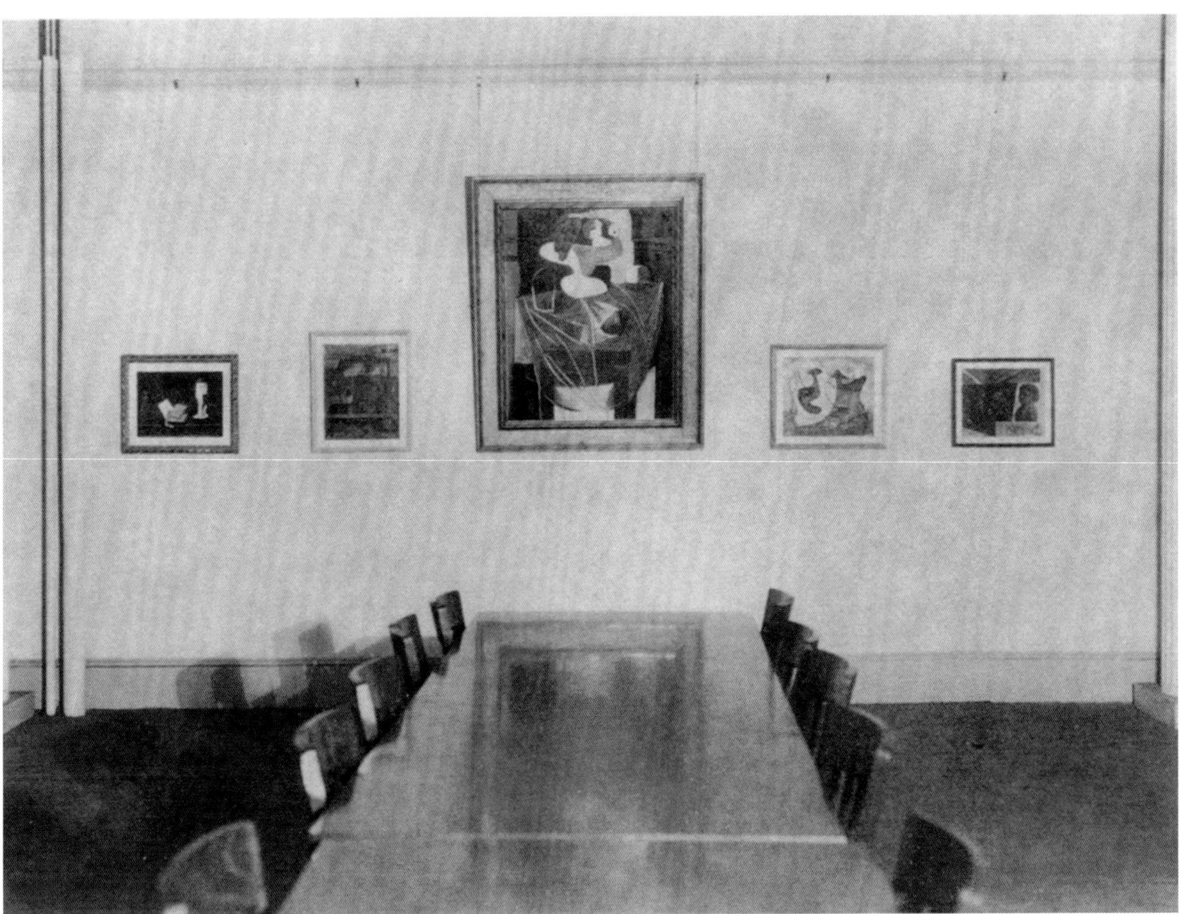

that signaled its knowledge of international styles even while remaining relevant at home.

Moreover, Davis had a vested interest in arguing for the continued importance of European modernist traditions: in May 1928 he had finally traveled to Paris, soaking in French culture for fifteen months before returning home to paint important works that synthesized his experiences, among them *New York–Paris No. 3* (1931; fig. 2). In this canvas, the last of a series, he combined images meant to evoke the Old World and the new in a language that was clearly indebted to European models. The artist arranged a disparate selection of motifs in a single plane against a flat, unmodulated background, toying with scale throughout, most notably in the pile of chairs and tables that are almost as tall as skyscrapers. The elements appear to bear little relationship to one another or to the background and were described by a contemporary critic as "a ticketing of mental images which he associates with a given set of experiences."[16] This nonlinear presentation of form has been attributed to the influence of the Dadaists and Surrealists, who freed their art from the need for narrative logic and specific spaces. Davis in particular admired the Surrealists' use of free association as a means of juxtaposing pictorial motifs.[17] His affinity for Fernand Léger's flat, linear forms has also been noted, and indeed, the two met and compared works during Davis's stay in Paris.[18]

Although Davis invigorated the composition of *New York–Paris No. 3* by infusing it with a modernist sense of pictorial construction, the jumbled array of motifs ultimately reinforces his native context—the "American" in his designation "Picasso-American." The street sign at the left immediately betrays the painting's New York origins; although the sign points to "Ticino," the tiny script above reads "Bleeker St.," firmly situating this as a reference to one of Davis's favorite Greenwich

**Fig. 2** Stuart Davis. *New York–Paris No. 3*, 1931. Private collection. Cat. 11.

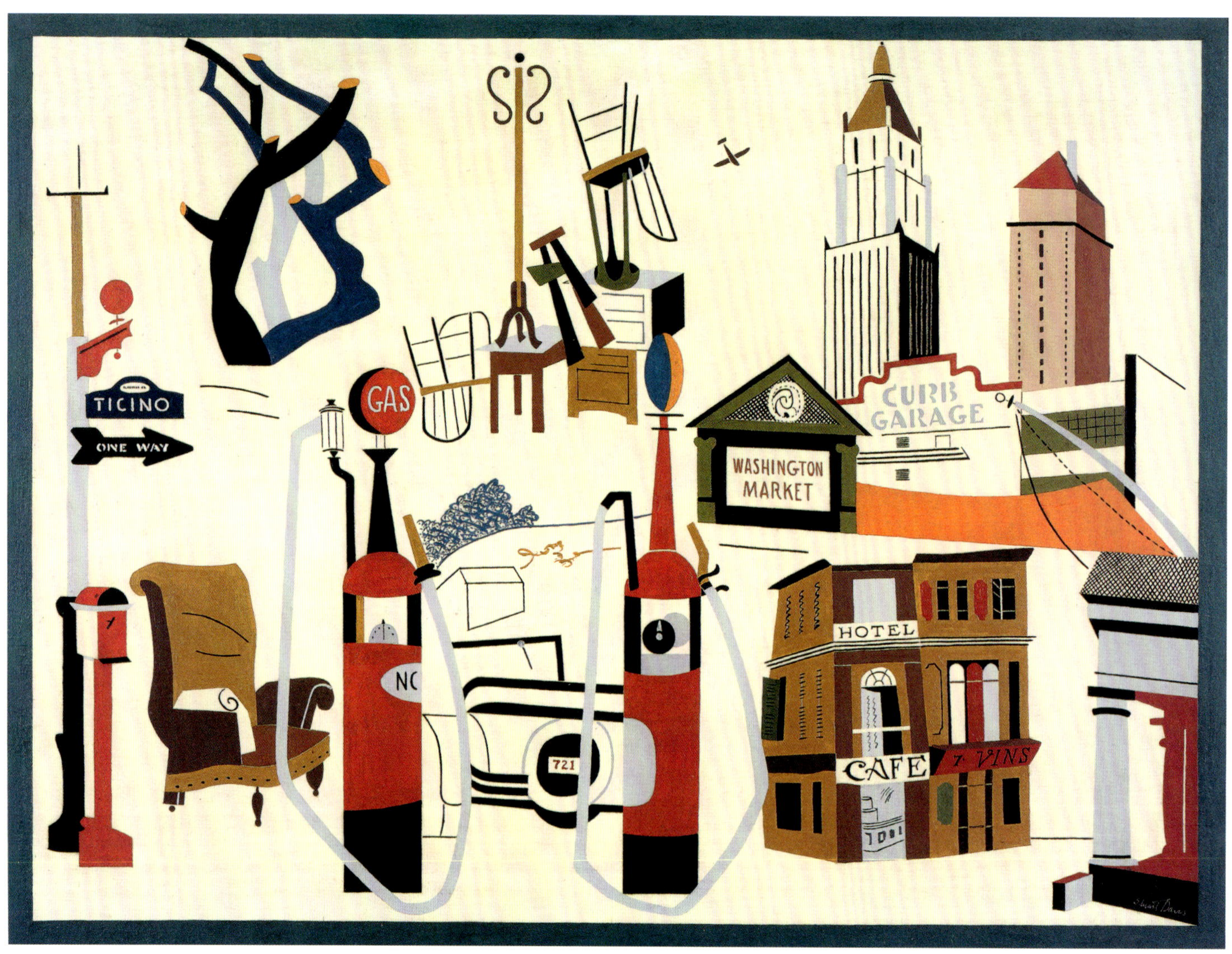

Village restaurants.[19] Indeed, despite the painting's title, the only recognizably French element is the typically Parisian hotel and café at lower right; it derives from a sketch made in Paris in 1928–29.[20] This structure is directly surrounded by emblems of Manhattan's past: Washington Market and a colonnaded building with flagpole. Davis sketched the latter in lower Manhattan around 1930 (fig. 3); perhaps he intended the neoclassical building to evoke the shared political and artistic histories of the two countries in the resulting painting.[21] Neoclassicism was, however, an architectural style that was quickly vanishing from New York's skyline as the modern city developed in the early 1930s, even if it was still visible in buildings such as Federal Hall and the New York Stock Exchange.[22] Davis's sketch shows the unknown building in close proximity to 120 Wall Street, a skyscraper completed in 1930.[23] Demolition also shown nearby implies that the structure will be torn down to make way for additional skyscrapers. Indeed, in the final painting, Davis overshadowed both the French café and the older New York buildings with unmistakable emblems of modern Manhattan: the Woolworth and Transportation skyscrapers, a parking garage, and gasoline pumps that frame a modern automobile.[24]

By juxtaposing Europe and the United States and ultimately favoring the latter's modernity, Davis's *New York–Paris No. 3* wittily echoes the evolution of the artist's attitude toward his home country. Initially infatuated with the idea of Europe, Davis reached a vital turning point during his stay there, which he articulated in an article published in 1931, the same year as the painting: "It allowed me to observe the enormous vitality of the American atmosphere as compared to Europe and made me regard the necessity of working in New York as a positive advantage."[25] Europe was crucial to the formulation of his aesthetic, yet it was only one factor in the complex makeup that Davis characterized as his American identity. He would spend the rest of his career formulating an American form of Cubism, a transatlantic modern language that he had synthesized from multiple influences.[26]

Davis was not alone in his exploration of a nationalized internationalism in 1930 and 1931. In those same years, Stieglitz's group produced a body of works (many of which were shown at An American Place) that are striking for their makers' deliberate negotiation of the boundaries between nationalism and modernism. They undertook this by developing an intense focus on place even as they repeatedly expressed their desire to conceive of painting as art first, subject matter second. This campaign had begun in the 1920s but intensified, particularly in the first years of the 1930s.[27] Not surprisingly, it occurred during the initial years of the Great Depression. The crash of 1929 had alarmed investors, but most Americans were untouched by the stock market. However, the country's economic slowdown—ongoing agricultural stagnation and growing unemployment in particular—became apparent in November and December 1930 with the catastrophic failure of six hundred banks. When, in 1931, a financial liquidity crisis crippled European nations and consequently affected the sluggish US economy, the impact of the Depression on everyday citizens could not be ignored.[28]

This economic free fall was the context for the key works that Demuth and O'Keeffe painted in the summer and fall of 1931. Although members of the Stieglitz circle are rarely discussed as Depression-era artists, their work clearly reflected

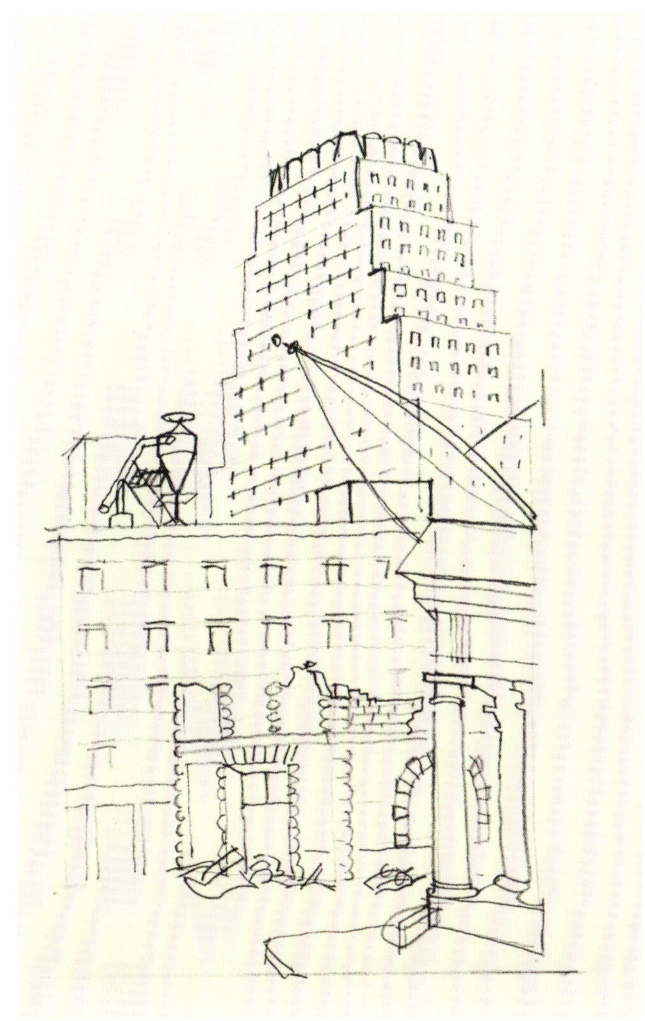

some degree of anxiety about the state of the nation. However, at no time did they allow this context to trump their aesthetic concerns; instead, they remained committed to modernist techniques that could be melded with American subject matter. In this way, they perceived their art as having continued relevance for a new reality. Instead of painting cartoonish representations of national pastimes, they believed their art heralded the "Great American Thing": a synthesis of native places and modern aesthetics.[29] To do anything else would have been to be considered unsophisticated.

In the summer of 1931, Demuth painted *. . . And the Home of the Brave* (fig. 4), one of a series of cubistic architectural

compositions that take as their subject the many factories of
his hometown, Lancaster, Pennsylvania.[30] This major group of
works was to be the artist's last before his early death from dia-
betes in 1935. As has been noted, the paintings complicate the
traditional distinctions between modernism and regionalism
in these years, for their intense focus on Lancaster manifests
Demuth's complex dedication to his home.[31] He referred to the
city as "the province" but resided there his entire life and frequently made it the focus of his work. He was equally intrigued
by Europe, traveling there three times between 1907 and
1921. On his last trip, he found, like Davis, that his European
sojourns only reaffirmed his desire to paint in a modern
American style: "What work I do will be done here terrible as
it is to work in this 'our land of the free.' . . . Together we will
add to the American scene."[32] He thus claimed a space for his
modernist art under the heading of American Scene, seeing no
discrepancy between the two.

    *. . . And the Home of the Brave* masterfully reveals the
precise, faceted aesthetic that Demuth had developed over the
course of his career. He is often associated with Precisionism, a
term coined in the late 1940s to describe the work of a number
of American artists of the previous decades. Characterized
by a streamlined, hard-edged, planar approach that blends
abstraction and representation, Precisionism was seen as an
American adaptation of Cubism, and this is evident here. The
painting depicts the Bayuk Brothers Cigar Company, one of the
many tobacco producers in Lancaster County. Demuth's family
had long been in the tobacco business (an ancestor had opened
the Demuth Tobacco Shop in 1770), and his choice of subject
undoubtedly held a personal resonance (see also the essay by
Annelise K. Madsen in this volume).[33] But despite this long history, he represented the factory as a series of geometric planes
that are immediately parallel to the picture plane, sharply
reducing the composition's pictorial depth and complicating its
legibility. Graphite lines delineate each block of color, further
heightening the overall two-dimensionality of the painting. As
critic Henry McBride noted of Demuth at the time, "He may
be said to have translated cubism 'into American,' and to have
added to it some of his native elegance."[34]

    The formal qualities of *. . . And the Home of the Brave*
attest to its origins in European modernism, yet its industrial
subject was understood to be distinctly American, and its
patriotic title firmly rooted it in an American context. In March
1931, just a few months before Demuth began the painting, "The
Star Spangled Banner" was formally adopted as the national
anthem of the United States.[35] This had not been without significant debate; many critics felt that the song was too militaristic
and advocated for other possibilities, among them "America the
Beautiful." Demuth's conception is likewise equivocal, for while
American industry was often glorified at this time, the painting
links the regimentation of factory work to the American lifestyle. Demuth's comments about the work reveal his hesitation:
"I think, really, my summer's painting—only one—is all right.
I think that you will like it too. It's an oil. And seems more to
the point than most,—different, I feel. Perhaps I'm just, in my
suffering, making myself feel this,—from my others. Anyway
it has a grand name—it's called 'And the Land of the Brave.'"[36]
Demuth's "grand title" conflated two of the phrases from the
anthem—the entire lyric is "O'er the land of the free and the
home of the brave"—which might just have been a simple
mistake on his part. But his correction of the title from "Land"
to "Home" is nevertheless telling; the "home of the brave" was
not a majestic landscape but a complicated modernist tobacco
factory in "the province."

    *. . . And the Home of the Brave* offers a subtle counter-
point to *American Landscape* (1930; fig. 5), Charles Sheeler's
celebratory vision of Ford Motor Company's River Rouge
plant. Painted in 1930, before the full depths of the Depression
became apparent, Sheeler's modern, hard-edged composition
depicts industry as ordered and pristine. He based the painting on photographs taken at the factory in 1927, a commission
offered to him by advertising firm N. W. Ayer, which sought to
excite interest in the not yet unveiled Model A Ford. However,
the photographs, although commercial in origin, also served
Sheeler in the realm of international modern art when he
showed them in influential European exhibitions such as the
1929 *Film und Foto* display in Stuttgart.[37] He also used them as
the basis for *Industry* (1927; fig. 6), a mural he created for the

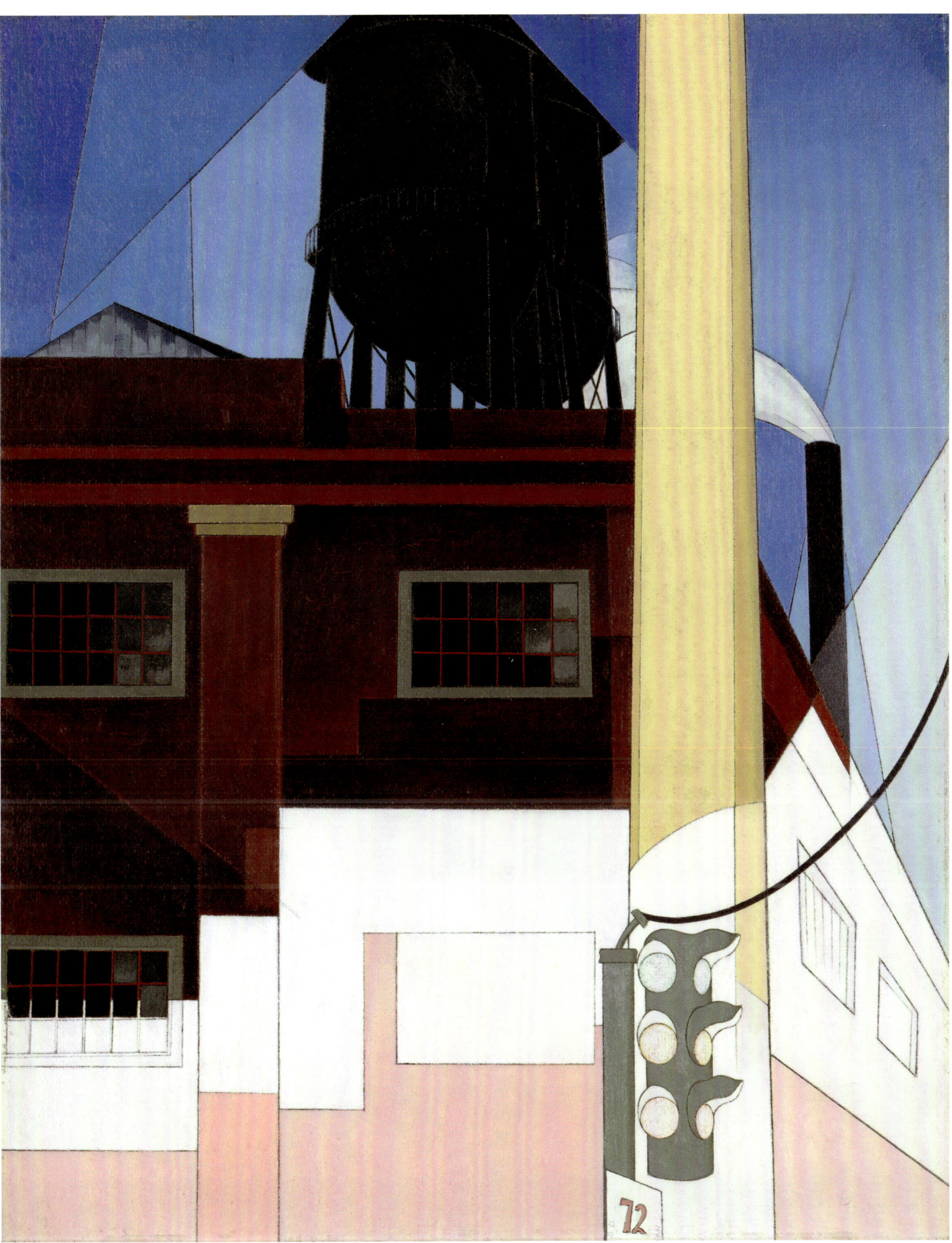

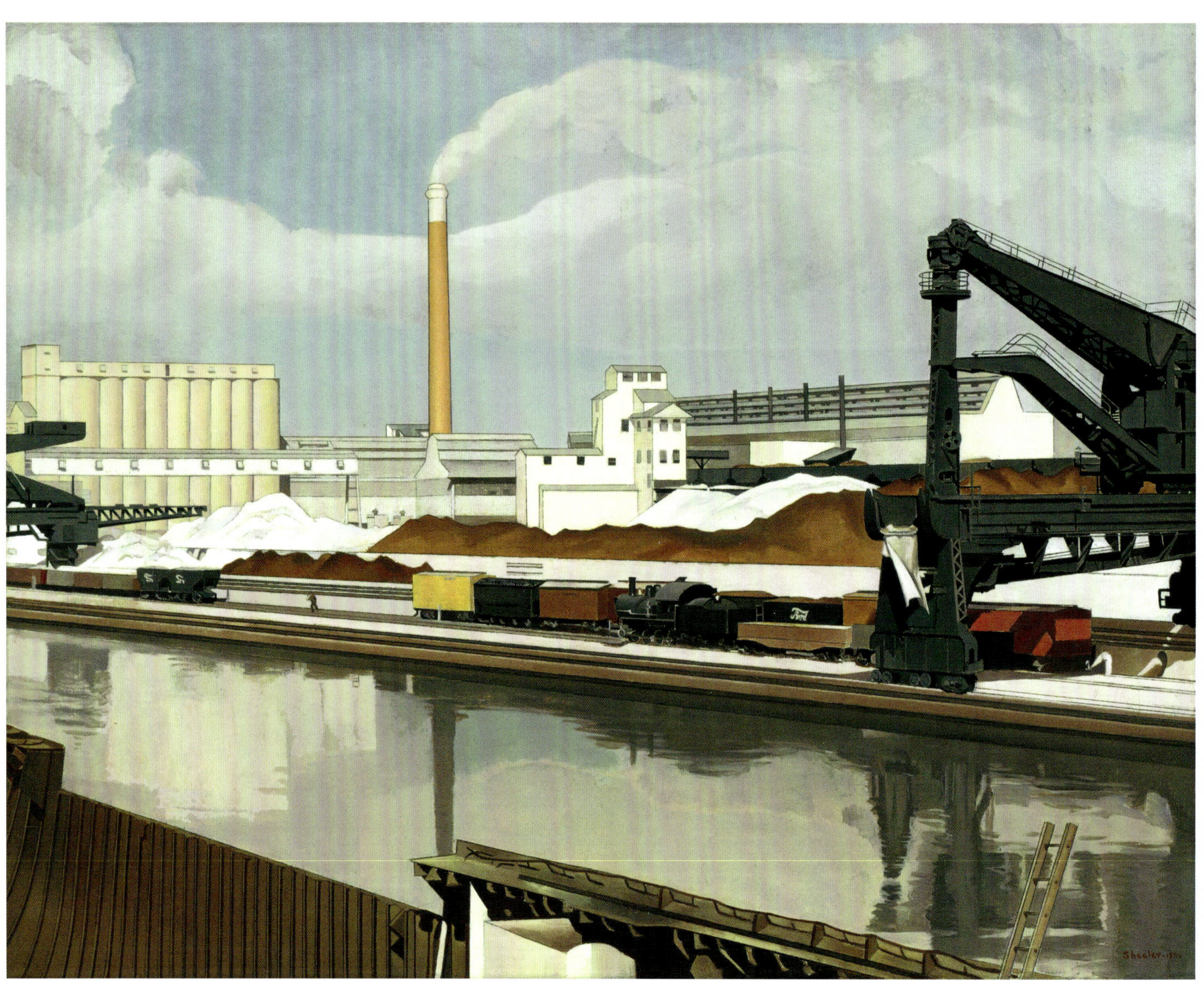

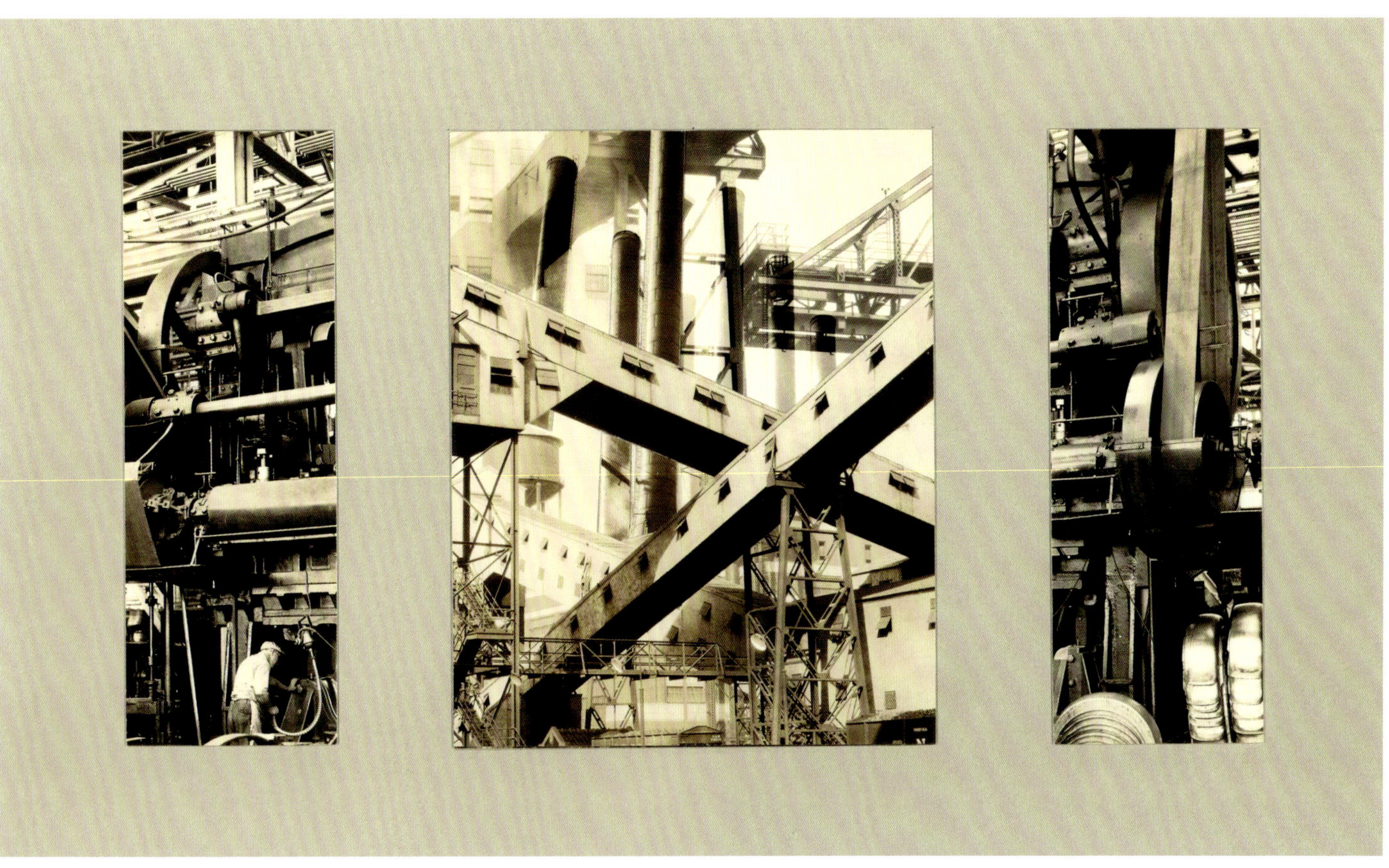

seminal Museum of Modern Art exhibition *Murals by American Painters and Photographers*. The abstracted industrial forms of the photographs helped promote his modernist reputation and enabled Sheeler to achieve an important breakthrough in his painting, uniting abstraction and realism. "I had come to feel," he later recalled, "that a picture could have incorporated in it the structural design implied in abstraction and be presented in a wholly realistic manner."[38] As the artist moved from photograph to oil painting, he eliminated details and purified form, further simplifying and stylizing the elements of the composition.[39] *American Landscape* and the related *Classic Landscape* (1931; p. 21, fig. 4) thus walk a tense line between abstracted and realistic form. This tactic would serve other modernists in the 1930s as well.

Shortly after Demuth completed . . . *And the Home of the Brave*, his friend O'Keeffe returned to Lake George, New York, from her summer's stay in Taos, New Mexico. The events of

1930 and 1931 had not gone unnoticed by O'Keeffe; her correspondence with her husband, Stieglitz, throughout the summer of 1931 acknowledged the financial difficulties facing them and the nation. For instance, Stieglitz wrote in June, "Wall Street is frightful. I adjust myself constantly—But the shrinkages are ghastly. I have gone through pretty tough times but none like this. To see all one's efforts wiped out gradually—to feel powerless in every respect."[40] A few weeks later, he reported on further financial setbacks: "I oughtn't to write you this. But you might as well know.—For awhile there is [food] to eat & a roof over the head.—Thanks to some monies *not invested*."[41]

Out in the Southwest, O'Keeffe was far from the financial center of the country and could pursue her painting in relative peace. But her return to New York was the catalyst for her next major subject: paintings of bones, among them *Cow's Skull with Calico Roses* (1931; fig. 7) and *Cow's Skull: Red, White, and Blue* (1931; p. 19, fig. 2).[42] These works were crucial in her artistic

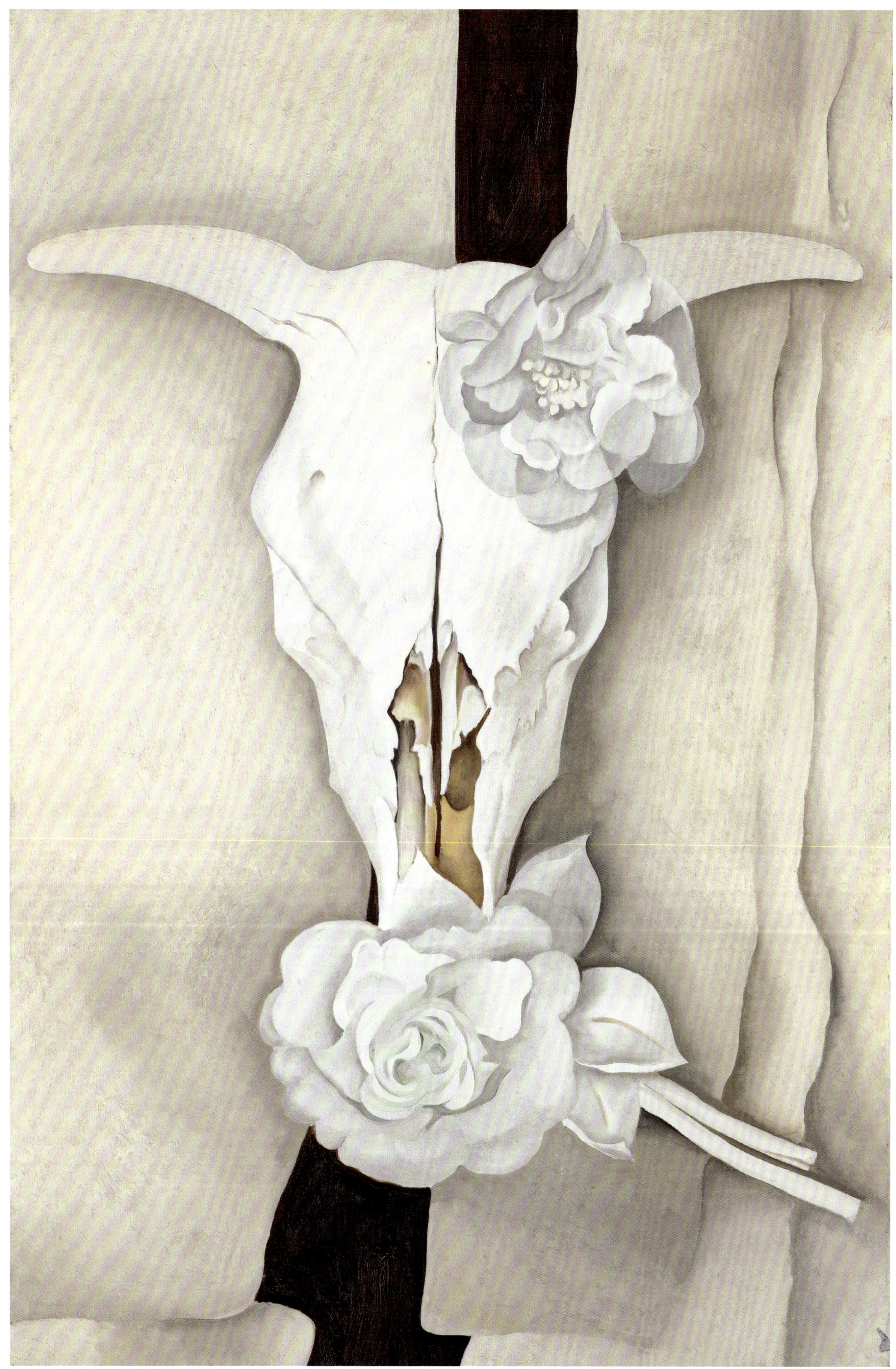

articulation of the "Great American Thing," as she provocatively described it. "As I was working [on the cow's skull paintings] I thought of the city men I had been seeing in the East. They talked so often of writing the Great American Novel—the Great American Play—the Great American Poetry. I am not sure that they aspired to the Great American Painting. Cézanne was so much in the air that I think the Great American Painting didn't even seem a possible dream."[43] Despite her reference to Cézanne, her solution was to create works that resonated with a specific sense of place—namely, the Southwest—and employed a distinctive modernist language. In such a manner her painting could break free of the confines of particular forms of European modernism and serve to define Americanness.

This challenging blend can be seen in *Cow's Skull with Calico Roses* and *Cow's Skull: Red, White, and Blue*. Although O'Keeffe opted for a highly representational depiction of the cow's skull in each composition, realism per se was not her goal. Instead, her reductive approach of eliminating details and abstracting form enabled her to achieve a monumental vision. In each, she thrust the stark bones up against the front of the picture plane. The shallow, abstract spaces behind the skulls—whether a blue and red ground reminiscent of a Navajo textile or overlapping fabric panels—thus insistently reinforce her prioritization of formal concerns. The gentle petals of the fabric flowers soften the hard edges of *Cow's Skull with Calico Roses* and further situate the painting in a Southwestern context: calico roses were used to adorn graves in the region. This strange pairing also amplifies the painting's status as an aesthetic object composed by the artist. However, it is the vibrant color scheme of *Cow's Skull: Red, White, and Blue* that most asserted her quest for Americanness. O'Keeffe saw it as a rebuttal to the jingoistic claims of conservative critics such as Thomas Craven, about which she later recalled, "People wanted to 'do' the American scene . . . and some of the current ideas about the American scene struck me as pretty ridiculous. To them, the American scene was a dilapidated house with a broken down buckboard out front and a horse that looked like a skeleton. . . . So, in a way, that cow's skull was my joke on the American scene, and it gave me pleasure to make it red, white, and blue."[44]

But this "joke" also evokes the troubled times of 1931. Although the overtly nationalistic palette would seem celebratory, the inchoate nature of the space, coupled with the bleached skull, lends the painting an almost surreal air. Indeed, O'Keeffe felt this herself as she completed the picture: "It is the kind of painting that makes me think many funny things about painting—Art—Myself—and maybe America—and then I look at it a bit cross-eyed and say to myself—that maybe it is just nothing after all—So that is that."[45] This very modern ambiguity of meaning can be seen as destabilizing purely nationalistic readings, underscoring the unsettled feeling of the era.

Hartley also pursued this quest for a localized modernism in the late 1930s, focusing on his home state for inspiration. Born in Lewiston, Maine, he returned to the state for good in 1937, which ended an extended period of expatriation from 1913 on that included stays in Germany, France, Bermuda, the Southwest, and points in between. As Donna Cassidy has described, Hartley had a desire for home, but his final move to Maine was also a response to the prevalent Regionalism of the 1930s. Beginning in the early years of the decade, the artist began to position himself first as a New Englander—with paintings of New Hampshire and Gloucester, Massachusetts—and then more specifically as a Mainer.[46] He cast his return in Biblical terms: "And so I say to my native continent of Maine, be patient and forgiving, I will soon put my cheek to your cheek, expecting the welcome of the prodigal, and be glad of it."[47]

Mount Katahdin became one of his most important subjects, presented in an equally spiritual light through his depictions of it as monumental and iconic. The peak was an important symbol of the Maine landscape, with a long history of artistic portrayals by such nineteenth-century painters as Frederic Edwin Church. But it also held great significance as a sightseeing destination. Designated a state park in 1931, it was central to Maine's tourism efforts, which surely contributed to Hartley's interest.[48] He camped there in October 1939, soon producing, among other works, the vibrantly bold *Mt. Katahdin (Maine), Autumn #2* (1939–40; fig. 8). Hartley depicted the view as a series of horizontally stacked bands of color, retaining a largely naturalistic if limited palette of red, white, blue, and

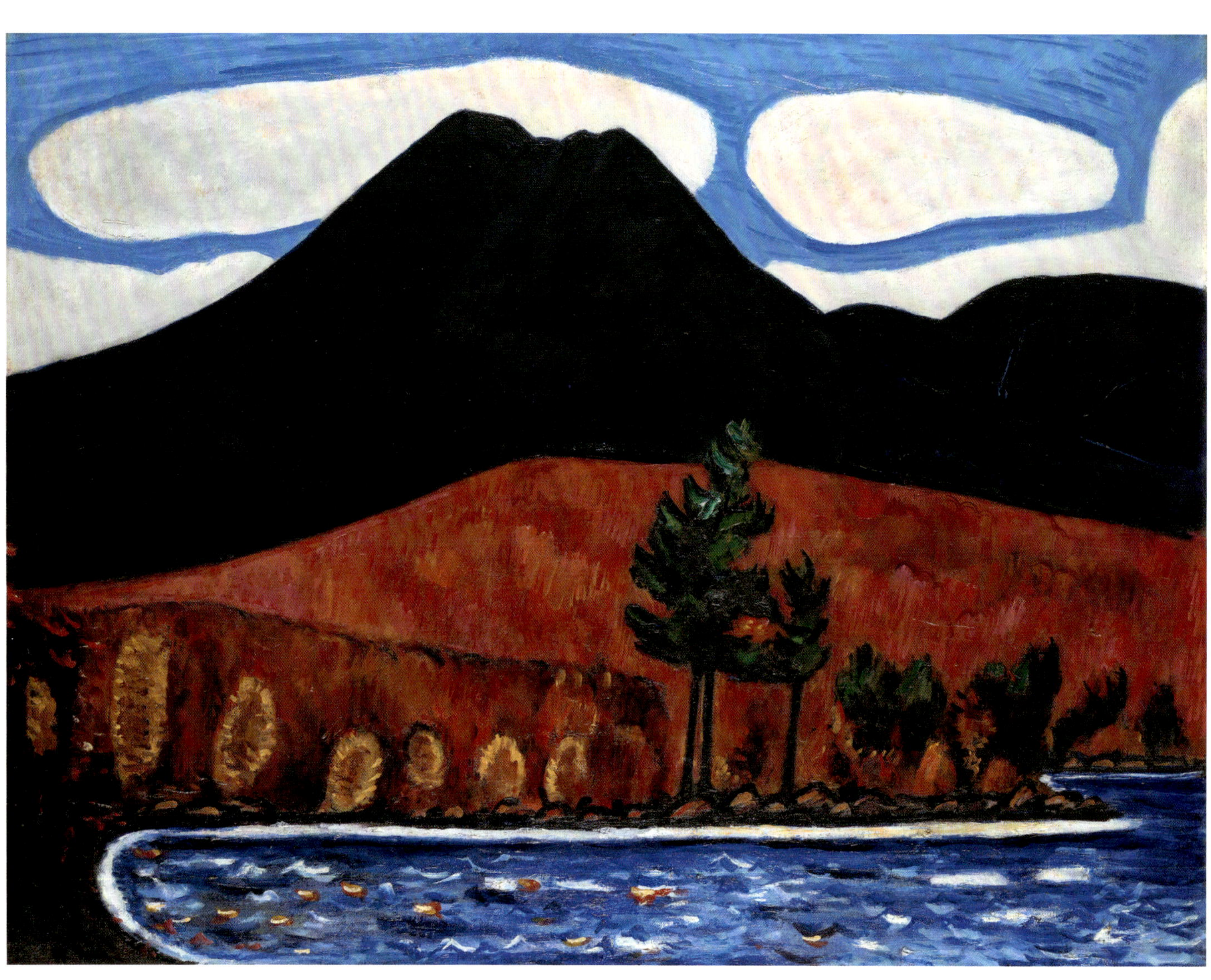

black. This color scheme bears nationalistic overtones, and it
seems likely that Hartley saw it as a rebuttal to the patriotic
claims of midwestern Regionalists such as Wood and Benton.
Indeed, Hartley undoubtedly had their public image in mind
when he posed for a publicity photograph with *Mt. Katahdin
(Maine), Autumn #2*, wearing a checked flannel shirt as a deliberate Maine counterpoint to Wood's Iowan overalls (fig. 9; see
also p. 40, fig. 7). But he made such arguments formally as well.
The artist varied his brushwork throughout the painting, constantly reinforcing the work's two-dimensional quality. Short
rhyming brushstrokes denote the feathery autumnal trees,
while flatly painted white patches indicate stylized clouds.
However, Hartley rendered the mountain itself with little
visible brushwork, allowing its dark pyramid to dominate the
composition without relief. Overall the composition reflected
his belief that "Maine is likewise a strong, simple, stately and
perhaps brutal country."[49]

Dove did not share O'Keeffe's preference for hard edges
and precise styles, or Hartley's preference for iconic images, but
his love of nature—specifically, the natural landscape around
his homes in Connecticut and New York—was a crucial point
of commonality. His passion for his home, his specific places,
was as intense as O'Keeffe's infatuation with the Southwest,
and it formed the core of his artistic expression. As she noted,
"Dove used to paint a lot of small pictures, little landscapes,
that didn't look particularly distinguished at first, but in them
he would get the feel of a particular place so completely that
you'd know you'd *been* there."[50] Like O'Keeffe as well, he often
turned to abstracted form to convey natural inspirations, as in
*Tree Trunks* (fig. 10), a lyrical work of 1934. This period was one
of great difficulty in Dove's life; several months before he had
moved, with great trepidation, back to his hometown of Geneva,
New York, following the death of his mother. He was impoverished but refused to apply for support from the Public Works
of Art Project, seeing it as a hindrance to creativity.[51] *Tree
Trunks* represented an aesthetic shift for Dove, as he moved
from depicting the landscape naturalistically to a more fluid
and abstracted approach. He swirled the trunks of the trees
into sinuous forms that dance across the picture plane, the dry

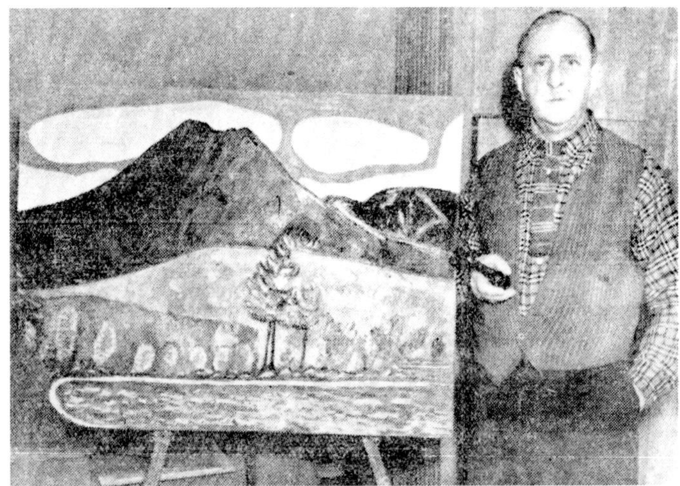

texture of the paint conveying an earthy quality. This new mode
of modernist expression did not go unnoticed when exhibited
at An American Place in 1934; one critic noted, "Dove's new
adventurous oils . . . denote embarkation upon a voyage of fresh
experimentation in the realm of design."[52] Indeed, the lyrical
abstraction of *Tree Trunks* evokes, although not precisely, the
organic forms seen in biomorphic paintings and constructions
by European artists such as Hans Arp, Jean Hélion, and Joan
Miró, all of which were displayed at Gallatin's Gallery of Living
Art in the first half of the 1930s.[53] Gallatin also acquired and
exhibited works by members of the Stieglitz circle, including
Dove, who was certainly familiar with the collection. *Tree
Trunks*, however, never abandons nature for an entirely nonobjective composition, instead moving between abstraction
and landscape in a manner that underscores the importance of
nature and place as an inspiration.

But Dove did not turn solely to the landscape to express
the Americanness of his work. In the 1930s, he also occasionally employed cultural references to connect his increasingly
abstract art to American life. An amateur musician and avid fan
of popular music, he translated the fast syncopation and joyous
rhythms of swing into paint in *Swing Music (Louis Armstrong)*
(1938; fig. 11).[54] Music was an important theme for Dove, and he
had produced a series of musical paintings around 1927, including *George Gershwin—I'll Build a Stairway to Paradise* (1927;

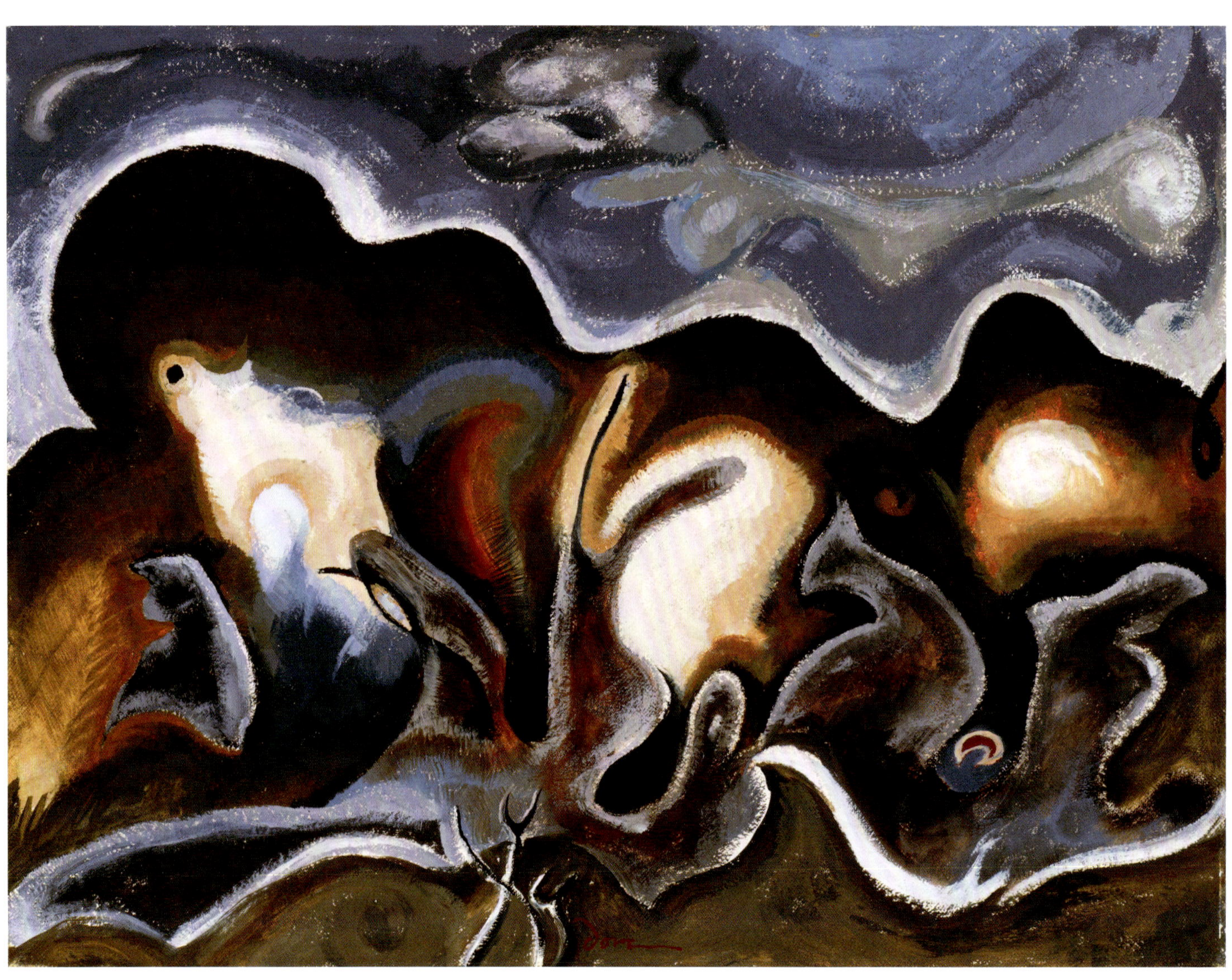

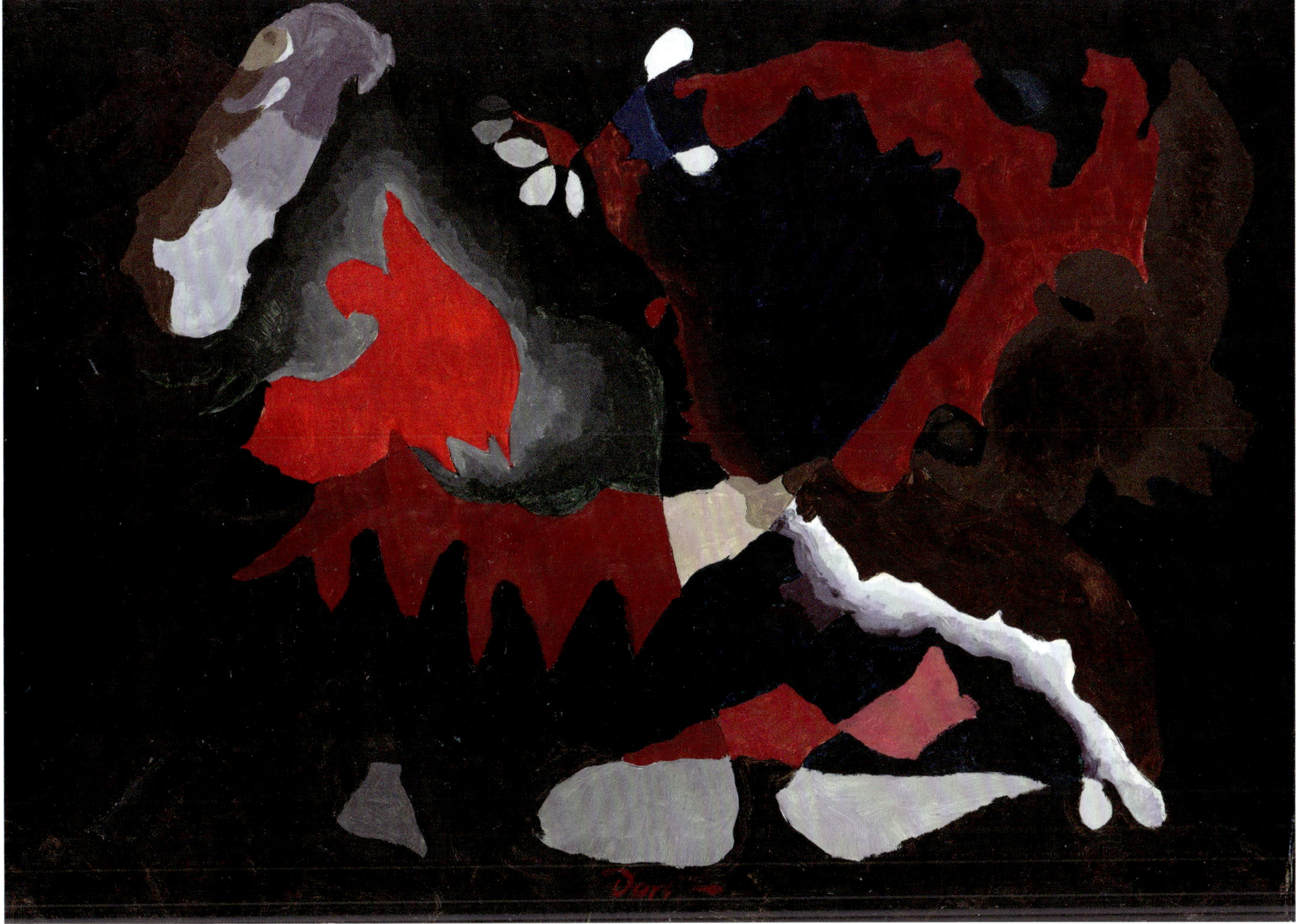

Museum of Fine Arts, Boston) and *Orange Grove in California, by Irving Berlin* (1927; Museo Thyssen-Bornemisza, Madrid).[55] In these works, he focused on white composers of popular songs, several of which were performed by the Paul Whiteman Orchestra on an album Dove owned. These men made jazz, born out of southern African American culture and brought north during the Great Migration, palatable to an unfamiliar nation by smoothing it out and taming its energy. Yet scholars have noted that even such sanitized music was understood as being definitely American and distinctly modern and rebellious.[56] Dove's paintings of 1927 were therefore a self-conscious display by a modernist artist of his nationalistic bona fides.[57]

This was equally true, if not even more so, of *Swing Music (Louis Armstrong)*, painted quickly in March 1938.[58] The completely abstract composition features blaring patches of red that erupt across the canvas, their jagged shapes suggesting that Dove sought to map the syncopation of Armstrong's music. Armstrong had achieved mainstream acceptance in the 1930s through his gravel-voiced singing and virtuosic trumpet playing, in which he always reached for the highest notes.[59] Likewise, the red notes of paint ascend higher and higher throughout Dove's painting, leaping out of darker areas as if to suggest the horn's dynamic sound in the midst of a nightclub. Dove, however, never heard Armstrong perform live; instead, he saw the 1937 film *Artists and Models*, which featured the musician.[60] The hit song "Swing That Music" (first recorded in 1936) might also have inspired Dove's painting. With the value of abstraction still highly contested, swing music offered Dove a means of tapping into American popular culture in his art. Indeed, the style reached its undisputed heyday in 1938, when *Life* magazine published "Swing: The Hottest and Best Kind of Jazz Reaches Its Golden Age."[61] The article declared Armstrong "the greatest of all Swing musicians," lauding his "unbelievable technique." By overtly linking his modernist abstraction to the hottest trend in music, Dove created a painting whose American quality could not be mistaken.

He might not have been aware of the racial implications of his work: *Swing Music (Louis Armstrong)* is an example of a white artist inspired by, and appropriating, African American culture to his own modernist ends.[62] However, the 1930s were notable for the number of important black artists who saw their creations as a means for advocating for the rights and freedom of their people in a still-segregated American society. Many found opportunities through the Works Progress Administration (WPA) to expose prejudice through paintings and prints in Social Realist styles. But others, most notably Aaron Douglas and William H. Johnson—both of whom worked for the WPA as well—used modernism to advance their personal, political, and social goals. In part, this was because of the connection at the time between leftist ideas and aesthetically progressive techniques.

The conflation of art and politics in the 1930s is crucial to understanding the stakes of the debate over the value of European modernism. In his public skirmish with the Regionalists, Davis positioned them as reactionary. Conversely, many European-inspired modernists (along with most Social Realists such as Ben Shahn) were seen as aligned with Communism and other leftist beliefs. Not all joined the Communist Party like Douglas did, but many believed more broadly in the goals of the Popular Front, the party's strategy to overthrow capitalism via cultural production.[63] Davis made his argument against the Regionalists in the journal *Art Front*, which represented the leftist voice in American art. It had been founded by members of the Artists Union and the Artists' Committee of Action (ACA), among them Davis. The ACA was organized in protest of the 1934 destruction at New York's Rockefeller Center of Diego Rivera's 1933 *Man at the Crossroads* mural, which had caused significant controversy due to its socialist message and inclusion of a portrait of Vladimir Lenin. As a result, the journal's editorial committee argued that the Depression era necessitated a louder voice: "The urgent need for a publication which speaks for the artist, battles for his economic security and guides him in his artistic efforts is self-evident. *Art Front* is the crystallization of all the forces in art surging forward to combat the destructive and chauvinistic tendencies which are becoming more distinct daily."[64] *Art Front* was one literary means by which leftist artists could affect society, but more importantly, many—whether immigrant, native-born white, or African American—believed that their work could serve in the struggle for a more just United States.

Douglas, one of the preeminent modernist painters of the 1930s, used a dynamic and unique visual language to symbolically chronicle black history as a means of promoting equality and introducing African American narratives into mainstream culture. *Aspiration* (p. 94, fig. 5), the last of a four-mural cycle painted in 1936 for the Texas Centennial Exposition, superbly reveals his adroit synthesis of multiple aesthetics, from Cubist geometric structure to ancient Egyptian art. The cycle portrayed how African Americans have affected American society through their labor, weaving together past and present to underscore the importance of their contributions.[65] Two of the paintings have been lost, but the second, *Into Bondage* (1936; fig. 12), was intended to evoke the early nation's dependence upon slave labor. In *Aspiration*, the artist depicted a trio of figures carrying attributes that mark them as educated: a compass and carpenter's square, a beaker, and an open book. They gesture toward a city on a hill, the modern metropolis to which they both aspire and contribute. But the trio is positioned above outstretched, manacled hands, suggesting that their lives are built upon a history of slavery.

Douglas buttressed these powerful images with a uniquely modern style that reinforces the narrative across the cycle. He had studied with the German-born modernist Winold Reiss in the 1920s and also stayed in Paris for a year in 1931 and 1932. He was therefore well versed in modernist techniques, including the use of so-called primitive art forms. Douglas drew

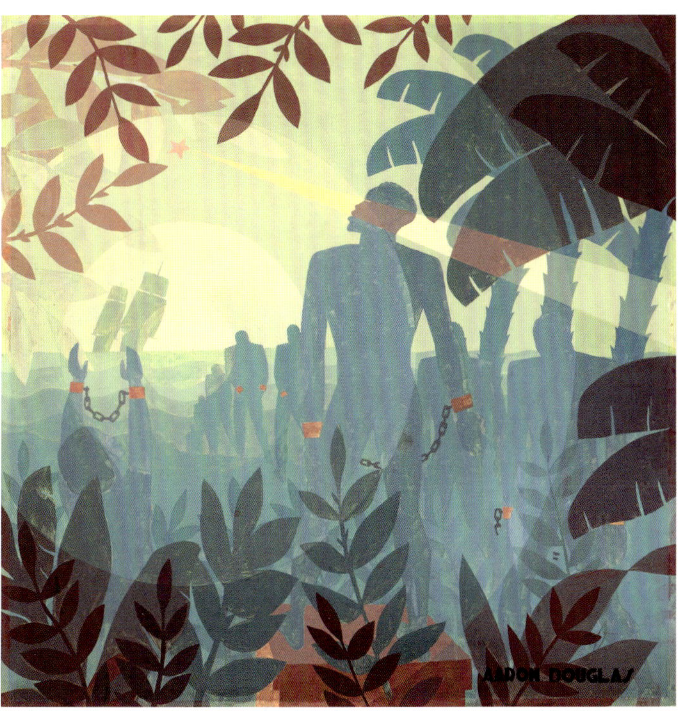


on ancient Egyptian and African art in his choice to silhouette the figures, endowing them with a monumental universality. More innovative are the concentric circles of light that radiate across the compositions, evoking a connection from one panel to the next. He also employed a friezelike format that was appropriate for mural painting but further enabled him to construct complex symbolic allegories across the cycle.[66] This is apparent with the presence of the small star that attracts the primary figure in *Into Bondage*; by *Aspiration*, it has become a major focal point (and possible emblem for the Lone Star State) that links the figures with the glowing city. Finally, the concentric elements of light work with the flattened, matte forms to fracture the space of the composition—an inventive rethinking of Cubist pictorial structure that gives Douglas's cycle a vivid dynamism.

Less monumental in his scope, Johnson developed a boldly colored and highly patterned modernist style to honor the daily lives of African Americans residing in Harlem at the end of the 1930s. The artist studied in France for three years in the 1920s but returned in 1929 and began exhibiting with the

Harmon Foundation, the leading supporter of black artists. His award-winning work of this period was highly expressionistic and was seen by some as trailblazing in its use of modernist language by an African American artist. Others criticized it as being too reminiscent of European styles—a common reproach at the time.[67] One journalist, however, echoed the thoughts of Davis when he defended Johnson with the words, "Negro artists are no more imitative than other American artists. Can we name one eminent painter who is not saturated with European influences?"[68] More so than most black artists, though, Johnson was firmly ensconced in European culture, for he crossed the Atlantic again in 1930 to marry the Danish artist Holcha Krake. They lived in Denmark and Norway for eight years, during which time he evolved an approach that was less reliant on flamboyantly decorative brushwork and more intent upon conveying forms as material, tangible entities, if still rendered in a modernist style. In 1938 the growing threat of war caused the Johnsons to return to the United States, where they settled in downtown New York.

Another motivation for Johnson's return was the desire to "come back to his own country and paint his own people."[69] He categorized his art as that of a "modern primitive," a term initially meant to suggest his authentic connection to nature but soon extended to African American culture. Although the idea of primitivism had held aesthetic currency for decades, initially deriving from Picasso's use of African masks, Johnson saw himself not as an outsider adapting the exotic forms of non-Western cultures but as an insider who possessed a direct understanding of and great sympathy for his own culture— despite having lived abroad for much of the decade. He was not alone in making such claims; the late 1930s saw the embrace of self-taught artists, among them the Pennsylvania painter Horace Pippin. Artists, curators, and collectors heralded such individuals as living symbols of an American past, linked to American modernism through folk art traditions. Johnson was highly trained yet nevertheless sought to tap into this vogue by exploiting his identity as an African American. In this, he was akin to Doris Lee, who adapted a folksy style as a signifier of authentic experience in *Thanksgiving* (c. 1935; p. 105, fig. 17).

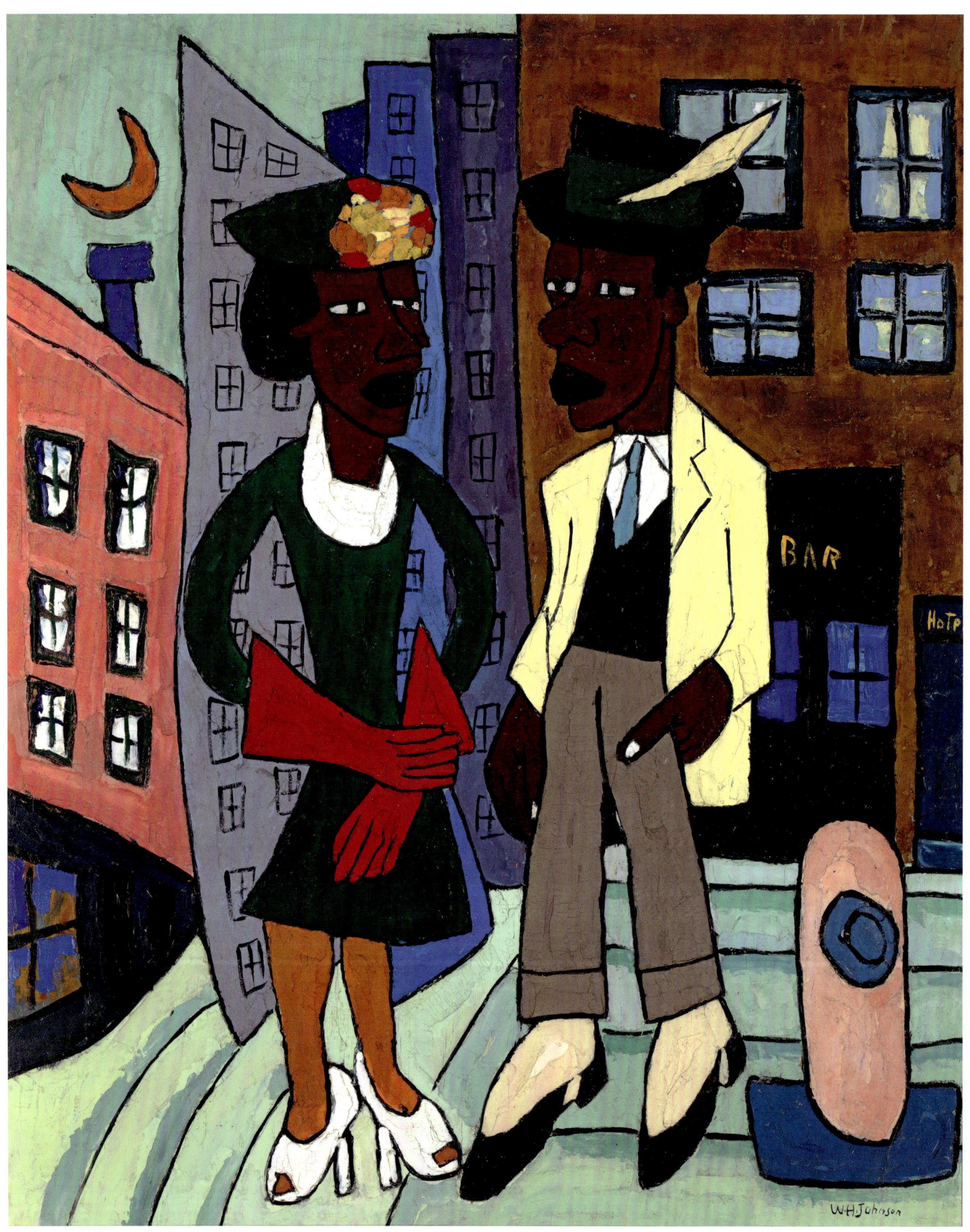

BAR
HOTP
W.H.Johnson

Several months after moving to New York, Johnson was able to join the WPA Federal Art Project (WPA/FAP) and began teaching at the Harlem Community Art Center. He soon embarked upon an extensive study of the people around him; he also began drawing African sculptures.[70] This investigation became the basis of a strong, seemingly untutored style that he used to great effect in *Street Life, Harlem* (1939; fig. 13), one of his most monumental and vivid paintings. The artist relied on thickly built up areas of paint, heavily outlined in black pigment, to endow the composition with a faux-naïve appearance. The angular, stylized figures suggest the influence of African sculptures, but Johnson's purpose is not entirely formal. Together, the subjects form a dapper couple, fashionably dressed in outfits that speak to their participation in the cool Harlem nightlife. The orange crescent moon and multicolored buildings around them contribute to the effect of a vibrant urban environment. By celebrating African American life in this "modern primitive" style, Johnson connected historical African art and the most au courant Harlem culture.

In the mid-1930s, even as numerous artists used nationalistic symbols, places, and different cultural expressions to carve out a space for distinctly American forms of modernism, a new group rebelled against representational art entirely.[71] These younger artists began to argue anew for nonobjective art, seeing it as an equally vital force. In contradiction of the trend toward American Scene painting, they believed art did not have to represent some aspect of everyday life; it could be culturally significant as a purely aesthetic object. Shaw, for example, articulated his commitment to formal concerns and visual interest regardless of subject matter:

**One seeks, for example, rhythm, composition, spacial [*sic*] organization, design, progression of color, and many, many other qualities in any aesthetic work. Indeed it is the perfection of these very qualities that constitute an aesthetic work and there is surely no earthly reason why a painting may not possess all such qualities and still be the most abstract picture ever.[72]**

Shaw and his fellow abstract artists represented a new wave of modernists who largely rejected naturalistic representation and looked more explicitly again to European styles. Many of them traveled to Paris and other cities in the 1930s, where they had contact with Piet Mondrian, Arp, Hélion, Miró, and others. They also responded to the increasing presence of European-born artists who had fled to the United States in the mid- to late 1930s due to the growing threat of war and Fascism in Europe.[73] Through such means, American artists, many of whom were earlier immigrants to the country, reinvigorated their interest in pure abstraction.

In November 1936, some of these abstractionists, among them Ilya Bolotowsky, Gallatin, Morris, and Shaw, banded together to form the American Abstract Artists (AAA), which sought to actively promote nonobjective art in the United States. The group was founded in response to the Museum of Modern Art's 1935 exhibition *Cubism and Abstract Art*, which included only one American artist, Alexander Calder. Members thus had two primary challenges: first, to prove the validity of abstraction to a still-conservative art world, and, second, to gain recognition specifically as American artists working in the idiom. Like Davis, they argued that it was a fallacy to think that artists could be immune to influences from outside national boundaries, yet they did so to support the idea that their mode of abstraction was just as relevant as that of Europeans. "No educated intelligence," wrote the editors of one of the group's catalogues, "can draw the so-called 'line of national culture' as an ambition and objective, without discerning its ambiguity. . . . [W]e can do nothing better than emphasize that the contemporary must respect the interpenetration and concatenation of all culture."[74] Despite these stated principles, a number of members nevertheless sought to distinguish their art from that of their European colleagues by blending American motifs and international styles into unique aesthetic objects.

*Wrigley's* (1937; fig. 14), Shaw's witty representation of the New York skyline depicted with a package of Wrigley's chewing gum hovering midair, exemplifies this fusion.[75] Despite the artist's published commitment to nonobjectivity, *Wrigley's* unites geometric abstraction with a cunning sense of consumer culture that would have been understood

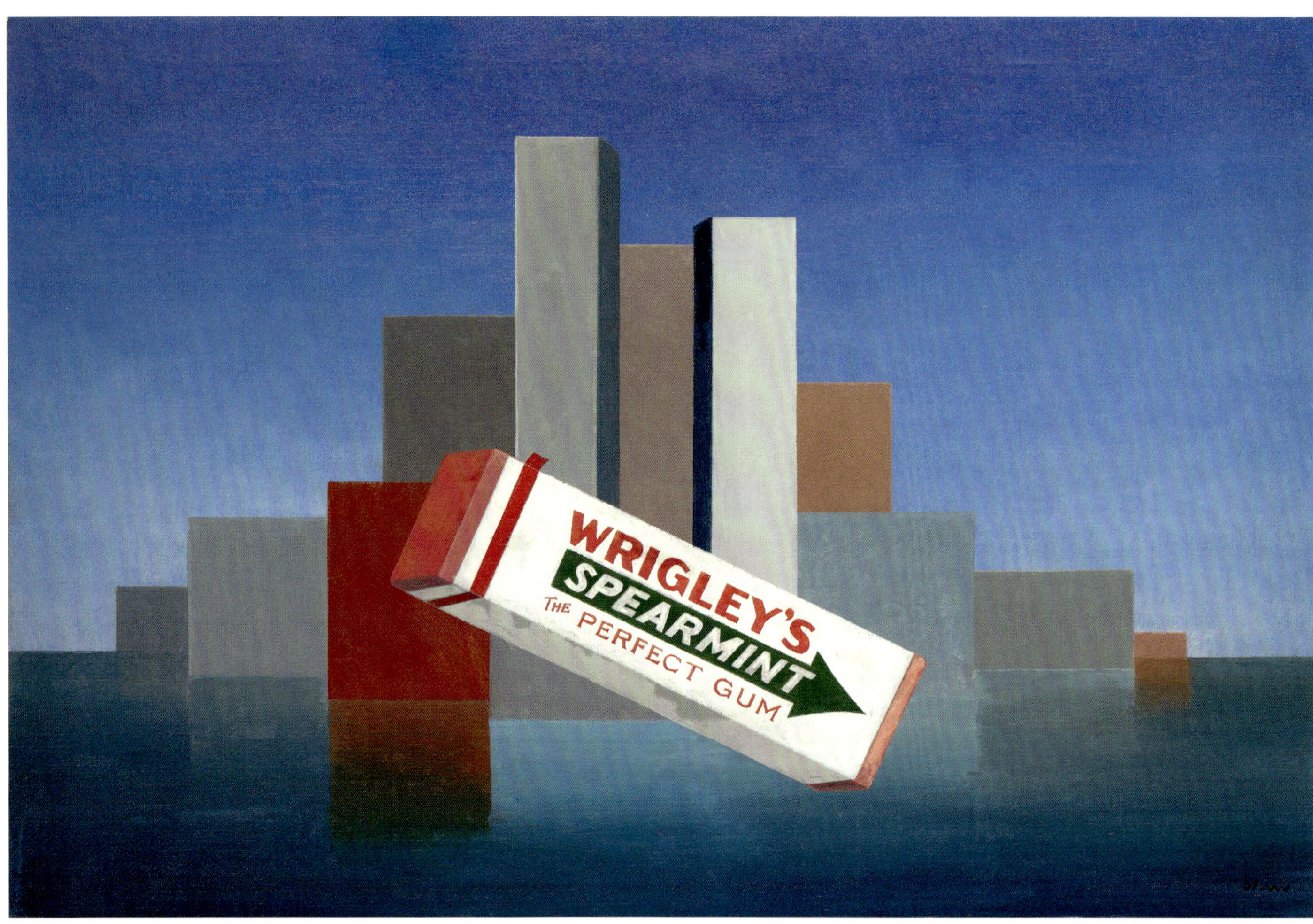


as distinctly American. As a work done on speculation, it also perhaps reflects his own social status: Shaw did not need to sell his paintings. In 1935 he forged friendships with Gallatin and Morris, and the three men, along with Morris's wife, Suzy Frelinghuysen, were soon called the "Park Avenue Cubists" because they possessed significant wealth and social connections.[76] Able to travel extensively despite the Depression, Shaw made several trips to Europe in the 1930s, where he met with artists and began collecting their works. He also collaborated with Gallatin on the organization of the influential exhibition *Five Contemporary American Concretionists*, which was shown at the Gallery of Living Art in 1936 and featured works by Charles Biederman, Calder, John Ferren, Morris, and Shaw.[77]

In December 1936, after seeing the landmark exhibition *Fantastic Art, Dada, Surrealism* at the Museum of Modern Art, Shaw conceived of a design for an advertising poster for Wrigley's chewing gum (fig. 15) by positioning a pack against a picture of the New York skyline and photographing it. He used *Wrigley's* to work the idea out on canvas, and although the poster was never produced, the painting remains a testament to his endeavor.[78] Although *Wrigley's* is not purely abstract due to the referential inclusion of the package of gum, its underlying structure is geometric and relates to a series of works the artist did that featured, as he wrote in an essay titled "The Plastic Polygon," the Manhattan skyline "treated semi-cubistically." He further asserted that the "polygon, sprouting, so to speak, from the steel and concrete of New York City, I feel to be essentially American in its roots."[79] *Wrigley's* thus overtly speaks to Shaw's desire to position his art within a specifically American context. Indeed, with its tongue-in-cheek reference to popular culture, his painting anticipates later works of Pop Art by Andy Warhol and Roy Lichtenstein.

Morris likewise sought to balance abstraction with American motifs, but instead of consumer culture, he repeatedly focused on Native American motifs in his painting, including *Indian Composition No. 6* (1938; fig. 16). Morris studied with Léger at the Académie Moderne in Paris in 1929 and again in 1930, which gave him a thorough grounding in the latest styles.[80] He also was one of the curators of Gallatin's Gallery of Living Art and thus was exposed to the most avant-garde European art then available in New York. *Indian Composition No. 6* represents his experimentation with biomorphic abstraction, which he would have seen in the work of Arp and Miró. However, although the work has no overt subject matter, Morris's inclusion of various patterned elements indicates his use of Native American visual culture, then considered primitive. Two wedge-shaped forms in the center of the painting have a pattern reminiscent of birch bark, which was used by northeastern and Great Lakes tribes to make canoes, while curving shapes at the top and bottom evoke a tooth and bear claws. Other forms could suggest arrows or a hatchet, but they are subsumed by the generally ovoid design of the composition. Native American art and artifacts were highly visible in New York in the 1930s; for example, Morris's mentor, John Sloan, helped organize the pioneering *Exposition of Indian Tribal Arts* in 1931, which undoubtedly prompted Morris's interest.[81]

The paintings also tapped into the long-standing vogue for primitivism in modern art. Although well versed in the employment of African art by modernist artists, Morris saw Native American forms as an equally valid part of international modernism.[82] Indeed, he believed that American modernists had an imperative to look to their own past as the basis for progressive art grounded in national culture: "If an authentic American culture is to arise, we must go back to a beginning. My work . . . is the attempt to find such a beginning."[83] He also

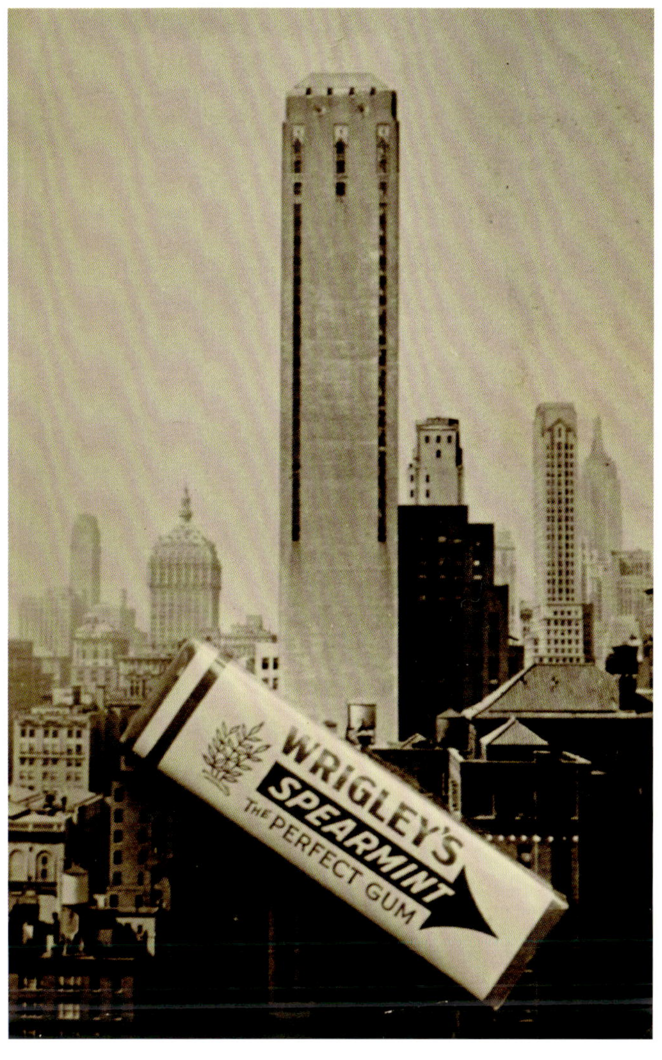



**Fig. 15** Idea for a montage showing a picture of the New York skyline photographed with a pack of Wrigley's gum. Charles Green Shaw Papers, Archives of American Art, Smithsonian Institution, Washington, DC.

saw this approach as a corrective to American Scene painting, which he described as "oppressive."[84] Native American art was a crucial part of his formulation. Morris also traveled to Santa Fe in the mid-1930s, where he copied Pueblo motifs that intrigued him. He employed these in a number of paintings, often in conjunction with motifs from other regions, later recalling, "I selected those which seemed to fit into the plastic scheme of the work on which I was engaged."[85] He thus clearly valued a variety of Native American designs for their abstract formal qualities but did not feel compelled to distinguish between them or isolate them from one another for the sake of authenticity. Thus, by synthesizing the latest in European

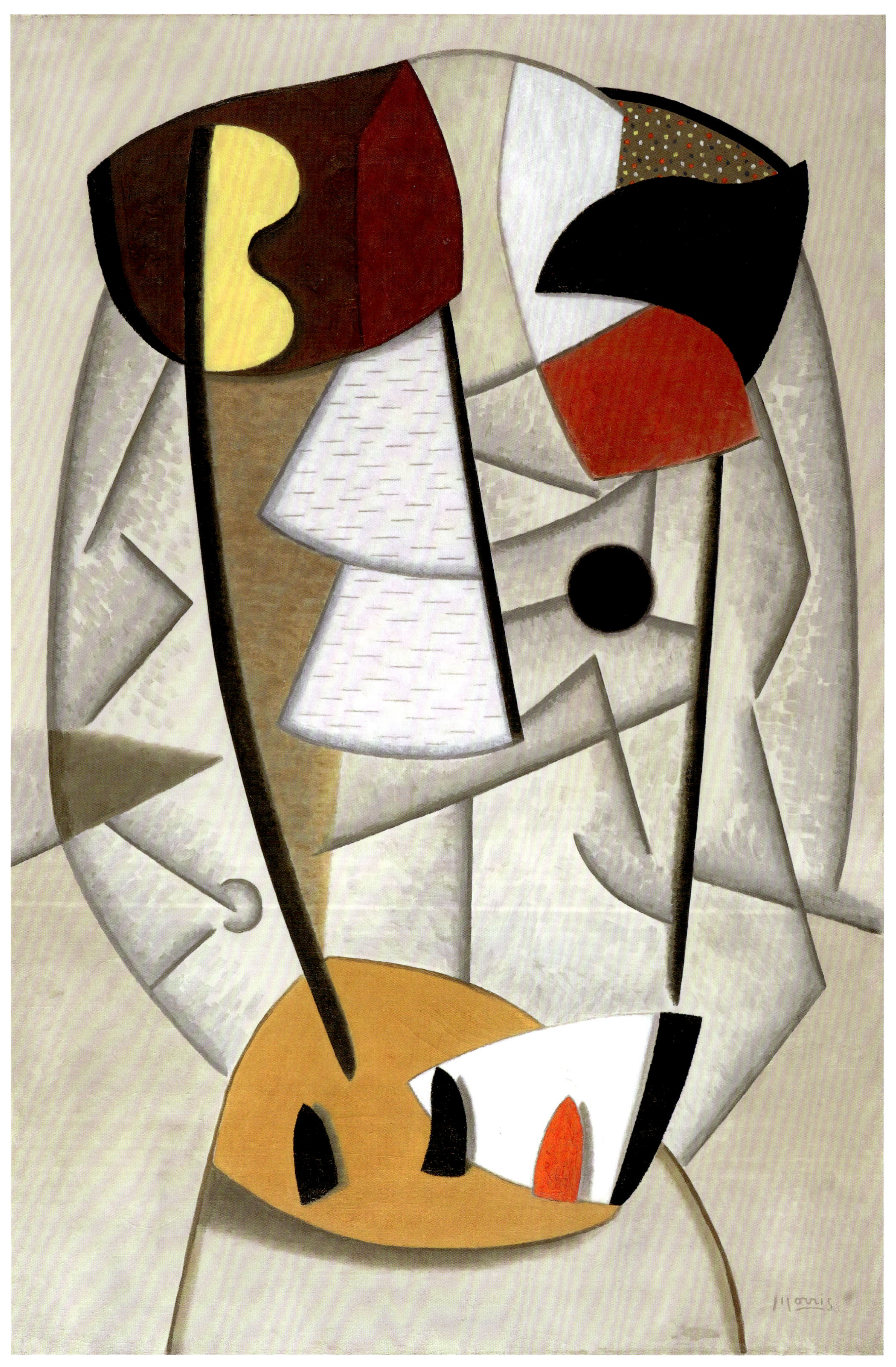

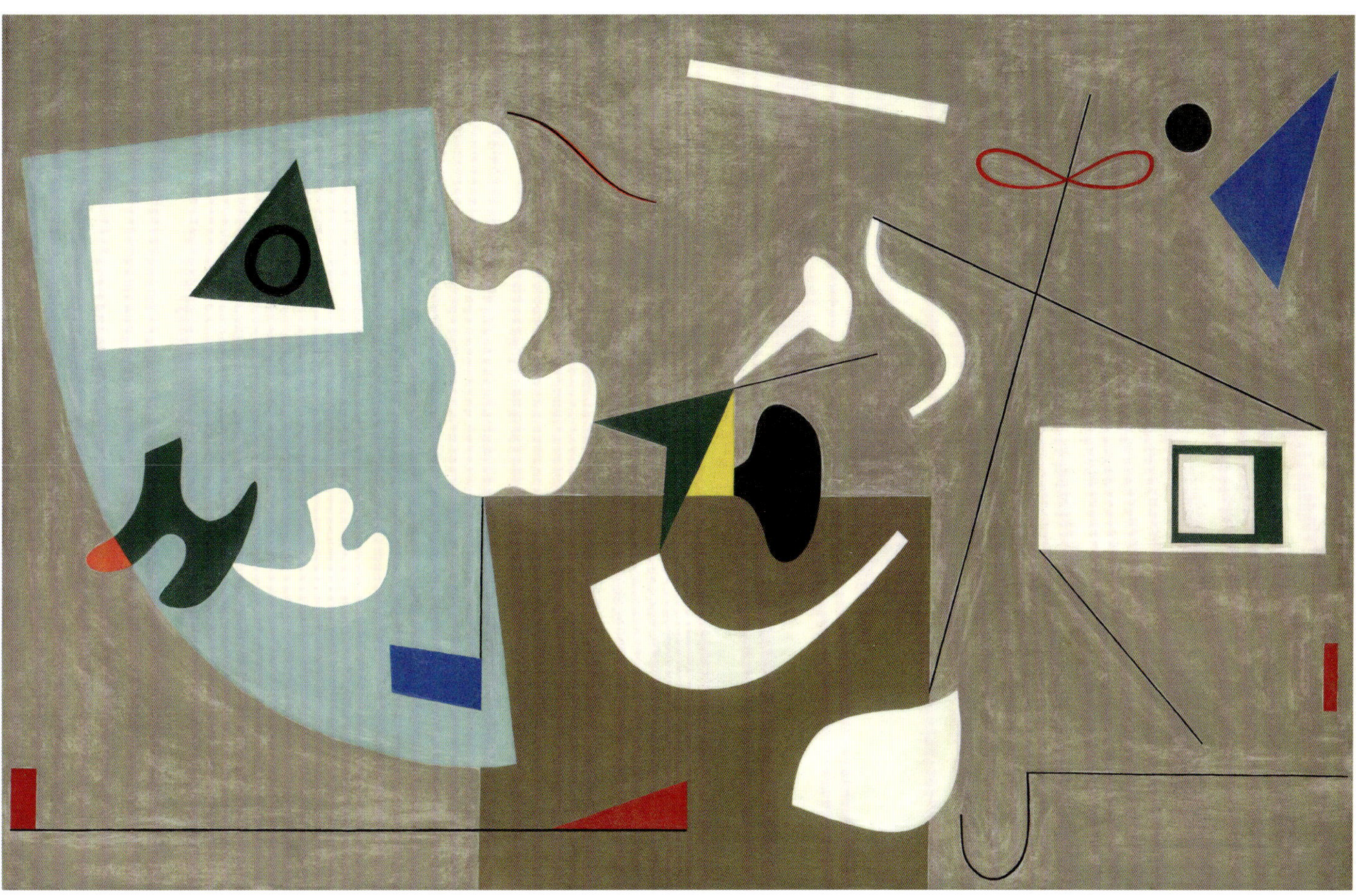

abstraction with what he perceived as distinctively original American motifs, he made his own foray into the critical dialogue about nationalism, American Scene painting, and the role that nonobjective art could play in that debate.

In contrast, the Russian-born abstractionist Bolotowsky eschewed recognizable motifs entirely, focusing on nonobjective imagery in early works such as the *Study for the Hall of Medical Sciences Mural at the 1939 World's Fair in New York* (1938/39; fig. 17).[86] Bolotowsky, whose family arrived in New York in 1923, returned to Europe in 1932, where he saw works by the Cubists and Surrealists.[87] He also recalled being inspired by Johnson, who was then living in Europe.[88] But this painting demonstrates the clear influence of the biomorphic works of Miró, which he saw, along with the geometric abstractions of Mondrian, in New York in 1933. Gallatin, for example, had numerous paintings by

Miró, among them *Painting* (1933; fig. 18). Over the course of his career, Bolotowsky would move between these two influences, the biomorphic and the geometric, always in search of a sense of equilibrium. He achieved this balance in his mural study, which juxtaposes curving and rectilinear forms in harmonious contrasts across the compositional field. Unlike Miró's work, in which abstract forms can appear almost figural, Bolotowsky refrained from endowing his shapes with anthropomorphic qualities. They do, however, spread across the picture plane with a whimsical rhythm, the white forms dancing in a diagonal from upper left to lower right, balanced by interspersed patches of blue and other colors. Although some forms overlap, the composition gives little indication of pictorial depth; the shapes consist of flat and unmodulated color against an equally two-dimensional neutral background.

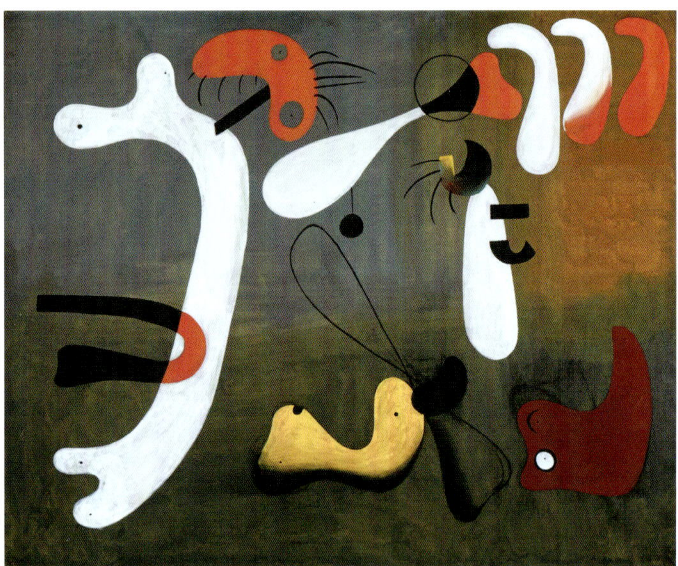

**Fig. 18** Joan Miró (Spanish, 1893–1983). *Painting*, 1933. Oil and aqueous medium on canvas; 130.5 × 163.2 cm (51 ³⁄₈ × 64 ¼ in.). Philadelphia Museum of Art, A. E. Gallatin Collection, 1952, 1952-61-85. Copyright Artists Rights Society (ARS), New York /ADAGP, Paris.

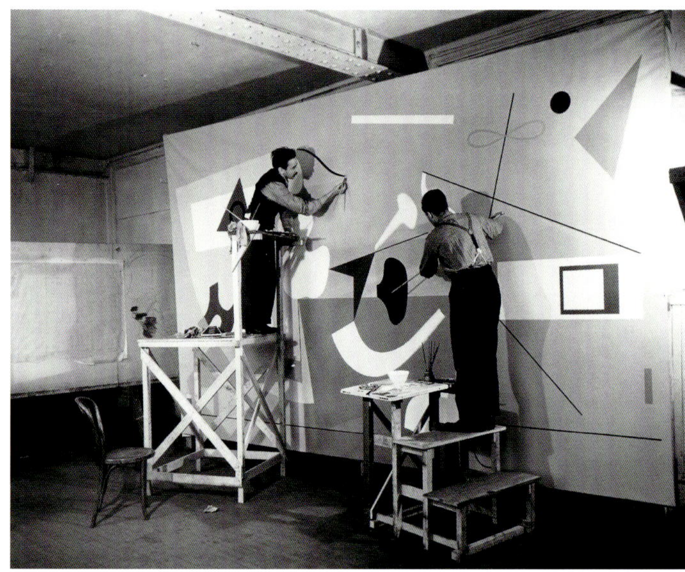

**Fig. 19** Ilya Bolotowsky, *Hall of Medical Sciences Mural*, 1939, installed in the Hall of Medicine and Public Health, New York World's Fair. Records of the Work Projects Administration, National Archives, College Park, Maryland.

Although the painting itself yields nothing to nationalistic rhetoric, its setting is significant. Bolotowsky executed this work as the final study for a mural intended for the Hall of Medical Sciences at the 1939 World's Fair (see fig. 19), where it hung along with three other abstract murals by Bolotowsky's fellow AAA members Byron Browne, Balcomb Greene, and Louis Schanker (all four were destroyed at the end of the fair along with many other representational murals).[89] The pieces had been commissioned by the WPA/FAP, which, in addition to supporting easel painting and printmaking divisions, ran a program to bring murals into public spaces. Most, although not all, of those were representational in nature, often following the model of Mexican modernists such as Diego Rivera, and were aligned with American Scene ideals. Bolotowsky had earlier painted an abstract mural for the Williamsburg Housing Project, but the Hall of Medical Sciences painting presented the seemingly radical idea of an abstract mural being used in a context of national progress.[90] With the theme "Building the World of Tomorrow," the fair promoted a vision of a prosperous United States and included numerous futuristic displays by architects, designers, and industrial manufacturers. Abstract murals would seem to have little place in this ideal world, but their acceptance suggests that by the end of the 1930s,

international modernism had overcome some (although by no means all) of its marginalization in American art. In addition to the murals, modernist painting could also be seen at the fair in *American Art Today*, a large loan show of contemporary art. While it remained less popular than American Scene painting, which dominated the exhibition, it nevertheless had a presence.[91]

Davis also participated in the fair; his *History of Communication* mural (fig. 20) adorned the Hall of Communications, and his easel painting *Gloucester Harbor* (1938; Museum of Fine Arts Houston) represented him in the *American Art Today* exhibition. Nearly a decade had passed since he had defended his heritage as a "Picasso-American," and in 1939 he mused once again about modernism, spurred by its presence at the World's Fair. In an essay titled "Abstract Art Today," he made the case, not for the first time nor for the last, that modernist art was a crucial barometer of advances in society:

**Abstract art has been and is now a direct progressive social force, not simply a theory about progress. . . . Abstract art in its mural, easel, and graphic forms has given concrete artistic formulation to the new lights, speeds, and spaces which are uniquely real in our time. . . . Modern art is not a spectator, it**

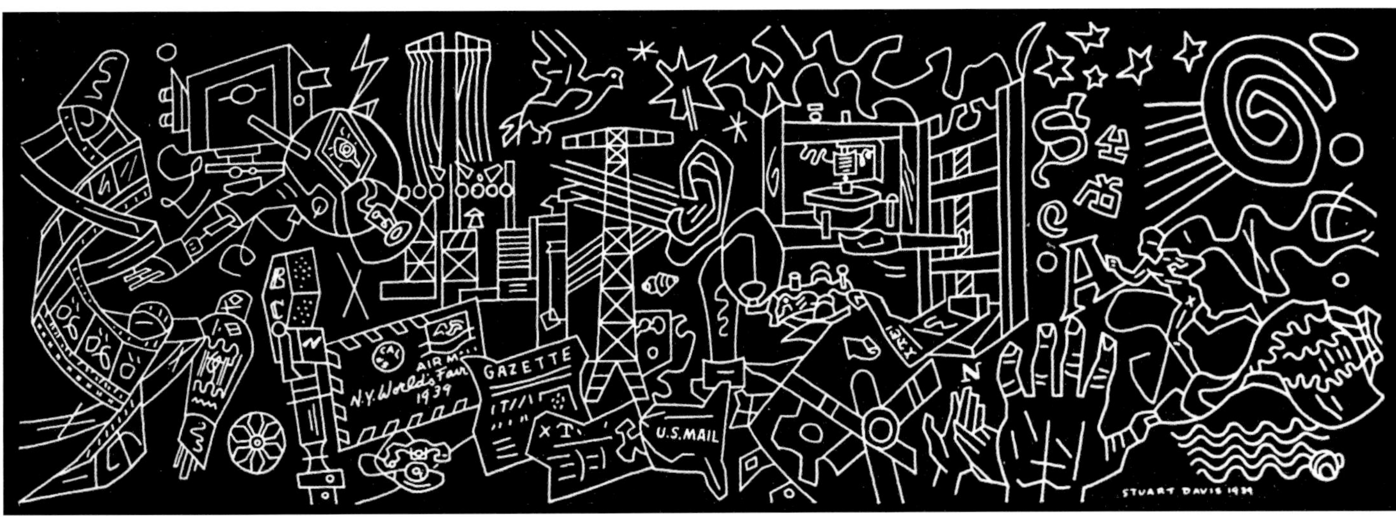


**is a participant. In other words, it not only reflects contemporary life but is an active agent in the direction of it.**[92]

Moreover, as he continued to advocate for modernism over representational styles, he explicitly linked its development to the freedom afforded by democracy in the United States: "American artists have the greatest potentialities of any artists in the world at the present time because of their relative political freedom."[93] In other words, as regimes in Europe grew more repressive, Davis believed it was precisely America's democratic structure that allowed artists to choose whether they wanted to be, as he had earlier said, a Rembrandt-American, a Renoir-American, or a Picasso-American. This idea—that the democratic nature of the United States encouraged the development of many different modes of art—permeated the culture of the 1930s, and it is the final key to understanding the persistence of transatlantic modernism. Although American Scene painting dominated the decade, modernists of all different stripes, from the Stieglitz circle to the American Abstract Artists, nevertheless continued to take inspiration from international styles because they knew they had the freedom to do so.

International modernism was therefore a flexible concept, allowing dedicated modernists to engage with American Scene painting even as the Regionalists—particularly Davis's longtime bête noire Benton—looked to modernism as a means of enhancing the aesthetic interest of their works. Even so, modernists were not immune to societal pressures; their careful negotiations between internationalism and nationalism suggest that they, too, felt the need to heighten the cultural relevance of their creations for American audiences. The 1930s were a complex decade in many ways: politically, socially, economically, and culturally. The American zeitgeist was fraught with debates over the role of government and the place of the individual in society. International modernism played an important role in cultural debates, and in this era of complexity, the manifold strategies employed by modernist artists to cope with real societal changes—to be, as Davis said, a "progressive social force"—were equally contentious.

**1** Stuart Davis, "Letter to Henry McBride," in Henry McBride, "The Palette Knife," *Creative Art* 6, no. 2 (February 1930), supplement, p. 35. Kelder reprints this letter as "The Place of Abstract Painting in America," in Diane Kelder, ed., *Stuart Davis* (Praeger, 1971), pp. 109–10.

**2** Davis, "Letter to Henry McBride," p. 34.

**3** Ibid.

**4** Thomas Craven, *Men of Art* (Simon and Schuster, 1931), p. 506.

**5** Stuart Davis, "Reviews: The New York American Scene in Art," *Art Front* 1, no. 3 (Feb. 1935), p. 6.

**6** Allen Jackson, "U.S. Scene," *Time* 24, no. 26 (December 24, 1934), p. 24.

**7** Davis, "Reviews," p. 6.

**8** This point has been made in numerous contexts; see, for example, Debra Bricker Balken, *After Many Springs: Regionalism, Modernism, and the Midwest*, exh. cat. (Des Moines Art Center/Yale University Press, 2009). In relation to Demuth in particular, see Betsy Fahlman, *Chimneys and Towers: Charles Demuth's Late Paintings of Lancaster*, exh. cat. (Amon Carter Museum of American Art, 2007), p. 97.

**9** Wanda M. Corn, *The Great American Thing: Modern Art and National Identity, 1915–1935* (University of California Press, 1999), pp. 288–89.

**10** Gail Stavitsky, "A. E. Gallatin's Gallery and Museum of Living Art (1927–1943)," *American Art* 7, no. 2 (Spring 1993), pp. 46–63; for Davis, see p. 62. See also John R. Lane and Susan C. Larsen, eds., *Abstract Painting and Sculpture in America, 1927–1944*, exh. cat. (Museum of Art, Carnegie Institute/Harry N. Abrams, 1983), pp. 18–19.

**11** An early history is given in *Modern Works of Art: Fifth Anniversary Exhibition, November 20, 1934–January 20, 1935* (Museum of Modern Art, 1934). See also Esther Adler, "The Problem of Our American Collection: MoMA Collects at Home," in Kathy Curry and Esther Adler, *American Modern: Hopper to O'Keeffe*, exh. cat. (Museum of Modern Art, 2013), pp. 126–27, for a discussion of early MoMA exhibitions.

**12** See Lyn Delliquadri, "A Living Tradition: The Winterbothams and Their Legacy," *Art Institute of Chicago Museum Studies* 20, no. 2 (1994), pp. 102–10.

**13** For an excellent discussion of the origins of the museum, see Avis Berman, *Rebels on Eighth Street: Juliana Force and the Whitney Museum of American Art* (Atheneum, 1990), esp. pp. 260–88.

**14** Stuart Davis, Introduction to *Abstract Painting in America, February 12 to March 22, 1935*, exh. cat. (Whitney Museum of American Art, 1935), n. pag.

**15** For information on Stieglitz's galleries, see Sarah Greenough et al., *Modern Art and America: Alfred Stieglitz and His New York Galleries*, exh. cat. (National Gallery of Art/Bulfinch, 2000); for the founding of An American Place, see pp. 320–22.

**16** Carlyle Burrows, "News and Comment on Current Art Events," *New York Herald Tribune*, April 5, 1931, section 8, p. 8.

**17** Bruce Weber, *Stuart Davis' New York*, exh. cat. (Norton Gallery and School of Art, 1985), p. 11; also p. 23 n. 34.

**18** Lewis Kachur, *Stuart Davis: An American in Paris*, exh. cat. (Whitney Museum of American Art at Philip Morris, 1987), p. 6.

**19** Weber, *Stuart Davis' New York*, p. 11.

**20** Ani Boyajian and Mark Rutkoski, eds., *Stuart Davis: A Catalogue Raisonné*, vol. 2 (Yale University Press, 2007), no. 287.

**21** Boyajian and Rutkoski, *Stuart Davis*, vol. 2, p. 157, no. 323.

**22** Lowery Stokes Sims has suggested that this building could be the New York Stock Exchange, but Davis's preliminary sketch indicates that this is unlikely. The Stock Exchange is blocks from 120 Wall Street, with many high-rise buildings in between. See Lowery Stokes Sims, "New York–Paris No. 3," in Lowery Stokes Sims et al., *Stuart Davis: American Painter*, exh. cat. (Metropolitan Museum of Art, 1991), pp. 206–07, cat. no. 91.

**23** With thanks to Alison Fisher, Harold and Margot Schiff Associate Curator in the Department of Architecture and Design, Art Institute of Chicago, for her assistance in identifying the skyscraper in this sketch as 120 Wall Street.

**24** Weber, *Stuart Davis' New York*, p. 12.

**25** Stuart Davis, "Self-Interview," *Creative Art* 9, no. 3 (September 1931), p. 211.

**26** For example, in 1943 Davis wrote, "Some of the things which have made me want to paint, outside of other paintings, are . . . the brilliant colors on gasoline stations; chain-store fronts, and taxicabs; the music of Bach; synthetic chemistry; the poetry of Rimbeau [*sic*]; fast travel by train, auto, and aeroplane which brought new and multiple perspectives; electric signs; the landscape and boats of Gloucester, Mass.; 5 & 10 cent store kitchen utensils; movies and radio; Earl Hines hot piano and Negro jazz music in general, etc." Stuart Davis, "The Cube Root," *Art News* 41, no. 18 (February 1–14, 1943), p. 34.

**27** For excellent essays on 1920s art and culture, see Teresa A. Carbone, ed., *Youth and Beauty: Art of the American Twenties*, exh. cat. (Brooklyn Museum/Skira Rizzoli, 2011).

**28** David M. Kennedy, *Freedom from Fear: The American People in Depression and War, 1929–1945* (Oxford University Press, 1999), pp. 65–79.

**29** "The Great American Thing" was the term used by Georgia O'Keeffe; see, for example, Georgia O'Keeffe, *Georgia O'Keeffe* (Viking, 1976), n. pag., cat. 58. See also Wanda M. Corn's chapter on O'Keeffe, "The Great American Thing," in Corn, *Great American Thing*, pp. 239–91.

**30** See also Ellen E. Roberts, "Charles Demuth (1883–1935)," in Judith A. Barter et al., *American Modernism at the Art Institute of Chicago: From World War I to 1955* (Art Institute of Chicago/ Yale University Press, 2009), pp. 162–66.

**31** Fahlman, *Chimneys and Towers*, esp. pp. 96–97.

**32** Charles Demuth to Alfred Stieglitz, November 28, 1921, in Bruce Kellner, ed., *Letters of Charles Demuth: American Artist, 1883–1935* (Temple University Press, 2000), p. 38.

**33** Fahlman, *Chimneys and Towers*, p. 120.

**34** Henry McBride, "Demuth Memorial Exhibition," *New York Sun*, December 18, 1937; reprinted in Kellner, *Letters of Charles Demuth*, p. 179.

**35** For a history of the anthem, see Marc Ferris, *Star-Spangled Banner: The Unlikely Story of America's National Anthem* (Johns Hopkins University Press, 2014).

**36** Charles Demuth to Alfred Stieglitz, September 10, 1931, in Kellner, *Letters of Charles Demuth*, p. 133.

**37** See Charles Brock, *Charles Sheeler: Across Media*, exh. cat. (National Gallery of Art/ University of California Press, 2006), pp. 77–78.

**38** Constance Rourke, *Charles Sheeler: Artist in the American Tradition* (Harcourt Brace, 1938), p. 143.

**39** Brock, *Charles Sheeler*, pp. 84–86.

**40** Alfred Stieglitz to Georgia O'Keeffe, June 2, 1931, in Sarah Greenough, ed., *My Faraway One: Selected Letters of Georgia O'Keeffe and Alfred Stieglitz*, vol. 1, *1915–1933* (Beinecke Rare Book and Manuscript Library/Yale University Press, 2011), p. 572.

**41** Alfred Stieglitz to Georgia O'Keeffe, June 24, 1931, in Greenough, *My Faraway One*, p. 583.

**42** For more on *Cow's Skull with Calico Roses*, see Ellen E. Roberts, "Georgia O'Keeffe (1887–1986)," in Barter et al., *American Modernism*, pp. 155–61.

**43** O'Keeffe, *Georgia O'Keeffe*, n. pag., cat. 58.

**44** Calvin Tompkins, "Profiles: The Rose in the Eye Looked Pretty Fine," *New Yorker*, March 4, 1974, pp. 48, 50.

**45** Georgia O'Keeffe to Alfred Stieglitz, October 20, 1931, in Greenough, *My Faraway One*, pp. 603–04.

**46** Donna M. Cassidy, "Localized Glory: Marsden Hartley as New England Regionalist," in Elizabeth Mankin Kornhauser, ed., *Marsden Hartley*, exh. cat. (Wadsworth Atheneum Museum of Art/Yale University Press, 2002), pp. 175–92. See also Donna M. Cassidy, *Marsden Hartley: Race, Region, and Nation* (University Press of New England, 2005), pp. 73–80.

**47** Marsden Hartley, "On the Subject of Nativeness—A Tribute to Maine," in *Marsden Hartley: Exhibition of Recent Paintings, 1936* (An American Place, 1937), p. 5.

**48** Cassidy, *Marsden Hartley*, pp. 74–75.

**49** Hartley, "On the Subject of Nativeness," p. 2.

**50** Tompkins, "Profiles," p. 62.

**51** For a discussion of Dove's time in Geneva, see Elizabeth Hutton Turner, "Going Home: Geneva, 1933–1938," in Debra Bricker Balken in collaboration with William C. Agee and Elizabeth Hutton Turner, *Arthur Dove: A Retrospective*, exh. cat. (Addison Gallery of American Art, Phillips Academy/Phillips Collection/MIT Press, 1997), pp. 100–03.

**52** Edward Alden Jewell, "Exhibition Shows Dove's Early Fine," *New Yorker*, March 4, 1974, pp. 48, 50.

**52** Edward Alden Jewell, "Exhibition Shows Dove's Early Art," *New York Times*, April 21, 1934, p. 13.

**53** See, for example, *Gallery of Living Art: A. E. Gallatin Collection* (Gallery of Living Art, 1933), for the record of Gallatin's holdings at this time.

**54** See Ellen E. Roberts, "Arthur Dove (1880–1946)," in Barter et al., *American Modernism*, pp. 247–49.

**55** For a discussion of the 1927 series, see Donna M. Cassidy, "Arthur Dove's Music Paintings of the Jazz Age," *American Art Journal* 20, no. 1 (1988), pp. 5–23; and Donna M. Cassidy, *Painting the Musical City: Jazz and Cultural Identity* (Smithsonian Institution Press, 1997), ch. 3. More recently, Rachael Z. DeLue has explored the group in "Arthur Dove, Painting, and Phonography," *History and Technology* 27, no. 1 (March 2011), pp. 113–21.

**56** On the whitening of jazz, see Cassidy, *Painting the Musical City*, pp. 95–102; for its connections to modernism, see pp. 71–72.

**57** Cassidy, "Arthur Dove's Music Paintings," p. 8.

**58** Helen Torr, diary, 1938, Arthur and Helen Torr Dove papers, 1905–1975, Archives of American Art, Smithsonian Institution, Washington, DC.

**59** A good history of swing in general can be found in Gunther Schuller, *The Swing Era: The Development of Jazz, 1930–1945* (Oxford University Press, 1989), including a chapter on Louis Armstrong, pp. 158–97.

**60** Cassidy, *Painting the Musical City*, p. 92.

**61** "Swing: The Hottest and Best Kind of Jazz Reaches Its Golden Age," *Life* 5, no. 6 (August 8, 1938), pp. 50–60.

**62** For a discussion of the racial connotations of Dove's work, particularly the 1925 assemblage *Goin' Fishin'* (Phillips Collection), see Lauren Kroiz, *Creative Composites: Modernism, Race, and the Stieglitz Circle*, exh. cat. (Phillips Collection/University of California Press, 2012).

**63** For a fine history of this, see Michael Denning, *The Cultural Front: The Laboring of American Culture in the Twentieth Century* (Verso, 1997).

**64** Editorial, *Art Front* 1, no. 1 (Nov. 1934), n. pag. (front page).

**65** For a discussion of the cycle and its role and reception at the centennial, see Renée Ater, "Creating a 'Usable Past' and a 'Future Perfect Society': Aaron Douglas's Murals for the 1936 Texas Centennial Exposition," in Susan Earle, ed., *Aaron Douglas: African American Modernist*, exh. cat. (Spencer Museum of Art/ Yale University Press, 2007), pp. 95–113.

**66** Susan Earle, "Harlem, Modernism, and Beyond: Aaron Douglas and His Role in Art/ History," in Earle, *Aaron Douglas*, p. 27.

**67** Richard J. Powell, *Homecoming: The Art and Life of William H. Johnson*, exh. cat. (National Museum of American Art, Smithsonian Institution, 1991), p. 42. See also Teresa G. Gionis, ed., *William H. Johnson: An American Modern*, exh. cat. (Smithsonian Institution Traveling Exhibition Service (SITES)/James E. Lewis Museum of Art, Morgan State University/ University of Washington Press, 2011).

**68** "Negro Artists," *New York Amsterdam News*, January 8, 1930, editorial page.

**69** Helen Harriton to Mary Beattie Brady, September 30, 1956, Harmon Foundation Papers, Manuscript Division, Library of Congress, Washington, DC, quoted in Powell, *Homecoming*, p. 123.

**70** Powell, *Homecoming*, pp. 124–25.

**71** See Lane and Larsen, eds., *Abstract Painting and Sculpture*, for an extended discussion of the movement toward abstraction in this period.

**72** Charles G. Shaw, "A Word to the Objector," in *American Abstract Artists* (AAA, 1938), n. pag., article 1. The group published this yearbook and two others in 1939 and 1946.

**73** For a still-useful discussion of immigrant artists, see Cynthia Jaffee McCabe, *The Golden Door: Artist-Immigrants of America, 1876–1976*, exh. cat. (Hirshhorn Museum and Sculpture Garden, Smithsonian Institution/ Smithsonian Institution Press, 1976).

**74** Editors' note to *American Abstract Artists*, n. pag.

**75** See Sarah E. Kelly, "Charles Green Shaw (1892–1974), in Barter et al., *American Modernism*, pp. 240–43.

**76** For biographical information on Shaw, see Buck Pennington, "The 'Floating World' in the Twenties: The Jazz Age and Charles Green Shaw," *Archives of American Art Journal* 20, no. 4 (1980), pp. 17–24, which focuses on his friendships with such notable figures as Cole Porter and F. Scott Fitzgerald. See also Leah Rosenblatt, "Charles G. Shaw: Life," in *The Park Avenue Cubists: Gallatin, Morris, Frelinghuysen and Shaw*, exh. cat. (Grey Art Gallery, New York University/ Ashgate, 2002), pp. 69–73.

**77** For the Concretionists exhibition, see Gail Stavitsky, "A Landmark Exhibition: Five Contemporary American Concretionists, March 1936," *Archives of American Art Journal* 33, no. 2 (1993), pp. 2–10.

**78** Emily Lenz, "Charles Green Shaw (1892–1974): Evolution of an Artist, 1926–1946," in Henry Adams and Emily Lenz, *Charles Green Shaw (1892–1974): The 1930s and 1940s* (D. Wigmore Fine Art, 2007), p. 78 n. 2. Shaw frequently made note of his progress on the *Wrigley's* project in his daily diary. On April 7, 1937, he recorded that he had finished the canvas, and on April 16 he wrote that he had received a letter from the Wrigley company asking to see the design; see Diaries, Charles Green Shaw Papers, 1874–1979, Archives of American Art Smithsonian Institution, Washington, DC.

**79** Charles G. Shaw, "The Plastic Polygon," *Plastique* 3 (Spring 1938), pp. 28–29.

**80** For biographical information on Morris and an analysis of his career, see Melinda Lorenz, *George L. K. Morris: Artist and Critic* (UMI Research Press, 1982).

**81** For a discussion of this exhibition, see W. Jackson Rushing, *Native American Art and the New York Avant-Garde: A History of Cultural Primitivism* (University of Texas Press, 1995), p. 103. Rushing also discusses Morris's Native American paintings; see pp. 90–95.

**82** Lorenz, *George L. K. Morris*, p. 11. See also Nicolai Cikovsky, Jr., "Notes and Footnotes on a Painting by George L. K. Morris," *Bulletin of the University of New Mexico Art Museum* 10 (1976–77), pp. 3–11.

**83** "G. L. Morris Holds Modern Art Exhibition," *Yale Daily News* 60, no. 44 (November 17, 1936), p. 1.

**84** Specifically, he wrote, "The exploitation of American local color is the most oppressive at the moment." George L. K. Morris, "The Quest for an Abstract

Tradition," in *American Abstract Artists*, n. pag., article 3.

**85**  George L. K. Morris to Van Deren Coke, November 27, 1975, quoted in Cikovsky, "Notes and Footnotes," p. 6.

**86**  For more on the painting, see Denise Mahoney, "Ilya Bolotowsky (1907–1981)," in Barter et al., *American Modernism*, pp. 260–62.

**87**  For biographical information on Bolotowsky as well as a good analysis of his work, see Deborah M. Rosenthal, "Ilya Bolotowsky," in Lane and Larsen, eds., *Abstract Painting and Sculpture*, pp. 51–54.

**88**  Louise Averill Svendsen with Mimi Poser, "Interview with Ilya Bolotowsky," in *Ilya Bolotowsky*, exh. cat. (Solomon R. Guggenheim Museum, 1974), p. 15. Both Bolotowsky and Johnson studied at the National Academy of Design.

**89**  For an excellent discussion of the murals at the Fair, including Bolotowsky's, see Jody Patterson, "Modernism and Murals at the 1939 New York World's Fair," *American Art* 24, no. 2 (Summer 2010), pp. 50–73.

**90**  For information on the Williamsburg murals, see Barbara Dayer Gallati, "The Williamsburg Murals: Five Monumental Works from the 1930s by Ilya Bolotowsky, Balcomb Greene, Paul Kelpe, and Albert Swinden" (Brooklyn Museum, 1990).

**91**  For illustrations of some of the included works, see *American Art Today: Gallery of American Art Today, New York World's Fair* (National Art Society, 1939).

**92**  Stuart Davis, "Abstract Painting Today," in Francis V. O'Connor, ed., *Art for the Millions: Essays from the 1930s by Artists and Administrators of the WPA Federal Art Project* (New York Graphic Society, 1973), pp. 126, 127. In the late 1930s, the WPA began soliciting articles, including Davis's, for a documentary report to be called *Art for the Millions*. It was never published. A different draft appears in Kelder, *Stuart Davis*, pp. 116–21.

**93**  Davis, "Abstract Painting Today," p. 127.

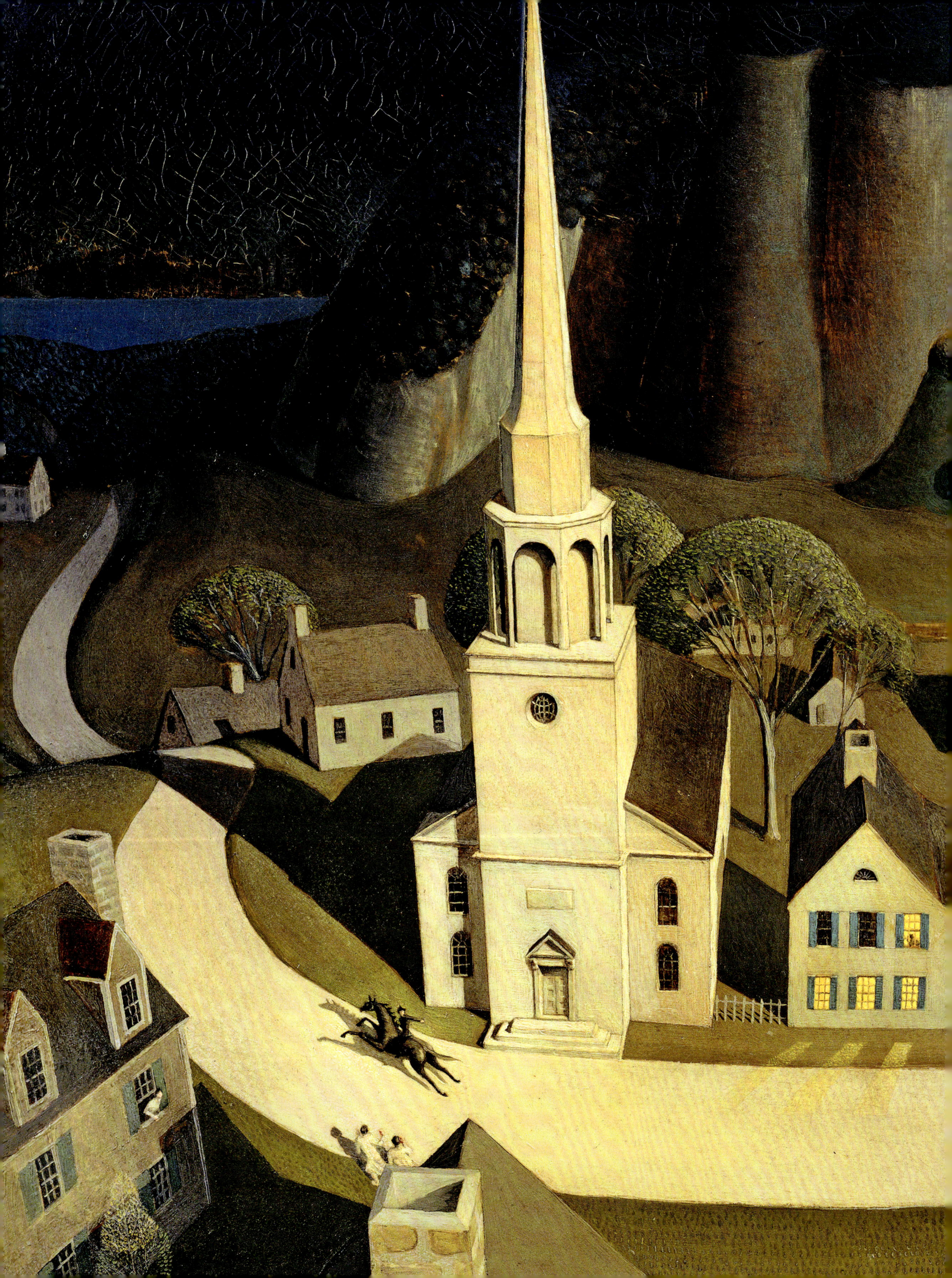

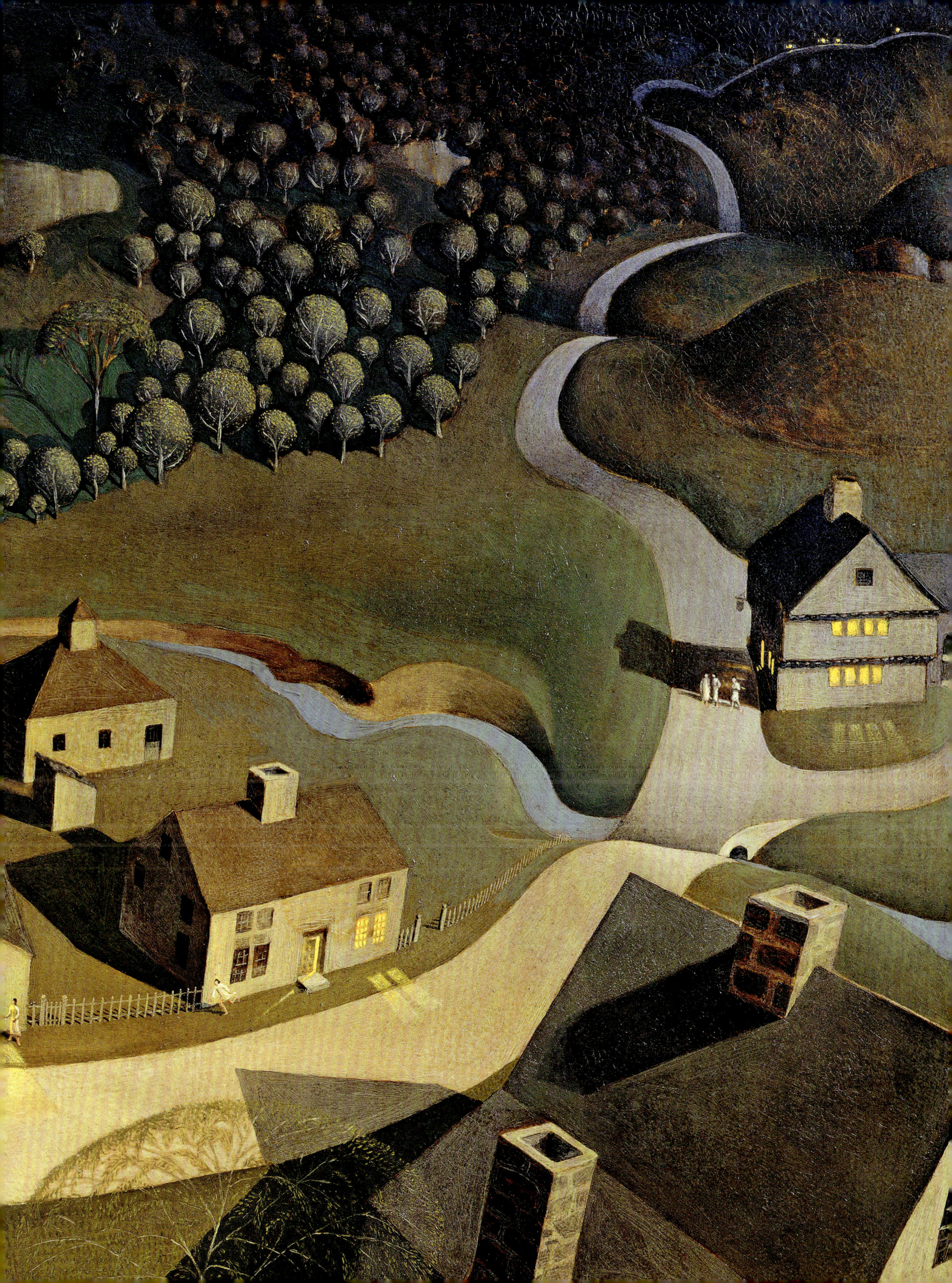

**ANNELISE K. MADSEN**

With tight lips and unblinking stares, the three women in Grant Wood's *Daughters of Revolution* (1932; fig. 1) confront the viewer with haughty self-possession and utmost seriousness. Standing in front of a print of Emanuel Leutze's famed 1851 painting *Washington Crossing the Delaware*, they silently declare their role as guardians of America's heroic origins. Depression-era women, they seem to fit more easily into the eighteenth or nineteenth century, relics of bygone generations. In this 1932 painting, Wood took aim at such ancestral pretentiousness, playing with the past for satirical ends to visually undercut the sense of ownership and entitlement that swelled among colonial societies such as the Daughters of the American Revolution. History, the artist made clear, did not

## THREE    *Reviving the Old and Telling Tales: 1930s Modernism and the Uses of American History*

need to be the stale, dusty version that these ladies aimed to safeguard. Wood served up the past with modern-day bite.

In works like *Daughters of Revolution*, Wood demonstrated that the nation's material culture and tales of old could breathe new life into an American painting rooted in figuration and narrative. The artist's brand of modernism drew upon the past to construct novel compositions that struck a chord with 1930s audiences. Making use of familiar, well-worn characters and story lines, Wood nevertheless crafted a send-up that was topical, humorous, and engagingly insightful. He brought the past into his painting in several ways, creating layers of visual history-telling—from heroic to genealogical, memorializing to satirical—that imbue the work's forms with a rich range of meanings.

For many painters of the Depression decade, the past served as a powerful resource for defining culture, inspiring artists who worked in a range of styles from realism to abstraction to shape an American modernism rooted in common, albeit often contested, experiences and values. The concept of a "usable past," initially outlined by the literary critic and historian Van Wyck Brooks in 1918, still resonated in the 1930s. Of an earlier generation, Brooks's project was motivated by a desire to revitalize the nation's literature by unmooring it from received traditions.[1] Seeing a national culture in need of remediation, Brooks sought to empower contemporary writers to discover or invent a past with "living value" for the present.[2] His ideas indeed held sway, elastic enough to accommodate the changing conditions and various agendas of cultural thinkers and professionals during the Great Depression.

Brooks endowed creative producers with unequivocal agency. One's stance toward the past should not be objective, he advised, but emphatically selective. A serviceable past, in his opinion, would take form by actively embracing some elements while discarding others. "The past is an inexhaustible storehouse of apt attitudes and adaptable ideals; it opens of itself at the touch of desire; it yields up, now this treasure, now that, to anyone who comes to it armed with a capacity for personal choices."[3] The past's value lay in how it could inform actions and enrich understandings in the present. Looking backward was a timeworn practice, yet how and to what extent cultural leaders engaged in that pursuit ebbed and flowed with the times. Brooks's call, at its core, rang optimistic—received history could be transcended and a new script written by his contemporaries. In the wake of World War I, however, the past seemed hardly usable. Life in the 1920s pulsed in the present. Writers and historians made heroes of their contemporaries and collectively worked to debunk the political and military leaders of yesteryear; an antihistorical strain colored 1920s scholarship, unraveling the grand narratives and myths of earlier eras. All the while, artists working in representational styles did engage with art history's past, drawing on the classical tradition in their aesthetic explorations of the figure in modern life. With the onset of the Great Depression, history gained renewed appeal more broadly among cultural tastemakers. Amid uncertain times, the nation's past registered as a source of guidance for the present; a pursuit of authenticity and shared experiences countered the debunking mindset of the previous decade.[4] Although a concern for objectivity accompanied this reinvestment in history, the search for a usable past in the 1930s was nevertheless a selective endeavor. Artists, writers, and other cultural stewards materialized not one past, but numerous pasts. As one critic put it in 1934, "Today the trouble seems to be that we have too many pasts and that the proponents of one will have nothing to do with the others."[5] Looking backward during the Depression decade offered a wellspring of possibilities.

This essay explores not only how the past paved connections to modernism for painters including Wood, Doris Lee, Aaron Douglas, Charles Sheeler, Charles Demuth, and Georgia O'Keeffe, but also the roles that history, myth, and material culture played in reimagining understandings of local and national identities in the 1930s. Artists revived the old in a variety of ways, marshaling diverse origin stories and historical artifacts to shape an array of American modernisms. The inclination to look backward was a broad cultural phenomenon. Under President Franklin Roosevelt, the federal government sponsored many historically spirited projects. New Deal murals were among the most visible of these, with the past taking center stage in many of the decorations in post offices and other public buildings produced as part of the Public Works of Art Project, the Works Progress Administration's Federal Art Project, and the Treasury Department's Section of Painting and Sculpture, among other agencies. A preservationist and documentary spirit motivated such efforts as the Index of American Design (part of the Federal Art Project) and the formation of the National Archives. Additionally, the colonial revival, in full swing in the 1930s, influenced the activities of architects, collectors and museums, historical and hereditary societies, and preservationists. From folk art and traditions to historical fiction, living history museums to bicentennials and regional expositions, Depression-era society discovered a host of usable pasts.

**Fig. 1**  Grant Wood. *Daughters of Revolution*, 1932. Cincinnati Art Museum. Cat. 51.

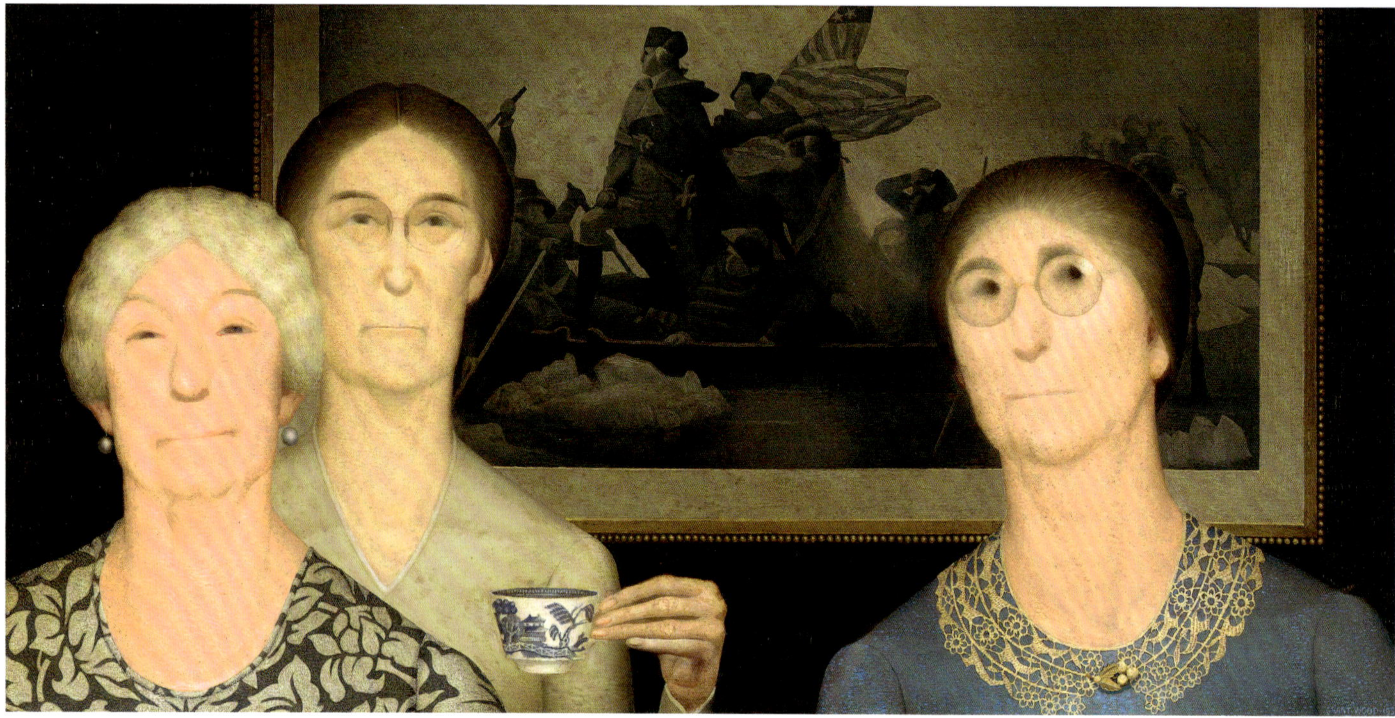

The strong narratives and relatable figures of Wood's Regionalist vision make clear his investment in the past. Born near Anamosa, Iowa, in 1891, Wood (see fig. 2) studied and practiced art in the Midwest beginning in the 1910s, traveling to Europe on several occasions the following decade. Upon his return to Iowa from Munich in 1928, he honed a distinctive style featuring strong geometric forms, hard edges, decorative patterning, and local subjects—an aesthetic informed by Northern Renaissance painting and by his abiding interest in Americana and midwestern life. With this new focus, success came quickly; *American Gothic* (p. 40, fig. 9) was an instant hit with audiences when it debuted at the Art Institute of Chicago in 1930. Wood soon emerged as a leader, along with Thomas Hart Benton and John Steuart Curry, of Regionalism.[6] Coinciding with the Great Depression, the movement offered a salve for the economic turbulence and social hardships of the times with reassuring visions of familiar folks, enduring ways of life, and agrarian bounty. By the middle of the decade, Regionalism had gained a reputation for being narrowly rural

and conservative. Wood himself did not conceptualize the movement as such, seeing it instead as a commitment to one's local subjects and surroundings, not as a stylistic or antiurban credo.[7] Recent scholars have broadened our understanding of the various regionalist practices of the era, from New England to the Southwest, suggesting that the midwestern impulse was but one of many efforts to negotiate local and national identities.[8] Further, they have emphasized connections between realism and abstraction, Regionalism and European-inspired modernism, arguing against tidy bifurcations of such terms, which flatten the dynamic, multivalent explorations of modernism by US artists in the 1930s.[9]

*Daughters of Revolution* is a productive place to launch our investigation of the past's vitality—both aesthetic and cultural—for modern American painters and their audiences. At the level of form, artifact, and context, the painting engages with shared histories to tell a tale as only Grant Wood could. An undoing of genealogical airs is at the heart of the artist's play with history. His shorthand title, a purposeful move to skirt

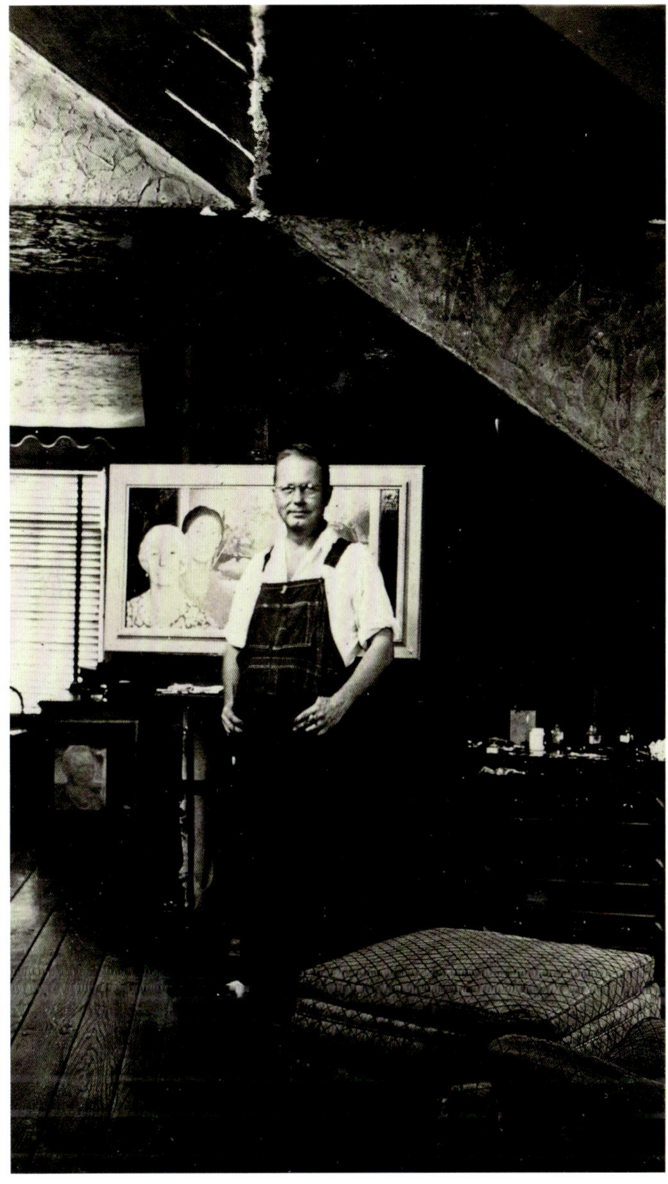

**Fig. 2** Grant Wood standing in front of *Daughters of Revolution*. Cedar Rapids Museum of Art Archives, Gift of John B. Turner II in memory of Happy Young Turner.

legal retaliation, did not fool audiences, nor was it intended to. These are three members of the Daughters of the American Revolution (DAR). Rather than individuals, Wood portrayed types, arriving at a kind of composite portrait by studying faces in contemporary DAR publications.[10] As one reporter wryly noted, "[Wood] says there is a particular kind of mouth exclusive with 'Daughters of Revolution.'"[11] In addition to physiognomy, the artist sharpened his commentary with the depiction of the central woman's bony, ringless fingers raising a tightly grasped teacup. One of the ancestral lines from revolutionary past to twentieth-century present—defining entry into the organization's ranks—ostensibly halts with this spinster Daughter. Further, the teacup she holds is itself an heirloom, valued for its ties to familial origin stories. For DAR types like those of Cedar Rapids, Iowa, where Wood resided, such a piece of blue willow china served as a material reminder of early settlement of the Midwest, when pioneer families brought precious few objects from the East with them.[12] Wood, like these figures, valued the material culture of yesteryear but objected to its use as a symbol or leverage of status. "I don't like to have anyone try to set up an aristocracy of birth in a republic," the painter declared. With his portrayal of three "tory gals," as he called them, Wood refashioned ancestral power into something deserving of scrutiny by Depression-era audiences.[13]

*Daughters of Revolution* also engaged with heroic and mythic retellings of the past. At the center of the composition stands George Washington leading the Continental Army across frigid waters on December 25, 1776, for a surprise attack on British troops. Leutze's monumental painting (fig. 3) is shown here in the form of a popular lithographic print, domesticated in size and reinterpreted once more in paint by Wood's brush. Grand manner history painting by Leutze and other nineteenth-century artists made icons of early American figures, ensuring that chiseled profiles, gallant poses, and crystallized acts of courage endured in the nation's collective memory. Washington's legacy was the subject of much interest and maneuvering in 1932, the bicentennial of his birth, with official celebrations—pageants, teas, schoolroom lessons, film screenings, public art dedications, and more—taking place nationwide

throughout the year under the guidance of the federal government's George Washington Bicentennial Commission.[14] Wood tapped into this mania, juxtaposing the founding father's larger-than-life persona with the three stolid dames raising a teacup in his honor. Neither party, Wood seems to say, has dibs on the whole story. It is in the conversations between them that the artist found richness.

Further, Wood's aesthetic satire in *Daughters* indirectly called upon a different mode of history-telling—one that

**Fig. 3**  Emanuel Leutze (American, born Germany, 1816–1868). *Washington Crossing the Delaware*, 1851. Oil on canvas; 378.5 × 647.7 cm (149 × 255 in.). Metropolitan Museum of Art. Gift of John Stewart Kennedy, 1897, 97.34.

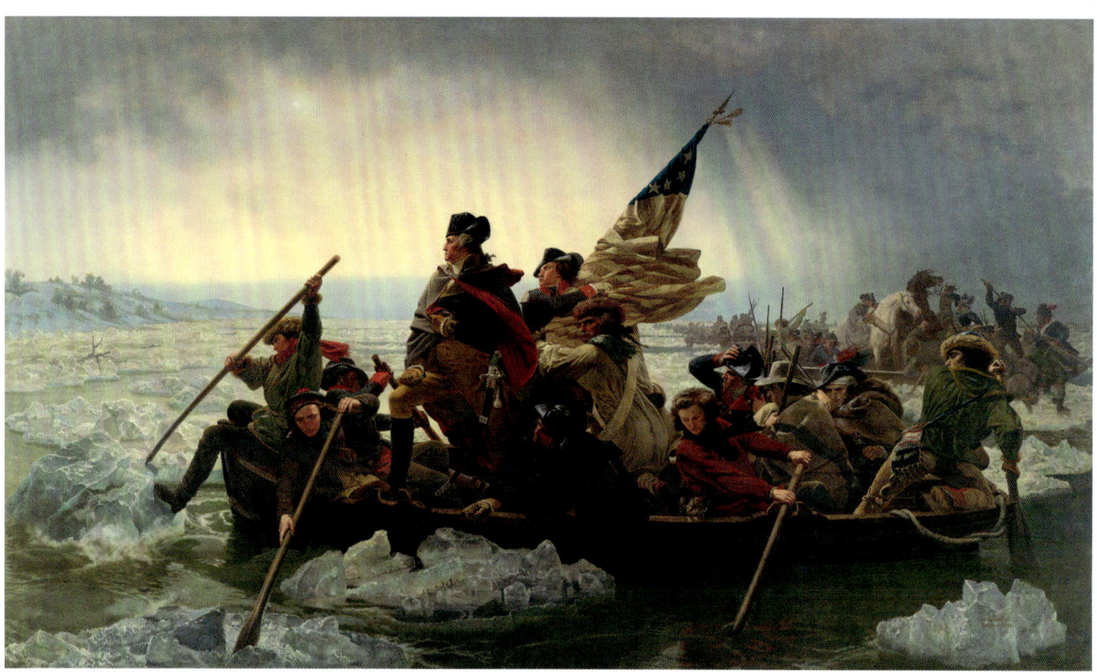

memorialized. In 1927 the artist was commissioned to create a monumental stained-glass window for the Veterans Memorial Building in Cedar Rapids, and a year later the project took him to Munich to oversee its production by glassmakers there. Local DAR members in Iowa voiced objections to the window's manufacture in Germany in the wake of the recent world war, and the controversy succeeded in delaying the dedication of the window for nearly thirty years, long after Wood's death.[15] The artist redirected the likely sting from this hubbub to his "tory gals" painting a few years later. As stern sentinels of the mythic figure of Washington behind them, the women stand seemingly unaware that they are safeguarding a German-American masterpiece. Born in Germany and raised in Philadelphia, Leutze returned to Europe to study in the 1840s. He painted *Washington Crossing the Delaware* in Düsseldorf, an international artistic community that included a strong contingent of Americans. Like Wood's *Memorial Window*, Leutze's painting had endured scrutiny amid anti-German sentiment during and after World War I.[16]

Despite the dames' tight-lipped demeanor, *Daughters of Revolution* had much to say, and contemporary audiences responded. The painting was immediately exhibited, traveling to New York, Chicago, Des Moines, Cedar Rapids, Pittsburgh, Baltimore, Los Angeles, and Paris over the next six years. DAR supporters across the United States were particularly vocal, their reactions amplified by reporters eager for good material. Members of the Pittsburgh chapter demanded its removal from the Carnegie International Exhibition in 1933, to no avail. A local DAR member in Cedar Rapids wrote a letter of protest to a gallery director there, likewise calling for it to be taken off public view; newspapers as far away as Albuquerque picked up the story. And Baltimore members somehow planned to ignore the painting when it went on display at the Baltimore Museum of Art in 1934.[17] Yet despite all the DAR indignation that made headlines, reaction to *Daughters* varied, with many among the organization's ranks relishing the lampoon. A journalist for the *Cedar Rapids Gazette* noted, "Only Iowa D.A.R.'s have been able to 'take it' from Grant Wood. A reproduction of it flashed on a screen at a state convention of the D.A.R.'s drew so much applause and laughter that it had to be brought back by two encores."[18] The general public flocked to the composition as well. According to the *Chicago Tribune*, *Daughters of Revolution*

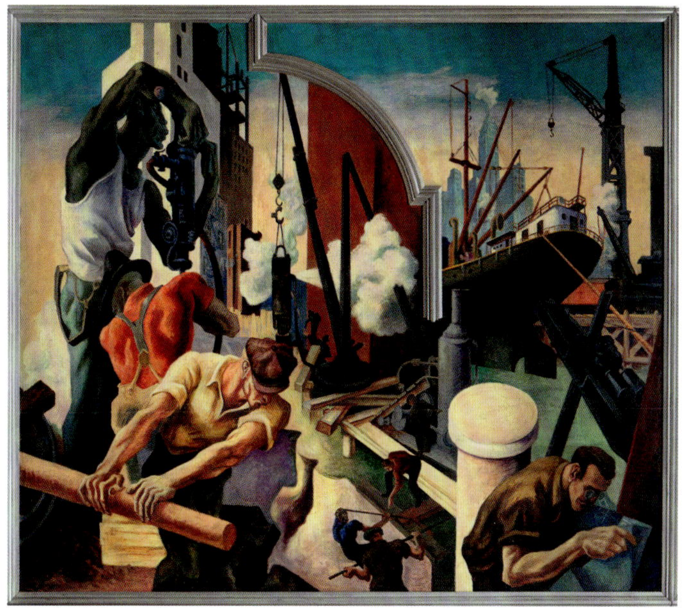

**Fig. 4**  Thomas Hart Benton (American, 1889–1975). *America Today: City Building*, 1930–31. Egg tempera with oil glazing over Permalba on a gesso ground on linen mounted to wood panels with a honeycomb interior; 233.7 × 297.2 cm (92 × 117 in.). Commissioned for the New School for Social Research, New York. The Metropolitan Museum of Art, New York, Gift of AXA Equitable, 2012, 2012.478i.

was the most popular painting at the Century of Progress Exposition in Chicago in 1934.[19]

By including a cropped and miniaturized version of grand manner history painting, Wood's easel-sized work drew attention to a category of art making whose status had changed significantly since its glory days in the eighteenth and the first half of the nineteenth centuries. By the 1930s, ennobling and didactic history paintings like Leutze's had long fallen out of favor with scholars, although they remained popular with the public. In fact, *Washington Crossing the Delaware* had been rolled up in storage at the Metropolitan Museum of Art for three years when in January 1932 the museum president mandated that it be rehung in time for that year's bicentennial celebrations, making clear in a press statement that the decision was guided by factors other than aesthetics. According to the museum president, Leutze's painting "cannot be classified as a masterpiece, nor is it an accurate historical record. Nevertheless, we believe that it is both fitting and desirable that this picture should be shown at the time of the Washington Bicentennial . . . because in spite of obvious defects it has great interest for many people in this country."[20] The monumental canvas and its mythic heroics drew crowds during the Depression.

Large-scale history painting did gain renewed visibility in the 1930s in the form of newly executed murals. The Mexican mural movement, well underway in the 1920s, proved an important model for the US government in its approach to the support of public art, including hiring artists as wage earners, favoring popular history-telling, and broadening public engagement with modernism.[21] The federal government sponsored both relief-work programs—the Works Progress Administration's Federal Art Project (WPA/FAP) the most famous of these—and commissioned employment, including the Treasury Department's Section of Painting and Sculpture (later called the Section of Fine Arts). Artists painted more than four thousand murals for municipal, state, and federal buildings between 1933 and 1943, adorning these communal public spaces with scenes of local histories, landscapes, and people.[22] Wood, Curry, Douglas, Lee, Peter Blume, Ilya Bolotowsky, Paul Cadmus, Stuart Davis, Philip Evergood, O. Louis Guglielmi,

Philip Guston, Alexandre Hogue, William H. Johnson, Joe Jones, Helen Lundeberg, Reginald Marsh, Archibald Motley, Alice Neel, Jackson Pollock, Paul Sample, and Ben Shahn were all counted among federal rolls.[23] Benton did not participate in a New Deal mural assignment, but he did tour the country to build support for WPA programs.[24] The artist was much invested in history and mural painting, shaping grand progress narratives as well as dynamic visions of the country's recent events. His commissions in 1930–31 for the New School for Social Research in New York (*America Today*, now at the Metropolitan Museum of Art) and in 1932–33 for the Indiana Hall at the Century of Progress Exposition (*Indiana Murals*, now at Indiana University) were two important, early examples of this modern interest in scaling up a version of the past for Depression-era audiences (see fig. 4). Benton's sinuous forms, muscular bodies, vivid palette, and inventive breaks and joins of compositional planes modeled an emphatic modernism rooted in figuration and narrative.

While New Deal–era murals were overwhelmingly representational in style, painters did demonstrate a range of artistic expression. A leading member of the Harlem Renaissance, Douglas applied his avant-garde European training to American

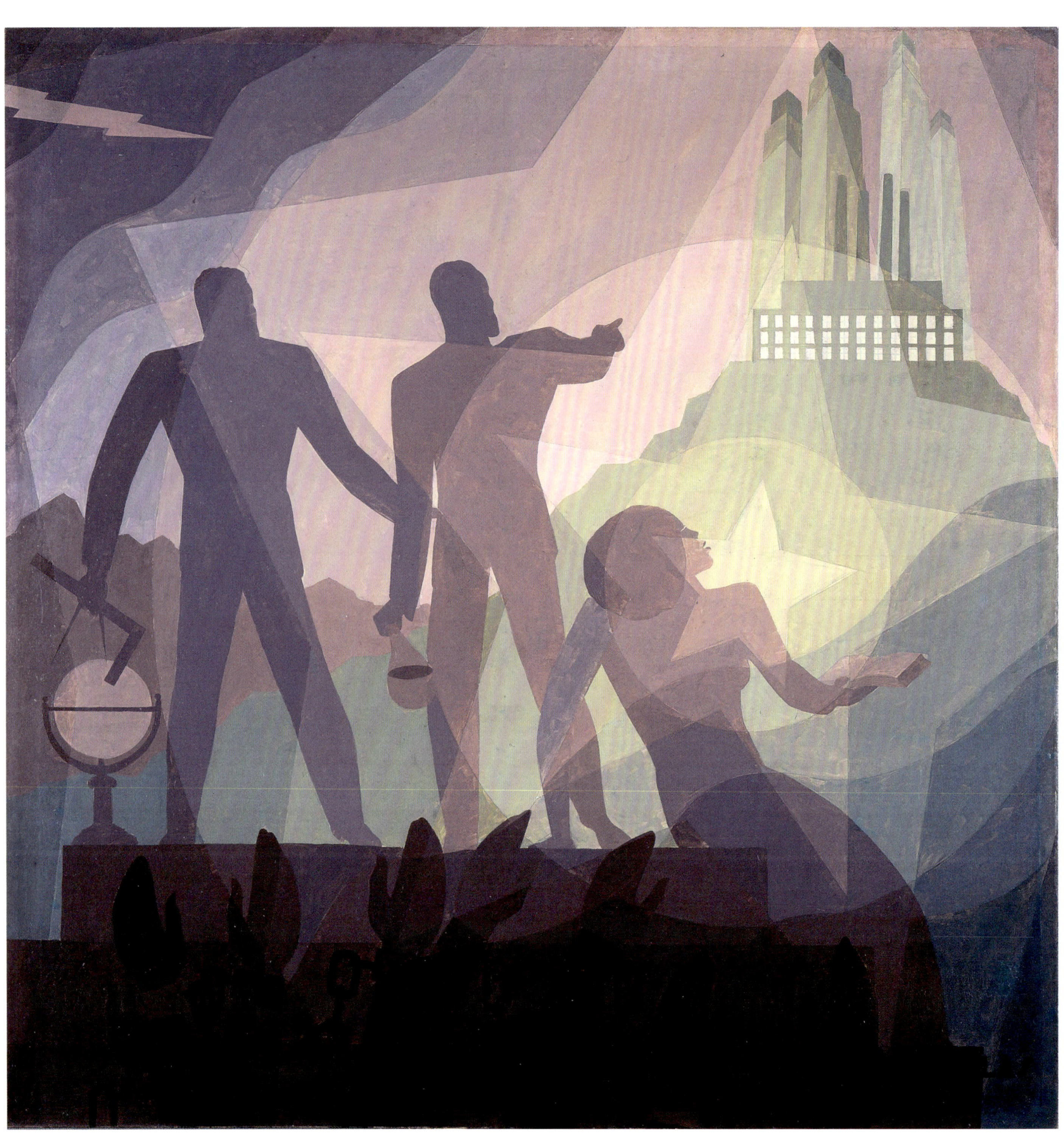

subjects, past and present. In a mural cycle for the Hall of Negro Life at the Texas Centennial Exposition in Dallas in 1936, the artist shaped a distinct modernist vision that brought together African American history, African iconology, humanistic themes, and geometric abstraction. His *Aspiration* (fig. 5) is the fourth and final panel in a series that showcased African American contributions to national life, from the forced labor of slavery (see p. 75, fig. 12) to the intellectual acumen of contemporary professionals in the arts and sciences. A seated woman and two standing men occupy the center of the composition, with manacled arms stretching across the foreground below and an industrial city on a hill capturing the figures' attention at upper right. Globe, compass, carpenter's square, beaker, and book signal the transformative power of education. The men wear contemporary suiting while the woman's profile recalls Egyptian art in relief. With silhouetted forms, overlapping planes, radiating stars and circles, and a palette of blues, mauves, and yellows, Douglas deployed an inventive vocabulary to address age-old themes of strife, self-betterment, and communal prosperity.[25]

The artist modeled an alternative and inclusive public history with his Texas Centennial murals, ennobling an American past built upon black agency and achievement. His usable past stretched from ancient Africa to the twentieth-century cities of the industrial north. The exposition itself was a grand undertaking in history-telling, as fair commissioners sought to demonstrate the state's economic and cultural progress since the end of Mexican rule one hundred years earlier. One of several world's fairs that took place during the Great Depression, the Texas Centennial Exposition was an effort to renew communal hope amid widespread hardship. The initial decision by white leaders to deny black participation was overturned when local African Americans successfully lobbied the federal government for funds to build the Hall of Negro Life. Douglas, in turn, gained the opportunity to realize this inclusive vision of American history, albeit working within the limits of a segregated exhibition space.[26]

Douglas was not alone in his attempts to broaden the country's shared narratives. Other muralists employed on

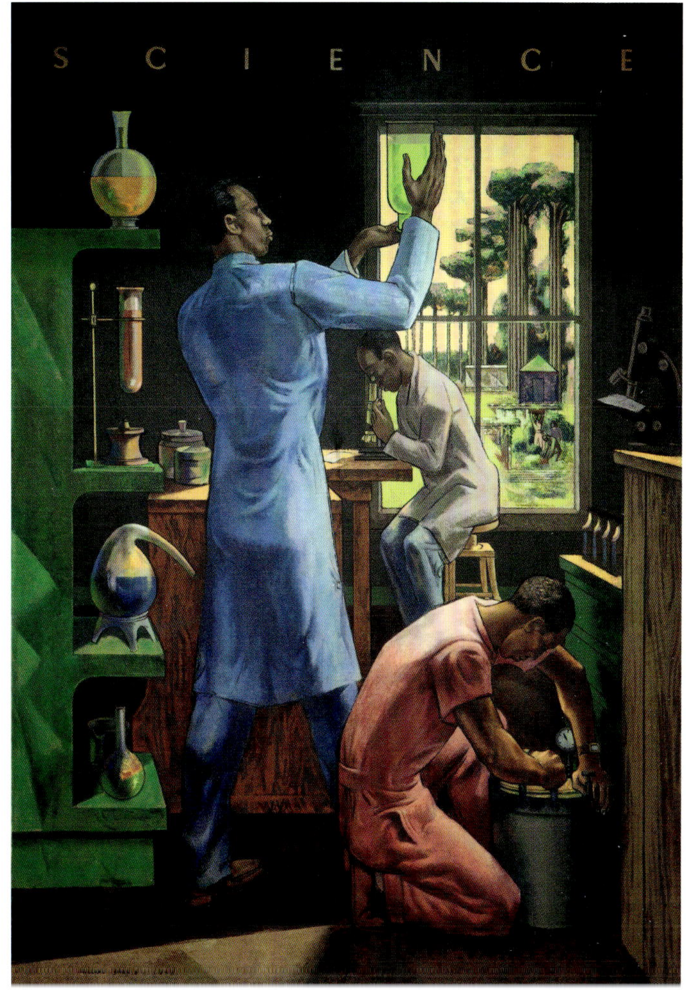


Depression-era assignments shaped revisionist histories both local and national. At the Kansas State Capitol in 1937–42, John Steuart Curry emphasized sixteenth-century Spanish exploration and antebellum abolitionism in the figures of Francisco Vázquez de Coronado and John Brown, endowing the midwestern state with an origin story that predated East Coast settlement and aggrandizing a particularly fiery vision of the entwined concerns of slavery and statehood.[27] In Washington, DC, in 1937–48, California artist Millard Sheets scaled up black achievements in the arts, education, religion, and science for his mural series *The Negro's Contribution in the Social and Cultural Development of America* in the Department of the Interior Building (fig. 6). Using a realist vocabulary comprising sturdy forms and strong lighting, Sheets focused on the talents of everyday African Americans to model a more inclusive historical vision.[28] And in small-scale, serial compositions, the Harlem-based painter Jacob Lawrence similarly expanded national narratives to include the dark struggles of slavery, chronicling the heroic lives of Toussaint L'Ouverture, Frederick Douglass, and Harriet Tubman before embarking on his celebrated series *The Migration of the Negro* (jointly held by the Phillips Collection, Washington, DC, and the Museum of Modern Art, New York) in 1940.[29]

Some painters turned their attention to the recent past as a worthy subject for artistic interpretation, including the Social Realist Ben Shahn, who created a series of works on the trial and 1927 execution of Nicola Sacco and Bartolomeo Vanzetti, a case of murder and social injustice that gripped the nation for many years. Italian immigrants and political radicals, they were sentenced to death for the armed robbery and murder of two men at a shoe factory in Massachusetts. Convicted on circumstantial evidence and denied a retrial, Sacco and Vanzetti became martyrs in the eyes of many contemporaries in the United States and around the globe, victims of the era's climate of suspicion surrounding leftist politics and radicalism.[30] In 1931–32, Shahn created *The Passion of Sacco and Vanzetti* (p. 16, fig. 1), a monumental canvas depicting the two executed men lying in their coffins in the foreground. The judge for the case appears in a background window while the three individuals who had rejected a new trial stand as attendants at the coffins, proffering lilies in mourning. With a vocabulary both economic and expressive, Shahn contrasted the calm dignity of Sacco and Vanzetti with the dressed-up authority—judicial robes, top hats, academic garb—of those empowered to pass judgment. His flat areas of color, calligraphic lines, and selective exaggerations of forms infuse the composition with directness and political charge. The artist's satiric vision stung all the more because such recent, polemical history still reverberated in the 1930s present. This was a usable past not quite past.[31]

While Shahn located source material in contemporary headlines and photographs, Wood turned to the well-worn objects found in local living rooms and attics. In *American*

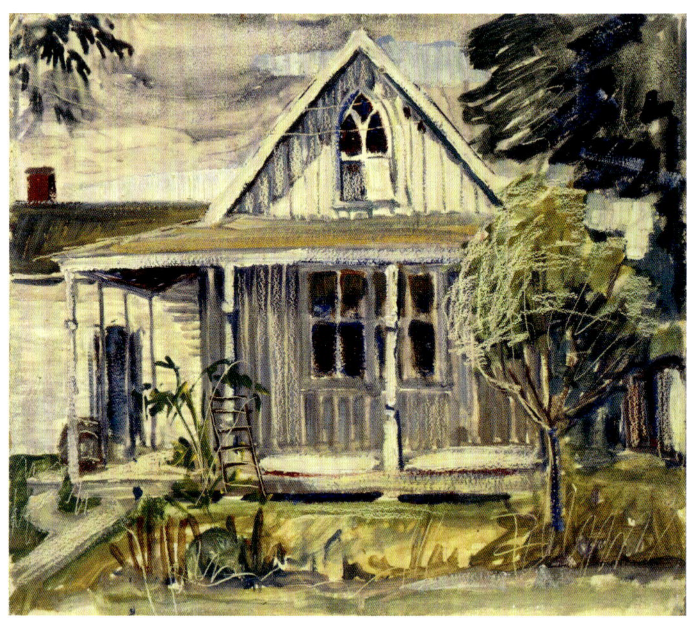



**Fig. 7**  Grant Wood (American, 1891–1942). Sketch for house in *American Gothic*, 1930. Oil on paperboard; 32.1 × 37.2 cm (12 ⅝ × 14 ⅝ in.). Smithsonian American Art Museum. Gift of Park and Phyllis Rinard, 1991.122.2R-V.

*Gothic*, his now-iconic portrait of a mum farming pair standing in front of their midwestern home, it is a Victorian past that the artist cultivates, bringing together old and new in a tightly controlled composition. Saving and repurposing a nineteenth-century past was itself a significant move in 1930, as widespread interest in the nation's colonial history far outweighed any positive attention given to the Victorian objects and lifestyles of one's parents and grandparents. Wood's archive was precisely that—the material culture of his childhood and connections to the people and artifacts of distinctly midwestern lives and memories.[32]

A particular house in Eldon, Iowa, inspired the picture (see fig. 7). Featuring white board-and-batten siding and a long and narrow window beneath a gable roof, it was an 1881–82 example of the timber construction then prevalent in rural areas, a style known as Carpenter Gothic. Further, elements such as the couple's outdated clothing, the woman's severe hairdo (the model, Wood's sister, had stylish marcelled locks at the time), and the man's three-tined pitchfork (a tool of the premodern, unmechanized farm) signal a backward glance.[33] Wood discerned aesthetic value in such objects of old, experimenting to create a variant of modernism that was representational

**Fig. 8** Passengers enjoying a trip on Steamboat Suwanee, Greenfield Village, c. 1935. The Henry Ford, Benson Ford Research Center. Edison Institute Photographs, 2012.0.17.2.

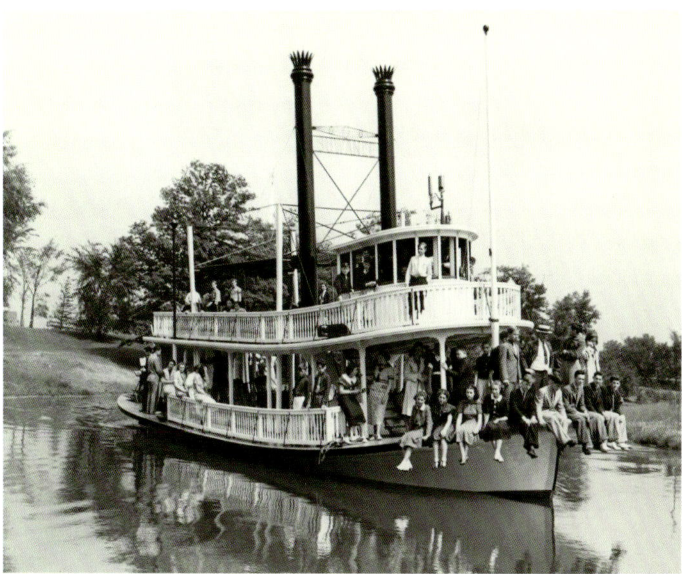

while also geometric, planar, and decorative: "I began to realize that there was real decoration in the rickrack braid on the aprons of the farmers' wives, in calico patterns and in lace curtains. At present, my most useful reference book, and one that is authentic, is a Sears, Roebuck catalogue."[34] For Wood, Victorian artifacts as well as contemporary midwestern types who still had one foot in an older way of life offered a point of departure, a circuitous way forward. With doses of fondness and commentary, *American Gothic* presents the viewer with an insular albeit endearing father and daughter, a self-reliant couple whose narrowness of vision can be felt in their frontal stance and crowding of the foreground. Yet their unspoken resilience and closeness to the land bespeak enduring characteristics of especial value during the shared hardships of the Depression years.

The Iowa landscape—its rolling, verdant contours synonymous with Wood himself—can also be thought of as part of the artist's search for a usable past. Wood retreated into nature, picturing the seasonal rhythms and bountiful yields of better days. The painter offered an optimistic, reassuring vision of midwesterners in harmony with the land rather than the bleak, devastating circumstances faced by many farmers in the wake of insect infestations, soil erosion, and dust storms.

In *Fall Plowing* of 1931 (p. 45, fig. 11), an elevated view reveals the quilt-like patterns of the undulating terrain. The plowed portion of the field takes the shape of vertical ribbons that lead the viewer's eye to the thimble-shaped corn shocks in the middle distance. Bulbous trees of autumnal hues dot the ridges and valleys, sheltering a red barn and farmhouse near the horizon. Prominently placed in the foreground is a walking plow, which was drawn by horses and guided by the hand of the farmer. The tool's steel blade is in the act of turning over the soil into furrows; Wood halts the manual labor midstream in a passage of still life that hints at a return to the work at hand. *Fall Plowing* germinates from the artist's own childhood, a vision of Victorian-era farming powered by men and draft animals but not by motorized equipment.[35] Although the late nineteenth century did witness advances in mechanized agriculture, Wood's backward glance omits such technology. And the tractors, cultivators, and combines prevalent on farms in the 1930s do not figure into the artist's pastoral vision. It is the plow as material connection to communal rituals and familial histories that roots this landscape. Wood's modernism, in turn, infuses the composition in stylistic plays of abstract forms, repeating geometries, and dreamlike illumination.

This fascination with tools and other objects of old motivated a variety of cultural projects in the early twentieth century. In Bucks County, Pennsylvania, beginning in 1897, archaeologist Henry Mercer collected a remarkable array of colonial- and early Federal-era tools, amassing some thirty thousand pieces by the time of his death in 1930. Mercer conceived of his activities as a new kind of historical scholarship, one that valued the primacy of the object and traced the forces of historical change through the tangible implements of yesteryear. His approach was scientific and classificatory in nature, driven by a desire to document and preserve known types of a particular tool, whether plows, hoes, andirons, wagons, cradles, mallets, scissors, or spoons.[36] Living history museums likewise participated in the preservationist impulse, including John D. Rockefeller, Jr.'s Colonial Williamsburg in Virginia (begun in 1926) and Henry Ford's Greenfield Village in Michigan (opened in 1929; see fig. 8). Such destinations created immersive

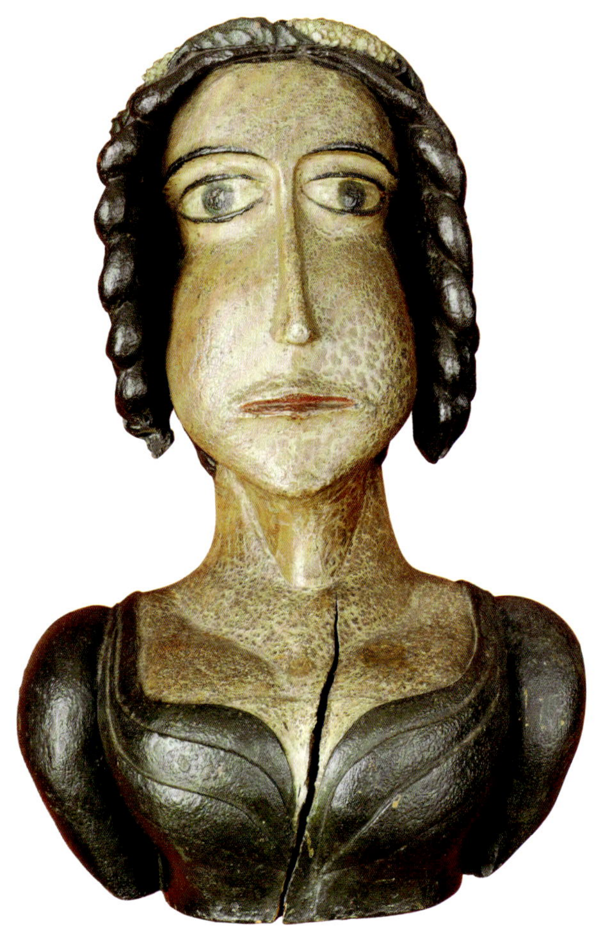

environments for visitors to study the American past, experiences structured to be more contextual, dynamic, and nostalgic than Mercer's typological displays.

In the arena of fine arts, the desire to save and interpret native traditions included such diverse projects as the establishment of museum period rooms of American decorative arts and the recovery of folk art. Curators, gallerists, antiquarians, collectors, and artists shaped a variety of usable pasts, tracing artistic lineages based on style and form, from the high to the vernacular, in attempts to define and value the nation's art making on its own terms, distinct from Europe's. The American Wing of the Metropolitan Museum of Art opened in 1924 with a suite of period rooms chronicling the advancement of native craftsmanship in wood, precious metals, ceramics, textiles, and the like from the colonial period to 1825. These

meticulously staged interiors exhibited the choicest examples of furniture, silver, and other decorative objects, assembling a material record of the most well-to-do members of the Eastern Seaboard's white merchant class.[37] American folk art traditions, in contrast, encompassed broader swaths of communities, with a diversity of regionally characteristic artifacts bespeaking the tastes and material environs of the middle classes and those with modest means. Rural art forms that were both functional and ornamental, folk art objects were made by craftsmen and artists with a range of talent and training, some self-taught, others highly skilled (see fig. 9). In the 1920s, a keen interest in folk art took hold among the nation's fine art professionals, who discerned something valuable for modernism in these vernacular forms. Centered in New York (and extending to areas in the Mid-Atlantic, Northeast, and beyond), tastemakers such as gallery and museum director Juliana Force, gallerist and dealer Edith Halpert, curator and Director of the Federal Art Project Holger Cahill, collector Abby Aldrich Rockefeller, and numerous practicing artist-collectors were instrumental in the elevation (and marketing) of folk art in kinship with modernism. Rather than spinning long narratives of progress connecting folk art ancestors to contemporary artists, they found and promoted stylistic continuities. Indigenous art proffered an immediacy, a physical connection to the country's unaffected aesthetic origins that was understood as evidence of an enduring national temperament. Chronology collapsed. Folk art was simultaneously old and modern. Past was present.[38]

Charles Sheeler stood at the center of such crosscurrents. Working in a variety of media, including painting, drawing, photography, and textile design, he honed a Precisionist aesthetic comprising clean lines, Cubist-inspired compressions of space, and geometric abstractions, which he applied to both industrial subjects (see p. 21, fig. 4; p. 23, fig. 6; and p. 64, fig. 5) and domestic interiors such as *Home, Sweet Home* (1931; fig. 10). Over the years Sheeler, an avid collector of folk art, furnished his residences in Pennsylvania, New York, and Connecticut with old, handcrafted objects, notably those made by Shaker communities and Pennsylvania Germans during the eighteenth and nineteenth centuries (see fig. 11). With these, the

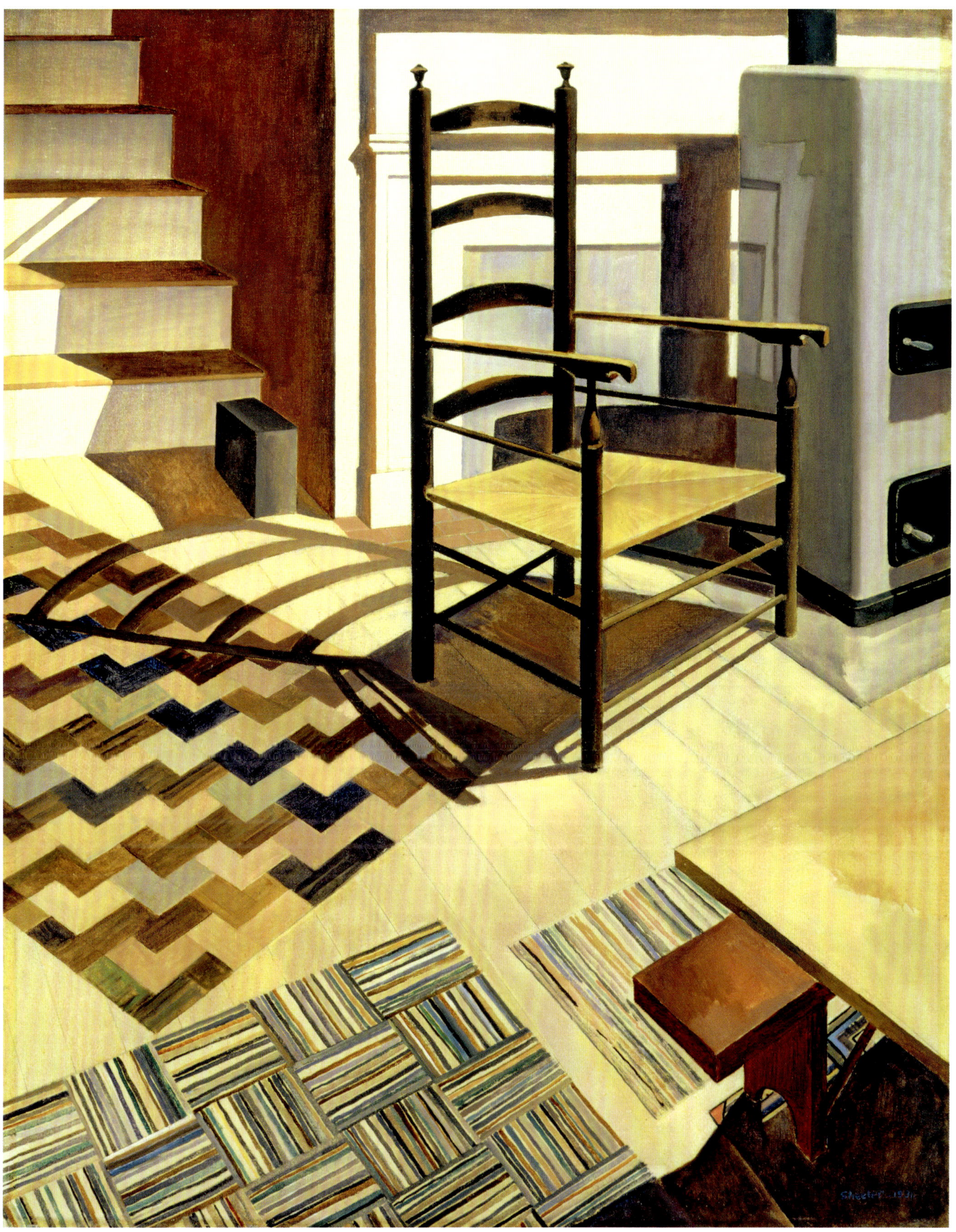

**Fig. 11**  Charles Sheeler (American, 1883–1965). *South Salem Interior*, 1929. Gelatin silver print; 19. 5 × 24.4 cm (7 ¹¹⁄₁₆ × 9 ⅝ in.). Lane Collection.

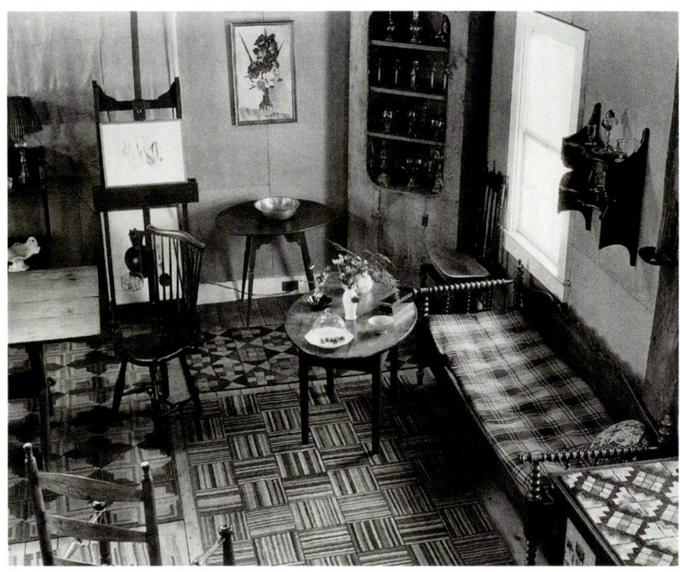

**Fig. 12**  Charles Goodwin (American, active c. 1935). *Fragment of Shaker Hall Rug*, c. 1937. Watercolor, graphite, and pen and ink on paper; 22.2 × 27.8 cm (8 ¾ × 10 ¹⁵⁄₁₆ in.). National Gallery of Art, Washington, DC, Index of American Design, 1943.8.13689.

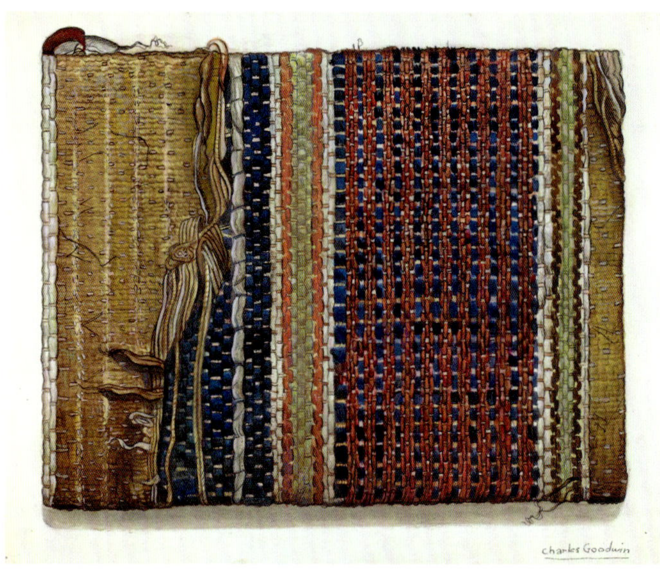

artist constructed a regionalist vision rooted in the rural East. In *Home, Sweet Home* he features his house in South Salem, New York, arranging color, form, and pattern in jigsaw-puzzle precision; Shaker rugs, table, and bench, all seen from above, function both as objects of Americana and as planar abstractions. An early American ladder-back chair, strong in stature, is drawn up closely to a modern furnace, which is positioned in front of the room's old wood-burning fireplace. Sheeler harmonizes the clean forms of this industrial machine with the plainspoken objects around it. Strong spotlighting casts exaggerated shadows behind the chair and onto the stairs, further animating the uninhabited room with an overlapping and interplay of formal elements.[39]

Sheeler's lovingly crafted paintings of American interiors brought together old and new in appealing ways. His collection drew the attention of Cahill, Ruth Reeves, and Constance Rourke, who served as administrators of the Index of American Design, an FAP unit that employed a cadre of artists to make exacting drawings—over eighteen thousand watercolors—of folk, popular, and decorative art objects from the past (see fig. 12). It was a modernist-inspired effort to archive the nation's material culture for contemporary artists. Sheeler made his own Shaker objects available for copying.[40] Further, *Home, Sweet Home* was included in the artist's solo

exhibition in the fall of 1931 at an important venue for modern art in New York, Halpert's Downtown Gallery; just upstairs was the newly launched American Folk Art Gallery, a commercial venture by Halpert and Cahill. Halpert soon became Sheeler's representative.[41]

Like Sheeler, painter Morris Kantor brought a modernist vocabulary to still lifes of domestic interiors replete with objects of old. A Russian immigrant born in present-day Belarus, he worked in both figurative and abstract modes during his career. His *Haunted House* (1930; fig. 13) is a fantastical rendering of a home that he had rented in rural Massachusetts. The room features two ladder-back chairs, a colonial portrait, and a marine painting of a schooner, flanked by two candlestick holders, over a large hearth. In the composition's darkened edges, Kantor sketched a nightscape of the town—building facades, roofs, and illuminated windows—creating an incongruous transition from interior to exterior space. Indeed, the shadowy form at right is that of a human figure, an unknown presence encroaching on the comforts of the sitting room. The artist later recounted, "The humble interior of the American farm house, old and quaint, with its peculiar moldy smell, the fading beauty of old plaster discolored by time and living, layers upon layers of wall paper, all turned my imagination to the past, to the people who had lived there and gone. My emotions were

**Fig. 13**  Morris Kantor. *Haunted House*, 1930. Art Institute of Chicago.
Cat. 28.

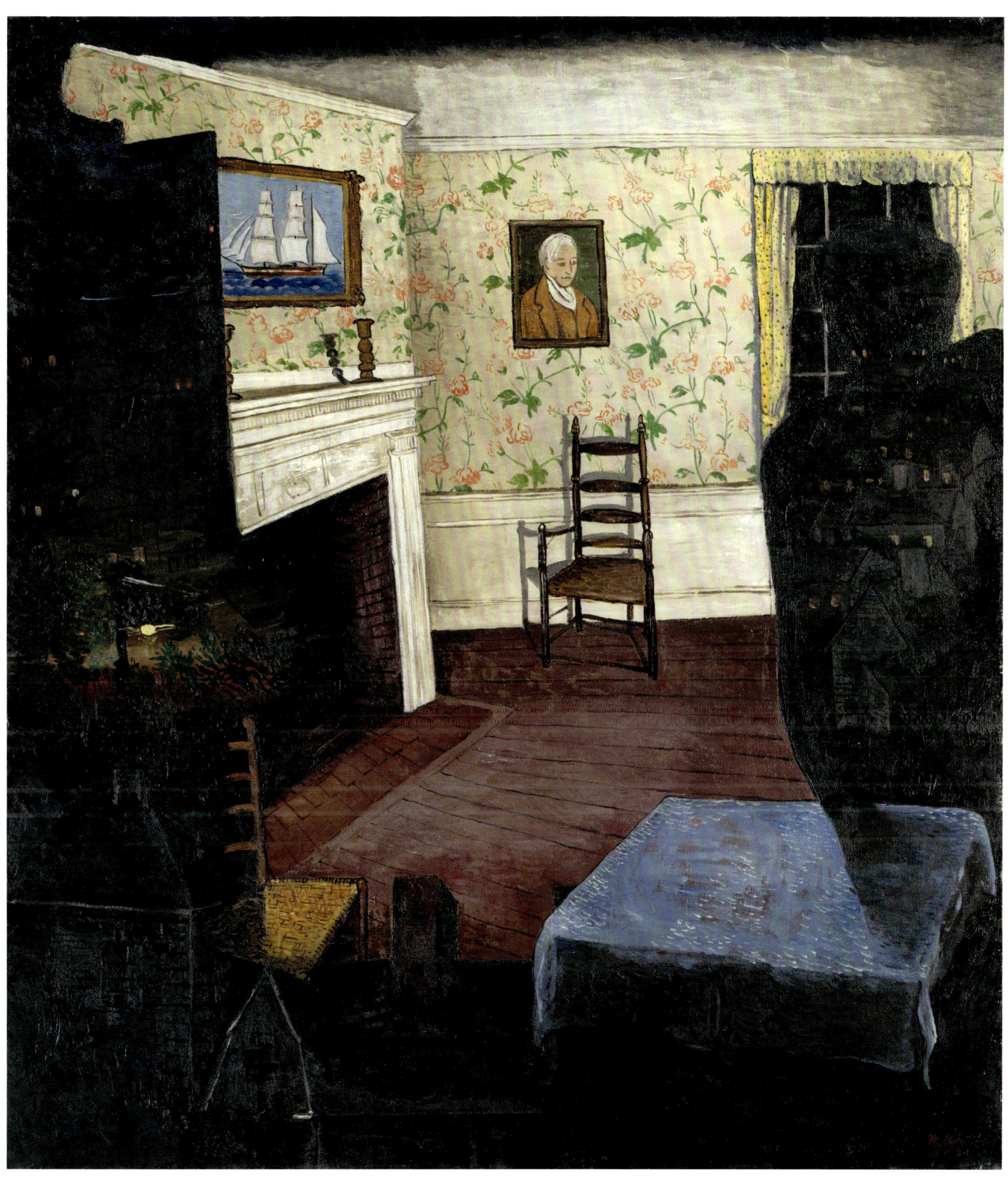

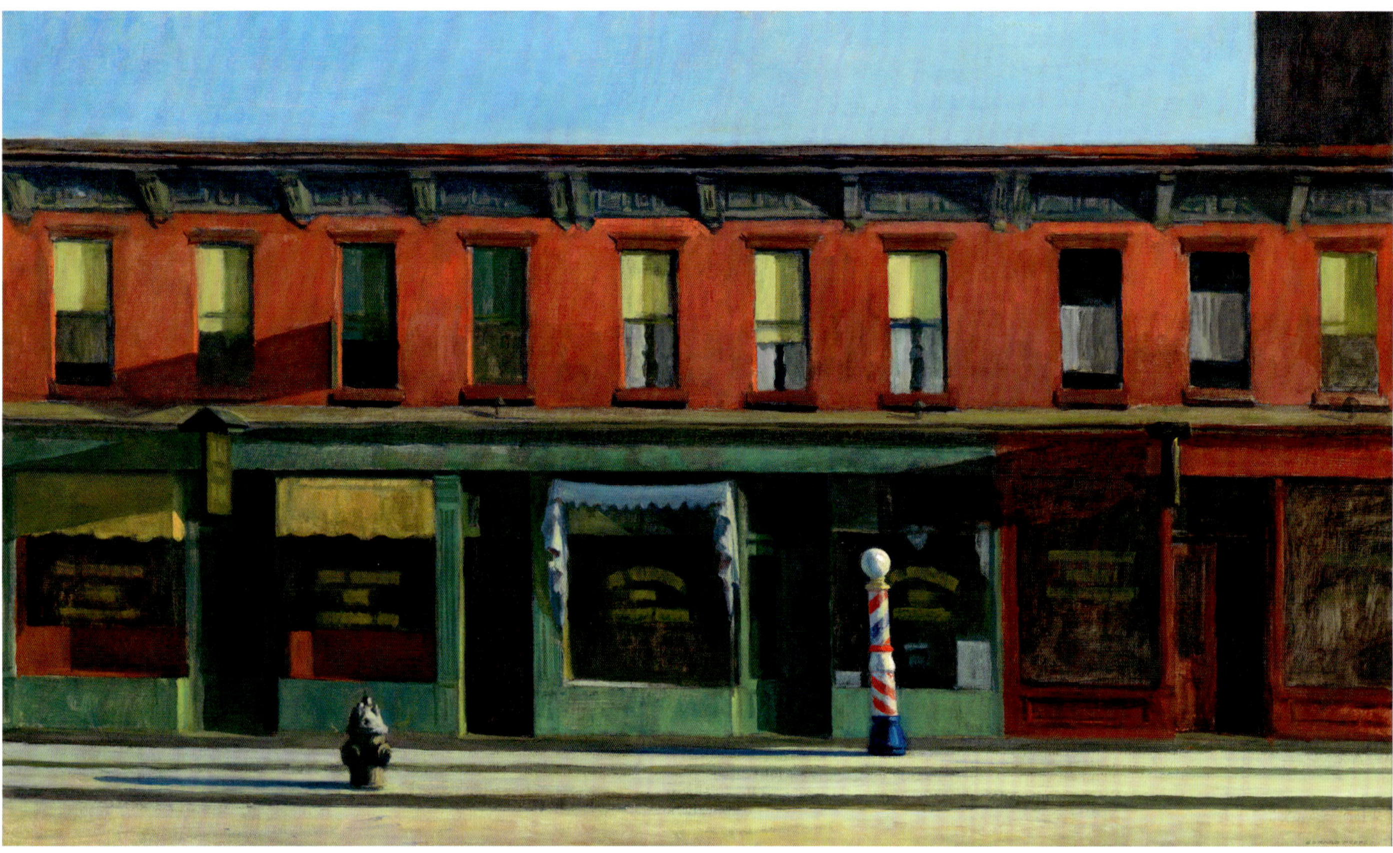

aroused."[42] Local legend had it that the house was haunted; such storytelling invited Kantor, in turn, to formulate a Surrealist musing on its residues of the past. His appropriation of a New England town's shared memories rings an eerie note, as this slice of Americana feels more strange than familiar. *Haunted House*, then, comments on inherited traditions, drawing attention to the constructed nature of national (and local) culture.

Explorations of a lived, felt past extended to the urban scene as well, as in Edward Hopper's *Early Sunday Morning* (fig. 14), likewise painted in 1930. Hopper turned to his immediate environs in lower Manhattan—streets that he walked and knew well—for source material, focusing on a modest, Victorian-era structure that housed shops at ground level and residential apartments above. Amid a rising city of skyscrapers, such architecture was a vestige of old New York. With an emphatically horizontal composition and frontal view— emptied of people and bustle but filled with sunlight—the

artist interwove present and past, stilling and aggrandizing a remnant of lived experience that was fast becoming outmoded.[43] As in Kantor's painting, memory and a sense of strangeness are at play in *Early Sunday Morning*. Yet instead of Surrealist hauntings, Hopper distilled, harmonized, and poeticized his subject, arranging ordinary shop fronts, barber pole, curtained windows, and corniced roofline into a serene streetscape that evokes both tangible familiarity and projected artifact.

As in this New York scene, an attachment to place anchored the expressions of many modern painters, with an array of regionalist visions informing artists' sense of national identity amid crisis and change. It was through a local lens that artists, other cultural stewards, and society more broadly oftentimes arrived at shared understandings of Americanness during the Depression decade.[44] Charles Demuth focused on his hometown of Lancaster, Pennsylvania, for a series of architectural paintings, including . . . *And the Home of the Brave* (p. 63,

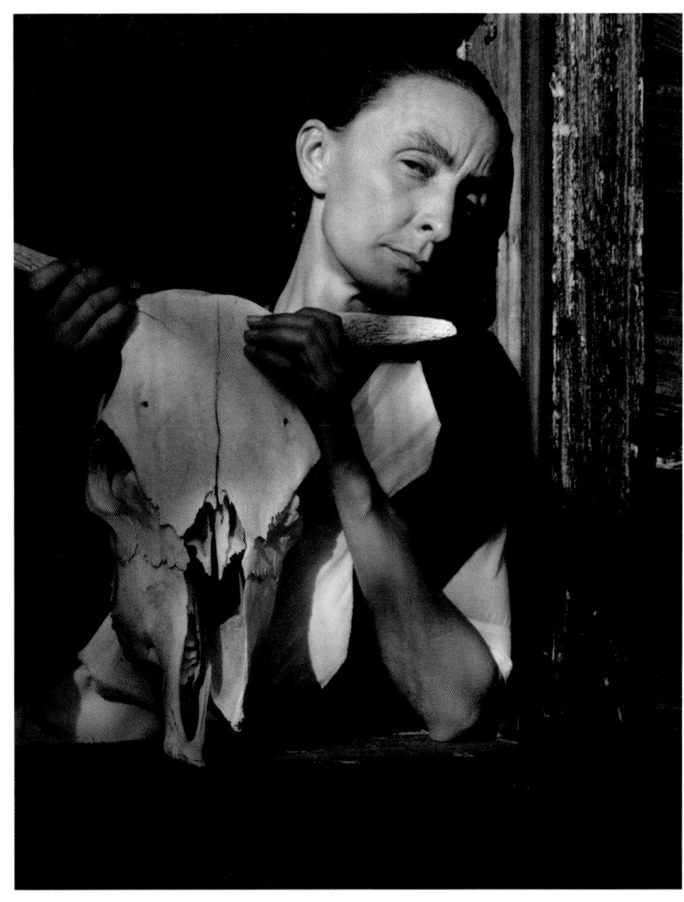

**Fig. 15** Alfred Stieglitz (American, 1864–1946). *Georgia O'Keeffe: A Portrait—With Cow Skull*, 1931. Gelatin silver print; 23.6 × 18.7 cm (9 ⁵⁄₁₆ × 7 ³⁄₈ in.). National Gallery of Art, Washington, DC. Alfred Stieglitz Collection.

fig. 4) of 1931, which takes its title from Francis Scott Key's 1814 "Star-Spangled Banner," named the national anthem by an act of Congress the same year that Demuth executed his work. His Precisionist technique emphasizes straight edges, the flatness of the picture plane, and simplified and repeating geometries. Seen from below, the building of a local cigar company fills much of the frame, its water towers, smoking chimney, and roofline contrasted against a crisp sky, which is animated by graphite lines and shades of blue. In locating his study in a structure of the tobacco industry, Demuth layered a municipal and familial past onto his red, white, and blue modernist rendition. Tobacco had deep roots in Lancaster County and in the Demuth family, who had operated a tobacco shop in the city since the eighteenth century. Originally titling the work *And the Land of the Brave*, Demuth later changed "land" to "home," making clear the work's nationalistic theme while also underscoring the importance of place and belonging. He did so with a measure of irony, as he situated his banner-waving in a center of industrial labor, not domestic life.[45]

Georgia O'Keeffe, a New York–based and Wisconsin-born painter, cultivated a regionalist vision grounded in what would become her adopted home, the Southwest. Summer trips to New Mexico beginning in 1929 opened up timeworn material—objects, customs, cultures, and landscapes—for O'Keeffe's modernist interpretations. In 1931 she painted *Cow's Skull: Red, White, and Blue* (p. 21, fig. 2) and *Cow's Skull with Calico Roses* (p. 68, fig. 7), still lifes featuring monumental, idol-like renderings of bleached bones. "Bones and flowers run together in my mind when I think of the desert," ther artist told a reporter that December when her recent compositions were on exhibition at An American Place, the New York gallery run by her husband, photographer Alfred Stieglitz.[46] In *Cow's Skull with Calico Roses*, a centered skull hangs trophy-like in front a nondescript background resembling layers of buff-colored fabric atop a black board or other flat surface. The two roses were painted from the sort of artificial flowers commonly used to adorn southwestern graves; they both contrast and harmonize with the bones, suggesting beauty and life while also serving as markers of time's passing, inorganic replicas set against skeletal forms from

nature. With the animal's horns arranged across the dark band behind, the composition recalls the Spanish Catholic crosses that dotted the region's wide-open landscape, a commonplace sight that so fascinated O'Keeffe. The background also brings to mind the designs of a Navajo blanket, another local artifact. At the conclusion of her New Mexico summer in 1930, O'Keeffe shipped back East bleached bones, cloth flowers, and a ceremonial blanket, working up her first bone still lifes in 1930–31 with bits of southwestern material culture in her New York studio (see fig. 15).[47]

In *Cow's Skull: Red, White, and Blue*, O'Keeffe framed her engagement with the Southwest through an emphatically nationalistic lens. Flat bands of red run along the left and right edges, and undulating passages of bright blue fill much of the canvas, divided by a black band. The distinctive white form of a skull, part smooth and part jagged, floats in front or above.

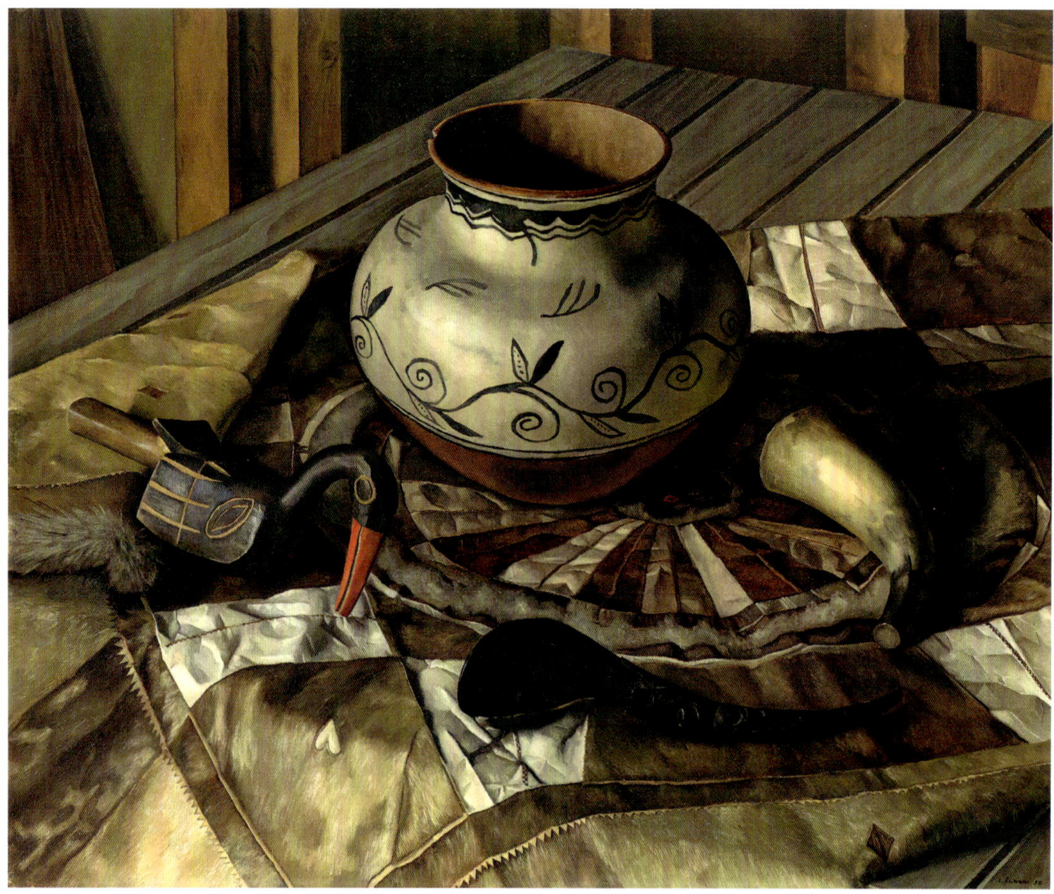

The canvas's patriotic palette signals an American theme, yet the spare compositional elements provide few clues to narrative or context.[48] While the artist employed a representational style for the large skull (albeit with some very flat areas, such as the horns), the rest of the composition approaches abstraction, evoking a Native American textile or the open skies of the Southwest but also existing as purely formal passages of color, shape, and movement.[49] O'Keeffe's modernism drew upon a usable past assembled from her experiences in New Mexico and with the objects she found there; rather than tell stories or archive native traditions, her bone pictures (and other southwestern subjects) weave material connections to place into grander visions concerning avant-garde art and national identity.

The Italian-born artist Luigi Lucioni likewise visualized foundational ideas through paintings about cherished objects. In his 1930 still life *Americana* (fig. 16), he arranged several Native American artifacts in a rhythmic composition of geometric patterns and curvilinear forms, executed in an earthy palette in the artist's signature style of heightened realism. On top of an Eskimo sealskin blanket rest four additional handcrafted pieces made of clay, wood, and animal horn: a San Ildefonso pot at center; a Tlingit oyster catcher rattle at left; a carved horn spoon made by Haida, Tlingit, or Tsimshian craftspeople in front; and a buffalo horn originating with a Plains tribe at right.[50] This image brings together Indian cultures from multiple regions—the Southwest, the Pacific Northwest Coast and Alaska, and the Great Plains. Assembling a usable past rooted in indigenous ways of life, Lucioni painted an inclusive vision of national history and identity.

The practice of treating national themes through regionalist expressions is evident as well in *Thanksgiving* (c. 1935; fig. 17), a bustling scene of holiday preparations in a midwestern kitchen by Doris Lee, a native of Illinois. Lee located this

**Fig. 17**  Doris Lee. *Thanksgiving*, c. 1935. Art Institute of Chicago. Cat. 30.

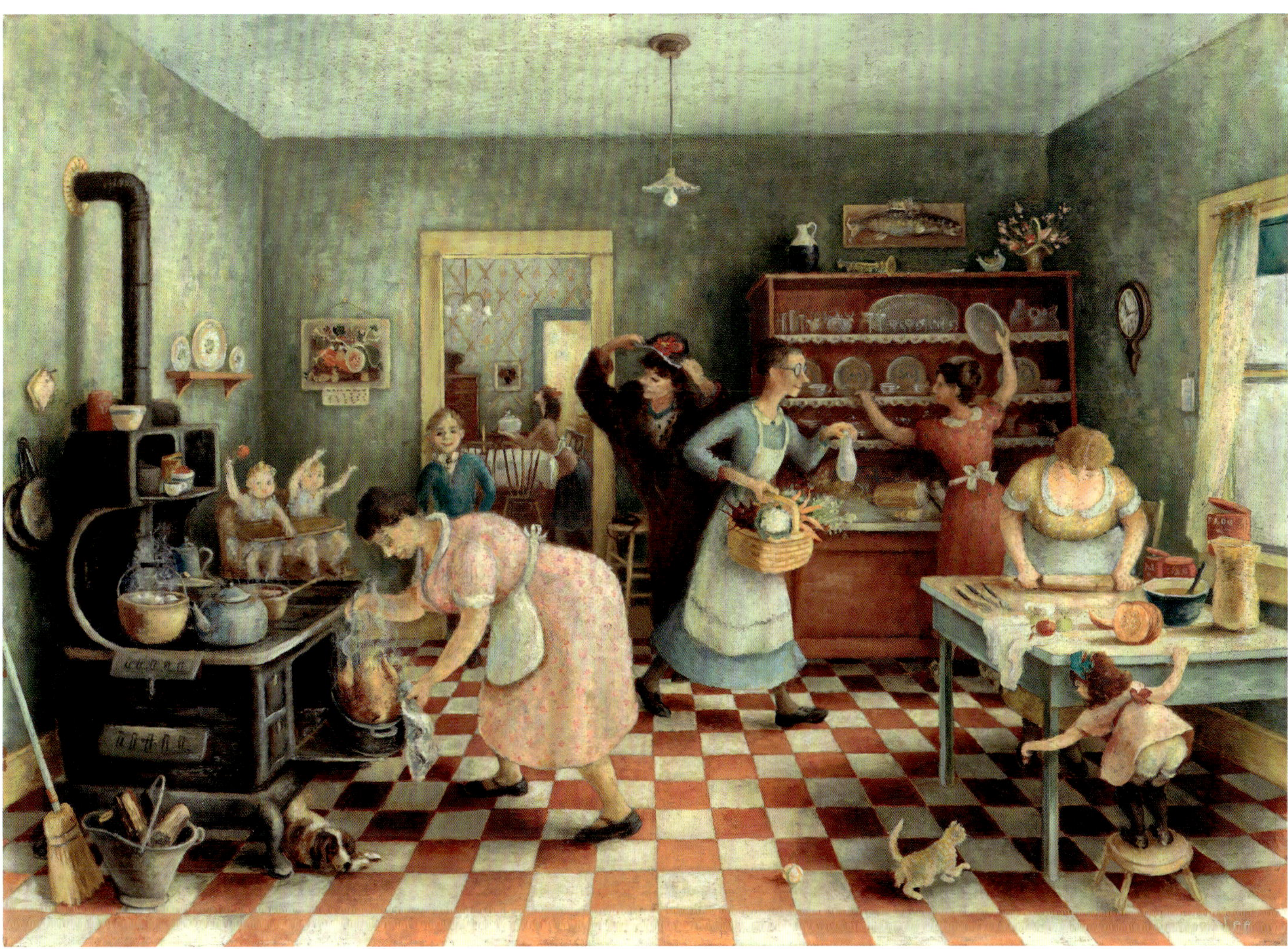

American ritual of family and food in a modest, folksy interior. The farmhouse kitchen, with its cast-iron stove, linoleum flooring, simple furniture, and fresh foodstuffs, serves as a nostalgic setting for Thanksgiving's shared traditions, revered all the more during the Great Depression's toughest years. Yet this vision of Americana is not unaffected. While the artist's deliberately broad and rough approach proffers directness and accessibility, the painting's naïve style was nonetheless filtered through a modernist lens. Working in a representational mode, Lee also explored the explicitly formal qualities of color, shape, movement, and patterning, bespeaking her avant-garde training in France. She achieved her first major success when *Thanksgiving* was included in the Art Institute of Chicago's Annual Exhibition of American Painting and Sculpture in 1935. Awarded the exhibition's foremost prize, the composition received uncommon publicity when the museum donor and namesake of the prize denounced it as "atrocious."[51] All the while, the painting drew crowds of visitors. Lee's brand of modernism put a vernacular twist on national rituals, locating Americana in the hinterlands.

Another of Wood's Depression-era paintings, *The Midnight Ride of Paul Revere* (fig. 18) of 1931, overlays local sensibilities on an episode of storytelling with national import. Here, the artist chose a subject from the country's revolutionary past, the legend of Revere racing on horseback through the countryside in April 1775 to alert the New England villages of Medford, Lexington, and Concord to the patriots' call to arms. Wood composed a bird's-eye view of a once-sleepy village, its

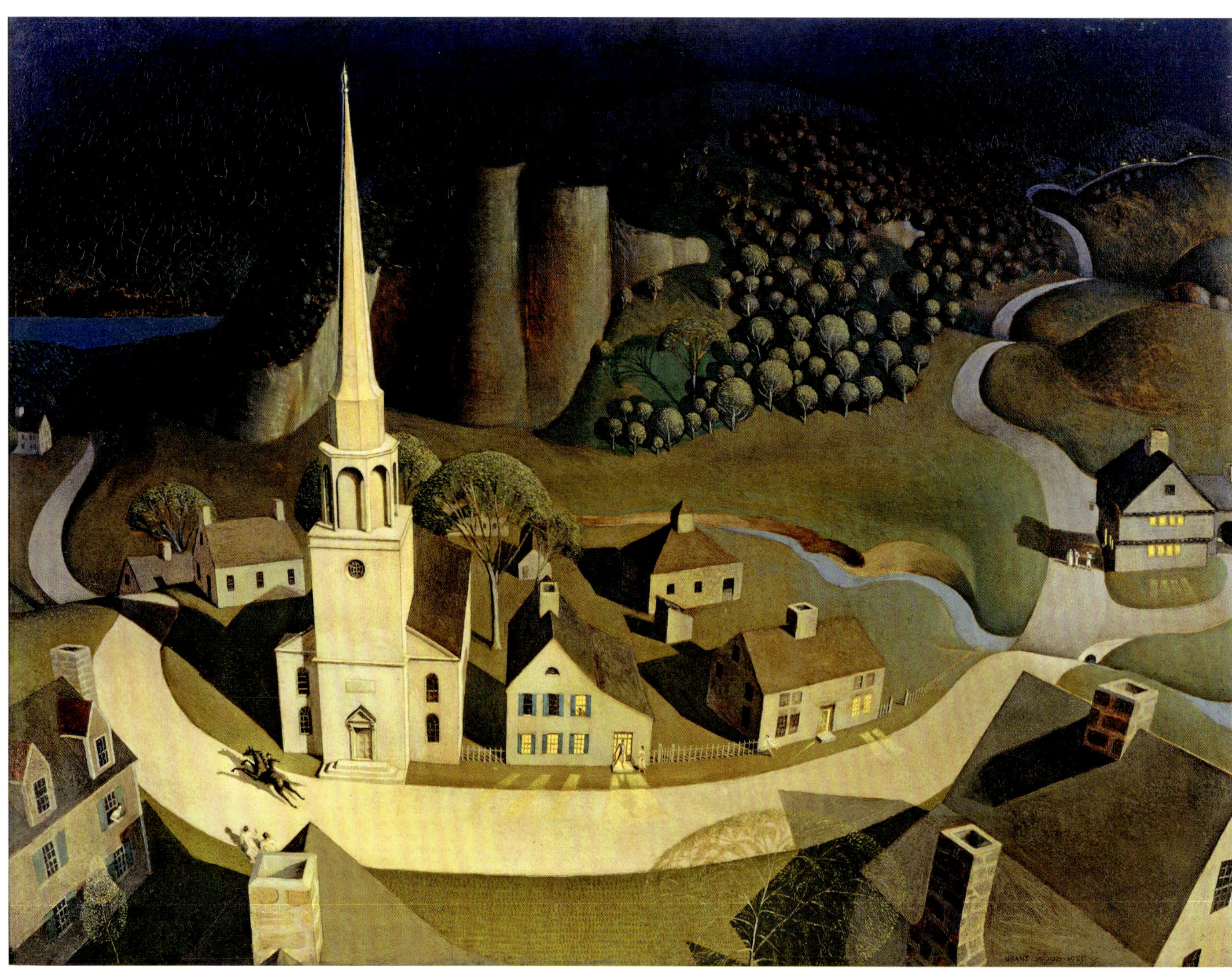

verdant landscape cut by a road that winds from upper right, through the foreground, and to the middle distance at left, past several homes and a steepled church. A handful of tiny figures stand outside, in doorways, and at windows, signaling that Revere, the miniature form atop a galloping horse, has communicated his fateful message. Although the myth takes place in colonial Massachusetts, the painted landscape, with its bluffs and rolling hills, comfortably resembles the artist's native Iowa, akin to such works as Wood's *Young Corn* (p. 44, fig. 12) and Marvin Cone's *River Bend No. 4* (p. 46, fig. 14). Yet the scene's dollhouse-like scale and dramatic illumination (with seemingly modern-day electric lighting emanating from several homes)

transform the locale into an almost otherworldly place, a fairy-tale stage set.[52]

Wood regarded the tale of Paul Revere as one of those "bits of American folklore that are too good to lose," in his words, taking up the material with a wink and nod toward the creative untruths that colored society's engagement with communal histories.[53] The Revere legend grew during the Civil War era, when Henry Wadsworth Longfellow penned "Paul Revere's Ride," which appeared in the *Atlantic Monthly* in January 1861 and in his *Tales of a Wayside Inn* in 1863.[54] Poet and mythmaker, Longfellow embellished history, canonizing Revere as singular messenger and symbol of civic duty, heroic action, and national character. The poem found its way into American curricula and history books in the late nineteenth century, becoming the stuff of a schoolchild's lesson during Wood's own youth.[55] The painting is an invitation to recollect, to dream, to knowingly indulge in a bit of nostalgia. Folkloric yarns, with their historic tenor and familiar heroics, offered a site for shared experiences. In *The Midnight Ride of Paul Revere*, the artist both honors the tall tale and reinvents it. Wood's playful engagement with history and myth marks a defining contribution to American modernism.

This enlivening of a shared past in paint resonated with an avid taste for historical fiction during the Depression years. Bestselling novels included Margaret Mitchell's *Gone with the Wind* (1936), a plantation story of the Civil War and Reconstruction eras, and Kenneth Roberts's *Northwest Passage* (1937), which unfolds in the 1750s and 1760s during the French and Indian War and its aftermath. Another bestseller was *Drums along the Mohawk* (1936), by Walter Edmonds, who chronicled the impact of the Revolutionary War on the farming communities of the Mohawk Valley in upstate New York. Edmonds, an area native, carefully researched his subject in order to build a "faithful presentation of a bygone time" out of documentary details of the daily lives of ordinary people.[56] Although Edmonds's investment in historical accuracy may seem at odds with Wood's investment in national myths, their creative endeavors share a popular aesthetic. Taking different tacks, both nevertheless opened up and revitalized the past for a broad public.

In *Parson Weems' Fable* (1939; fig. 19), Wood upped the ante, playing with the past in a composition that not only presents the story of the young George Washington, his hatchet, and the cherry tree, but also stages the act of spinning the tall tale itself. Before a cherry-fringed curtain stands Mason Locke Weems, the eighteenth-century figure who penned the famous tale and first published it in the 1806 edition of his biography of Washington.[57] Acknowledging the viewer's presence, Weems guides our attention to the drama unfolding behind him. A small-statured George points to the clutched hatchet, while his father, supporting the wounded tree, demands that his son hand over the tool. Wood depicts the crucial moment in the fable when George admits his misdeed and declares, "I cant tell a lie."[58] The scene ostensibly takes place on a southern plantation, with the homestead pictured at center and a male and female slave picking fruit from another tree in the middle distance. The verdant landscape is illuminated from the left from what appear to be spotlights more than sunlight, adding to the composition's theatricality.

*Parson Weems' Fable* serves as a visual primer on how the artist could mine a usable past to shape American culture. The painting is not simply about the myth of Washington but about mythmaking itself as a distinct historical event.[59] An array of antiquated elements function as compositional building blocks, fit together with the seams still visible so that the viewer, like Wood the painter and Weems the fabler, can partake in the crafting. Wood collapsed chronologies, intermingling personages and artifacts of the eighteenth, nineteenth, and twentieth centuries. He placed the head from Gilbert Stuart's iconic painting of President Washington atop a boy's body, the six-year-old persona of Weems's tale. This image, known as the Athenaeum portrait, would likely have been in the mind's eye of 1930s viewers, who were well versed in this particular likeness of the president due to its prevalent use during bicentennial celebrations and ongoing Washingtoniana. While the fable transpires in Virginia, the brick house in the scene is Wood's own home in Iowa City, a Civil War–era structure that the artist had restored recently.[60] With *Parson Weems' Fable*, Wood clearly asserted his own role as interpreter and storyteller, aiming to preserve "something of color and imagination" from the past for the present. "As I see it," said Wood, "the most effective way to do this is to frankly accept these historical tales for what they are now known to be—folklore—and treat them in such a fashion that the realistic-minded, sophisticated people of our generation can accept them."[61] Wood, too, took liberties with the stuff of history, not to pull the wool over his audiences' eyes but to rekindle a common American heritage through doses of fact, fiction, humor, and artistry.

At decade's end, amid a changing international climate, Wood's project did not resonate as intended. Although *Parson Weems' Fable* sold immediately, it was not well received by the public.[62] Was the artist debunking history, unraveling myth, celebrating them both, or revising them? The wit and

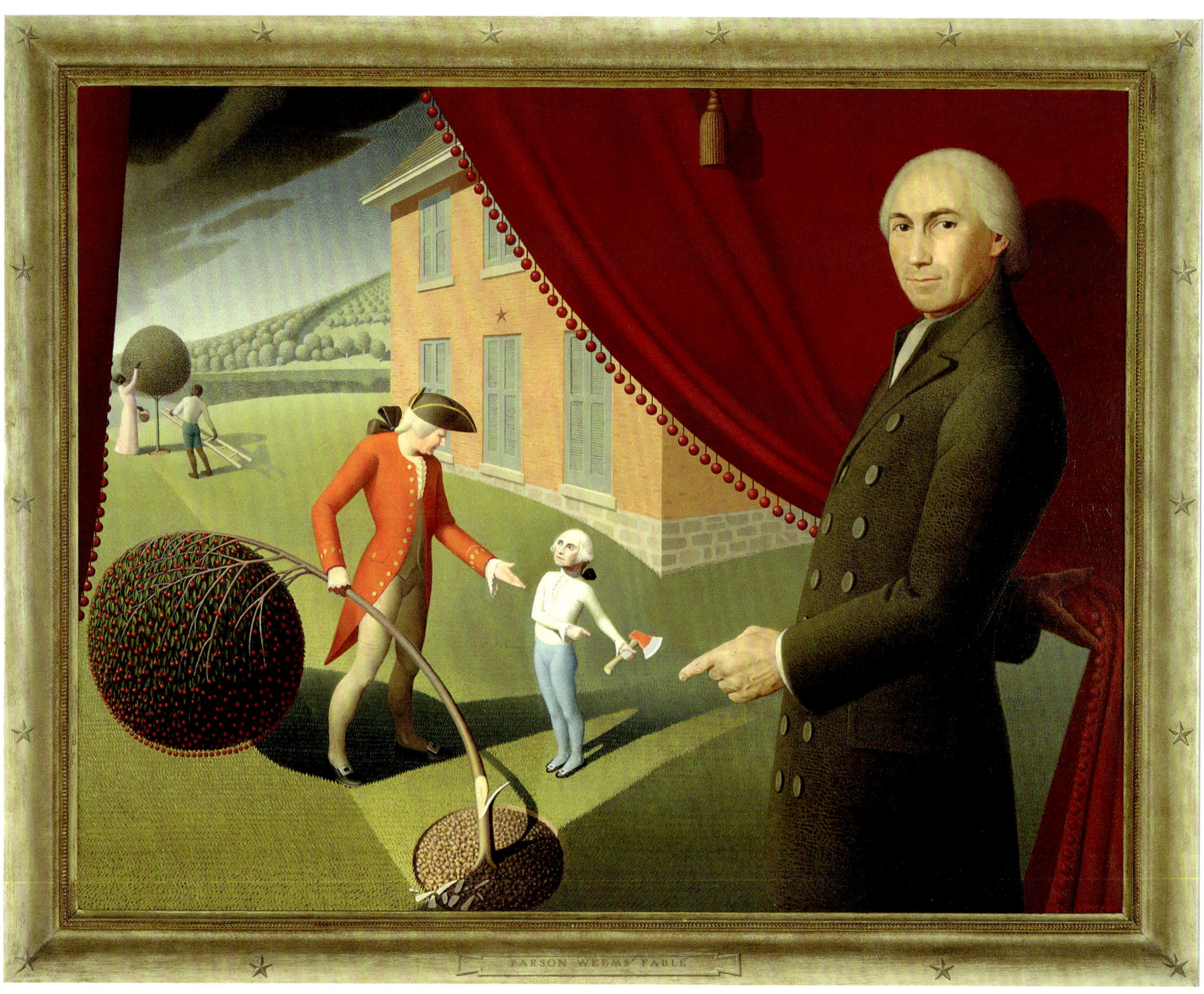


nuance of the composition made Wood's intentions hard to place. Further, Regionalism, of which Wood was a key leader, faced intense scrutiny during the march to war in Europe. The movement's figurative (read conservative) style, distance from European-inspired modernism, midwestern origins, and strongly national subjects led to a broadly accepted understanding of Regionalism as deplorably in step with Fascism and the nationalistic fervor of enemy regimes.[63] The movement's fall from grace in the late 1930s was an uncanny development, given both the popularity of earlier paintings by Wood and other Regionalists and the entwined national/regional impulse demonstrated by many period artists, who worked in a stylistically varied range of modernisms. Wholly unsympathetic to Fascism, Regionalists attempted, in turn, to visualize a response to the threat. Wood, for his part, employed anti-Fascist strategies in his Parson Weems painting, as art historian Cécile Whiting has shown.[64] His look backward stood in distinction to Magic Realist Peter Blume and Surrealist Federico Castellón, for example, who confronted the global threat head on in brooding paintings of a devastated, war-torn

**Fig. 20** Gertrude Abercrombie (American, 1909–1977). *The Past and the Present*, c. 1945. Oil on Masonite; 55.9 × 68.6 cm (22 × 27 in.). The Art Institute of Chicago, gift of the Gertrude Abercrombie Trust, 1978.398.

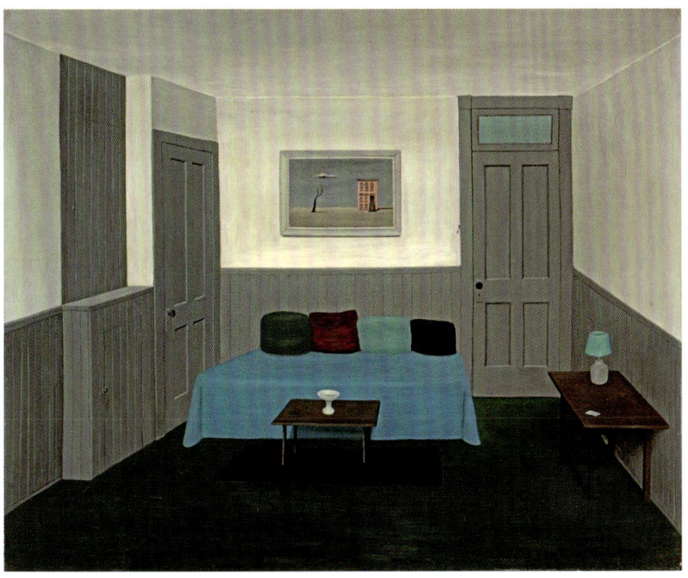

future (see p. 132, fig. 14; p. 134, fig. 16; and the essay by Sarah L. Burns in this volume). Wood's engagement with contemporary politics was more circuitous. Saving folklore was itself an act of patriotism, a means of uniting citizens through shared histories (embellishments and all) amid a new crisis. Just such a call to shore up patriotism through a revival of American mythologies came from Howard Mumford Jones, a scholar at Harvard University, in a November 1938 article in the *Atlantic Monthly*.[65] Wood saw *Parson Weems' Fable* as answering that call. Unlike the propaganda artists of Nazi Germany, for instance, Wood did not portray history as unmitigated truth but as an admixture of truth and artifice.[66] Storytelling—history or otherwise—was craft, process, production. As the Great Depression lifted and the war effort took hold, Wood's painting fell flat. But with the advantage yet again of historical distance, viewers in the late twentieth century and today have come to appreciate the work and its keen and mirthful engagement with myths and narratives that are recognizably American.

During the 1940s, a usable past continued to take shape, from large communal expressions executed as part of the final wave of federally sponsored public murals to more subtle resonances of the past—for instance, in easel paintings by Edward Hopper. Yet changes within modernism were afoot as the country entered World War II, industry and commerce ramped up, and the communal spirit of the Depression years gave way to more individualistic and psychological probing. In Hopper's *Gas* (1940; p. 179, fig. 4), the older architectural structure of the station house at right contends with the shiny red, metallic pumps at center, their modern-day branding quite visible amid the otherwise quaint, rural setting. Painter Jackson Pollock would push abstraction to new, nonobjective ends, such experimentation already underway in the late 1930s (see pp. 176–77, fig. 1). With the rise of Abstract Expressionism, the art world would come to exalt form, material, and process above content. Alternatively, postwar figurative art—from realism to Surrealism to Magic Realism—often traced connections to the past in deeply personal, coded formulations (see fig. 20).[67]

Yet throughout the 1930s, the past proved a tangible, important, and remarkably varied point of departure for modern American artists. While Wood looked to national folklore and the Victorian-era material culture of his native Iowa as threads of continuity amid the changes of modern life, Shahn translated recent headlines about working-class immigrants and social injustice into a memorializing, monumental composition with decided historical weight. Both Douglas and Demuth embraced abstract vocabularies composed of crisp lines, planar geometries, and bold color. Scaling up grand progress narratives of African American achievement, Douglas made the human figure an integral component of his modernist aesthetic. Demuth, in contrast, drew more obliquely from a smaller-scale past—one that was local and personal—for his easel-sized compositions of modern industry. A collector, Sheeler made new objects about old objects; his paintings did not tell stories like those by Wood or Kantor but rather served as invitations to discern harmonies of form and craftsmanship across time. O'Keeffe similarly tamped down narrative in favor of a celebration of timeworn forms, hers monumental, spare, partially described, and emblematic of the Southwest. American histories—shared, contested, discarded, mythologized, reinvented, and renewed—provided fertile terrain for Depression-era painters to root aesthetic experimentation and related explorations of artistic, regional, and national identity.

**1**  For Brooks, it was the nation's Puritan past that needed revamping. See Van Wyck Brooks, "On Creating a Usable Past," *Dial* 64 (April 11, 1918), pp. 337–41; reprinted in Claire Sprague, ed., *Van Wyck Brooks: The Early Years, A Selection of His Works, 1908–1925* (1968; repr., Northeastern University Press, 1993), pp. 219–26, and introduction, pp. xxxvii–lix; and Warren I. Susman, *Culture as History: The Transformation of American Society in the Twentieth Century* (1974; repr., Smithsonian Institution Press, 2003), p. 45.

**2**  Brooks, "On Creating a Usable Past," p. 223.

**3**  Ibid., pp. 223–24.

**4**  Alfred Haworth Jones, "The Search for a Usable American Past in the New Deal Era," *American Quarterly* 23, no. 5 (December 1971), pp. 710–24; see especially pp. 712–16; and Teresa A. Carbone, ed., *Youth and Beauty: Art of the American Twenties*, exh. cat. (Brooklyn Museum/Skira Rizzoli, 2011), esp. pp. 15–111.

**5**  Joseph Wood Krutch, "The Usable Past," *Nation* 138, no. 3580 (February 14, 1934), p. 191. An important voice of the period was that of historian and critic Lewis Mumford, whose early writings were influenced by Brooks. In *The Brown Decades*, his 1931 study of the Gilded Age, Mumford resuscitated painters including Thomas Eakins and Albert Pinkham Ryder, valuing artists whom he thought of as working against the grain of the nation's colonial and capitalist traditions. Mumford's usable past proffered independence of spirit and antimaterialism. See Eddy Dow, "Van Wyck Brooks and Lewis Mumford: A Confluence in the 'Twenties," *American Literature* 45, no. 3 (November 1973), pp. 407–22; and Lewis Mumford, *The Brown Decades: A Study of the Arts in America 1865–1895* (Harcourt, Brace, 1931).

**6**  On Wood and Regionalism, see, for example, Wanda M. Corn, *Grant Wood: The Regionalist Vision*, exh. cat. (Minneapolis Institute of Arts/Yale University Press, 1983); and James M. Dennis, *Renegade Regionalists: The Modern Independence of Grant Wood, Thomas Hart Benton, and John Steuart Curry* (University of Wisconsin Press, 1998).

**7**  Corn, *Grant Wood*, pp. xiv, 40, 43.

**8**  See, for example, Julia B. Rosenbaum, *Visions of Belonging: New England Art and the Making of American Identity* (Cornell University Press, 2006), pp. 151–73.

**9**  Dennis, *Renegade Regionalists*; Debra Bricker Balken, *After Many Springs: Regionalism, Modernism, and the Midwest*, exh. cat. (Des Moines Art Center/Yale University Press, 2009); and Randall R. Griffey, "Reconsidering the 'Soil': The Stieglitz Circle, the Regionalists, and Cultural Eugenics in the Twenties," in Carbone, *Youth and Beauty*, pp. 245–76.

**10**  James M. Dennis, *Grant Wood: A Study in American Art and Culture* (Viking, 1975), p. 110; and Corn, *Grant Wood*, pp. 98–100.

**11**  "Grant Wood's New Picture Causes Talk," *Evening World-Herald* (Omaha), November 23, 1932, clipping, Grant Wood Scrapbook 1, comp. Nan Wood Graham, Figge Art Museum Grant Wood Digital Collection, University of Iowa Libraries (hereafter Wood Digital Collection), http://digital.lib.uiowa.edu/cdm /compoundobject/collection /grantwood/id/1030/show/957 /rec/9/.

**12**  Corn, *Grant Wood*, p. 100.

**13**  Unmarked clipping, Grant Wood Scrapbook 1, Wood Digital Collection, http://digital.lib .uiowa.edu/cdm/ref/collection /grantwood/id/956/rec/2/.

**14**  Formed in 1926, the Bicentennial Commission embraced the debunking spirit of that decade, celebrating Washington while also seeking to undo the myths and legends surrounding him, including Leutze's vision of the general standing upright in his boat during a secret military maneuver. See Corn, *Grant Wood*, p. 98; Karal Ann Marling, "Of Cherry Trees and Ladies' Teas: Grant Wood Looks at Colonial America," in Alan Axelrod, ed., *The Colonial Revival in America* (Winterthur Museum/W. W. Norton, 1985), pp. 294–319; and Karal Ann Marling, *George Washington Slept Here: Colonial Revivals in American Culture, 1876–1986* (Harvard University Press, 1988), pp. 325–64.

**15**  The window was finally dedicated in 1955; Wood died of cancer in 1942. Corn, *Grant Wood*, pp. 66–67, 100–101; and Nan Wood Graham, with John Zug and Julie Jensen McDonald, *My Brother, Grant Wood* (State Historical Society of Iowa, 1993), pp. 60–65.

**16**  Corn, *Grant Wood*, pp. 100–01. On Leutze's painting, its creation (in two versions), and its political significance for both German and American audiences in the mid-nineteenth century, see Barbara Groseclose, "*Washington Crossing the Delaware*: The Political Context," *American Art Journal* 7, no. 2 (November 1975), pp. 70–78.

**17**  "D.A.R.'s of Baltimore to 'Ignore' Grant Wood's Painting," *Cedar Rapids Gazette*, January 8, 1934, clipping, Grant Wood Scrapbook 1, Wood Digital Collection, http://digital.lib.uiowa .edu/cdm/ref/collection/grant wood/id/997/rec/12/; "The Painting That Made the Ladies Indignant," clipping, Grant Wood Scrapbook 1, Wood Digital Collection, http://digital.lib.uiowa .edu/cdm/ref/collection/grant wood/id/961/rec/4/; and "Artist Arouses Wrath of Daughters of Revolution," *Albuquerque Tribune*, June 3, 1933, p. 8, clipping, Grant Wood Scrapbook 1, Wood Digital Collection, http://digital.lib .uiowa.edu/cdm/ref/collection /grantwood/id/975/rec/7/.

**18**  "D.A.R.'s of Baltimore."

**19**  "Painting by Iowa Artist Proves Most Popular in a Century of Progress Art Exhibition," *Chicago Tribune*, clipping, Grant Wood Scrapbook 1, Wood Digital Collection, http://digital.lib .uiowa.edu/cdm/ref/collection /grantwood/id/986/rec/10/.

**20**  The painting remained on view until 1946. Carrie Rebora Barratt et al., "*Washington Crossing the Delaware*: Restoring an American Masterpiece," *Metropolitan Museum of Art Bulletin* 69, no. 2 (Fall 2011), pp. 11–13; quote on p. 12. On the changing tastes and critical assessments of history painting, see Jochen Wierich, *Grand Themes: Emanuel Leutze,* Washington Crossing the Delaware*, and American History Painting* (Pennsylvania State University Press, 2012); and William Ayres, ed., *Picturing History: American Painting 1770–1930*, exh. cat. (Fraunces Tavern Museum/Rizzoli, 1993).

**21**  Artist George Biddle, a former schoolmate of Franklin Roosevelt, wrote to the president in 1933 about enlisting the government's support to build a national school of mural painting and specifically mentioned the example of the Mexican mural movement. See George Biddle, *An American Artist's Story* (Little, Brown, 1939), pp. 263–75; letter on pp. 268–69. Further, Diego Rivera, José Clemente Orozco, and David Alfaro Siqueiros brought Mexican muralism, with its leftist

politics and avant-garde aesthetics, to the United States. The *tres grandes,* as they were known, had embraced cultural nationalism and historical subjects in state-sponsored commissions at home; in the United States, they largely undertook private commissions. See Anna Indych-López, *Muralism without Walls: Rivera, Orozco, and Siqueiros in the United States, 1927–1940* (University of Pittsburgh Press, 2009).

**22**  Marlene Park and Gerald E. Markowitz, *Democratic Vistas: Post Offices and Public Art in the New Deal* (Temple University Press, 1984), p. 5.

**23**  See ibid.; see also New Deal Art Registry, http://www.newdealart registry.org/.

**24**  Kathleen A. Foster et al., *Thomas Hart Benton and the Indiana Murals* (Indiana University Art Museum/Indiana University Press, 2000), p. 23.

**25**  On Douglas's mural cycle, see Renée Ater, "Creating a 'Usable Past' and a 'Future Perfect Society': Aaron Douglas's Murals for the 1936 Texas Centennial Exposition," in Susan Earle, ed., *Aaron Douglas: African American Modernist,* exh. cat. (Spencer Museum of Art/Yale University Press, 2007), pp. 95–113; and Timothy Anglin Burgard, ed., *Masterworks of American Painting at the de Young* (Fine Arts Museums of San Francisco, 2005), pp. 342–46.

**26**  Ater, "Creating a 'Usable Past,'" pp. 95–105. Historically at world's fairs, marginalized groups, including African Americans and women, had faced exclusion or segregation when they pushed to participate in planning, activities, and displays.

**27**  See Sue M. Kendall, *Rethinking Regionalism: John Steuart Curry and the Kansas Mural Controversy* (Smithsonian Institution Press, 1986).

**28**  See Sara A. Butler, "Reimagining the Movement: Beyond the Art of Negro Advancement at the Interior Building, 1937–1948," *American Art* 28, no. 2 (Summer 2014), pp. 70–87.

**29**  See Patricia Hills, *Painting Harlem Modern: The Art of Jacob Lawrence* (University of California Press, 2009), pp. 57–133. In 1941 Lawrence painted a historical series on the abolitionist John Brown; see Ellen Sharp, "The Legend of John Brown and the Series by Jacob Lawrence," *Bulletin of the Detroit Institute of Arts* 67, no. 4 (1993), pp. 14–35.

**30**  For more on Ben Shahn's artistic engagement with the Sacco and Vanzetti case, see Alejandro Anreus et al., *Ben Shahn and the Passion of Sacco and Vanzetti*, exh. cat. (Jersey City Museum, 2001).

**31**  When the painting was exhibited at the Museum of Modern Art in New York in 1932, two trustees threatened censorship of Shahn's work and those of Hugo Gellert and William Gropper; all of the objects

remained on view. See ibid., pp. 99 and 118–19; and Hugo Gellert, "We Captured the Walls! The Museum of Modern Art Episode," *Art Front* 1, no. 1 (November 1934), p. 8. For another example of Shahn's use of history in the 1930s, one that was socially conscious and community-centered yet not polemical, see Susan Noyes Platt, "The Jersey Homesteads Mural: Ben Shahn, Bernarda Bryson, and History Painting in the 1930s," in Patricia M. Burnham and Lucretia Hoover Giese, eds., *Redefining American History Painting* (Cambridge University Press, 1995), pp. 294–309.

**32**  Wanda M. Corn, "Grant Wood: Uneasy Modern," in Jane C. Milosch, ed., *Grant Wood's Studio: Birthplace of American Gothic*, exh. cat. (Cedar Rapids Museum of Art/Prestel, 2005), pp. 116–18; and Corn, "The Birth of a National Icon: Grant Wood's *American Gothic*," *Art Institute of Chicago Museum Studies* 10 (1983), pp. 252–75, especially 256–60.

**33**  Sarah E. Kelly, "Grant Wood (1891–1942)," in Judith A. Barter et al., *American Modernism at the Art Institute of Chicago: From World War I to 1955* (Art Institute of Chicago/Yale University Press), pp. 178–81.

**34**  Irma Rene Koen, "The Art of Grant Wood," *Christian Science Monitor*, March 26, 1932, clipping, Grant Wood Scrapbook 1, Wood Digital Collection, http://digital.lib .uiowa.edu/cdm/compoundobject /collection/grantwood/id/1030 /show/944/rec/3/.

**35** Corn, *Grant Wood*, p. 90.

**36** For more on Mercer, see Steven Conn, "Henry Chapman Mercer and the Search for American History," *Pennsylvania Magazine of History and Biography* 116, no. 3 (July 1992), pp. 323–55.

**37** R. T. Haines Halsey and C. O. C., "The American Wing," *Metropolitan Museum of Art Bulletin* 19, no. 11 (November 1924), pp. 251–65; and Wanda M. Corn, *The Great American Thing: Modern Art and National Identity, 1915–1935* (University of California Press, 1999), pp. 309–13.

**38** Corn, *Great American Thing*, pp. 319–27; and Victoria Grieve, *The Federal Art Project and the Creation of Middlebrow Culture* (University of Illinois Press, 2009), pp. 40–58.

**39** For an extended reading of "Home, Sweet Home" and Sheeler's role in salvaging a past for modernists, see Corn, *Great American Thing*, pp. 293–337. For more on Sheeler's paintings, drawings, and photographs of his domestic settings, see Susan Fillin-Yeh, *Charles Sheeler: American Interiors*, exh. cat. (Yale University Art Gallery, 1987).

**40** Virginia Tuttle Clayton et al., *Drawing on America's Past: Folk Art, Modernism, and the Index of American Design*, exh. cat. (National Gallery of Art/ University of North Carolina Press, 2002), pp. 1–10, 23. Sheeler's taste for collecting grew after meeting Henry Mercer, his neighbor when he lived in an eighteenth-century farmhouse in Doylestown, Pennsylvania, in the 1910s and 1920s. Sheeler also likely learned of Henry Ford's plans for Greenfield Village when he was on assignment at the River Rouge plant in 1927–28. In addition to her efforts for the Index of American Design, Constance Rourke cultivated a usable past in her own writing projects, including a history of humor in American folk tales and literature, *American Humor* (1931), as well as a study on Sheeler; see Joan Shelley Rubin, "A Convergence of Vision: Constance Rourke, Charles Sheeler, and American Art," *American Quarterly* 42, no. 2 (June 1990), pp. 191–222.

**41** H. V. D., "Charles Sheeler's Exhibition," *New York Times*, November 19, 1931, p. 32; and Grieve, *Federal Art Project*, p. 47. For a reading of Sheeler's interiors that emphasizes their consumer appeal for contemporary viewers, see Kristina Wilson, "Ambivalence, Irony, and Americana: Charles Sheeler's 'American Interiors,'" *Winterthur Portfolio* 45, no. 4 (Winter 2011), pp. 249–76.

**42** Morris Kantor, "Ends and Means," *Magazine of Art* 33, no. 3 (March 1940), p. 144. See also Sarah E. Kelly, "Morris Kantor (1896–1974)," in Barter et al., *American Modernism*, pp. 181–83.

**43** Carol Troyen, "'The Sacredness of Everyday Fact': Hopper's Pictures of the City," in Carol Troyen et al., *Edward Hopper*, exh. cat. (Museum of Fine Arts, Boston, 2007), pp. 111, 115, 136–39; and Carter E. Foster, ed., *Hopper Drawing*, exh. cat. (Whitney Museum of American Art, 2013), pp. 101–105.

**44** Rosenbaum, *Visions of Belonging*, pp. 3–5, 166–67; Park and Markowitz, *Democratic Vistas*, pp. 9, 30; and Dennis, *Renegade Regionalists*, p. 197.

**45** Barbara Haskell, *Charles Demuth*, exh. cat. (Whitney Museum of American Art/Harry N. Abrams, 1988), p. 198; Betsy Fahlman, *Chimneys and Towers: Charles Demuth's Late Paintings of Lancaster*, exh. cat. (Amon Carter Museum of American Art, 2007), pp. 36–39, 92, 119–23; Corn, *Great American Thing*, pp. 222–23; and Ellen E. Roberts, "Charles Demuth (1883–1935)," in Barter et al., *American Modernism*, pp. 162–66.

**46** Ishbel Ross, "Bones of Desert Blaze Art Trail of Miss O'Keeffe," *New York Herald Tribune*, December 29, 1931, p. 3.

**47** Ellen E. Roberts, "Georgia O'Keeffe (1887–1986)," in Barter et al., *American Modernism*, pp. 155–61; and Corn, *Great American Thing*, pp. 252–53, 256–60, 265–66. On the landscape of New Mexico as generative material for O'Keeffe's modernist paintings, see Barbara Buhler Lynes, Lesley Poling-Kempes, and Frederick W. Turner, *Georgia O'Keeffe and New Mexico: A Sense of Place*, exh. cat. (Georgia O'Keeffe Museum/ Princeton University Press, 2004).

**48** For a reading of O'Keeffe's nationalistic palette as accompanied by a sense of ambivalence and unease, see the essay by Sarah Kelly Oehler in this volume.

**49** For an extended reading of *Cow's Skull: Red, White, and Blue* and O'Keeffe's decades-long engagement with the Southwest, see Corn, *Great American Thing*, pp. 239–91. See also Rosenbaum, *Visions of Belonging*, pp. 163–66.

**50** I thank Julie Aronson and Anne Buening at the Cincinnati Art Museum for their assistance in identifying the objects in Lucioni's painting.

**51** Sarah E. Kelly, "Doris Lee (1905–1983)," in Barter et al., *American Modernism*, pp. 183–85; Virginia Gardner, "Society Donors Join Fiery Art Show Dispute," *Chicago Tribune*, November 7, 1935, p. 2; and "Institute Buys 'Thanksgiving' for Galleries," *Chicago Tribune*, December 11, 1935, p. 21.

**52** Dennis, *Grant Wood*, p. 109; and Corn, *Grant Wood*, p. 86.

**53** "Artist Denies Intent to 'Debunk' Legend, 'Clarifies' Picture of Washington and the Cherry Tree," *New York Times*, January 3, 1940, p. 18.

**54** [Henry Wadsworth Longfellow], "Paul Revere's Ride," *Atlantic Monthly* 7, no. 39 (January 1861), pp. 27–29; and Henry Wadsworth Longfellow, *Tales of a Wayside Inn* (Ticknor and Fields, 1863), pp. 18–25.

**55**  See, for example, the textbook by John Fiske, *A History of the United States for Schools* (1894; repr., Houghton, Mifflin, 1899), p. 204. Marling, "Of Cherry Trees," pp. 312–13.

**56**  Walter D. Edmonds, *Drums along the Mohawk* (1936; repr., Syracuse University Press, 1997), quote on p. xv. See also Lionel D. Wyld, "History and Humanism: A Novelist's Portrayal of the American Revolution," *North Dakota Quarterly* 51, no. 4 (Fall 1983), pp. 174–82; and Jones, "Search for a Usable American Past," p. 719.

**57**  Corn, *Grant Wood*, p. 120.

**58**  M. L. Weems, *The Life of George Washington* (1800; repr., R. Cochran, 1808; sixth ed.), p. 14.

**59**  Cécile Whiting, *Antifascism in American Art* (Yale University Press, 1989), p. 102.

**60**  Corn, *Grant Wood*, pp. 122–23; and Marling, *George Washington Slept Here*, p. 345.

**61**  "Artist Denies Intent," p. 18.

**62**  Corn, *Grant Wood*, p. 123; and Whiting, *Antifascism in American Art*, p. 111.

**63**  One of Regionalism's most vocal critics was art historian H. W. Janson; see his "Benton and Wood, Champions of Regionalism," *Magazine of Art* 39, no. 5 (May 1946), pp. 184–86, 198–200.

**64**  Whiting, *Antifascism in American Art*, pp. 98–111.

**65**  Howard Mumford Jones, "Patriotism—But How?" *Atlantic Monthly* 162, no. 5 (November 1938), pp. 585–92.

**66**  Whiting, *Antifascism in American Art*, pp. 100–02, 106–08.

**67**  Pollock's pictures did resonate with the political and social climate of Cold War America; see Erika Doss, *Benton, Pollock, and the Politics of Modernism: From Regionalism to Abstract Expressionism* (University of Chicago Press, 1991), pp. 328–62. On postwar representational art, see Greta Berman and Jeffrey Wechsler, *Realism and Realities: The Other Side of American Painting, 1940–1960*, exh. cat. (Rutgers University Art Gallery, 1982); I thank Angela Miller for suggesting this resource.

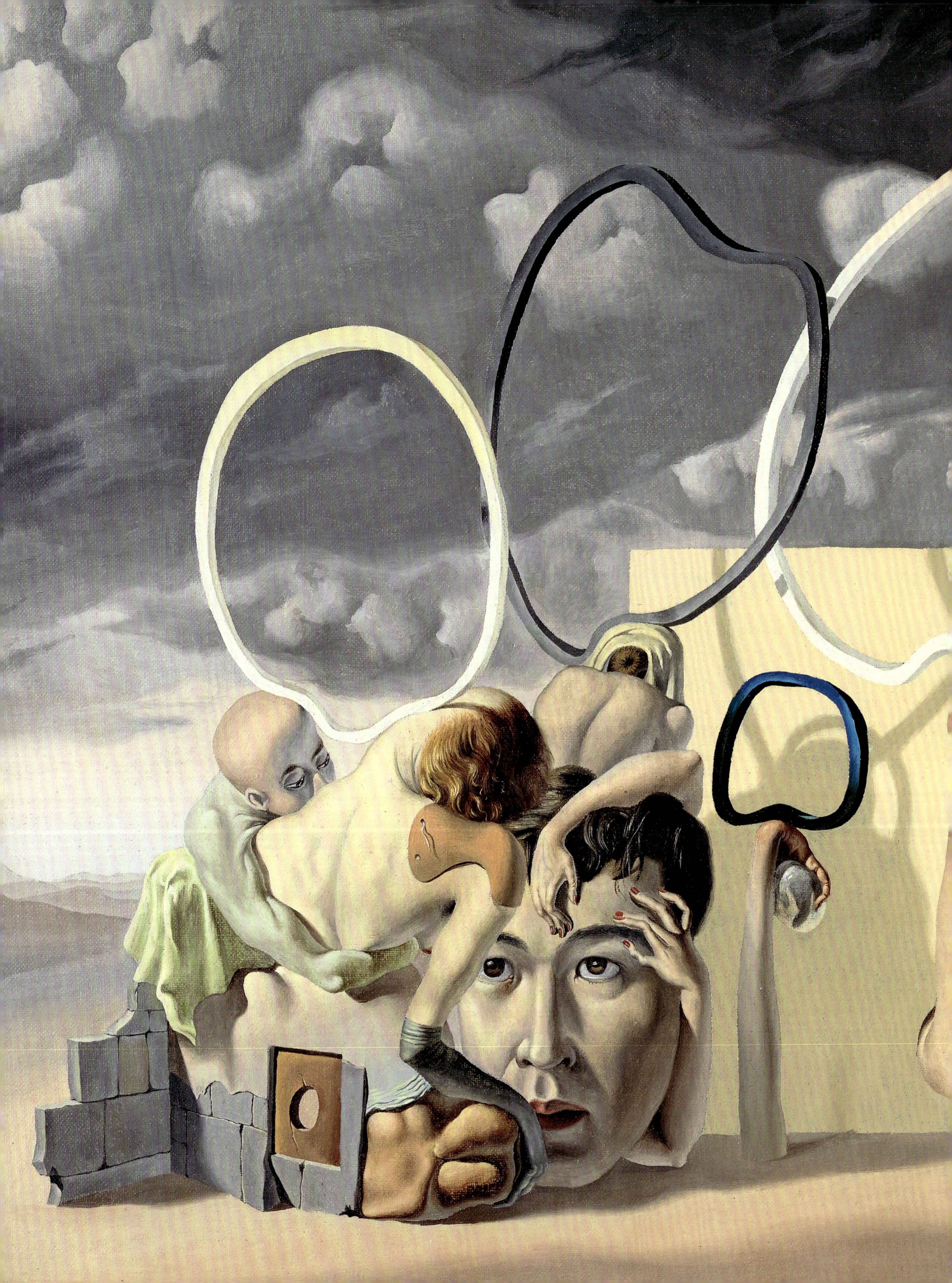

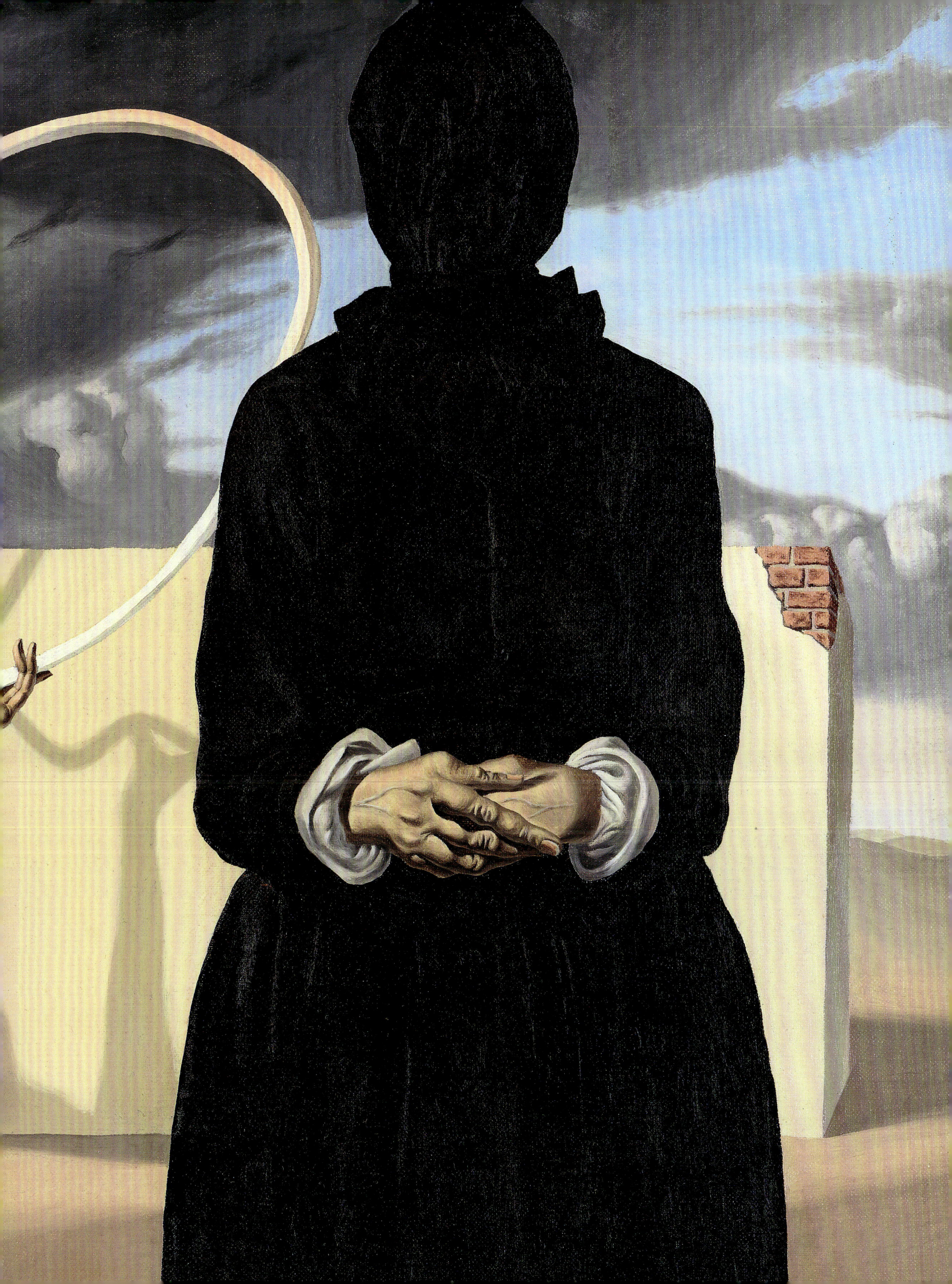

**SARAH L. BURNS**

**H**orror and violence pervaded Depression America in the 1930s. Fired up by the mass media, fears of social collapse preyed on minds already beset by economic anxiety and apprehension for the future. Journalists surveyed the social landscape with foreboding, extrapolating ominous general meanings from gruesome individual events. The kidnapping and murder of famed aviator Charles Lindbergh's young son in 1932, gangland assassinations, and the seemingly intractable spate of lynchings all over the country became potent symbols of a nation in steep decline. Depression America had become a "sad spectacle" for the whole world to see, to be horrified by the "savagery" now running rampant in the land. America seemed little better than Germany under Adolf Hitler and his brutal henchmen, who—as one writer imagined—would

FOUR

# *Death, Decay, and Dystopia: Painting the American Wasteland in the 1930s*

have read recent reports of atrocious crime in America "with wry smiles." American civilization had somehow fallen victim to a deep and perhaps fatal sickness. The shining city on a hill had morphed into a dark dystopia.[1]

Not surprisingly, perhaps, horror movies became mainstream popular entertainment the 1930s. *Frankenstein,* the Universal Pictures hit released in 1931, gave rise to the "great horror epidemic" that gripped audiences nationwide. Released to a "horror-struck world," the film attracted some fifteen million people to shudder at the "horror-heavy spectacle." After *Frankenstein,* horror films became so profitable that industry insiders dubbed them "Midas productions."[2] At the same time, millions of readers devoured cheap pulp-fiction magazines, which purveyed murder, monsters, and outrageously gruesome deeds of violence. The primary reason for their popularity was

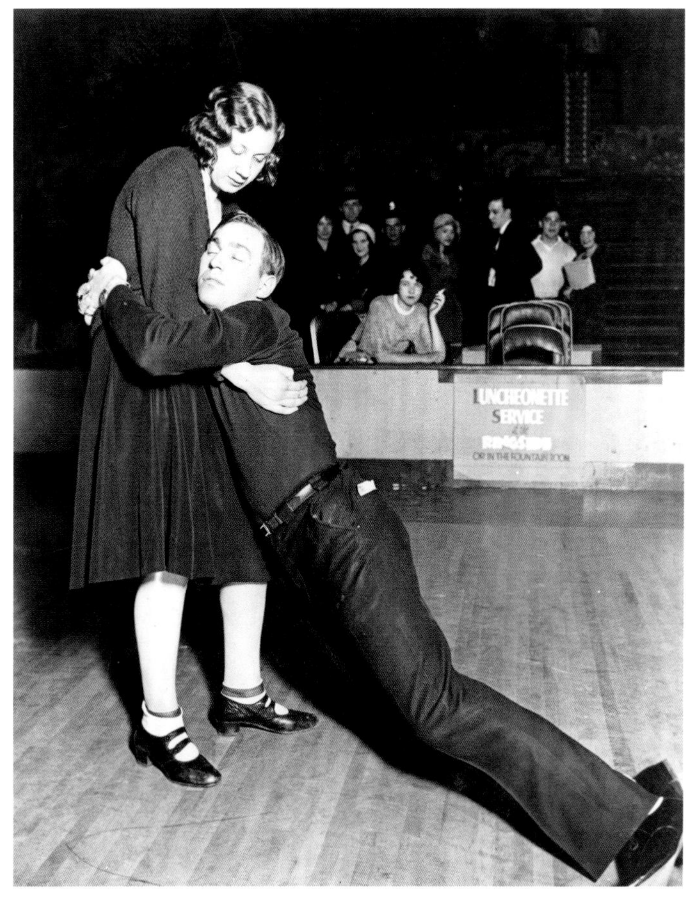

**Fig. 1** Underwood and Underwood. *Marathon Dancers Still Going*, 1930. Ann Lawanick holds up her partner, Jack Ritof, after he has fallen asleep during a marathon dance at the Merry Garden Ballroom, Chicago, IL. Prints and Photographs Division, Library of Congress, Washington, DC.

escape: for pulp readers, "There is no Depression," as *Vanity Fair* put it in 1933. Even so, for the majority of Americans—elite and proletarian alike—the Depression remained all too real: it was an inescapable "rite of passage . . . into an unknown realm of terror."[3] Those uneasy moods and haunting anxieties crept into the world of painting, too, often in dreamlike—or nightmarish—forms. The fine arts, of course, purportedly ranked far above the popular and the commonplace. Yet many paintings of the 1930s occupied the same or proximate ground as the detective thriller, the pulps, or the monster movie. Fear and foreboding demanded phantasmagoric visions of violence, suffering, corruption, and destruction. For anxious artists, even picturing the "real" world demanded wild exaggeration or lurid distortion for maximum impact.

Philip Evergood's *Dance Marathon* (1934; p. 156, fig. 8) is a case in point. Born into affluent circumstances but radicalized in the early 1930s, Evergood in his art launched a sustained assault on social oppression under capitalism. While *Dance Marathon* is not overtly political, it dramatizes the plight of ordinary people driven to extremes by economic hardship. Dance marathons began in the 1920s and evolved into grueling endurance contests that required competitors to dance twenty-four hours a day, sometimes for weeks on end. The rules allowed fifteen minutes of rest for every forty-five minutes on the dance floor; otherwise, dancers had to stay in continuous motion even when eating. Added to chronic muscle strain and swollen feet was the torture of sleep deprivation. One participant recalled a man "dragging behind his sleeping partner . . . bent double, her fingers scraping the floor, head lolling, one foot scraping after the other" (see fig. 1). Marathons attracted audiences that often took sadistic pleasure in the dancers' pain. As Horace McCoy put it in his 1935 novel *They Shoot Horses, Don't They?*: "Customers at a marathon dance do not have to be prepared for their excitement. When anything happens they get excited all at once. In that respect a marathon dance is like a bull fight."[4]

Evergood drew the details of *Dance Marathon* straight from actuality. There is a bandstand, a first aid station staffed by a nurse, a clock, and a sign announcing that the contest is now in its forty-ninth day. Most topical of all is the word "Walkathon" emblazoned in huge red letters on the back wall. At the start of the Depression, event organizers restyled marathons as "walkathons" to assuage moralists who believed that marathon dancing encouraged loose sexual conduct that posed grave dangers to young women in particular.[5] Evergood's loud colors, cartoonish exaggerations, and fantastic symbolic flourishes, however, transmute the scene into a morbid dance of death. He elongated and grossly distorted the dancers' muscle-bound bodies and emphasized their rumps with skintight skirts and trousers. The couple in the foreground rivets the eye, he in glaring blue, she clashing in garish, "nasty" red.[6] Sagging with exhaustion and dangling her manicured claws, she falls against her swarthy partner's bulging body as he props her up with huge, meaty hands. All around them stagger other couples— literally on their last legs—with fright-mask faces and clownish hats. Under the clock stands Mickey Mouse, grinning, while a skeletal hand brandishes a thousand-dollar bill in the upper left corner. The spiderweb pattern of the crimson dance floor further underscores the dancers' hopeless entrapment. For Evergood, the sight of "people flopping around on their behinds on the floor tired out after 49 days of dancing" epitomized "the violence of that age, of this beginning age that is so violent today."[7]

Of a different order entirely was the atrocious violence of the Ku Klux Klan, the hate group founded after the Civil War to carry out a bloodthirsty "reign of terror" against blacks and their supporters.[8] Abolished by law in 1871, the organization regrouped in 1915 as a white supremacist band of avengers that over the next two decades unleashed a scourge of grisly murders, torturing, hanging, incinerating, and dismembering their victims. The press widely reported and vehemently condemned lynching—the *Nation*, for example, deploring the lynch mob's "unbelievable extremes of savagery . . . reminiscent of primitive orgy, maniacal frenzy, and holy combat." Such brutality was a sign that the whole life of man was "'dropping back to a lower level.'"[9]

In the 1930s, left-wing American painters and printmakers also took on the Klan, exhibiting graphic representations of frenzied rabble, faceless killers, anguished victims, and violated bodies.[10] Seeking to expose and condemn the practice, both the NAACP and the John Reed Club held antilynching exhibitions in 1935. Joe Jones was in the vanguard, creating *American Justice* (p. 34, fig. 4) in 1933. A native of Saint Louis, the working-class Jones was a self-taught painter and a Communist. He conceived of and painted *American Justice* in Provincetown, Massachusetts, where instead of doing seascapes, he got "class consciousness."[11] Jones's ghastly nocturne is both a lynching scene and an allegory of justice gone bad in modern America. In the foreground lies the body of a young black woman stripped to the waist. Nearby, a dog howls, and a noose dangles from a spectral tree. Behind the victim are white-sheeted Klansmen, robes emblazoned with black crosses. One of them holds the firebrand used to ignite the blazing house beyond.

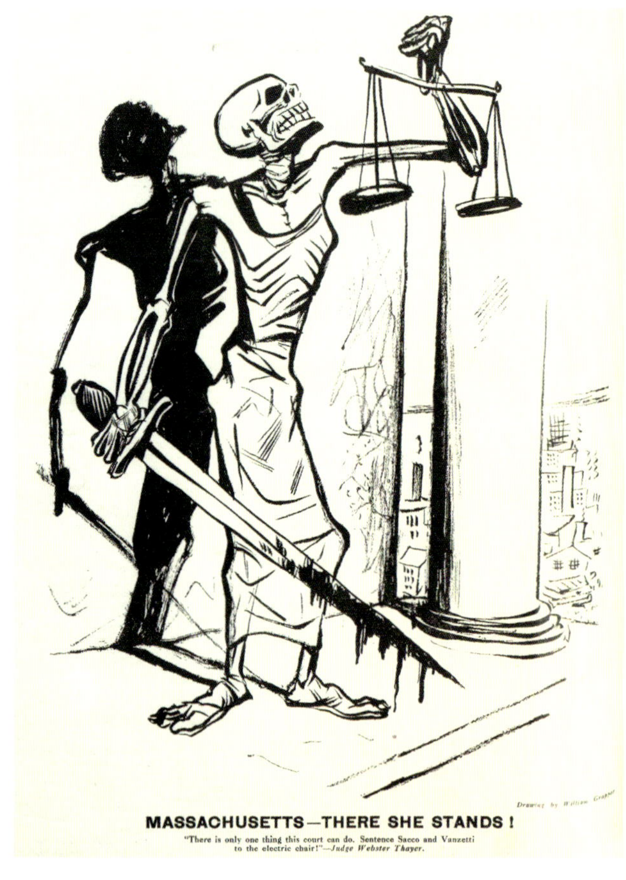



Jones's title is deeply ironic. All too obviously, this is an exposé of gross injustice. The dead woman's partially draped body recalls the classical personification of Justice, but in the most perverted sense. It bears comparison with radical cartoons like William Gropper's *Massachusetts—There She Stands,* representing Justice in her classical raiment as the Grim Reaper holding a long and bloody sword in addition to the customary scales (fig. 2). Drawn for the Marxist magazine *New Masses* in 1927, the cartoon is an indictment of the Massachusetts justice system for the execution of the Italian anarchists Nicola Sacco and Bartolomeo Vanzetti (see p. 16, fig. 1). Cartoon and painting alike condemn modern America, where there is no justice for those who are powerless, poor, foreign, or black.

Jones claimed that he intended *American Justice* as a modern martyrdom with its own strange if disturbing beauty.

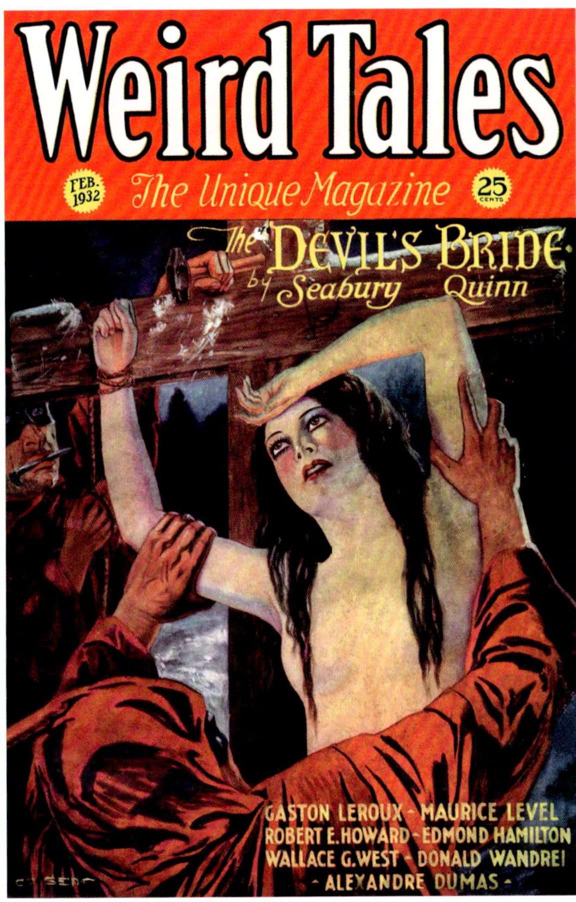


He wrote, "I want to ask a question, why do people who find beauty and love in a picture of a crucifixion painted by an Italian master . . . why do they avoid a lynching? (which is exactly the same thing)."[12] But was it the same? The Klansman's all-too-phallic firebrand suggests that the woman has been raped.[13] Her exposed and vulnerable body, moreover, generates erotic undercurrents that complicate the connotations of the scene and augment its horrors. In its insidious suggestiveness, indeed, *American Justice* straddles the border of fine art and sensational popular entertainment.

Jones's shocking tableau is hardly more than a step away from the typical pulp magazine cover. Offering escape and cheap thrills, pulps transposed real terrors into a different and seemingly innocuous register in which black—literally— became white. The art of *Dime Mystery*, *Horror Stories*, *Weird Tales*, and the like repeatedly deployed reversals, distortions, and transpositions that displaced *actual* menace—lawlessness, racial oppression, violence, class war—into a world of fantastic horror, where sheeted ghosts or hooded assassins stand in for Klansmen and cowering damsels in distress replace (and erase) black victims. C. C. Senf's lurid *Weird Tales* cover from 1932 typifies the genre, showing diabolical masked torturers in the act of crucifying their prey, a young white woman stripped naked and helplessly casting her eyes heavenward while one of her captors prepares to hammer home the first nail (fig. 3). Of course they are not the same, exactly. Jones's painting speaks a revolutionary and bitterly oppositional language. The pulps, by and large, neutralized and rechanneled contemporary violence by disavowing and relocating it into an ironically "safe," fantastic, and pleasurable space. Yet Jones's painting and the tawdry art of pulp magazines occupied points on a continuum, inhabiting the same dark world of 1930s terror and trafficking in the pornography of violence.[14]

In 1933 there were twenty-six documented deaths by lynching. That same year, 31,363 Americans died in motor vehicle accidents, and in the next, the number jumped to 36,101.[15] However horrendous the crimes of the Klan, the automobile was a far more deadly, and ubiquitous, killer—"another murderer of growing importance," as one report put it in 1935.[16] It brought a uniquely modern form of death into daily life. As the toll mounted, worries about highway safety, excess speed, and the staggering death toll generated an outpouring of articles, propaganda, and films intended to frighten drivers into awareness of the danger they courted every time they slid behind the wheel.

No one deployed better scare tactics than J. C. Furnas, commissioned by *Reader's Digest* in 1935 to expose the realities of automobile accidents in unsparing detail. Furnas boasted that no artist would dare to paint such scenes, but *he* was ready to make readers sick to their stomachs. He was good for his word. Among his object lessons was the old mother with a "splinter of wood" driven "four inches into her brain" because her son had sped around a curve. Then there was the driver who had recklessly passed another car without checking the road ahead and ended up with the steering column buried in his abdomen. Some bodies were so horribly mutilated that there was "no point in an autopsy" to determine if a broken neck or ruptured heart had killed them. Shattered glass, too, was lethal: "A leg or arm stuck through the windshield will cut clean to the bone through vein . . . like a piece of beef under a butcher's knife." Even the new, shatterproof "safety" glass could kill: someone might break through the windshield only to have his shoulders stick and the "raw, clean edges of the hole" behead the body "as neatly as a guillotine."[17]

Furnas's "—And Sudden Death" was an immediate sensation, probably the "most widely read and hotly debated article of the decade," in historian Peter D. Norton's view.[18] Barely two weeks after it appeared in *Reader's Digest*, *Time* magazine ran a generous (and gory) excerpt, urging automobile clubs, women's clubs, and any other groups interested in public welfare to distribute copies as widely as possible. Reprints issued by Scribner's reached a circulation of five million. Judges handed out copies to traffic offenders, and representatives of the auto industry hurried to flood the popular press with self-serving articles on improving highway safety.[19] Furnas himself quickly capitalized on his notoriety by publishing *Sudden Death and How to Avoid It*, which included "Better Off Dead," an even more lurid piece on car crashes that scarred and maimed people for life. One of these was a beautiful woman so irreparably damaged that she eventually poisoned herself in despair. "At her funeral nobody wondered why the coffin was not left open. . . . They all knew she had no face."[20] Thanks to Furnas and his advocates, horror had insinuated itself into everyday life.

Death on the highway was also on Iowa Regionalist painter Grant Wood's mind in 1935, when he completed *Death on the Ridge Road* (fig. 4). The imagery is not at all gory, but the title, the suspenseful pictorial narrative, and the eerie atmosphere combine to instill uneasy feelings of dread. The scene shows a narrow country road, where a sleek black sedan has just passed a boxy older-model car on a blind curve. Around that curve hurtles a red truck on certain collision course with the sedan, which straddles both lanes as it crests the hill. On either side are rounded green fields fenced with barbed wire. Two tautly strung telegraph poles stand like crosses, one near and one far. Storm clouds gather on the right, and thick darkness creeps up from below. Stretched perspective, dramatic chiaroscuro, and vertiginous viewpoint amplify the tension. The truck's windshield and the sedan's windows are opaque, as if to underscore the fact that the drivers are fatally blind to each other. Only the viewer, suspended above, can see what is about to happen.[21]

*Death on the Ridge Road*, exhibited at New York's Ferargil Gallery, preceded Furnas's "—And Sudden Death" by several months, but it touched a nerve. *Scholastic* magazine reproduced it in a reprint of Furnas's article in October 1935. In March 1936, a cartoon version of Wood's painting accompanied Furnas's "Death's Harvest Time" in *Rural Progress* magazine.[22] The following year, the painting itself appeared in *Death Begins at 40*, an illustrated booklet issued by the Travelers Insurance Company. Among the other images in the booklet is a moonlit auto graveyard populated by ghosts of accident victims. Over their heads, thought bubbles recall what went wrong on that fatal day: "He dared me to go fast!" "I had the right of way." "He thought he could make it." Even more chilling is *You Change Drivers at 40* (fig. 5), showing Death, cloak swirling, at the wheel of a speeding coupe, the ousted driver in the passenger seat, helpless and terrified. The songwriter Cole Porter bought *Death on the Ridge Road* straight out of the Ferargil Gallery in 1935. Celebrated for his glamorous lifestyle and witty musical comedies, the urbane Porter on the face of it would hardly seem a likely purchaser for such a morbid and macabre painting. But the subject may have hit close to home: his wife's ex-husband, an automobile enthusiast, was reportedly the first American to kill someone in an auto accident.[23]

The subject came uncomfortably close to home for Wood, too. *Death on the Ridge Road* originated in an accident that befell writer Jay Sigmund, a close friend active in Wood's Stone City Art Colony in the summers of 1932 and 1933. One day in August 1933, Sigmund and his wife, Louise, were driving home on a rural road after one of the colony's Sunday gatherings when their car, sideswiped by an oncoming truck, rolled over

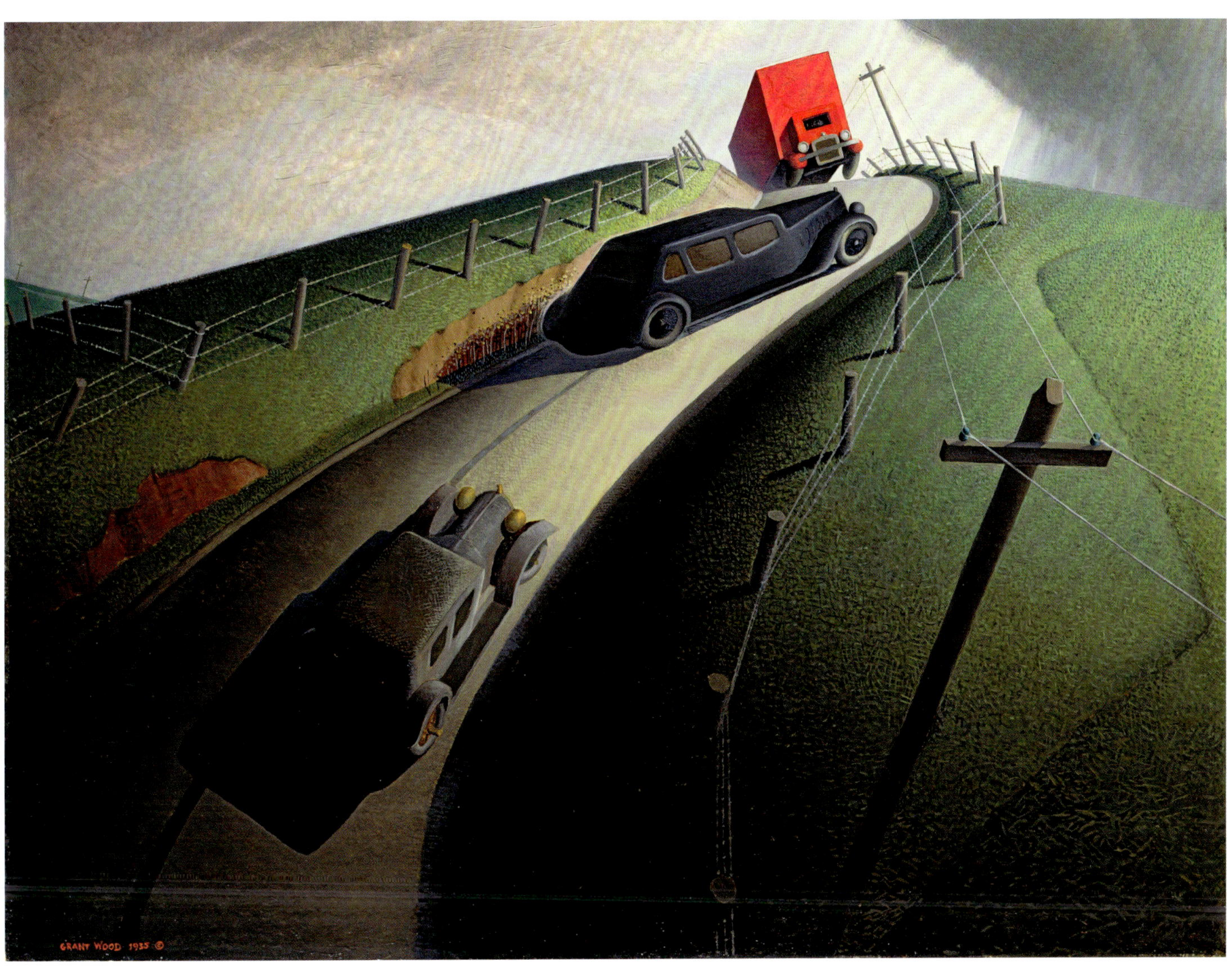

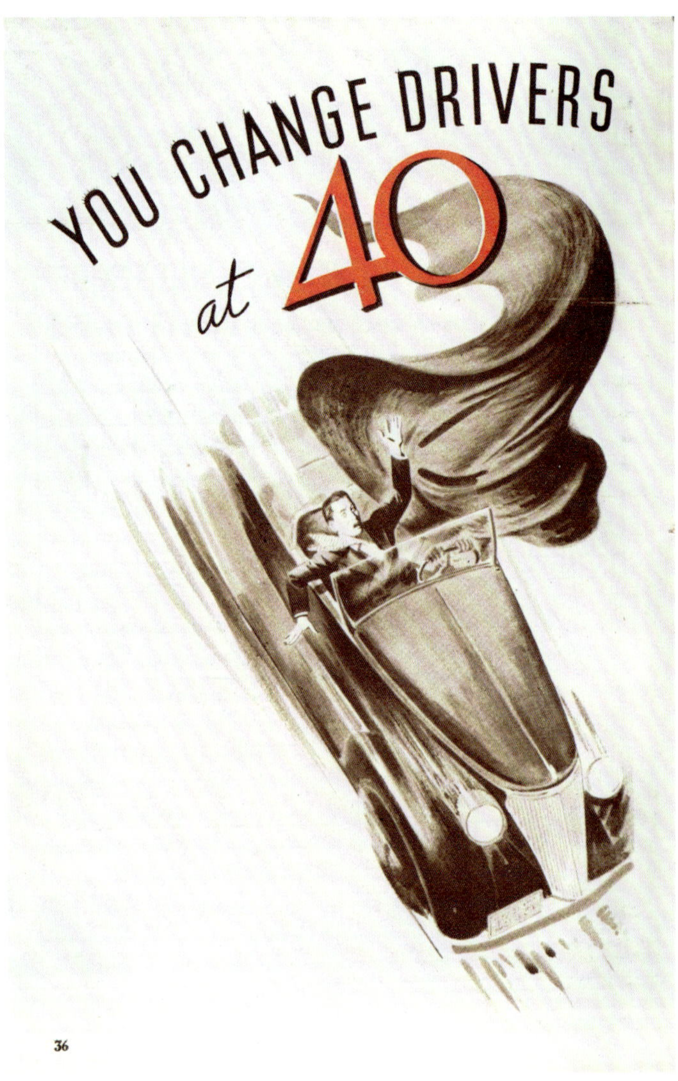

**Fig. 5**  *You Change Drivers at 40*. From *Death Begins at 40* (Travelers Insurance Co., 1937), p. 5. Collection of Greg Van Antwerp.

had personal resonance for Wood, a closeted gay man living in ever-increasing fear of exposure, is an open question.[26]

Reflecting on his own brush with mortality, Sigmund—despite his mutilated hand—wrote "Death Rides a Rubber-Shod Horse" (1934). In the poem, Death has abandoned his one-time mount to ride a "devil-horse of steel and brass /. . . Supplied with lances made of glass." Electric eyes flashing, the "rubber-footed silvered steed" glides through the countryside along the rippling gray ridge roads that now line the sod. Death is out to kill in his up-to-date motorcar.[27] Sigmund's poem and Wood's painting perfectly complement each other. In both, the automobile, symbol of modernity and mobility, has become the vehicle of doom.

Where to retreat from the ills of modernity and the bleak realities of the Depression? Fantasies of an ideal American past offered one way out. Beginning in the 1920s, the celebration of colonial antiques, folk art, Shaker crafts, and the preindustrial world of the handmade and the homemade grew rapidly to cult status.[28] But the past harbored danger and darkness, too, nowhere more artfully than in the ancient houses of New England. Here lingered the memory of Nathaniel Hawthorne's *The House of the Seven Gables* (1851), cursed by ancestral evil and haunted by an "odious and abominable past."[29] Current too was the widespread concern that New England—site of the Puritans' shining city on a hill—was in decline as the immigrant population swelled and vital industries fled the region.

Pulp writer H. P. Lovecraft probably did more than anyone to crystallize that foreboding vision. A native of Providence, Rhode Island, Lovecraft had from an early age steeped himself in ghost stories and Gothic novels. As an adult, he fell under the influence of Oswald Spengler, whose *Decline of the West* (1918) foretold the ultimate collapse of Western civilization. Galvanized by Spengler, Lovecraft began to write tales of terror based on his own perception of New England's fall. Inbreeding and degeneration, he believed, had all but obliterated the last drops of old New England blood, while masses of immigrants— the barbarians—now threatened what little remained. Worse, the decay of New England and the decay of the nation were coextensive. Alienated from the present, Lovecraft craved

twice and crashed. Louise suffered broken ribs, and Jay's right hand—his writing hand—was so badly mangled that doctors had to amputate the index finger.[24] Wood visited the crash site and over the following months developed ideas for the painting, beginning to work on it seriously in the late summer of 1934—after he had purchased his first car. Before completing the painting, Wood (a chronically nervous driver) skidded on an icy road while en route to Iowa City and went over a twelve-foot embankment. In a letter to Ferargil, he reported that the car "was practically standing on its radiator when it ended up in a snow bank."[25] Whether the scene of impending disaster also connection with the past. His first visit to the quaint old town of Marblehead, Massachusetts, in December 1922 gave him the jolt he longed for: "God! Shall I ever forget my first stupefying glimpse of MARBLEHEAD'S huddled and archaick [*sic*] roofs . . . [It was] the most powerful single emotional climax experienced during my nearly forty years of existence. In a flash, all the past of New England . . . swept over me. . . . That was the high tide of my life."[30]

Several years after Lovecraft's visit, the painter Morris Kantor rented a house in Marblehead. He too responded to the allure of long-ago times. As he recalled, "The humble interior of the American farm house, old and quaint, with its peculiar moldy smell, the fading beauty of old plaster discolored by time and living, layers upon layers of wall paper, all turned my imagination to the past, to the people who had lived there and gone. My emotions were aroused."[31] A Russian immigrant who had come to New York in his teens, Kantor was Lovecraft's antithesis. Yet his Marblehead experience made as profound an impression as it had on the deep-rooted New Englander.

Stirred by his epiphany, Kantor began to paint New England interiors that merged past and present in an uncanny amalgam. *Haunted House* (1930; p. 101, fig. 13), exemplifies that strange blend. The room is simply furnished with two rush-bottomed ladder-back chairs and a cloth-draped table. Above the classical fireplace hangs an ornately framed painting of a sailing ship; on the wall adjacent is the portrait of a colonial gentleman. The floor is bare and the ceiling dingy, but the wallpaper sports a lively pattern of oversized pink blooms and emerald green foliage. The edges of the room dissolve into glimpses of nocturnal Marblehead, ancient houses under the faint beam of a modern streetlight. On the right hovers a ghost that seems to have taken shape out of the darkness itself: in its shadowy form, we can make out a huddle of old houses with steep roofs and dim windows. Harsh lighting, incongruities of scale, and skewed perspective heighten the disorienting effect.

*Haunted House* won the Logan Purchase Prize at the Art Institute of Chicago in 1931. Viewers and critics alike responded to its mysterious imagery and atmosphere. One writer marveled at the painting's popularity: it drew crowds at any hour of the day. But its allure had less to do with vividly rendered antiquarian details than the simple fact that the house was haunted. Critic Eleanor Jewett ruminated on the way the artist had combined the charm of an early American period room with the ghostly figures, crumbling walls, and mystifying spatial dislocations of a top-notch literary thriller. "The first step has been made in publicly acknowledging the value of spooks in art," she wrote. "Now we can look forward to all kinds and types of 'thrill' pictures."[32]

During the 1920s and into the 1930s, a number of plays and movies featured old (and more often than not dark) houses as settings for narratives of mystery and terror. In Paul Leni's 1927 film *The Cat and the Canary*, for example, hapless guests endure the night in a brooding mansion, where, in one reviewer's words, "ghosts, greed, a house with secret doors, a maniac, a murder, jewels and a slight love story winding thru [*sic*] the whole are the ingredients of the plot."[33] Mystery novels also soared in popularity, one subgenre featuring titles such as *House of Mystery, House of Horror, House of Death,* and *House of Doom.* And on the extreme literary edge, the pulp magazine *Weird Tales* served up Lovecraft's horror stories set in Marblehead (fictionalized as "Kingsport"), Salem, Boston, Providence, and other decaying New England towns where the old, dark houses contained dreadful secrets.[34] Little wonder, perhaps, that Kantor's *Haunted House* fascinated viewers in 1932: they came preconditioned to appreciate it as an eerie period piece hinting of sinister deeds in a dark American past that could still be sensed, hauntingly, in the present.

In 1930s America, artists tended to dwell on their *own* lives past and present, too. That subject was on Helen Lundeberg's mind in 1935, when she created *Double Portrait of the Artist in Time* (fig. 6). Born in Chicago, Lundeberg at age four had moved with her family to Pasadena, California. As an adult in Los Angeles, she became (with Lorser Feitelson) a founding member of the Post-Surrealist group.[35] Lundeberg was to a large degree insulated from the turmoil and anxiety of the Depression that affected so many painters farther east. Yet her pictorial strategy of incorporating time's passage into a self-portrait suggests how some artists of that troubled era

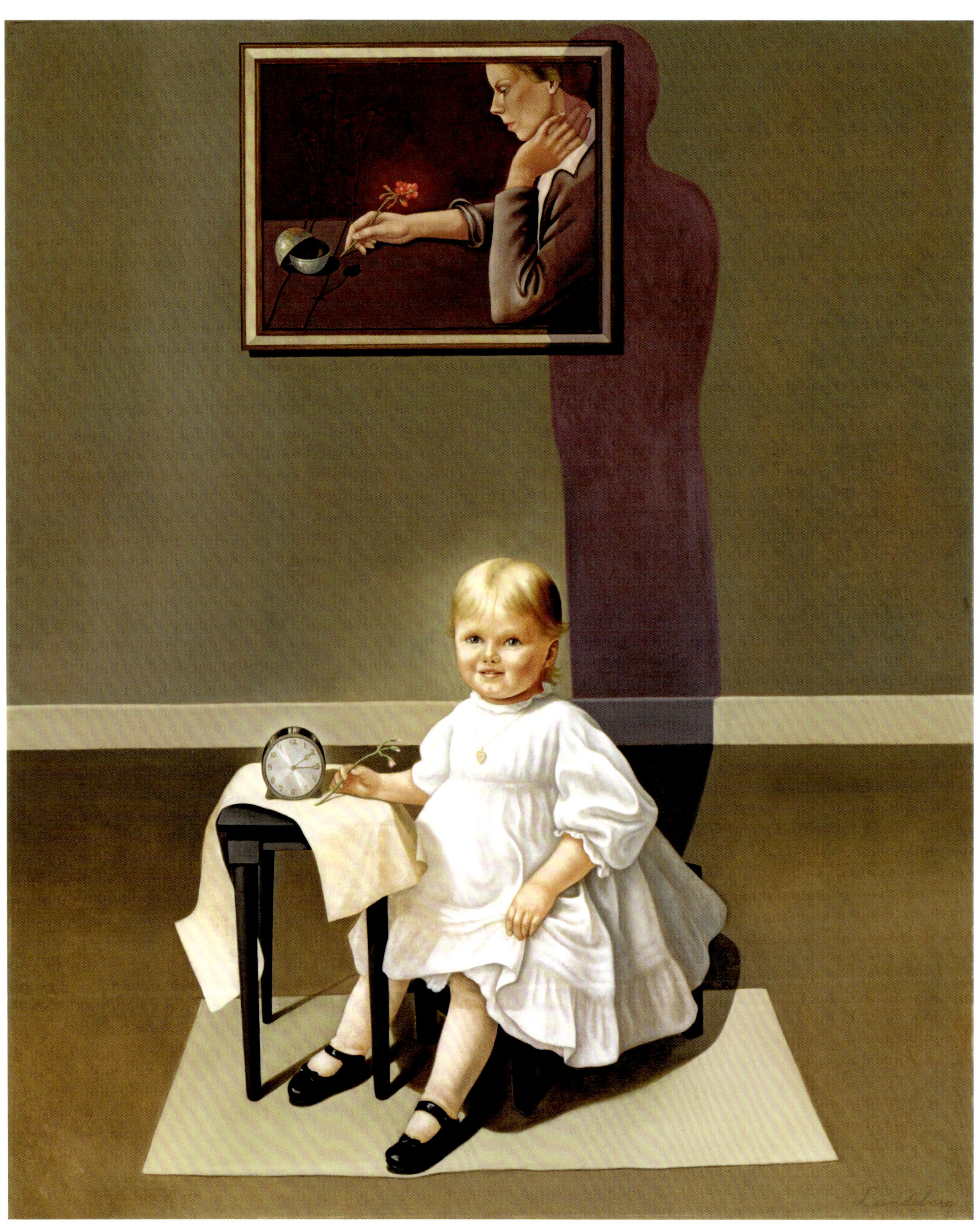

conceived of themselves (like old houses, perhaps) as beings subject to the changes and ravages of time.

Crisp and clear, Lundeberg's realist style belies the surreality, indeed the impossibility, of her subject. Surrealism became widely known in the United States only in 1936, when Alfred Barr mounted the exhibition *Fantastic Art, Dada, Surrealism* at the Museum of Modern Art. Many American artists had already encountered Surrealism in Europe in the 1920s, and as early as 1931, the Wadsworth Athenaeum in Hartford, Connecticut, showed Surrealist work. In America, however, Surrealism—irrational and libidinous—shifted shape as artists retooled it either to serve as a vehicle for social and political critique or, as in Lundeberg's case, to encourage rational meditation on cosmic themes such as love, genesis, and eternity.[36]

In *Double Portrait* the artist represented herself simultaneously as child and as grown woman. The little girl casts a shadow, which, as the artist explained, is that of the adult—herself—who appears in the portrait on the wall. Paradoxically, the child of the past, based on a photograph, is physically present, while the here-and-now Lundeberg appears only in two dimensions. The room is otherwise bare, its dim greenish floor and wall interrupted only by a line of white baseboard. Holding a sprig of pink buds, the child sits at a low table with a blank sheet of paper anchored by an alarm clock. The time, two fifteen, corresponds to Lundeberg's age when the photograph was taken (two years, three months). In the painting on the wall, the artist, in profile, holds the now blooming sprig like a pencil as if about to begin drawing. On the table before her sits a miniature globe of the Earth, hemispheres cracked apart like two bowls.[37]

On the surface, the symbolism seems transparent. The virginal buds have flowered into maturity; the blank page has become the artist's sketchpad, and the globe the wider (or wide open) world into which she has moved. But there are darker dimensions. Lundeberg told an interviewer that her early memories of Chicago were of interiors, "all very closed in" because the outside world was so dangerous. "At that time in Chicago, there'd been a lot of kidnappings, and people with small children were terrified that their children would be snatched

away if they weren't kept under close supervision," she said in an interview. Aggravating the worry was her mother's fragile health. In Chicago, with its "fierce climate," there were "black fogs, fogs cum coal dust, coal smoke" that gave rise to attacks of terrible bronchitis every winter.[38] The move to Pasadena was thus a deliverance into healthful sunlight and open air. But in life, and in the *Double Portrait*, time did not stop, and youth was finite. The toddler is sunny and bright, the mature Lundeberg faded and drab. Confined to a tight space, she contemplates the world before her, reduced to an empty box. What haunts *Double Portrait* is the future, which will, sooner or later, come to an end.

Walt Kuhn was pondering that same nebulous future when he created *Portrait of the Artist as a Clown (Kansas)* in 1932 (fig. 7). The actual model for the painting was Ralph Osgood, a real circus clown, and during Kuhn's lifetime, it bore the title *Kansas*, referring to the notion that circus clowns hailed from that part of the country.[39] The artist stipulated that after his own death, the painting was to be retitled as a self-portrait. And indeed, whatever the original Ralph Osgood looked like, the glowering face is clearly that of the artist himself, as photographs attest (see fig. 8). A native New Yorker, Kuhn played a major role in organizing the 1913 Armory Show and spent the next decade and more trying to hit his artistic stride. For several years, he made ends meet by writing, designing, and directing revues and circus skits, thus becoming a true insider and aficionado of the circus world.

Curator Lloyd Goodrich celebrated the circus as an antidote to the drab solemnity of modern life. "Against all these humorless and anti-artistic tendencies," he wrote, "the circus clown, with his insanely painted face and his grotesque costume stands as a living denial of the commonplace values of everyday life."[40] But Kuhn's *Portrait of the Artist* is nothing if not humorless. The artist represented himself (or Osgood) in the guise of Pierrot, the sad clown of the commedia dell'arte, widely appropriated in the nineteenth and early twentieth centuries as a signifier of the artist's alienation from bourgeois life.[41] Kuhn's clown wears Pierrot's conical hat, ballooning white jacket, and white face paint. Staring out at us with hard

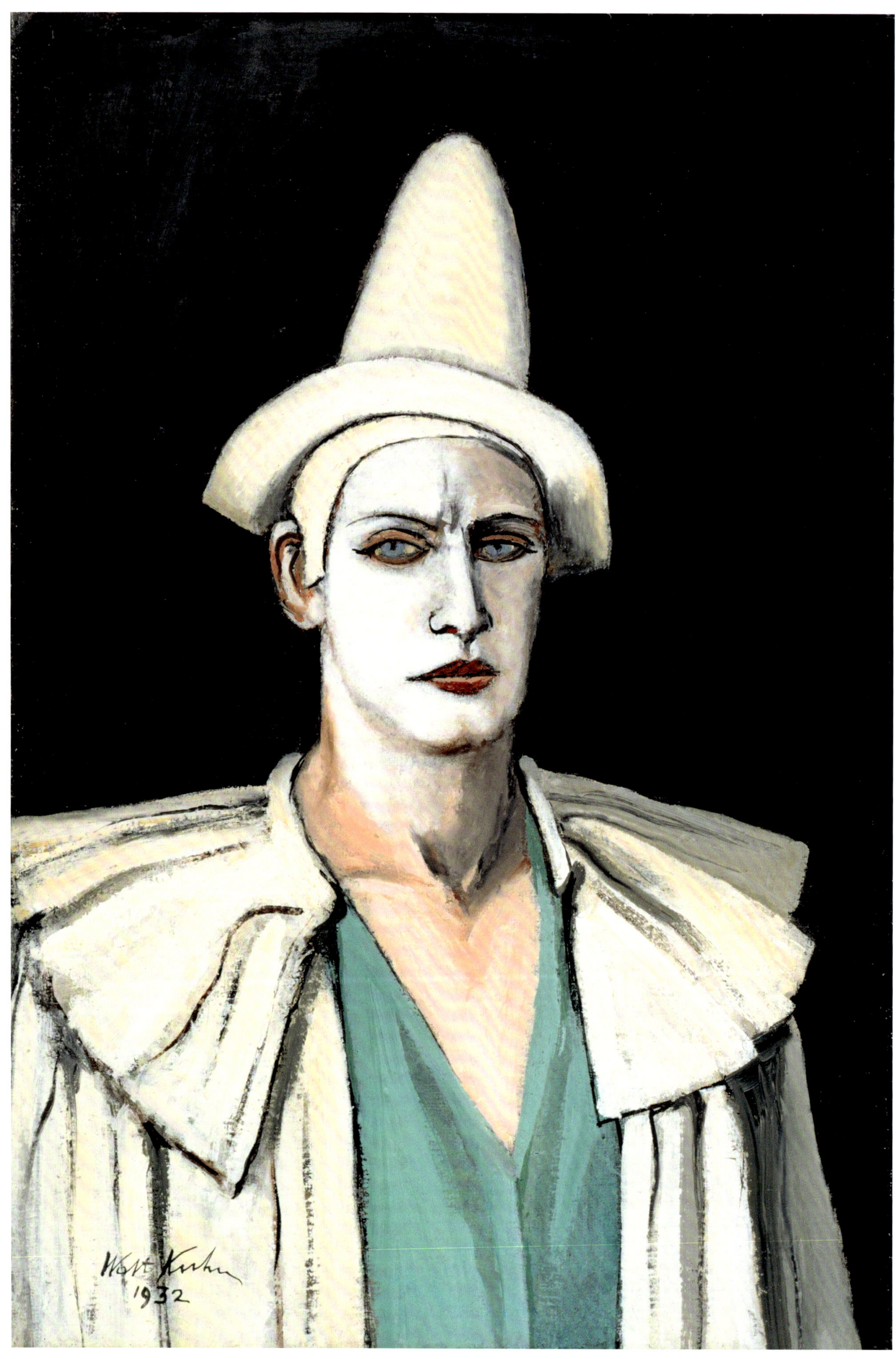

**Fig. 7** Walt Kuhn. *Portrait of the Artist as a Clown (Kansas)*, 1932. Collection of Barney A. Ebsworth. Cat. 29.

**Fig. 8** Walt Kuhn, c. 1948. Labeled "Last photo made Oct. 1948." Walt Kuhn, Kuhn Family Papers, and Armory Show Records, Archives of American Art, Smithsonian Institution, Washington, DC.

blue eyes and a forbidding scowl, he is more of a mad clown than a sad one.

Fifty-five when he painted this work, Kuhn had spent a great deal more than half his life in search of a uniquely individual style. With three successful shows at New York's Harriman Gallery in 1932 alone, he was at last on the rise as an artist known for his monumental renderings of melancholy showgirls and solemn circus performers. The Depression had not affected him deeply. Nonetheless, he was a troubled man, aloof, contrary, and pathologically private. Frosty and fierce, he is emphatically the artist-clown as Other in the self-portrait. At the same time, his plunging V-neck revealing the border between white paint and bare skin hints of a certain vulnerability. Perhaps Kuhn was already feeling signs of the emotional instability that would eventually relegate him to a mental hospital the year before his death in 1949.[42] Whatever the case, in 1932, death was already on his mind, his white clown a ghost in waiting.

Death was also, and always, on the mind of Chicago's Ivan Albright. He aged himself by decades in his self-portraits, notably the one commissioned in 1935 by Chicago ad man Earle Ludgin (fig. 9).[43] In it, Albright, thirty-eight at the time, could easily be taken for ninety. Dressed in a dinner jacket, the artist sits in an ornate Victorian chair and lifts a wineglass in one puffy hand while putting the other to his sagging cheek as if lost in thought. Before him on a turbulently rumpled tablecloth is an array of objects: a red glass ashtray and goblet, a cigarette box with a mirrored top, a cut-glass vase containing a bouquet of pansies, a halved lime, a wine decanter, and, finally, another wineglass at bottom right. Everything is rendered in painstaking detail, culminating in the decanter's stopper, in which we see the artist's tiny, inverted reflection. Despite spots of bright color, the predominantly sooty tonality casts a dingy pall over the scene. The face under its thatch of wild gray hair maps the ravages of age with excruciating precision: the discolored skin with its livid patches and reddish eruptions, the hairy ears and wiry brows, the sunken eyes, blank and bleary. It is a death's head in the making.

Son of a painter who had studied under the renowned Philadelphia realist Thomas Eakins, Albright during World

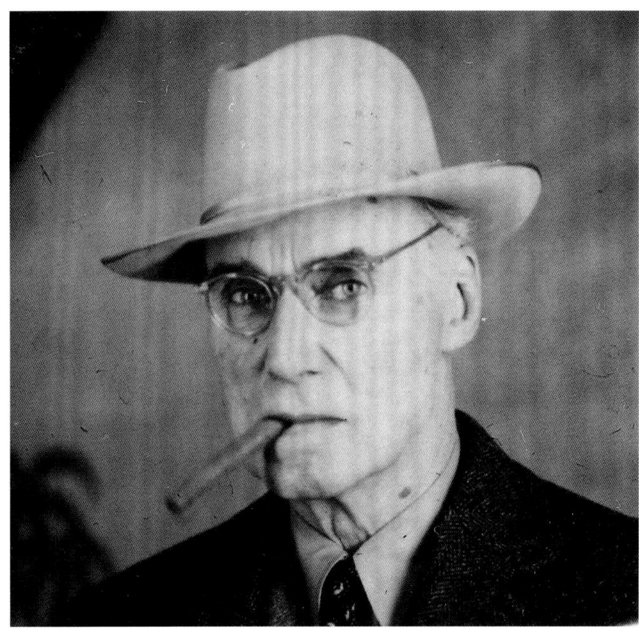

War I served as a medical draftsman at the American field hospital in Nantes, France. In the course of duty, he filled eight sketchbooks with detailed drawings of bloody limbs, shattered bones, and ghastly disfigurements. Reluctant, perhaps, to reveal how deeply these sights affected him, he later denied that they had any impact upon his art. Still, his war experience made an indelible impression, leading, directly or indirectly, to the artist's conviction that "the body is our tomb."[44] After the war, Albright set about developing a dark vision of bodies that seemed to be in the advanced stages of decay and putrescence (see fig. 10). At once disgusting and enthralling, his paintings, as one critic put it, fell into "the same category as Poe's tales of horror." As with Poe, there was a "frightful fascination" about Albright's art that compelled beholders return to the "scene of the torture," no matter how gruesome. His flesh was "the color of a corpse drowned six weeks"; his figures were like cadavers just dug up from "newly opened graves." While some sensed a deep sympathy in the artist's vision of sagging and vulnerable bodies, most surrendered themselves to the shuddery pleasures of revulsion at the spectacle of rotting flesh.[45]

Critics used strikingly similar terms when writing about horror movies, notably *Frankenstein*. Played by Boris Karloff,

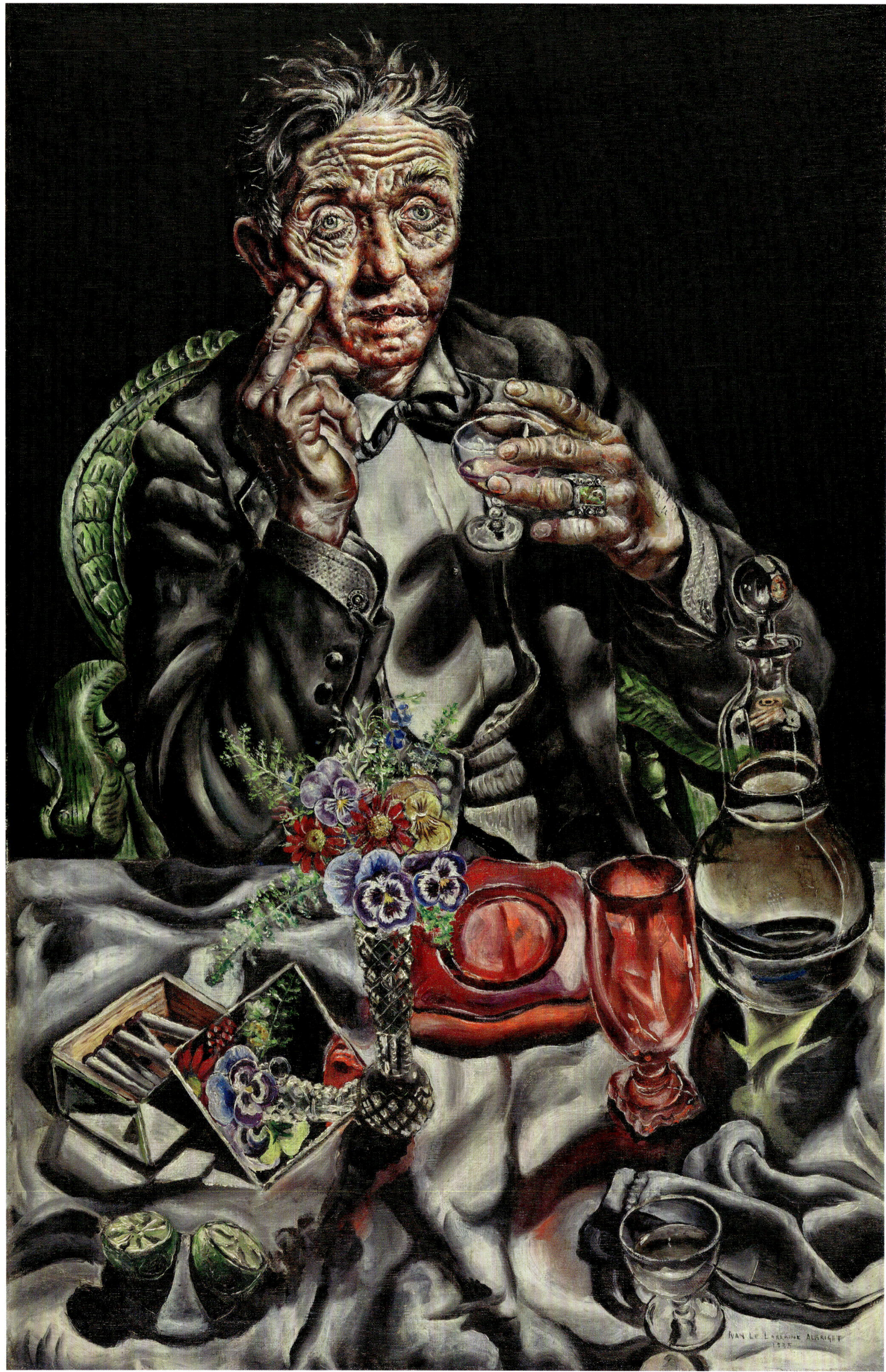

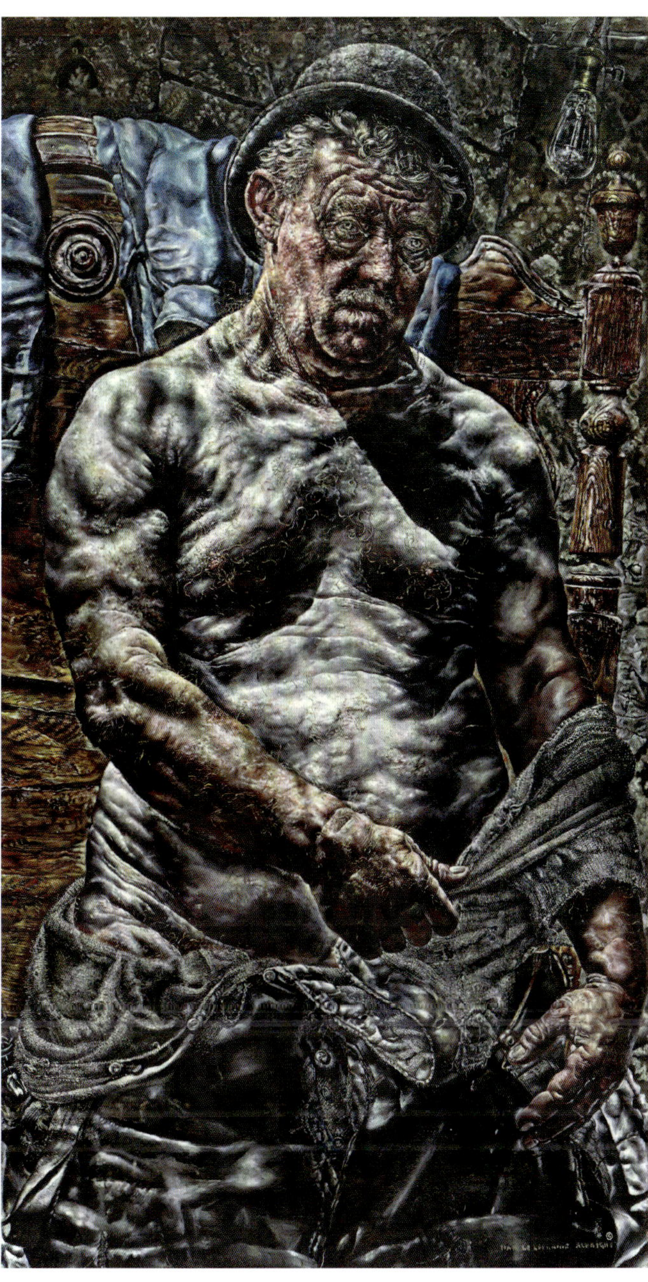

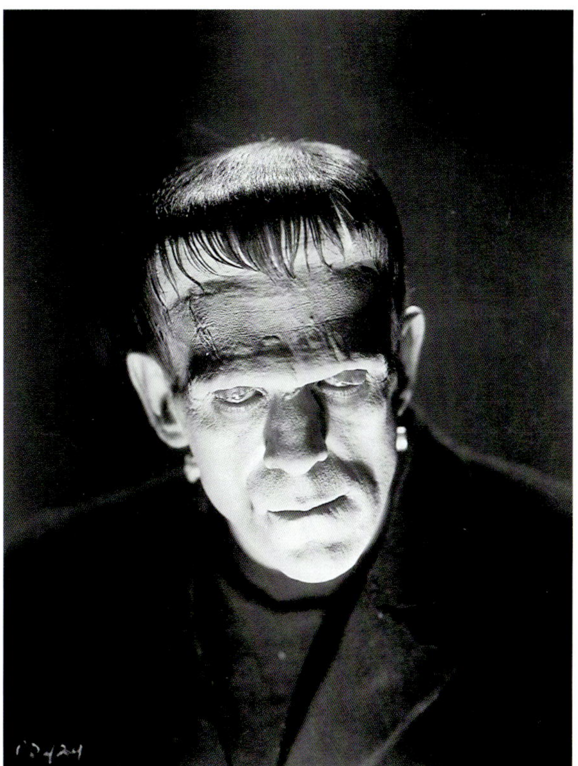

the monster—Dr. Frankenstein's Creature, assembled piece-meal out of cold, dead flesh dug from the graveyard—wore elaborate makeup devised by Jack Pierce, who had picked up his ideas from books on cranial surgery and "a picture he had seen of a Mexican buried alive," the drooping eyelids giving the dead face a "weird expression." By applying putty to Karloff's eyelids, Pierce achieved just the right cadaverous look (see fig. 11). For the flesh, he sprayed on a gray-blue compound that photographed "like the pallor of a corpse."[46] Thus incarnated, Frankenstein's monster was a "terrible, terrible THING," repel-lent yet all the more "grimly fascinating" because of its effect: it enabled viewers to stand safely (and therapeutically) on one side of the boundary separating living and dead, bodily integrity and decay.[47]

Aggressive publicity made *Frankenstein* a household word long before its release, and early on, critics began to see Albright's paintings through horror-movie lenses. Wrote one, "His works have a power of a sort—even though it be the power, as we believe, of . . . a Frankenstein monster." Another warned that if Albright inspired a school of painters like himself, "the ground would tremble . . . and all opposition seek shel-ter. His art has the Gargantuan roll of a Frankenstein."[48] Like Frankenstein's creation, Albright's bodies in decay were ter-rible things that nonetheless had a powerful allure. Importing the spirit of the horror movie into the gallery, his art offered

**Fig. 12**  O. Louis Guglielmi. *Phoenix*, 1935. Sheldon Museum of Art, University of Nebraska-Lincoln, NAA-Nelle Cochrane Woods Memorial. Cat. 17.

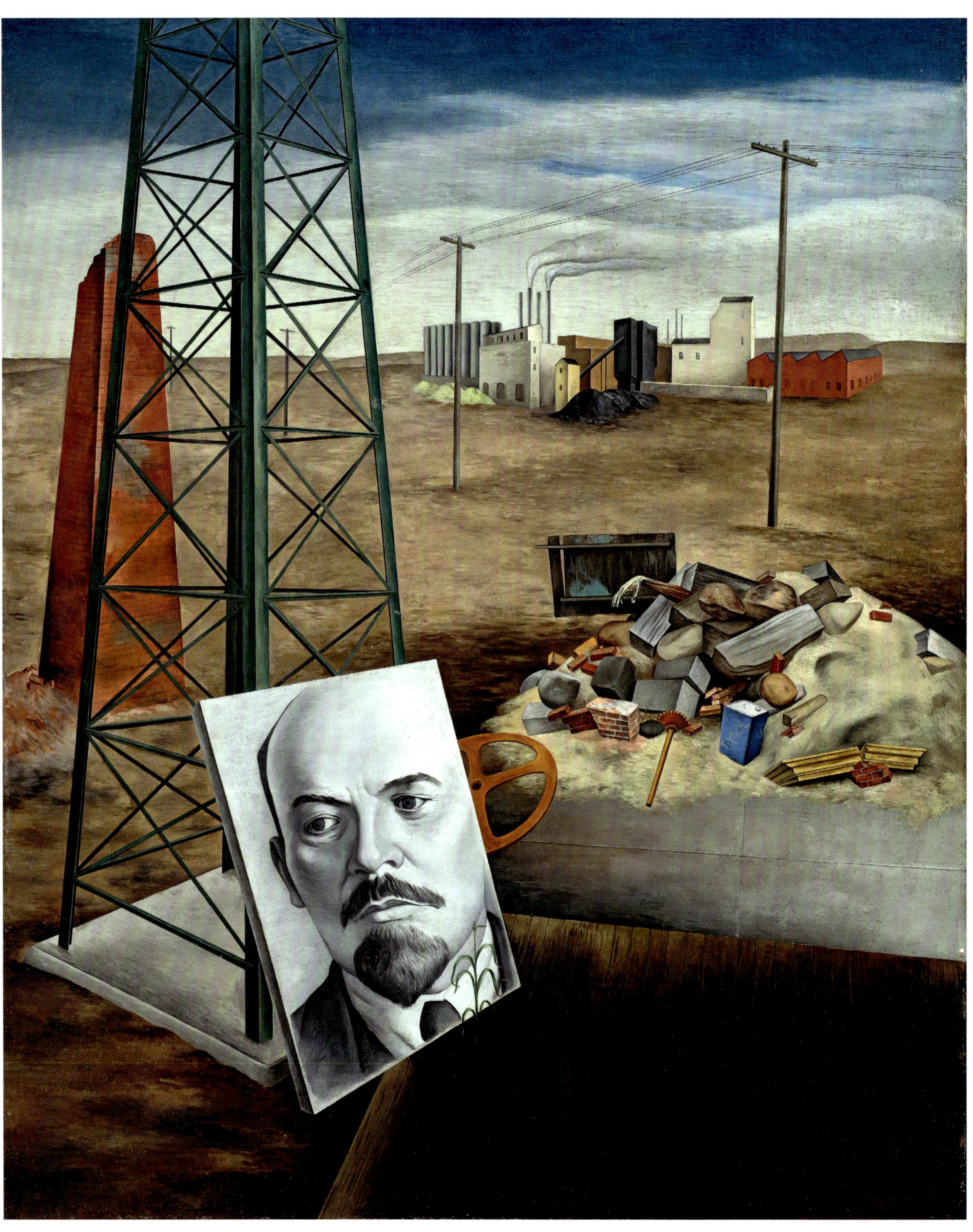

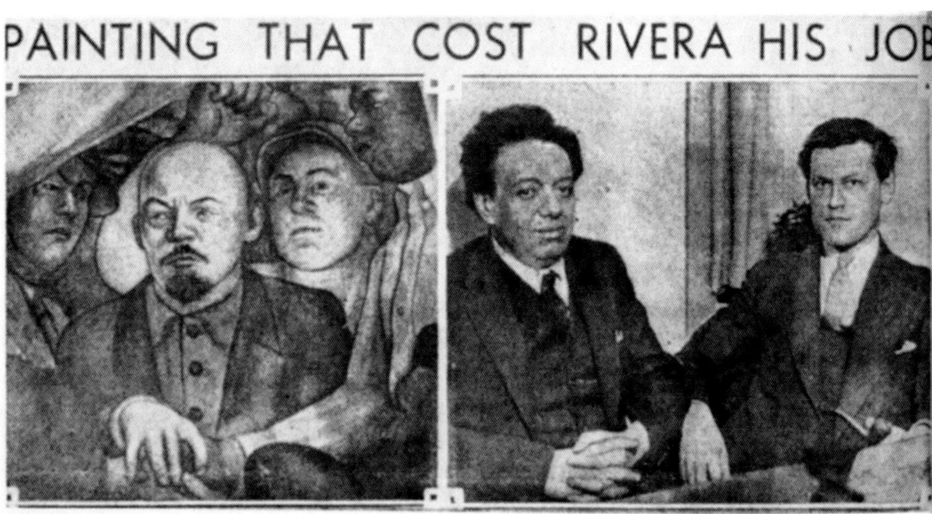


viewers the same delicious shudders and pleasurable revulsion. The 1935 self-portrait might well be entitled *Portrait of the Artist as Monster.* At one level, of course, the work functions symbolically as a traditional vanitas, the wine, cigarettes, and flowers signifying the transient pleasures of the flesh. In its implicit alignment with modern horror, though, it is very much a product of its time.

There were real monsters, however, far more threatening than anything in the make-believe world. In 1922 Fascist dictator Benito Mussolini had risen to power in Italy; in 1933, Adolf Hitler became chancellor of Nazi Germany, now militarized and poised to invade, conquer, and crush surrounding nations. So grave was the danger that in 1935 the Comintern, or Communist International, called for a Popular Front uniting all Communist parties to fight the spread of Fascism worldwide. New York's John Reed Club stood prepared. Established in 1929, the group had vowed to defend the Soviet Union and join the struggle against imperialist war and Fascism. The club's 1932 manifesto drafted art to its cause, calling for a "new art that would be a weapon in the battle for a new and superior world."[49]

O. Louis Guglielmi heeded that call. In 1935 he exhibited *Phoenix* (1935; fig. 12) at the John Reed Club and other left-wing venues. A radical Italian-American "Proletarian Surrealist" dedicated to social justice, Guglielmi developed a hyperrealistic style laced with Surrealist incongruity, because,

he argued, Surrealism expressed "our decaying society."[50] In *Phoenix*, an outsized portrait of Vladimir Lenin propped against an oil derrick dominates the foreground. All about is desolation: a truncated industrial chimney, a heap of construction rubble, and tall telegraph poles punctuating an expanse of brown desert. On the horizon huddle smoke-belching factories flanked by a mountain of coal. The only trace of human presence is a flayed hand protruding from the rubble. Still, there is a sign of life: before Lenin, a spindly stalk of corn has taken root.

*Phoenix* was topical and timely. The image of Lenin refers to the strikingly similar portrait in Diego Rivera's controversial Rockefeller Center mural, *Man at the Crossroads* (1933), which was destroyed on the night of February 10, 1934, after Rivera refused to follow patron Nelson Rockefeller's order to expunge the offending likeness of the revolutionary leader. The defiant Rivera announced that he would leave his case in the hands of the American masses: "They will yet take over industry and public buildings," he predicted, "and guarantee the productive development of man's creative powers." Of the mural, only black-and-white photographs remained (see fig. 13). It was common knowledge that the Rockefellers had amassed their huge fortune in the oil business. How appropriate, then, that in *Phoenix*, Guglielmi juxtaposed the black-and-white portrait of Lenin with an oil derrick. The "phoenix" is Lenin, his image and ideology destined to rise again, just as the corn has sprouted from the wasteland of capitalism.[51]

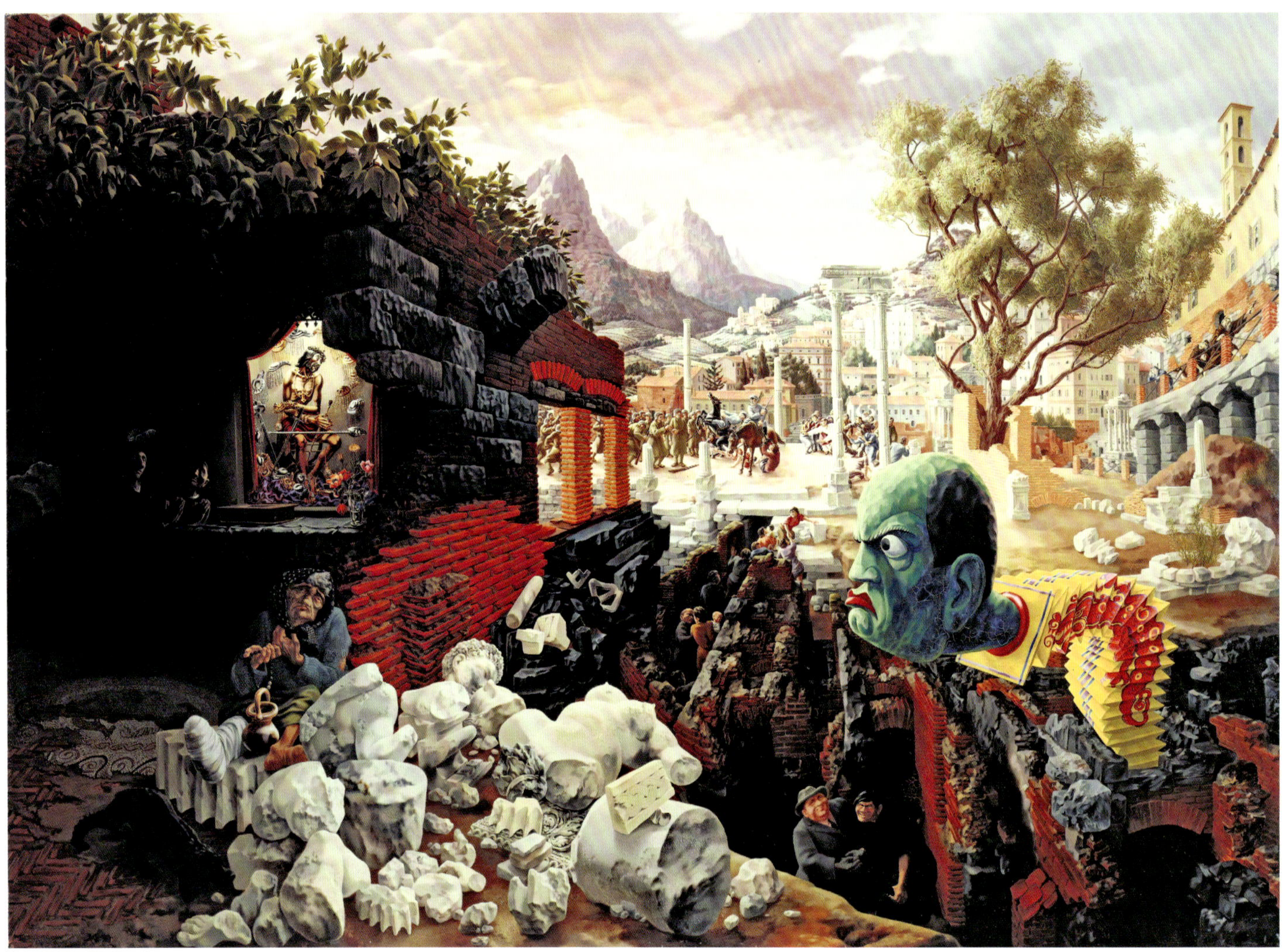

Equally topical was Peter Blume's *Eternal City* (1934–37; fig. 14). Blume was born in Russia and at age six immigrated to the United States with his family; he grew up in Brooklyn and trained at the Art Students League. A Guggenheim Fellowship enabled him to travel around Italy in 1932–33. In Rome one winter afternoon, he visited the Forum and was "moved by a strange light illuminating the ruins." That feeling inspired what became in the end a complex surrealistic allegory. The painting took three years to complete and incited fierce controversy on its exhibition at New York's Julien Levy Gallery in 1937. The setting, a composite of the Forum, the Coliseum, and the Catacombs, is dreamlike. But the enormous, green jack-in-the-box head of Mussolini springing from the rubble is the nexus of a nightmare that unfolds, detail by detail, across the scene. In the depths below the glowering effigy are the dictator's partners in crime: a beaming capitalist and a grinning Blackshirt thug. Fragments of antique sculpture and bits of architectural ornament lie in the foreground. At the far edge of the detritus sits a raddled beggar, bandaged foot propped upon a chunk of fluted column. Directly above is a brilliantly lit shrine, where an emaciated Christ—Mussolini's antithesis—is awash in worldly offerings: swords, epaulets, and jewels. Farther back, bold civilians stream out of the murky catacombs to taunt the Fascist troops in the bright Forum, while women on hands and knees struggle against sword-waving mounted officers. To the right, terrified monks flee along a balcony, leaving behind a female tourist who avidly takes in the violent commotion. The background is incongruously serene, its cultivated fields and sun-bleached hill town dwarfed by towering mountains that close off the view.[52]

Blume based his caricature of Mussolini on a colossal papier-mâché effigy he had seen at the Decennial Exposition celebrating the tenth anniversary of the 1922 Fascist March on Rome. The colors were intrinsic to the meaning: "I made the red lips clash with the green of the head," he explained. The combination had to be "strident and like nothing else in the picture: antithesis, dissonance." No compromise was possible.[53] More than anything else in the painting, it was the lurid head—and its explicitly anti-Fascist polemics—that sparked critical uproar and led to the exclusion of the work from the 1939 Corcoran Biennial in Washington, DC.[54] The rejection spurred a number of artists, critics, and organizations to fire off a telegram in protest. The museum's refusal to hang Blume's picture, they maintained, was "so dangerously akin to the treatment of art in Fascist countries as to be fraught with grave implications . . . to all American people."[55] If such an important work of art could be subject to censorship, how long before other liberties came under threat? *The Eternal City* does not warn explicitly of Fascism as a force with the potential to destroy the American republic. Still, it seems to have struck a nerve close to home.

While Blume was working on *The Eternal City*, Sinclair Lewis's *It Can't Happen Here* (1935) became a bestseller. The novel opens with the 1936 defeat of President Franklin Roosevelt by Senator Buzz Windrip. Once in power, President Windrip establishes a dictatorship, abolishes civil liberties, consigns dissidents to concentration camps, and spreads terror with a band of armed thugs. Before the fateful election, journalist Jessup Doremus predicts what will happen if Windrip wins. "People will think they're electing him to create more economic security. Then watch the Terror! God knows there's been enough indication that we *can* have tyranny in America—the fix of the southern share-croppers, the working conditions of the miners and garment-makers, and our keeping

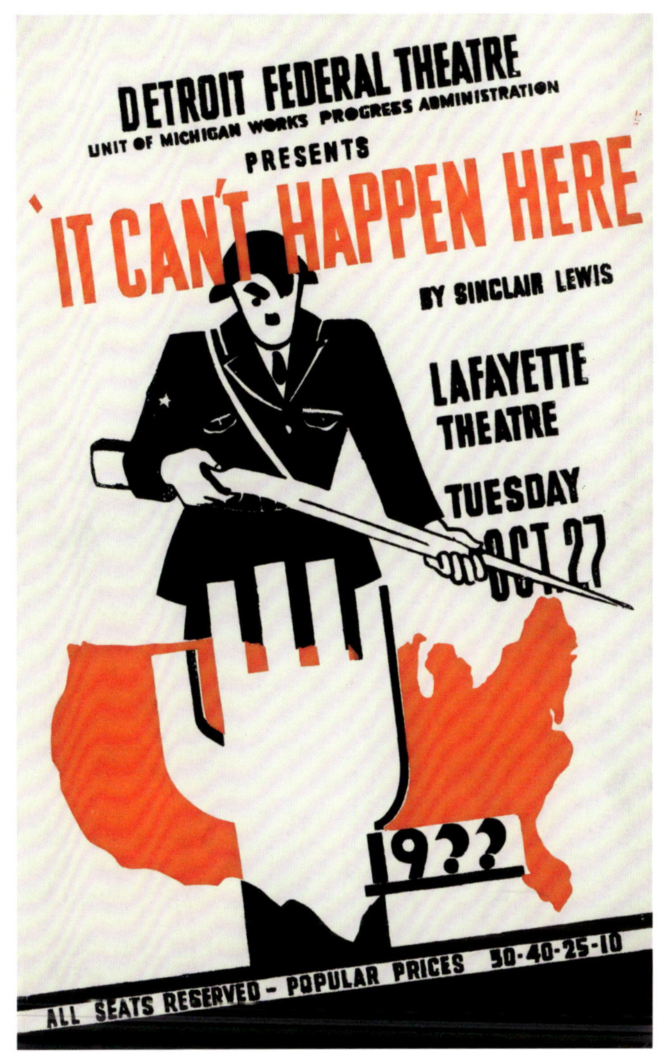


**Fig. 15** *Detroit Federal Theatre Unit of Michigan Works Progress Administration Presents "It Can't Happen Here" by Sinclair Lewis,* 1936/37. Poster, silkscreen print on board; 35.5 × 55.8 cm (14 × 22 in.). Library of Congress Prints and Photographs Division, Washington, DC.

Mooney [a labor leader] in prison so many years. But wait till Windrip shows us how to say it with machine guns! . . . Wait till Buzz takes charge of us. A real Fascist dictatorship!" Someone blusters, "Nonsense! . . . That couldn't happen here in America, not possibly! We're a country of freemen." But it can, and does, happen. By the end, the country is chaos, torn by murderous power struggles, riots, rebellions, and, finally, civil war.[56]

Lewis adapted the novel for the stage in 1936, and the production opened simultaneously at twenty-one Federal Theaters. Over the course of a 260-week run, it reached half a million people nationwide.[57] A boldly designed poster (fig. 15) for the Detroit production depicts a uniformed figure armed

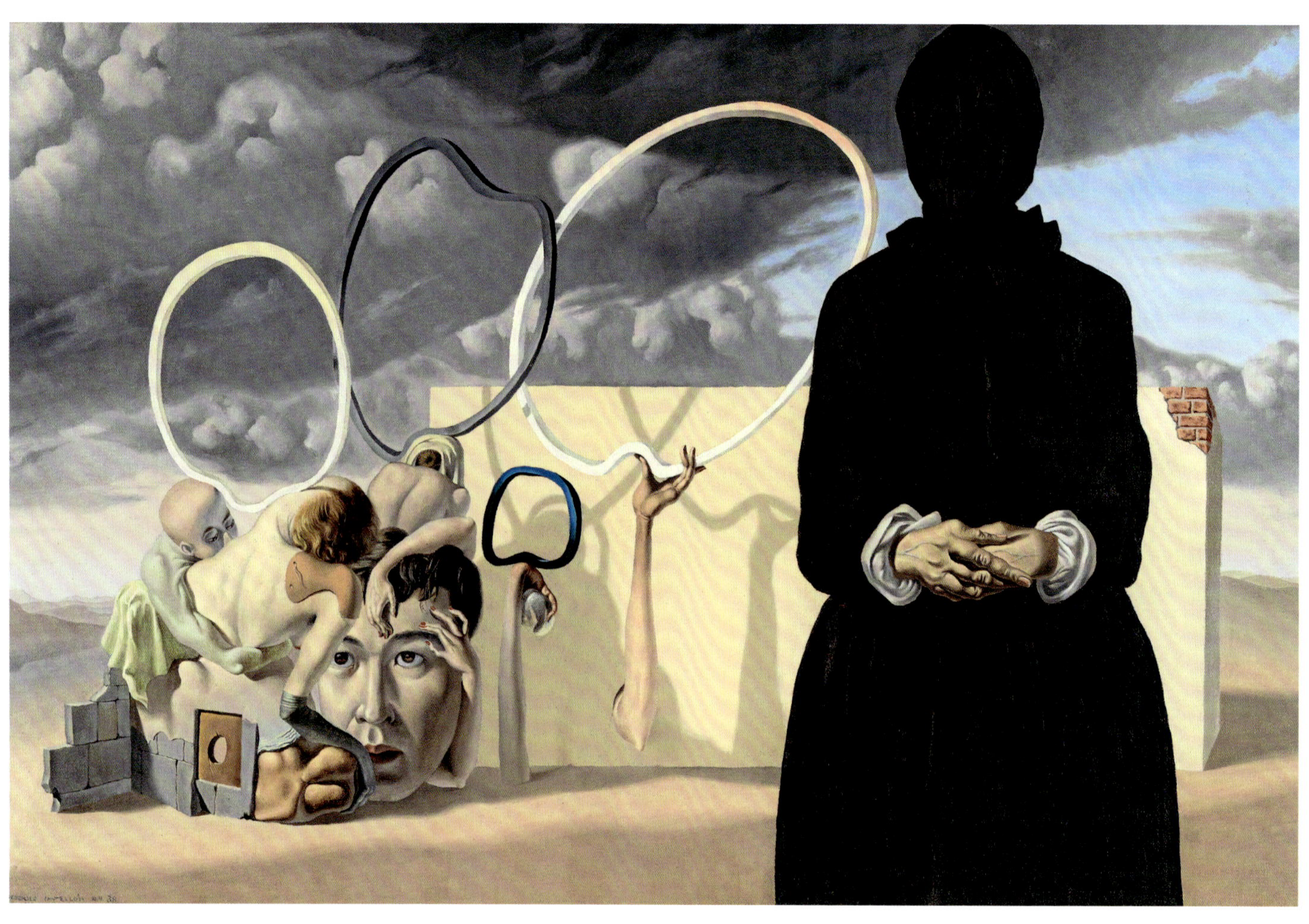

with a bayonetted rifle and towering over a map of the United States. The scowl and the black dab of moustache immediately call Adolf Hitler to mind. In the foreground is a hand, raised as if to push the menacing figure away. However, the date—"19??"—insinuates that Fascism will come to America. It is merely a question of when.

Other events soon reinforced Lewis's dystopian predictions. By the middle of the 1930s, it seemed more and more likely that war in Europe was inevitable. In February 1937, the American Artists' Congress against War and Fascism held its inaugural meeting. Opening the conference, the historian Lewis Mumford warned of a coming "world catastrophe" and urged listeners to oppose war and Fascism by whatever means necessary. Subsequent speakers, artists and critics alike, followed suit.[58] How long would it be before some monstrous dictator's head loomed on the American horizon?

In July 1937, the outbreak of the Spanish Civil War seemed like one more step toward Mumford's world catastrophe. Almost immediately, it refocused the attention, and fears, of radical American artists. *The Dark Figure* (1938; fig. 16) by Federico Castellón evokes both the dread of encroaching civil war and the artist's own hair's-breadth escape from it. Born in Spain, Castellón came with his family to Brooklyn when he was seven years old. Diego Rivera inspired him to become a painter, and with Rivera's help, Castellón won a fellowship from the Spanish Republican government. In 1934 he spent four months in his native country and then moved on to Paris, where Surrealism, in particular the work of Salvador Dalí, made a strong impact on his style. But in 1936, he fled back to New York, having narrowly eluded the Spanish draft.[59]

In *The Dark Figure*, Castellón portrayed himself as a disembodied head against a crumbling wall in a Dalíesque desert landscape. Mysterious human shapes and hands caress the head while holding aloft four rubbery hoops. On the other side stands an enigmatic female form, masked and shrouded in deepest brown save for stark white cuffs framing her clasped hands. It is impossible to tell whether *The Dark Figure* is personal, or political, or both. Whatever the case, the ominous apparition was a harbinger of terrible things to come.

One of those terrible things happened on April 26, 1937, when a coordinated bombing raid by allied German and Italian forces destroyed the Basque town of Guernica. The next day, the *New York Times* ran an eyewitness report, which described how the planes had "slowly and systematically" pounded the town to pieces, leaving nearly every structure reduced to glowing heaps of embers and trapping victims under burning wreckage. So horrendous was the abomination that both houses of Congress condemned it, Senator William Borah of Idaho decrying the savagery of the Fascist airplanes "like winged monsters," swooping down to slaughter innocent children and leave the streets "covered with charred bodies."[60]

Philip Guston created *Bombardment* (1937; fig. 17) directly in response to the atrocity.[61] Born in Montreal to Ukrainian Jewish parents and raised in Los Angeles, the largely self-taught Guston was committed to radical causes. Before moving to New York in 1935, he had been in Morelia, Mexico, where, in collaboration with Reuben Kadish, he painted *The Struggle against Terrorism* (1934–35), a monumental anti-Fascist mural. He was thus primed to attack the latest Fascist outrage. Using a Renaissance tondo format, Guston depicted the moment of impact as a bomb explodes dead center, its concussive force hurling bodies—men, women, children—in every direction. On the right, a weirdly elongated figure in a death's-head gas mask hurtles outward into our space. Beyond is a street bestrewn with the dead and dying, and in the somber sky an endless cavalcade of bombers rains death upon the stricken city. Exhibited first at a show mounted by the League Against War and Fascism and later at the Whitney Annual in late 1938, *Bombardment* also appeared as a full-page reproduction in the mass-market pictorial magazine *Look*.[62] No art museum could contain the horrors of Guernica.

Nor could such horror be confined to the far side of the ocean. That was Guglielmi's message in *Mental Geography* (1938; fig. 18), a fantasy of the Brooklyn Bridge in ruins after an air raid. In so-called "program notes" composed for its first exhibition at the Downtown Gallery in 1938, the artist made his meaning clear. "Headliners, eloquent loudspeakers of fascist destruction scream out the bombing of another

Fig. 17  Philip Guston. *Bombardment*, 1937. Philadelphia Museum of
Art. Cat. 19.

Fig. 18  O. Louis Guglielmi. *Mental Geography*, 1938. Collection of
Barney A. Ebsworth. Cat. 18.

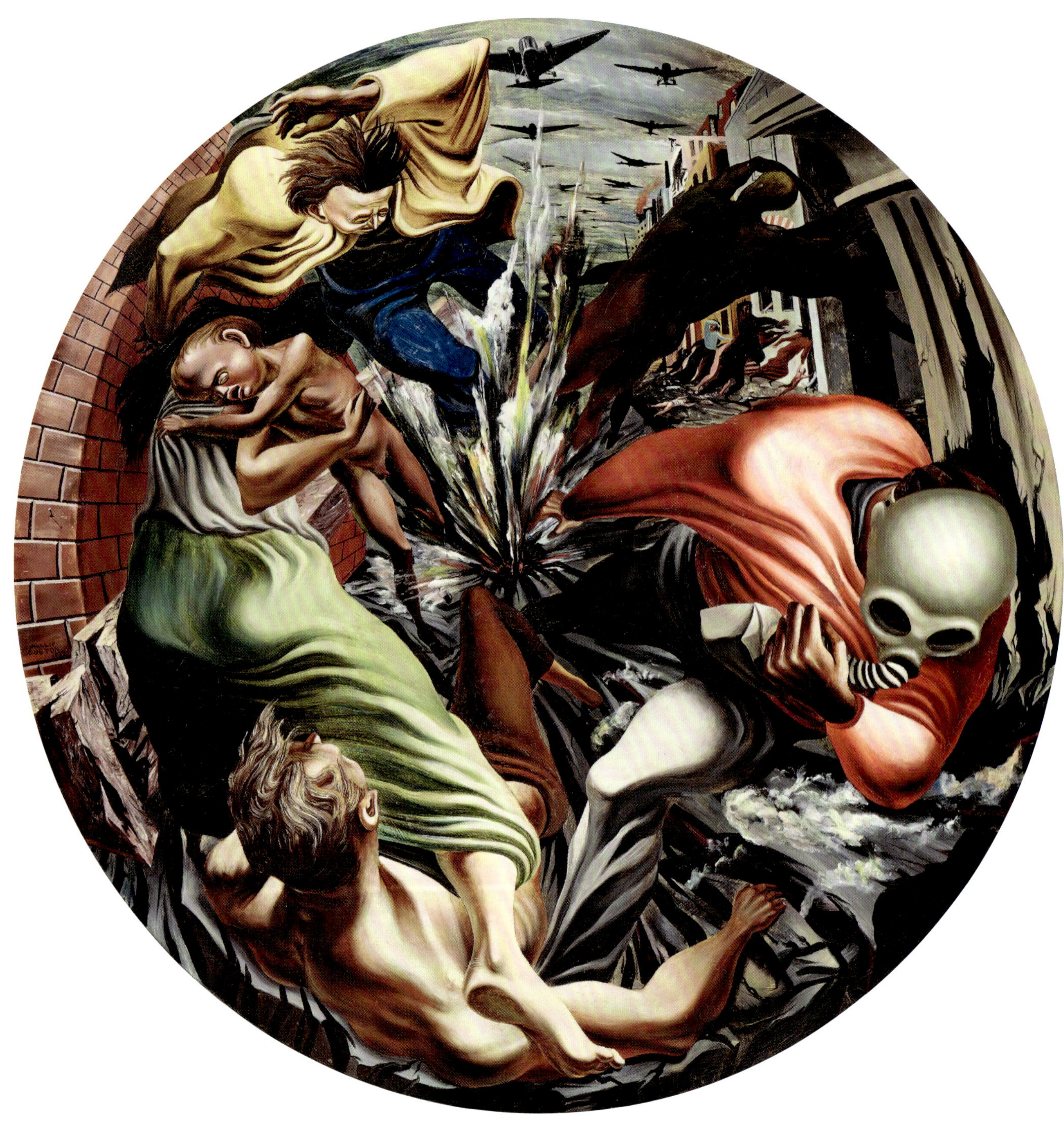

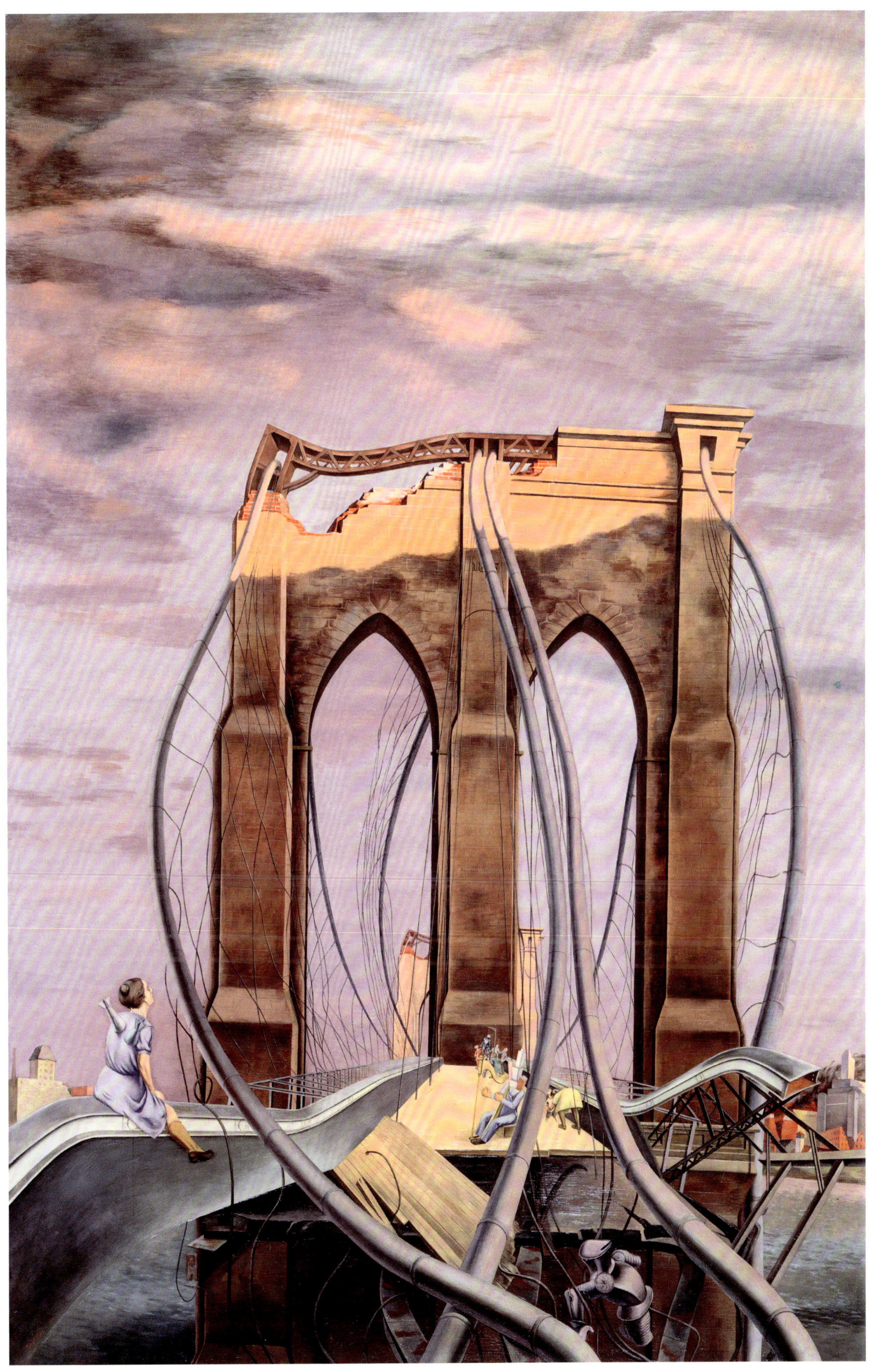

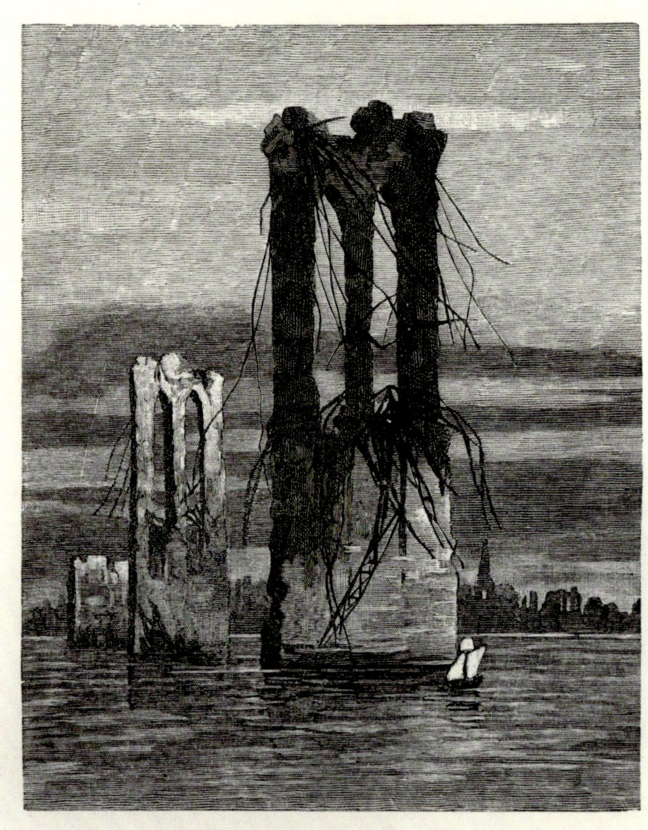

**Fig. 19** John Ames Mitchell (American, 1845–1918). *The Two Monuments in the River*. From *The Last American* (Frederick A. Stokes, 1889), p. 37. The Newberry Library, Chicago, IL.

only two lofty towers left standing, cables trailing like seaweed over the murky waters (see fig. 19). By 1937, however, the prospect of its destruction was all too believable. Only months before *Mental Geography* went on view, the *Saturday Evening Post* published Stephen Vincent Benét's story "The Place of the Gods," directly inspired by the catastrophe in Guernica. The setting is New York in the distant future, long after the fall of industrial civilization. In Benét's tale, a young man sets forth on a spiritual quest to find the fabled—and forbidden—city where dwell the mysterious gods. After a long journey, he arrives at a great river and sees that "once there had been god-roads across it, though now they were broken and fallen like broken vines. Very great they were, and wonderful and broken—broken in the time of the Great Burning when the fire fell out of the sky." Compelled against all better judgment to cross over, the youth builds a raft. As he draws nearer the Place of the Gods, huge ruins rise before his eyes.[65]

Guglielmi's *Mental Geography* envisions that "great burning" in the immediate present or near future. The bridge is falling down, towers crumbling, roadway collapsing, cables snaking free just as in the earlier illustration. A woman in a housedress straddles a beam on the left, two bombs protruding from her back like stubby wings. On what remains of the deck sits a harpist, shoulders supporting a cluster of jazzy skyscrapers in place of a head. Another woman bends over to tend a child, and at the opposite end, people dance around a gallows, from which hangs a figure in a full suit of medieval armor. A second armored figure dangles precariously from the loose cables at bottom right. Cartoonists of the 1930s used the suit of armor to symbolize Fascism, as in Mabel Dwight's lithograph *Danse Macabre* (c. 1934; fig. 20), representing world powers as grotesque puppets on stage. Hitler is among them in just such a shiny metallic shell, clutching a Jew's decapitated head; Mussolini stands by his side in modern military uniform. Watching them is Death in helmet and gas mask, one skeletal hand clutching a sword.[66] But in *Mental Geography*, some semblance of life goes on. Is there hope of averting the apocalypse? Or are these people merely playing—or plucking—while New York burns?

city. . . . A hundred dead, a thousand violated bodies. Valencia, Madrid, Barcelona, Guernica. Yesterday Toledo, the Prado—Tomorrow, Chartres—New York: Brooklyn Bridge is by process of mental geography a huge mass of stone, twisted girders, and limp cable." The "rivers of Spain," he said later, "flowed to the Atlantic and mixed with our waters as well." It was a new and perilous age.[63]

The Brooklyn Bridge had been a New York icon almost from the moment of its conception. As a towering emblem of American modernity, technological ingenuity, and engineering prowess, it inspired painters, poets, and novelists alike.[64] From the beginning, though, the bridge also appeared—or disappeared—in dystopian fantasies of New York's demise. In his novel *The Last American* (1889), author-illustrator John Ames Mitchell represented the mighty span as a desolate ruin,

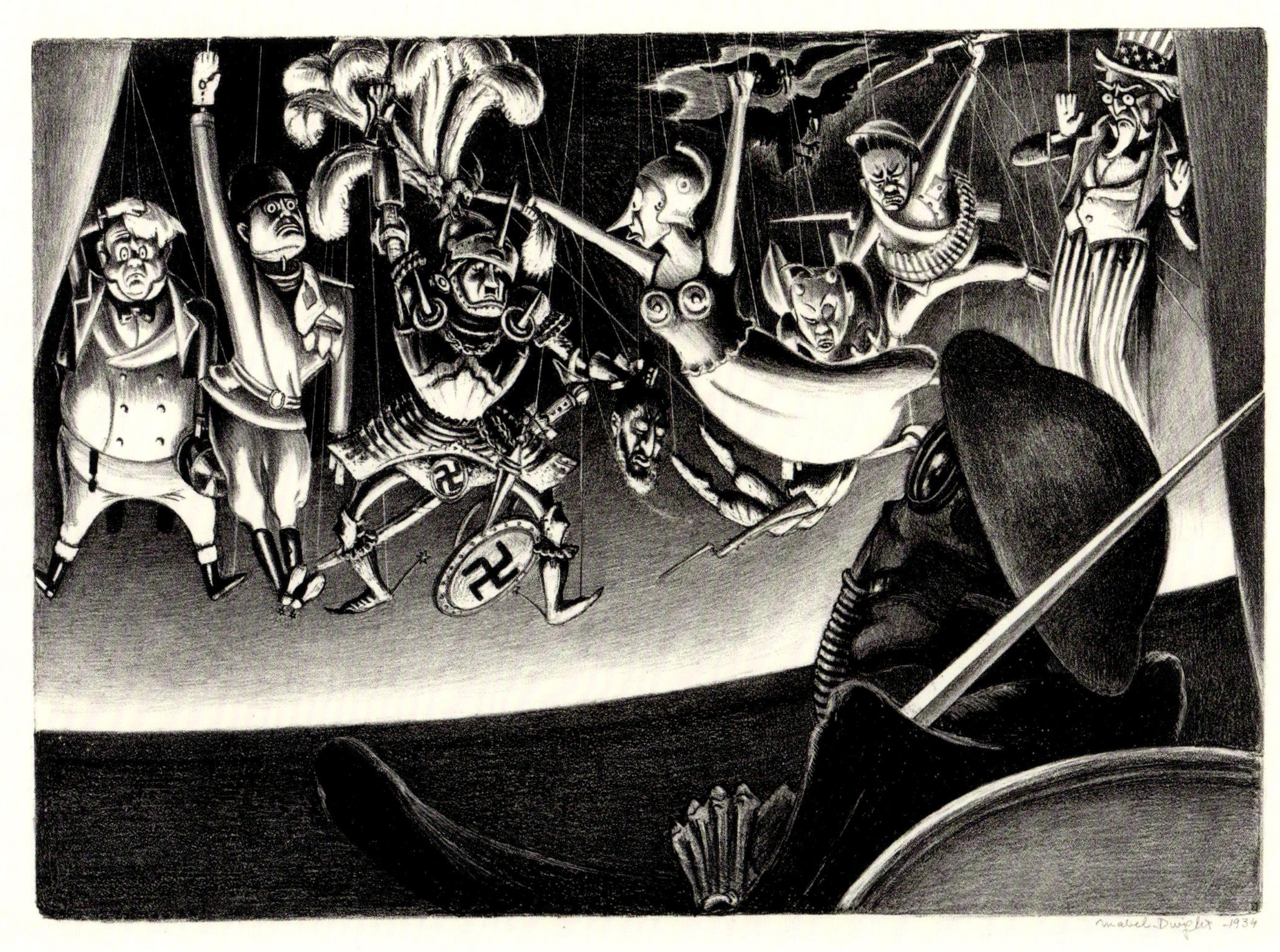

The onset of war radically refocused American culture. When Castellón's *Dark Figure* was on view at the 1941 Whitney Annual, the Japanese bombed Pearl Harbor and propelled the United States into World War II. Whatever *The Dark Figure* portended had come to pass—not only in Europe, beset by Nazi armies, but also on the island of Oahu and beyond.[67] Two years later, the Museum of Modern Art purchased Blume's *Eternal City* for the permanent collection. The painting—recently so hotly disputed—was now hailed as "remarkably prophetic" of the "coming doom of Mussolini and the Fascist regime."[68] No longer was there much possibility that *it* could happen *here*. The war effort had dispelled the pall of horror and violence overshadowing Depression America and displaced it to distant shores. Far away, horrors of unimaginable magnitude would play themselves out as America emerged from its dystopian decade and reclaimed the high ground it had lost. For a time, at least, mythic American heroes would prevail over monstrosity and evil.

**1** L. Martin Chauffier, "As Others See Us," *Living Age* 350 (June 1936), p. 348; "Mass Murder in America," *New Republic*, December 13, 1933, p. 117.

**2** Oden and Olivia Meeker, "Screamy-weamies," *Collier's* 117 (January 12, 1947), p. 55; Richard G. Hubler, "Scare 'Em to Death—and Cash In," *Saturday Evening Post*, May 23, 1942, pp. 20–21.

**3** Marcus Duffield, "The Pulps: Day Dreams for the Masses," *Vanity Fair*, June 1933, p. 51; David J. Skal, *The Monster Show: A Cultural History of Horror* (W. W. Norton, 1993), p. 159.

**4** June Havoc, *Early Havoc* (Hutchinson, 1960), p. 42; on the rules of the marathons, Carol J. Martin, *Dance Marathons: Performing American Culture of the 1920s and 1930s* (University Press of Mississippi, 1994), p. xxi; Horace McCoy, *They Shoot Horses Don't They?* (1935; repr., Serpent's Tail, 2010), p. 28. See Martin, *Dance Marathons*, especially ch. 3, pp. 40–67, for an overview of such events during the Depression years. For another view of Evergood's *Dance Marathon,* see Andrew Hemingway, "Realism under Duress: The 1930s," in John Davis, Jennifer A. Greenhill, and Jason D. LaFountain, *A Companion to American Art* (Wiley-Blackwell, 2015), pp. 626–31, which analyzes the painting in light of 1930s American debates about realism spurred by the new Socialist Realist painting in Soviet Russia.

**5** Martin, *Dance Marathons*, p. xix.

**6** John I. H. Baur, *Philip Evergood*, exh. cat. (Whitney Museum of American Art/Frederick A. Praeger, 1960), p. 50. Evergood himself used the adjective "nasty" to characterize that particular shade of red.

**7** Philip Evergood, "Oral history interview with Philip Evergood, 1968 Dec. 3," by Forrest Selvig, Archives of American Art, Smithsonian Institution, Washington, DC, http://www.aaa.si.edu/collections/interviews/oral-history-interview-philip evergood-12410/.

**8** Harold W. Stephens, "Mask and Lash in Crenshaw," *North American Review* 225 (April 1928), p. 437.

**9** Howard W. Odum, "Lynchings, Fears, and Folkways," *Nation* 133, no. 3469 (December 30, 1931), p. 719.

**10** See Dora Apel, *Imagery of Lynching: Black Men, White Women, and the Mob* (Rutgers University Press, 2004), pp. 82–132.

**11** "Housepainter," *Time* 25, no. 22 (June 3, 1935), p. 32.

**12** Joe Jones to Elizabeth Green, n.d. (1933), Green Papers, Dr. John Green Collection, Missouri History Museum, Saint Louis, Missouri, quoted in M. Melissa Wolfe, "Joe Jones: Worker-Artist," in Andrew Walker and Janeen Turk, *Joe Jones: Radical Painter of the American Scene*, exh. cat. (St. Louis Art Museum/University of Washington Press, 2010), pp. 39–40.

**13** See Wolfe, "Joe Jones: Worker-Artist," pp. 44–45, on the sexual implications of the scene. Also see Frances Pohl, *In the Eye of the Storm: An Art of Conscience, 1930–1970* (Pomegranate Artbooks, 1995), p. 50.

**14** For an overview, see Robert Kenneth Jones, *The Shudder Pulps: A History of the Weird Menace Magazines of the 1930s* (Plume, 1978).

**15** "Lynching Statistics by Year," University of Missouri-Kansas City School of Law, http://law2.umkc.edu/faculty/projects/ftrials/shipp/lynchingyear.html; *Leading Causes of Death, 1900–1998*, United States Centers for Disease Control and Prevention, http://www.cdc.gov/nchs/data/dvs/lead1900_98.pdf, p. 56. Two of the lynching victims in 1933 were white; the other twenty-four, black.

**16** "The Drive on Death: An Editorial," *Scholastic* 27 (October 5, 1935), p. 3.

**17** Joseph Chamberlain Furnas, "—And Sudden Death," *Reader's Digest* 27, no. 160 (August 1935), pp. 21–26.

**18** Peter D. Norton, *Fighting Traffic: The Dawn of the Motor Age in the American City* (MIT Press, 2008), p. 246.

**19** "Blood and Agony," *Time* 26, no. 7 (August 12, 1935), p. 21; Anedith Jo Bond Nash, "Death on the Highway: The Automobile Wreck in American Culture, 1920–40," Ph.D. diss., University of Minnesota, 1983, p. 59 n. 15; Norton, *Fighting Traffic*, p. 247. Nash amply documents the impact of the Furnas article; see pp. 38–42, 59–60.

**20** Joseph Chamberlain Furnas and Ernest N. Smith, *Sudden Death and How to Avoid It* (Simon and Schuster, 1935), p. 10.

**21** Ridge roads followed the paths made by pioneers, who sought the highest ridges in order to avoid muddy lowland areas. On this painting, see especially Nash, "Death on the Highway," ch. 4, pp. 100–31; also Nash, "*Death on the Ridge Road*: Grant Wood and Modernization in the Midwest," *Prospects: An Annual of American Cultural Studies* 8 (1983), pp. 281–301; and Wanda M. Corn, "Grant Wood (1892–1942), *Death on the Ridge Road*, 1935," in *American Dreams: American Art to 1950 in the Williams College Museum of Art* (Hudson Hills, 2001), pp. 158–61. Both Nash and Corn regard *Death on the Ridge Road* as an expression of the clash between city and country that became acute in the modern, mechanized era.

**22** Nash, "Death on the Highway," p. 120.

**23** William McBrien, *Cole Porter: A Biography* (Alfred A. Knopf, 2011), p. 65.

**24** On Sigmund's accident, see Zachary Michael Jack, ed., *The Plowman Sings: The Essential Fiction, Poetry, and Drama of America's Forgotten Regionalist Jay G. Sigmund* (University Press of America, 2008), p. 7; and Ed Ferreter, "Jay Sigmund and Grant Wood," *Books at Iowa* 42 (April 1985), http://digital.lib.uiowa.edu /bai/books_iowa42_04.htm.

**25** Nash, "Death on the Highway," p. 103; Grant Wood to Ferargil Gallery, December 22, 1934, cited in ibid., p. 106. On Wood's nervousness about driving, see R. Tripp Evans, *Grant Wood: A Life* (Alfred A. Knopf, 2010), p. 195.

**26** By 1934 Wood was under increasing threat of exposure by enemies at the University of Iowa, where he had just been promoted to associate professor. In 1935 he made an ill-fated marriage to Sara Maxon, and his painting production dried up almost completely for some time after that. On Wood's sexuality and its impact on his social and professional life, see Evans, *Grant Wood*, esp. ch. 4, pp. 197–293; and James H. Maroney, Jr., *Hiding in Plain Sight: Decoding the Homoerotic and Misogynistic Imagery of Grant Wood* (Gala Books, 2013), http:// jamesmaroney.com/art/grant wood/hiding_in_plain_sight_full .pdf.

**27** Jay G. Sigmund, "Death Rides a Rubber-Shod Horse," *American Poetry* 16, no. 6 (October 1934), p. 152.

**28** See William H. Truettner and Thomas Andrew Denenberg, "The Discreet Charm of the Colonial," in William H. Truettner and Roger B. Stein, *Picturing Old New England: Image and Memory*, exh. cat. (National Museum of American Art, Smithsonian Institution/Yale University Press, 1999), pp. 105–07, for an overview of the taste for colonial antiquity in the early twentieth century.

**29** Nathaniel Hawthorne, *The House of the Seven Gables* (Ticknor, Reed, and Fields, 1851), p. 199.

**30** H. P. Lovecraft to James Ferdinand Morton, March 12, 1930, in August Derleth and Donald Wandrei, eds., *H. P. Lovecraft: Selected Letters,* vol. 3 (Arkham House, 1971), p. 126. On Lovecraft's application of Spengler's theories to New England's decline, see Faye Ringel, "The Local Color Is Black—H. P. Lovecraft," in *New England's Gothic Literature: History and Folklore of the Supernatural from the Seventeenth through the Twentieth Centuries* (Edwin Mellen, 1996), pp. 157–201.

**31** Morris Kantor, "Ends and Means," *Magazine of Art* 33, no. 3 (March 1940), p. 114.

**32** C. J. Bulliet, "The Annual Exhibition at Chicago Art Institute," *New York Times*, November 8, 1931; Eleanor A. Jewett, "American Exhibition at Institute," *Chicago Tribune*, November 1, 1931.

**33** "The Cat and the Canary," *Universal Weekly*, April 23, 1927, p. 33.

**34** See Allen J. Hubin, *The Bibliography of Crime Fiction, 1749–1975* (University of California at San Diego, 1979), for a comprehensive listing of "haunted house" titles. For a thorough examination of Lovecraft in context, see J. T. Joshi, *A Dreamer and a Visionary: H. P. Lovecraft in His Time* (Liverpool University Press, 2001).

**35** On Post-Surrealism, see Susan Ehrlich, ed., *Pacific Dreams: Currents of Surrealism and Fantasy in California Art, 1934–1957*, exh. cat. (UCLA at the Armand Hammer Museum of Art and Cultural Center, 1995); and Michael Duncan, ed., *Post Surrealism*, exh. cat. (Pasadena Museum of California Art, 2003).

**36** On the movement in America, see Isabelle Dervaux et al., *Surrealism U.S.A.,* exh. cat. (National Academy Museum, 2005).

**37** "Feitelson-Lundeberg," *Sourcebook* 20, no. 4 (April 1973), p. 35.

**38** Fidel Danieli, "Interview of Helen Lundeberg," June 4, 1974, Los Angeles Community Group Portrait, Center for Oral History Research, UCLA Library Special Collections, http://oralhistory .library.ucla.edu/viewItem.do? ark=21198/zz0008z9qd&title =Lundeberg,%20Helen/.

**39** Paul Bird, *Fifty Paintings by Walt Kuhn* (Studio, 1940), no. 20, n. pag. The standard work on Kuhn is Philip Rhys Adams, *Walt Kuhn, Painter, His Life and Work* (Ohio State University Press, 1978). Also see Franklin Kelly, "Walt Kuhn (1877–1949), *Portrait of the Artist as a Clown (Kansas)*, 1932," in Bruce Robertson et al., *Twentieth-Century American Art: The Ebsworth Collection* (National Gallery of Art, 1999), pp. 159–61.

**40** Lloyd Goodrich, "The Circus in Paint," exh. brochure, Whitney Studio Galleries, April 1929, p. 1; Whitney Museum Library, Whitney Studio Club and Galleries, 1907–1930, http:// cdm16694.contentdm.oclc.org /cdm/compoundobject/collection /p15405coll1/id/126/rec/47/.

**41** See Francis Haskell, "The Sad Clown: Notes on a Nineteenth-Century Myth," in *Past and Present in Art and Taste: Selected Essays* (Yale University Press, 1987), pp. 117–28.

**42** Adams, *Walt Kuhn*, pp. 232–33.

**43** Ludgin saw Albright's 1934 *Self-Portrait* (New Trier Township High School, District 203, Winnetka, Illinois) at the Chicago Century of Progress exposition and so admired it that he asked Albright to paint something similar for him. See Courtney Graham Donnell, Susan S. Weininger, and Robert Cozzolino, *Ivan Albright*, exh. cat. (Art Institute of Chicago/ Hudson Hills, 1997), cat. 29, n. pag.

**44**  Ivan Albright, "Reflections by the Artist," in Frederick A. Sweet et al., *Ivan Albright: A Retrospective Exhibition*, exh. cat. (Art Institute of Chicago/Whitney Museum of American Art, 1964), p. 17. For Albright's war experience, see Robert Cozzolino, "Every Picture Should Be a Prayer: The Art of Ivan Albright," Ph.D. diss., University of Wisconsin–Madison, 2006, pp. 63–73.

**45**  Irwin St. John Tucker, "'Horror' Features Exhibit," *Chicago Herald Examiner,* August 31, 1930; "Lavender and Old Bottles," *Time* 38, no. 21 (November 24, 1941), p. 81.

**46**  Hubler, "Scare 'Em to Death," p. 76; Skal, *Monster Show*, p. 133. See Skal, pp. 113–59, for an overview of horror movies and their impact in the early 1930s.

**47**  "Horror, Thrills Compose Plot of Frankenstein," *Chicago Daily Tribune*, December 4, 1931; Mordaunt Hall, "The Screen," *New York Times*, December 5, 1931.

**48**  C. J. Bulliet, "Albright Tames Wild Baers," *Chicago Evening Post,* July 28, 1931; Eleanor Jewett, "Annual Exhibition at the Art Institute: Chosen by Directors of Four Prominent Museums," *Chicago Tribune*, n.d., 1931, clipping in scrapbooks maintained by Ryerson and Burnham Libraries, Art Institute of Chicago.

**49**  Cécile Whiting, *Antifascism in American Art* (Yale University Press, 1989), p. 21.

**50**  On Proletarian Surrealism, see Gerrit L. Lansing, "Surrealism as a Weapon," in Dervaux, *Surrealism U.S.A*, p. 31; O. Louis Guglielmi, "After the Locusts" [1939], in Francis V. O'Connor, ed., *Art for the Millions: Essays from the 1930's by Artists and Administrators of the WPA Federal Art Project* (New York Graphic Society, 1973), p. 113.

**51**  "Rivera RCA Mural Is Cut from Wall," *New York Times*, February 13, 1934. There has been some debate about the meaning of Guglielmi's enigmatic picture. One camp interprets it as a Marxist allegory celebrating the triumph of the Russian Revolution over capitalism. Another construes it as a critique of the revolution's failure to bring about a working-class, Communist Utopia. See Ilene Susan Fort, "American Social Surrealism," *Archives of American Art Journal* 22, no. 3 (1982), p. 14, and Gerrit L. Lansing, "'A Neurotic Mirror': The Painting of O. Louis Guglielmi, 1932–1943," Ph.D. diss., New York University, 1999, pp. 99–141.

**52**  See James Thrall Soby, "Peter Blume's 'Eternal City,'" *Bulletin of the Museum of Modern Art* 10, no. 4 (April 1943), pp. 2–6, for a vivid contemporary description of the painting.

**53**  Soby, "Peter Blume's 'Eternal City'," p. 3.

**54**  For detailed analyses of the critical reception and the controversy, see Frank Trapp, *Peter Blume* (Rizzoli, 1987), pp. 56–66; Whiting, *Antifascism in American Art*, pp. 54–64; and Sergio Cortesini, "Battling over the *Eternal City*," in Robert Cozzolino, ed., *Peter Blume: Nature and Metamorphosis*, exh. cat. (Pennsylvania Academy of Fine Arts/University of Pennsylvania Press, 2015), pp. 59–83.

**55**  "Gallery Rejects Anti-Fascist Art," *New York Times*, April 3, 1939.

**56**  Sinclair Lewis, *It Can't Happen Here* (Sun Dial, 1936), pp. 20–21.

**57**  Lorraine Brown, "Federal Theater: Melodrama, Social Protest, and Genius" (1979), in *The New Deal Stage: Selections from the Federal Theatre Project, 1935–1939* (Library of Congress, 2012), http://memory.loc.gov/ammem/fedtp/ftbrwn00.html.

**58**  Lewis Mumford, "Opening Address," in Matthew Baigell and Julia Williams, eds., *Artists against War and Fascism: Papers of the First American Artists' Congress* (Rutgers University Press, 1986), p. 63. On the American Artists' Congress, see Andrew Hemingway, *Artists on the Left: American Artists and the Communist Movement, 1926–1956* (Yale University Press, 2002), pp. 123–25.

**59**  Federico Castellón, "Oral history interview with Federico Castellón, 1971 April 7–14," by Paul Cummings, Archives of American Art, Smithsonian Institution, Washington, DC, http://www.aaa.si.edu/collections/interviews/oral-history-interview-federico-castellon-5452/. Castellón did not become an American citizen until 1943.

**60**  "The Tragedy of Guernica, Town Destroyed in Air Attack, Eye-Witness Account," *New York Times*, April 27, 1936; *Congressional Record, Senate,* May 6, 1937, pp. 5521–22, cited in Herbert Rutledge Southworth, *Guernica! Guernica!: A Study of Journalism, Diplomacy, Propaganda, and History* (University of California Press, 1977), pp. 186–87.

**61**  On Guston's politics and his experience in Mexico, see Ellen G. Landau, "Double Consciousness in Mexico: How Philip Guston and Reuben Kadish Painted a Morelian Mural," *American Art* 21, no. 1 (Spring 2007), pp. 74–97.

**62**  Musa Mayer, *Night Studio: A Memoir of Philip Guston* (Da Capo, 1997), p. 18.

**63**  "Guglielmi's 'First,'" *Art Digest* 13 (November 15, 1938), p. 20; Guglielmi, "I Hope to Sing Again," *Art Digest* 37 (May 1944), p. 175.

**64**  See Richard Haw, *The Art of the Brooklyn Bridge: A Visual History* (Routledge, 2008), and *The Brooklyn Bridge: A Cultural History* (Rutgers University Press, 2005).

**65**  Stephen Vincent Benét, "The Place of the Gods," *Saturday Evening Post* 210, no. 5 (July 31, 1937), p. 59. See Max Page, *The City's End: Two Centuries of*

*Fantasies, Fears, and Premonitions of New York's Destruction* (New Haven: Yale University Press, 2008), pp. 76–82, for a discussion of Benet's apocalyptic vision in relation to Guglielmi's *Mental Geography*.

**66** Lansing, "Surrealism as a Weapon," p. 33. For a thorough analysis of the symbolism see Nicolai Cikovsky, Jr., "O. Louis Guglielmi (1906–1956), *Mental Geography*, 1938," in Robertson et al., *Twentieth-Century American Art*, pp. 120–24.

**67** Patricia Hills and Roberta Tarbell, *The Figurative Tradition and the Whitney Museum of American Art: Paintings and Sculpture from the Permanent Collection*, exh. cat (Whitney Museum of American Art, 1980), p. 89; note that Castellón's painting was on view at the time of the Japanese attack on Pearl Harbor.

**68** "Museum Here Buys Anti-Fascist Painting That Corcoran Gallery Barred in 1939," *New York Times*, March 3, 1943.

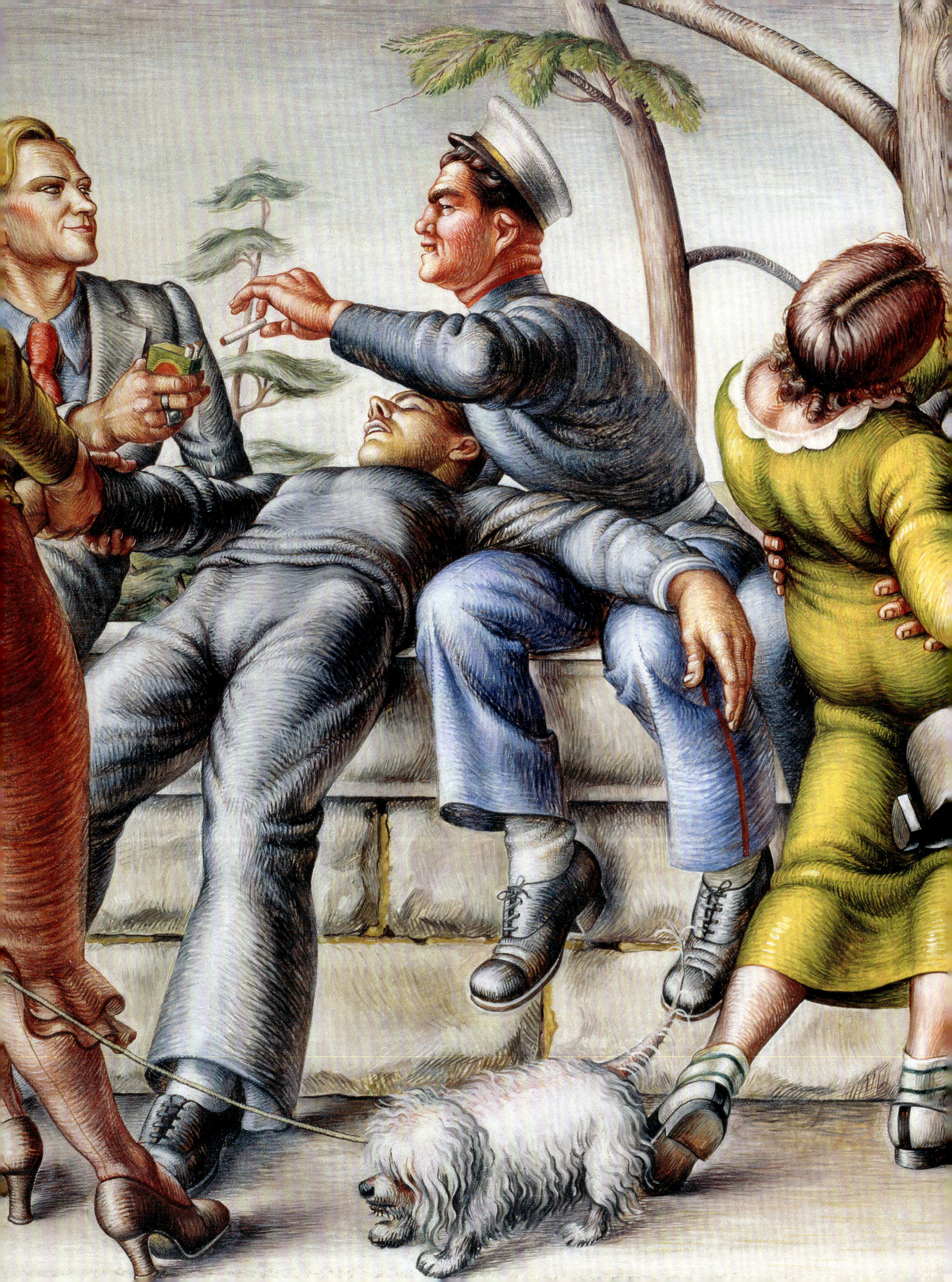

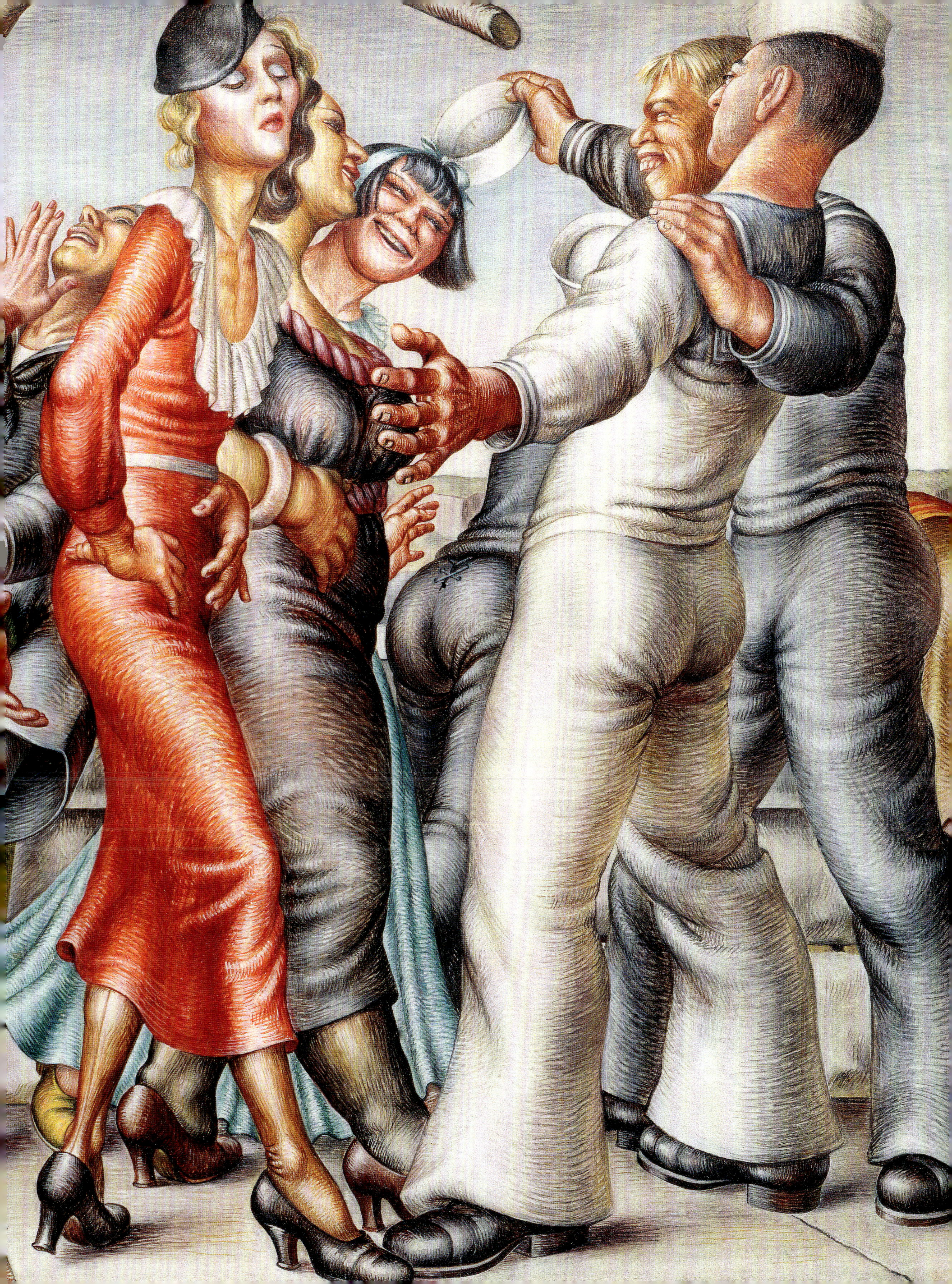

**These were the people he felt he must paint. He would never again do a fat red barn, old stone wall, or Nantucket fisherman. From the moment he had seen them, he had known that, despite his race, training and heritage, neither Winslow Homer nor Thomas Ryder could be his masters and he turned to Goya and Daumier.**

—Nathanael West, *The Day of the Locust*[1]

*H*e is Tod Hackett, a young painter discovered at the Yale School of Fine Arts by a talent scout for "National Films" who finds himself cast as both a set designer and witness to the bizarre and desperate counterculture of Depression-era Hollywood. Novelist Nathanael West created Hackett as the

**FIVE**  *Busted Seams and Bad Behavior: Bodies for the 1930s*

protagonist of his 1939 novel *The Day of the Locust*, calculating that a visual artist would be obsessively attentive to the strangeness of a place whose inhabitants fabricated alternative realities to entertain a public scarred by struggle, need, and dislocation. Hackett's ambition is to create a canvas, *The Burning of Los Angeles*, to prove that he remains a serious artist. He intends to capture Hollywood's carnivalesque environment, employing his friends—a helpless blonde who impersonates a 1930s screen siren and with whom he falls in love, and a dwarf con man—as his key figures. He turns to Honoré Daumier and Francisco de Goya as his artistic models—apt choices for an artist bent on representing the tragic human comedy through devices including the extremes of caricature and expressionism. In content and in form, the two European masters serve to guide the young American in the delineation of the misshapen, the ill-fortuned, and the chaotic.

West's choices on behalf of Hackett were no doubt inspired by the stylistic models to which actual artists gravitated throughout the 1930s, as they undertook subjects capable of conveying that the foundations of American life had been broken apart and that rules, norms, expectations, and futures had been summarily erased. Almost as if a switch had been thrown, the year 1930 brought with it a startlingly immediate recalibration of figurative styles in the United States. The distilled ideals formulated over the course of the 1920s evaporated almost instantly, no longer acceptable to a society undermined. Artists in the 1920s, faced with the aftermath of World War I and the onslaught of the machine age, had channeled the precisely graceful lines and polished volumes of Italian Renaissance models into quietly sensual forms evocative of physical beauty and power, and bodily integrity. The bodies they rendered, often as nudes, were clean, fit, lithe, and natural—ideals resistant to the wear and overstimulation of urban life, automated labor, and consumer culture.[2]

And then the 1930s happened. The perfection of healthfully fed, well-exercised and sleekly dressed bodies, to which so many had aspired, suddenly became less relevant than survival in the face of the stresses and deprivation that accompanied unemployment and poverty. The majority of figurative artists reacted quickly to the overwhelming new threats to physical and psychological well-being, calling upon the likes of post-Renaissance European masters—including Peter Paul Rubens, El Greco, Goya, and Daumier—to guide their representations of struggle and disorder. Drawing on these demonstrative baroque styles and ultimately on modernist expressionism, they recalibrated human forms to convey the strain, restlessness, fatigue, and disorientation of this new, if not better, version of American life.

The representation of labor was central to the reconceptualization of American figurative art in the 1930s. As unemployment grew increasingly dire and activism was catalyzed by the Communist Party and trade unionists, acceptable modes for labor-related imagery were highly contested even among the politically like-minded, and opinions shifted almost continuously over the course of the decade. When the openly Communist John Reed Club organized an exhibition in support of labor in 1933, comments in the accompanying catalogue set out requirements for acceptable subject matter yet remained entirely neutral on the question of style:

**We cannot say what style, manner, school or form is best suited to the artistic expression of the struggles of the oppressed. That is the artist's problem. We do say, however, that it is not sufficient merely to record the scene, to describe it or illustrate it. The artist to be artistically and socially vital must use his art forms to comment, to satirize, to condemn or praise. . . . He takes sides, not only through his subject matter, but in his treatment. He is on one side or the other of the historic class struggle.[3]**

Most American artists had limited experience in the production of openly political works and relatively little inclination to gain it. Those engaged in printmaking were the exception, and many quickly adopted imagery that featured militant workers and took formal cues from newly minted Soviet art. Activist critics targeted certain variations on the labor theme, however, such as portrayals of labor abuses that were criticized for framing workers as passive or disempowered.[4] They leveled equally pointed critiques at the hundreds of artists who signed on to federally funded payrolls to produce public murals in which narratives of the American worker were safely couched in local histories or rosy cultural myths.[5]

Particularly as the decade opened, the ways in which artists approached the subject of labor and described working bodies depended on political loyalties and sources of inspiration. The Saint Louis native Joe Jones is an interesting case of a virtually self-taught painter working far from artistic centers such as New York or Chicago. Initially an apprentice with his house-painter father, Jones soon began to produce easel paintings and exhibited them with the Saint Louis Art Guild.[6] He sought his sources in illustrated art journals and in the frequent exhibitions of works by living American and foreign painters at the Saint Louis Art Museum. Beginning in 1931, he demonstrated an attention to progressive styles with his entry into the New Hats, an association that promoted aesthetic modernism in the Midwest. He may have been inspired by any number of

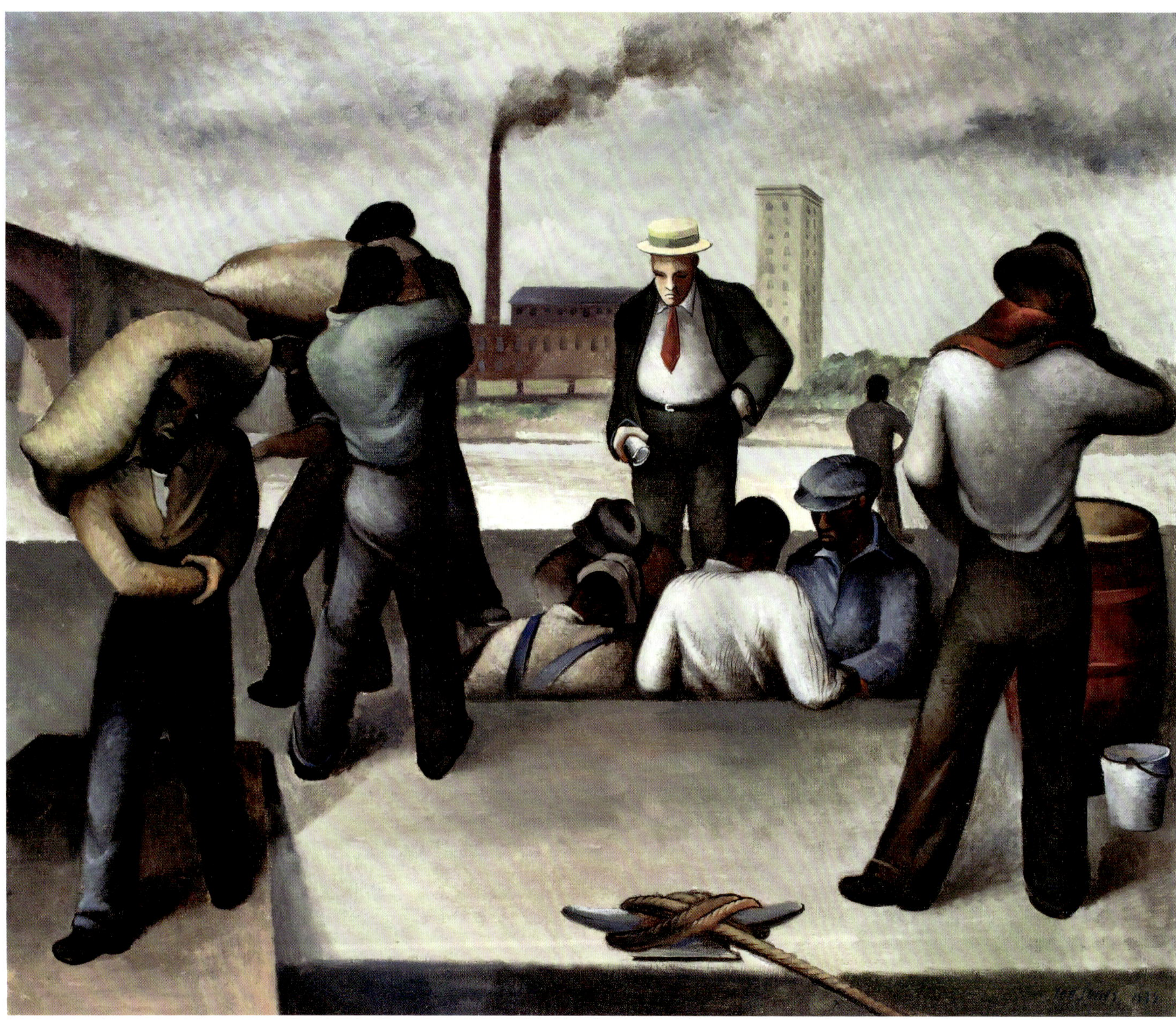

works included in the Saint Louis Art Museum exhibitions from 1930 to 1934; paintings exhibited by Boardman Robinson or Edward Bruce, respectively, in 1932 and 1933, contained the generalized volumes and architecture-based compositions typical of art of the 1920s and apparent in Jones's early efforts.[7]

Jones's single-minded address of the subject of labor emerged from a deeply felt identification with Depression-era workers in Saint Louis; it undoubtedly was fortified by his friendship with Jack Conroy, a proletarian writer who published his best-known novel, *The Disinherited*, in 1933. Jones allied himself more openly with Communism while at work at the distinctly political art colony in Provincetown, Massachusetts, in the summer of that year. His subsequent move to a houseboat moored in downtown Saint Louis, near a riverside Hooverville populated by the unemployed poor, was a demonstration of his deeper commitment. In December, with

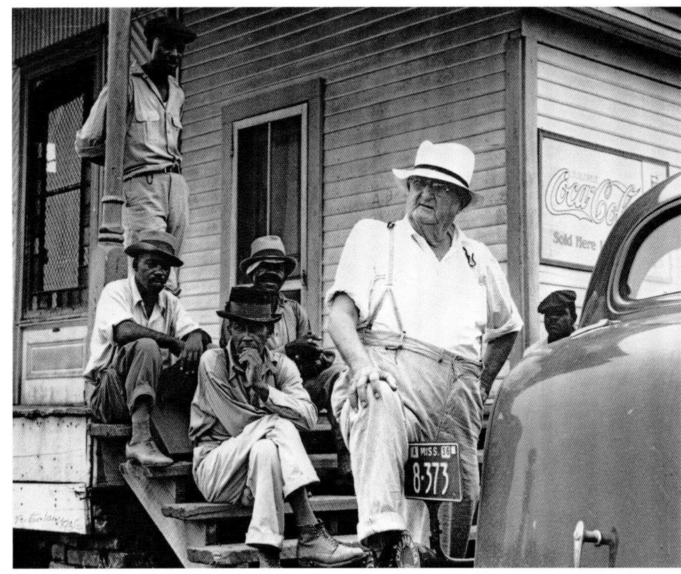



the support of his patron Elizabeth Green, Jones also organized the Unemployed Art Class, a racially integrated group that met in a former courthouse used by the city's Art League. In keeping with his politics, he led their production of an activist mural entitled *Social Protest in Old Saint Louis* (1934; destroyed), in which a central scene of African American dockworkers loading cargo onto a riverboat was flanked by a composition of unemployed laborers near a pawn shop and paired images of an African American river baptism and the Communist-led nut pickers' strike of 1932.[8] Jones was attentive to the plight of the African American population of Saint Louis, 80 percent of whom were unemployed at the time.

In 1934 the artist painted *Roustabouts* (fig. 1) as a study for a mural in which he revisited the riverfront labor theme.[9] Still relatively inexperienced, he utilized generalized forms, derived from the late-1920s Precisionist works by artists like Bruce, that were well suited for enlargement to mural scale. The backdrop of the industrialized Saint Louis waterfront in *Roustabouts* is entirely in keeping with the geometrical simplifications typical of the Precisionist approach to form and subject, as are the figures, who appear to be simplified and generally modeled stock types. The standing dockworkers, only one of whom faces the viewer, orbit around a central group of seated black men whose activities—a card game?—are observed by a standing white man dressed in a suit, tie, and boater and holding a rolled newspaper in one hand. His position, pose, clothing, and girth denote his supervisory role, as does his formal identification with the factory and freight yard in the distance; the black men around him are anchored to the docks themselves.

Jones's chosen aesthetic of muted generalities in both form and expression was limited in its ability to convey the depth of his political commitment and activism. One need only compare *Roustabouts* with one of the seminal documentary photographs taken by Dorothea Lange for the Farm Security Administration, whose mission was to produce visual documentation of dire need in order to argue for the renewal of the federal programs that sustained many of the unemployed poor by mid-decade.[10] In Lange's *Plantation Overseer and His Field Hands, near Clarksdale, Mississippi* (1936; fig. 2), the power

dynamic is comparable to that in *Roustabouts*, but the photographic record of bodies, clothing, and demeanor conveys more trenchant proof of the strain and stresses of the workers' lives than Jones's adopted manner of formal simplifications. Jones's politics were, in fact, entirely clear to his Saint Louis audience, to the extent that city officials turned his class out of their courthouse rooms in December of 1934. Perhaps out of caution, he avoided the John Reed Club when he set out to find a New York venue for a solo exhibition later that winter. He was exposed to a broader array of activist art there, however, leading him to observe, "The revolutionary pictures here are full of political satire or on the other hand sickles and hammers."[11] Critics observed a sense of moderation in his own political work when it went on view at the ACA Galleries, a venue increasingly active and influential in the rising field of Social Realist art. Responding to the exhibition, which included the mural-scaled version of *Roustabouts*, the *New York Times* critic Edward Alden Jewell noted both Jones's relative inexperience and his measured approach. Although the exhibition could be viewed as a "Left Wing show," Jewell wrote, "In his case one never suspects that painting, as an art, has figured exclusively, for him, as a crude machine by means of which propaganda broadsides may be catapulted into the face of the public."[12]

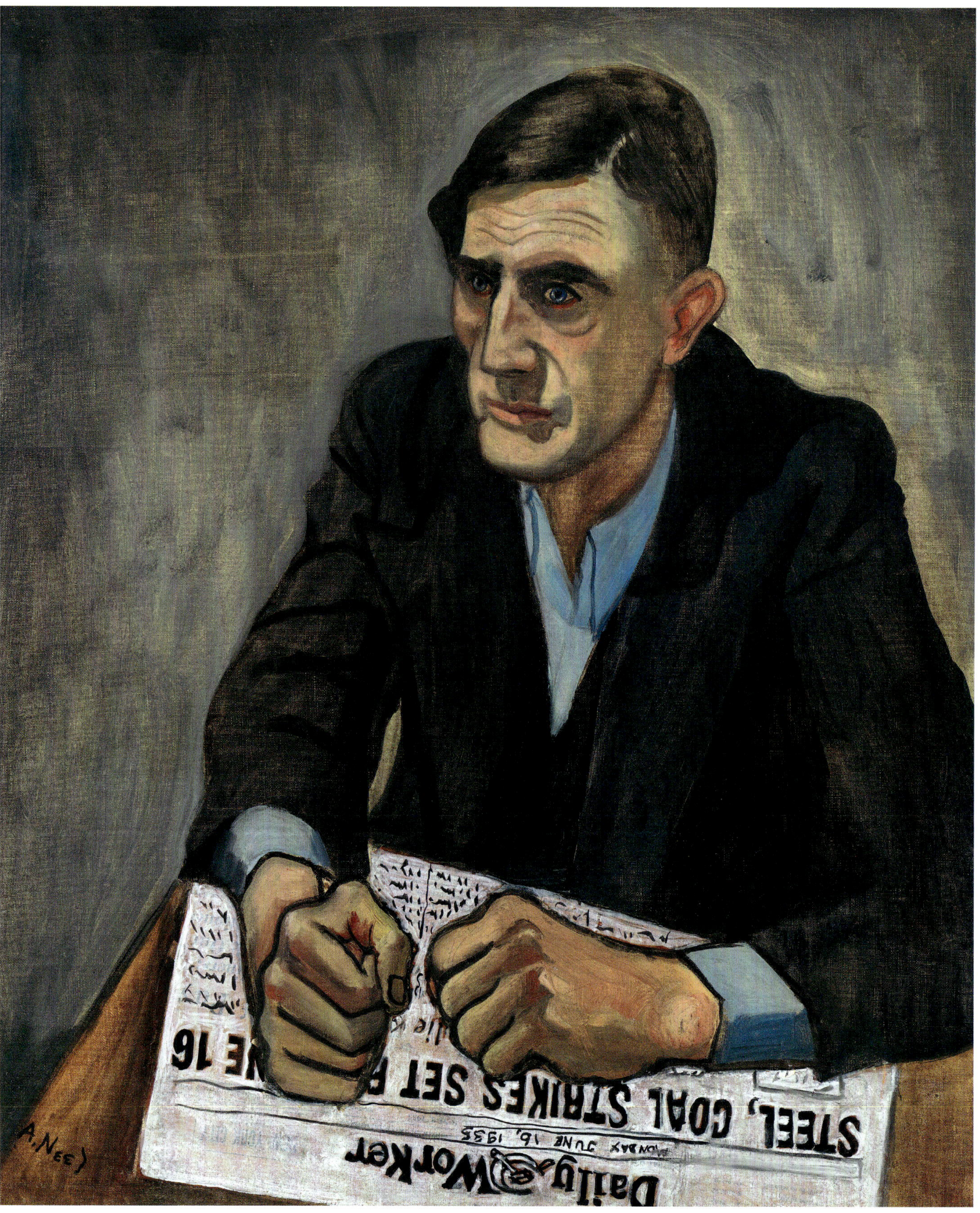

Daily Worker
STEEL, COAL STRIKES SET FOR JUNE 16
MONDAY, JUNE 15, 1935

The painter Alice Neel also sought her own aesthetic route in furthering the cause of American labor. Her most forceful political statements of the 1930s emerged in portraits, including an aggressive likeness of the longshoreman and militant Communist organizer Pat Whalen (1935; fig. 3). Neel, who began her artistic training in the early 1920s at the Philadelphia School of Design for Women (eventually Moore College of Art), was first exposed to the idea of socially relevant art after her marriage to the Cuban painter Carlos Enriquez de Gomez. From 1926 to 1927, the pair lived in Havana and participated in the activities of a rising avant-garde determined to expose social inequities wrought by capitalism and colonialism.[13] In 1932, after several turbulent years, Neel established herself independently in Greenwich Village, living with the sailor and Communist activist Kenneth Doolittle. She found her footing within the radical bohemian left, joining other struggling artists who participated in the *First Washington Square Outdoor Art Exhibit*. After showing work both there and in a 1933 exhibition organized by the relief-oriented Artist's Aid Committee, Neel garnered an invitation to enroll in the Public Works of Art Project (PWAP) that December. The federal agency's New York office was overseen by Juliana Force, director of the new Whitney Museum of American Art and an active supporter of the various New York relief exhibitions in which Neel had shown. Neel thus joined the ranks of artists who were paid thirty dollars a week to paint a 23-by-30-inch canvas every six weeks; her arrangement lasted until April of 1934, when she was removed from the payroll for having submitted a work that was deemed inappropriate.[14]

The artist later recalled that she had started "doing revolutionary paintings" by 1933, when she was still living in the Village on Cornelia Street.[15] She doubtless counted among them her *Synthesis of New York—The Great Depression* (1933; fig. 4), in which she used a naïve figure style and expressionist palette to render skull-headed human specters passing through an empty urban crossroads. By 1935 Neel's political commitment to the cause of labor had grown stronger. She had joined the Artists Union, formed in 1934 out of the Emergency Work Bureau Artists' Group, to monitor the treatment of artists by

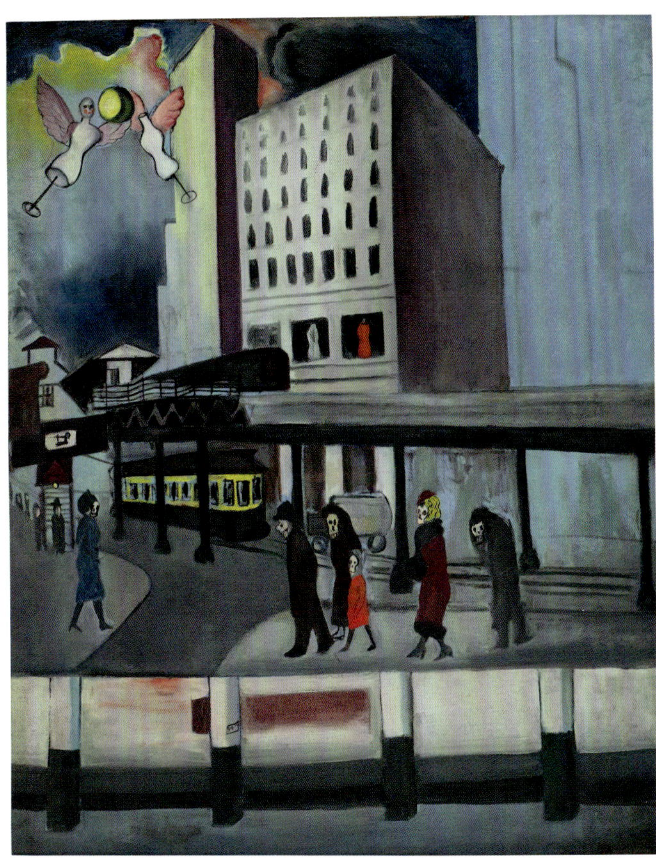

the WPA. Neel herself was picked up by the WPA in September of 1935 and began to receive about one hundred dollars a month in relief. That year she joined the Communist Party and thus forged a more definitive alliance with the activists whose portraits she undertook after her move to West Seventeenth Street. Newly focused on the longshoremen who traversed the area, she undertook the portrait of Whalen, the man best known for defending their rights.

Decades later, Neel's recollections of Whalen were colored by her customary acidity: "Patty Whalen was the organizer on the waterfront. . . . Ryan's men used to really beat him up. . . . Look how he cut his hair—like a dope. He had that thing shaven right off, right up to where the hair got thick. He was just an ordinary Irishman except for one thing: He was absolutely convinced of Communism, and he could convince other longshoremen."[16] Born in the Midwest in 1884, Whalen had joined his father in a locomotive engineers' union until he found him-self at loggerheads with his employers.[17] By the time he began working in the engine room of merchant ships out of New York harbor in the early 1930s, he was well versed in radical labor activism. He was recruited into the aggressively Communist-leaning Marine Workers Industrial Union, and when it was disbanded in 1935, Whalen, who had joined the Communist Party, was among those chosen to organize its realignment as the International Seamen's Union. His prolabor authenticity was underpinned by his leadership of a Hooverville of shanties on the New Jersey flats.

Neel portrayed the famously short and slight Whalen as a powerful man whose intense gaze is matched by the aggressive prominence of his large-fisted hands. She treated the figure with a brusque realism that is predictive of her later, iconic style. The artist's use of heavy outlines and broad modeling fortified the characterization she constructed around the deeply lined face, the workingman's haircut, and the unadorned clothing. At the time he sat for her, Whalen was riding the wave of rising work unrest that had swelled dramatically in 1934, when about one-third of the labor force was unemployed and wages were under assault. Neel announced his activism with the placement of his outsized hands on top of an issue of the Communist newspaper *Daily Worker*, a tool of resistance and activism, here dated June 16, 1935, and bearing the headline "Steel, Coal Strikes Set for June 16."[18] The message resonated with the newest labor legislation, the National Labor Relations Act (or Wagner Act), which at the time awaited only signing by the president. The law granted laborers the right to form and join unions, required employers to engage in collective bargain-ing, and created the National Labor Relations Board to enforce the rights of workers. Neel's orchestration of the portrait revised the dominant convention for the representation of the laborer's power: she resisted the propagandistic form of the hypermuscular worker promoted paradoxically by Communist ideologies and New Deal strategies, made an unvarnished reference to the dire conditions of American labor, and rebutted the Communist dismissal of portraiture as subservient to the individual rather than the revolutionary common good.[19]

During her long tenure on the WPA payroll, Neel was defended by the Artists Union when her works were deemed by the New York office of the Federal Art Project to be inappro-priate—too openly sexual or Communist—and thus were not "allocated," meaning not credited as submissions or designated for installation.[20] The agency was not entirely consistent, however, as is apparent in the case of Paul Cadmus's "accepted" 1934 canvas *The Fleet's In!* (fig. 5) and the national scandal it ignited. Cadmus had been working as a painter for only a short time when he dared to produce the bawdy and garish scene of sailors cutting loose in New York's Riverside Park. Trained at the National Academy of Design and the Art Students League during the 1920s, he had taken a job as a sketch artist and layout designer at the Blackman Company in 1928, benefitting from the first heyday of the American advertising industry.[21] In 1931, as the effects of the Depression were beginning to deepen, he and his lover, artist Jared French, booked passage to Europe on an oil tanker. They bicycled throughout France and Spain and ultimately set up a studio in Mallorca, where Cadmus executed his first mature oils in 1933. These included the ribald American subjects *YMCA Locker Room* (Collection of John P. Axelrod) and *Shore Leave* (Whitney Museum of American Art, New York), which prefigured the theme and treatment of *The Fleet's In!* Inspired by the European art he and French continued to seek out on forays to Austria, Germany, and Italy, Cadmus had reinvented his stylistic approach, developing a masterful facility with the human form and a scathingly satirical eye. He and French returned to New York after having received news of the shifting New York art world from his sister, Fidelma. By December of 1933, he was among the first artists to join the rolls of the Federal Art Project.

Cadmus found ample material for his art in a city that revealed both the privations of the deepening Depression and the cathartic release triggered by the repeal of Prohibition. He soon produced the small but complex *The Fleet's In!*, based on his own observations of the liberated behavior of navy men and the locals willing to show them a good time. Within a knot-ted frieze of seven women and seven men, Cadmus described the figures in exaggerated postures reminiscent of Italian

**Fig. 5**  Paul Cadmus. *The Fleet's In!*, 1934. Collection of the US Navy. Cat. 7.

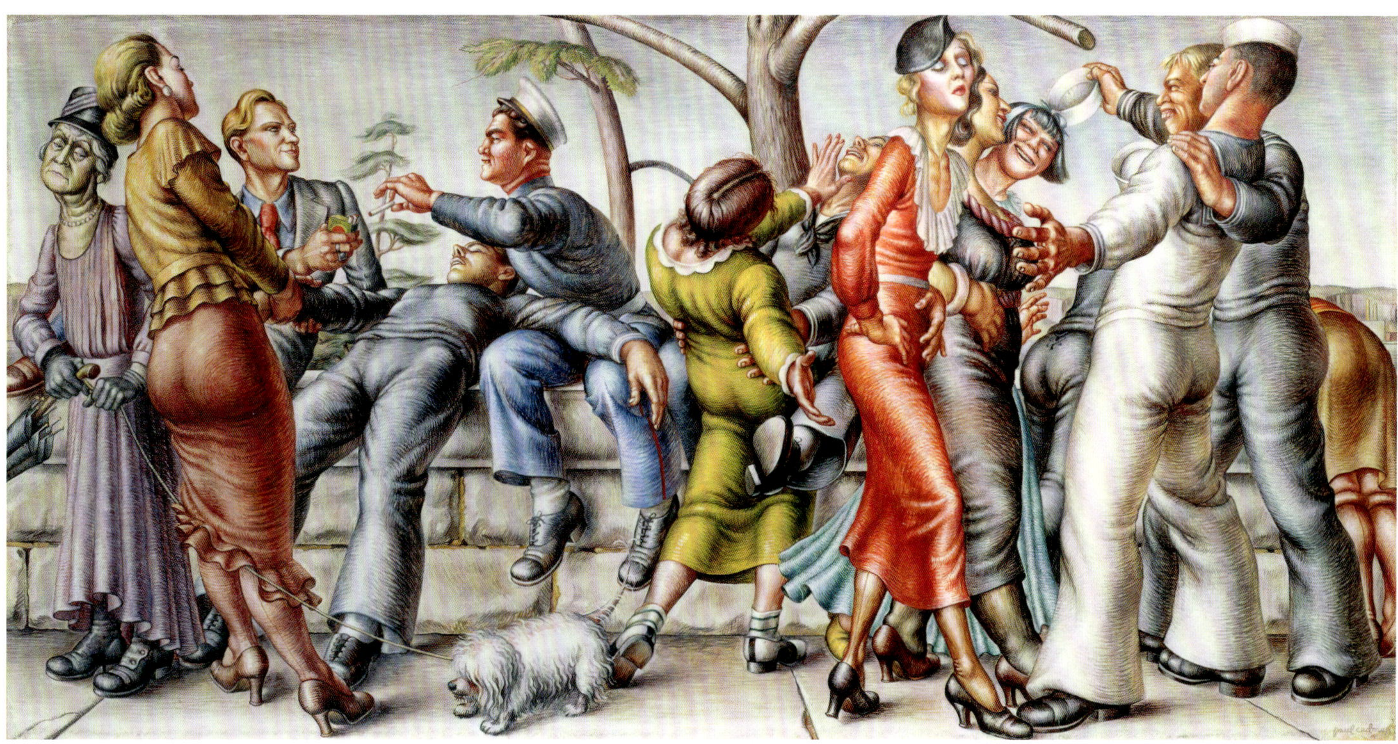

Mannerist and Dutch Baroque compositions, enacting a repertoire of uncensored behavior, from flirtations to solicitations to the drinking that lubricated the interactions. He delineated the faces as uniformly coarse or unattractive, with the exception of the well-groomed gay man at the far left, who offers a cigarette to one of the sailors. Cadmus pulled out all the stops in this raucous scene, barring only the element of nudity that was expressly forbidden by the federal guidelines. He went as far as he dared to flout that rule as well, emphatically delineating various muscular buttocks that appear to transcend clothing.

*The Fleet's In!* might have had an ordinary history were it not for the decision by the director of the PWAP, artist Edward Bruce, and his colleague, critic Forbes Watson, to include the painting in the *National Exhibition of Art by the Public Works of Art Project*, which opened at the Corcoran Gallery of Art in Washington in early April of 1934 with the aim of encouraging a congressional extension of the relief programs in the arts.[22] A tempest was released, however, when retired navy admiral Hugh Rodman saw the painting reproduced in a Washington newspaper and charged the Assistant Secretary of the Navy,

Henry Latrobe Roosevelt, with demanding its withdrawal before the opening of the exhibition and preventing its further display. Although Bruce promptly agreed to pull the picture at once, Roosevelt personally confiscated the canvas before Bruce could act. This preemptive act of censorship was seized upon by dozens of American newspapers, catapulting *The Fleet's In!*, and Cadmus, to instant fame. It has been suggested that Rodman and Roosevelt reacted hastily in order to uphold the navy's reputation at a moment when they were actively promoting legislation to fund an expanded force.[23] Their sense of urgency in the matter may have been heightened by the fact that news had just broken of Hitler's intent to rearm Germany and vastly expand its army and navy.[24]

Whatever the stakes, the navy's objections to the painting centered on the behaviors that Cadmus dared to record. In the comments Rodman released to the press, he called the painting an insult and a fabrication that "evidently originated in the sordid, depraved imagination" of the artist. Cadmus had gone too far in picturing "a disgraceful, sordid, disreputable, drunken brawl, wherein apparently a number of enlisted men

are consorting with a party of streetwalkers and denizens of the
red-light district."[25] Cadmus confidently stated that he had wit-
nessed all of this and more on his frequents visits to Riverside
Park as a youth and that the very truth of his representation
was what the navy brass found objectionable. The experience
immediately galvanized his artistic priorities, as stated for
an article published in his defense by the *New York Evening
Journal*: "[F]rom now on I'm painting the truth. I used to paint
pretty things. The ugliness of life hasn't been painted nearly so
much."[26] The *New York Daily News* defended both the painting
and the behavior it depicted: "If most of our sailors have come
to the point where they hurry alone to the Public Library or the
museums on shore leave, instead of finding themselves some
girlfriends and doing a little drinking, dancing, and the rest of
the things that he-men do when they want to relax, then it's too
bad for us and for our navy. The shore leave activities so vividly
pictured by Mr. Cadmus go with the fighting man's trade."
Quoted elsewhere in the *New York Daily News* the same day,
Cadmus suggested that he had used restraint in executing the
work: "I used to live out there and if I had painted what I really
saw, they would have hung me instead of the canvas."[27]

Several recent discussions of *The Fleet's In!* have suggested that the inclusion of the gay man—meticulously
groomed, sporting a signal red tie, and interacting with one
of the sailors—triggered Rodman's extreme reaction. There
was no subtlety in Cadmus's arrangement of the vignette—the
splayed position and well-endowed body of a drunken sailor
between the two conversing men provides a blatant cue. In his
well-documented analysis of the picture, Richard Meyer has
noted that the silence of both Rodman and Cadmus around
this feature of the composition underscores its centrality in
the controversy.[28] While the depiction of homosexual behavior may have been of issue, Cadmus's overarching immersion
in "the ugliness in life" in *The Fleet's In!* offers stiff competition. Here and in other Depression-era canvases, Cadmus
represented unbridled public behavior in the orbit of which
his ubiquitous gay man is often the embodiment of reserve. In
doing so, he supplemented his formal sources in Italian and
Dutch art—on which he typically modeled his highly articulated

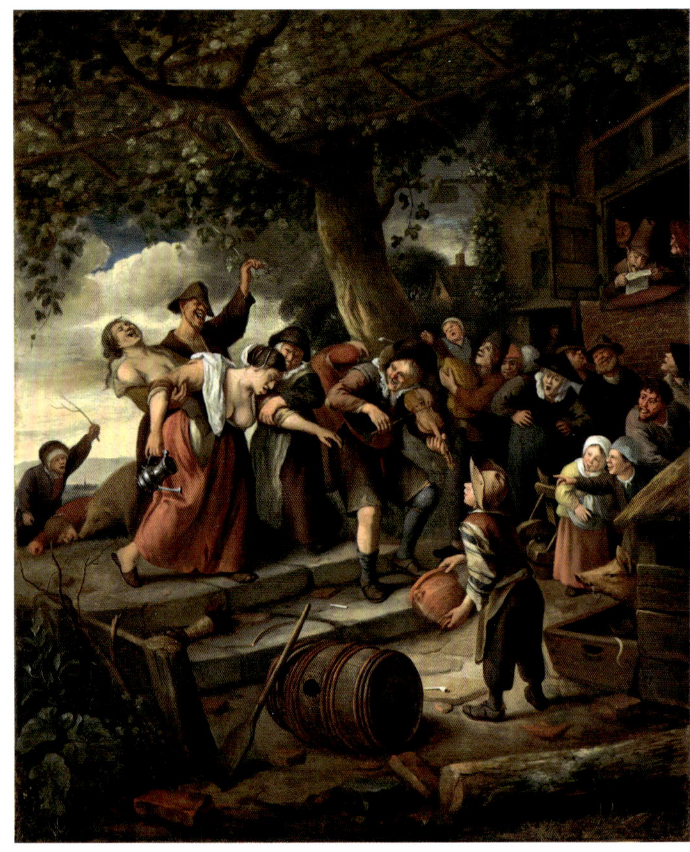



and exaggeratedly foreshortened figures—with subject matter inspired by the raucous Dutch Baroque figure subjects for
which painters such as Jan Steen were well known, in which
those on the lowest rung of the social ladder overindulge all of
their senses in every way (see fig. 6).

While disinclined to shed caution and decorum in his
own public behavior, Cadmus, along with other artists, writers,
and filmmakers of the decade, framed excess as a liberating
escape from the fateful conditions to which Americans were
subjected at the height of the Depression. His representations
of the down-and-out, including the women soliciting sailors in
*The Fleet's In!* and the regulars who seek a raucous good time in
his *Greenwich Village Cafeteria* (1934; Museum of Modern Art,
New York)—also painted for submission to the WPA—suggest
an almost enviable disregard for personal or public propriety. In
a comparable 1934 Hollywood feature titled *Happiness Ahead*,
a young heiress in the act of sneaking away from her family's

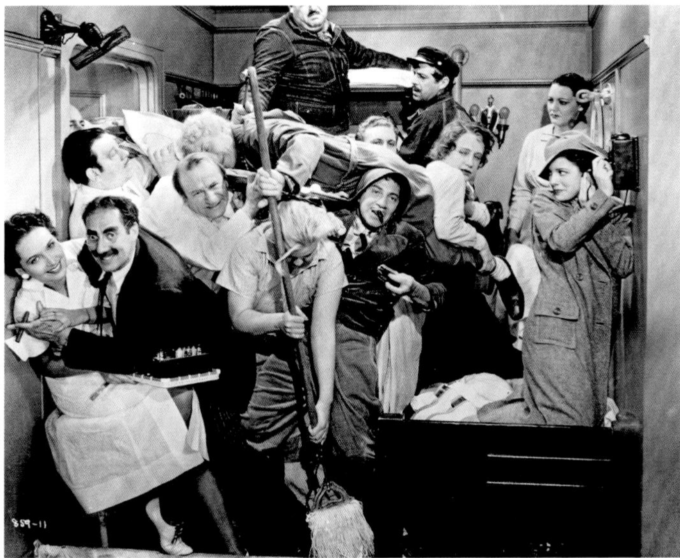

lavish townhouse and New Year's Eve festivities confides to her complicit father that she is desperate to go someplace where people "have real fun" and "make noise." Her wish comes true when she follows a group of boisterous young working men and women into a Chinese restaurant and joins them in pooling their pennies to eat and drink too much and to make a great deal of noise. The viability of representing off-color behavior in mainstream American painting in the 1930s undoubtedly owed something to the rising taste for such irreverently improper behavior in popular films including an array of Marx Brothers features (see fig. 7). In painting, film, and fiction throughout the 1930s, such grossly comedic devices mediated the potentially threatening overthrow of long-standing rules and conventional expectations. Interpreted more recently as an aesthetic of the "grotesque," this mode of representation offered audiences humor as a crutch with which to bear the unsettling realities of an upturned social order.[29]

The inclusion of *The Fleet's In!* would not likely have altered the overwhelmingly positive reception of the Corcoran exhibition by leading newspapers. A majority of the more than five hundred works of art on view offered somber but not abrasive American Scene narratives of daily life and proved the value of relief for artists under the auspices of the New Deal. The critic Emily Genauer described the works as uniformly "of,

by and for the people . . . created by their own artists and depicting their own lives."[30]

Playing against this tendency for restrained sobriety, the painter Philip Evergood, like Cadmus, mastered the comical grotesque by mid-decade. Evergood had found religion in the matter of social causes in 1933, after a midwinter meeting with a group of homeless people camped in makeshift shelters near the Hudson River off Christopher Street. He later recalled, "That's what brought me to life."[31] The transformative encounter also led him to ask himself, "Are you going on painting your centaurs and men . . . ? Or are you going to express life like Goya did, and like Daumier did? . . . What use are you going to be to humanity if you can't be a little part of your age?"[32] If Evergood was drawn to the same pictorial models as Nathanael West's Tod Hackett, he was motivated by altruistic concerns rather than by morbid fascination. Although he never signed on to the Communist rolls, he committed himself entirely to art attuned to the struggles of the impoverished and disenfranchised lower classes. He began to frequent the forums held by the John Reed Club and contributed to its 1933 exhibition on the theme "Hunger Fascism War."[33]

Evergood had signed on to the PWAP payroll early in 1933, owing in part to the good offices of the New York realist John Sloan, who had introduced him to Juliana Force. A year later Evergood painted the jarringly macabre *Dance Marathon* (1934; fig. 8), a subject that was entirely of the moment. By the 1930s, dance marathons were at best commercially driven endurance contests and at worst outright cons staged by out-of-towners.[34] Aptly described as part of the "culture of poverty," the marathons preyed on the unemployed and the idle. As the decade progressed, they were increasingly seen as a pernicious influence, encouraging inappropriate associations or even prostitution and tempting poor girls in particular into illicit or pointless behavior. Vigorous objections by local authorities led to the passage of legislation banning them, including a 1933 New York law prohibiting the organization of, or participation in, dance marathons lasting more than eight hours.[35] By the time Evergood undertook the subject, in New York it represented an even edgier choice.

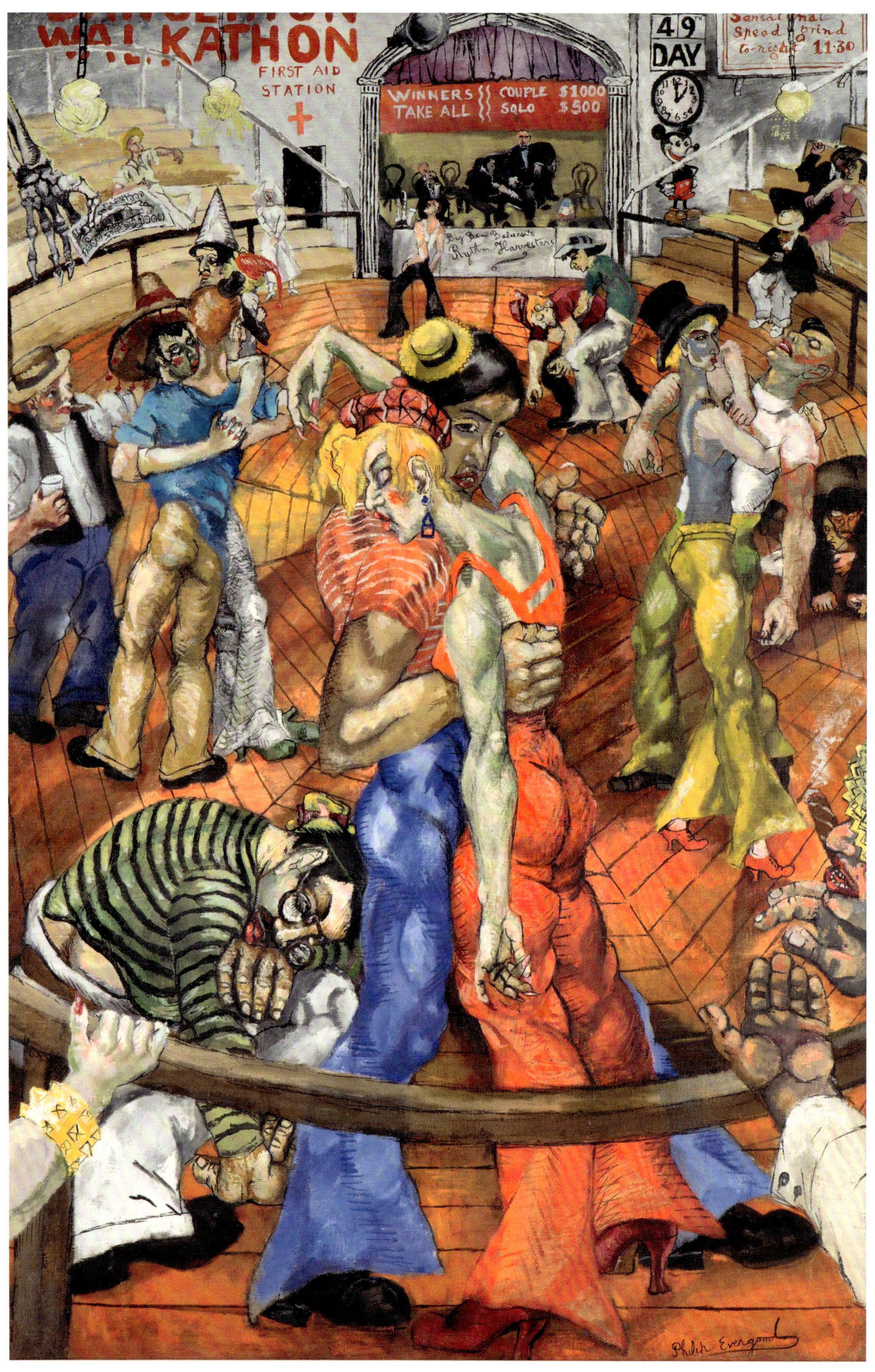

WALKATHON
FIRST AID
STATION
49 DAY
Sensational
Speed Grind
to-night 11:30
WINNERS
TAKE ALL
COUPLE $1000
SOLO $500
Philip Evergood

That the artist set out to invest *Dance Marathon* with a disturbing gravity is evident in his selection of pictorial sources. For the central figure alone, he echoed the emaciated contortions of Matthias Grünewald's Northern Renaissance crucified Christ in the Isenheim Altarpiece (1512–16; Musée Unterlinden, Colmar) in the clawlike, red-nailed hand; and in the face, the sharply profiled and harshly rouged, red-lipped prostitutes depicted by Henri de Toulouse-Lautrec. For bodies throughout the scene, the attenuated and overarticulated anatomy employed by the Spanish Mannerist artist El Greco was his model. Evergood later remarked that the paintings by El Greco that he had seen in Spain in 1931 had affected him "more than anything has ever impressed me."[36] One sees time and again in Evergood's work references to the Spaniard's signature elongation, bizarre musculature heightened by extreme modeling, and unhealthy grayish tonalities, combined in such masterworks as *Adoration of the Shepherds* (1612–14; fig. 9). The harsh formal exaggerations make many of the figures in *Dance Marathon* appear vaguely androgynous, as do the pants and jumpsuits, short haircuts topped with odd little hats, and coarse features. Evergood's gender-vagueness was in keeping with one of the more habitual critiques of marathon dancing, which held that the contests perverted gender roles by reducing men to seek income on a dance floor and forcing women to abandon all feminine grace and propriety.

The manipulative power of money (offered by a disingenuous skeletal hand) is embodied in the unsavory, partial forms of the rapt spectators in the foreground, whose attributes are a gaudy bracelet and a cigar. If the tilted perspective of the web-patterned floor suggests the spinning deck of an amusement ride, Evergood's dance marathon was the antithesis of the exuberantly democratic Coney Island amusement ride known as the Human Roulette Wheel, whose vertiginous spinning offered girls a momentary thrill and a taste of exhibitionism. The combined effect of the smoldering reds and the depleted surrender of the bodies transform *Dance Marathon* into an infernal vision—a sort of Last Judgment for the New Deal era, in which the pact to compete in the contest suggests a faithless and ultimately ill-fated life.

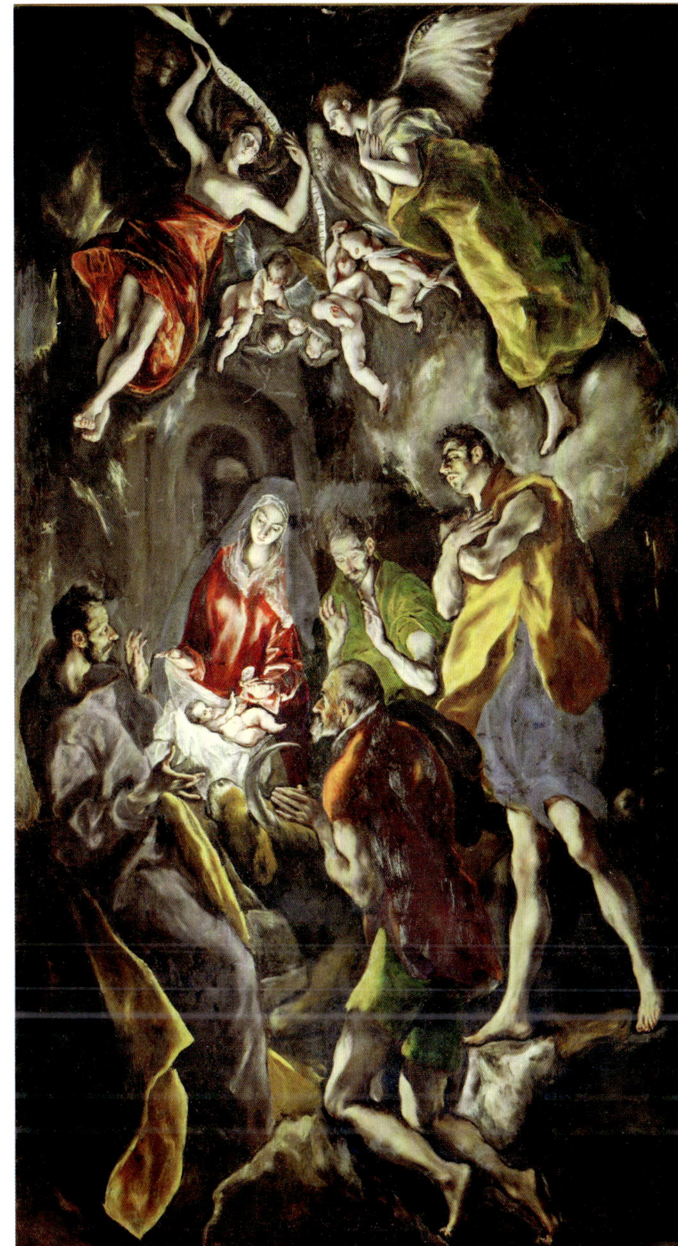

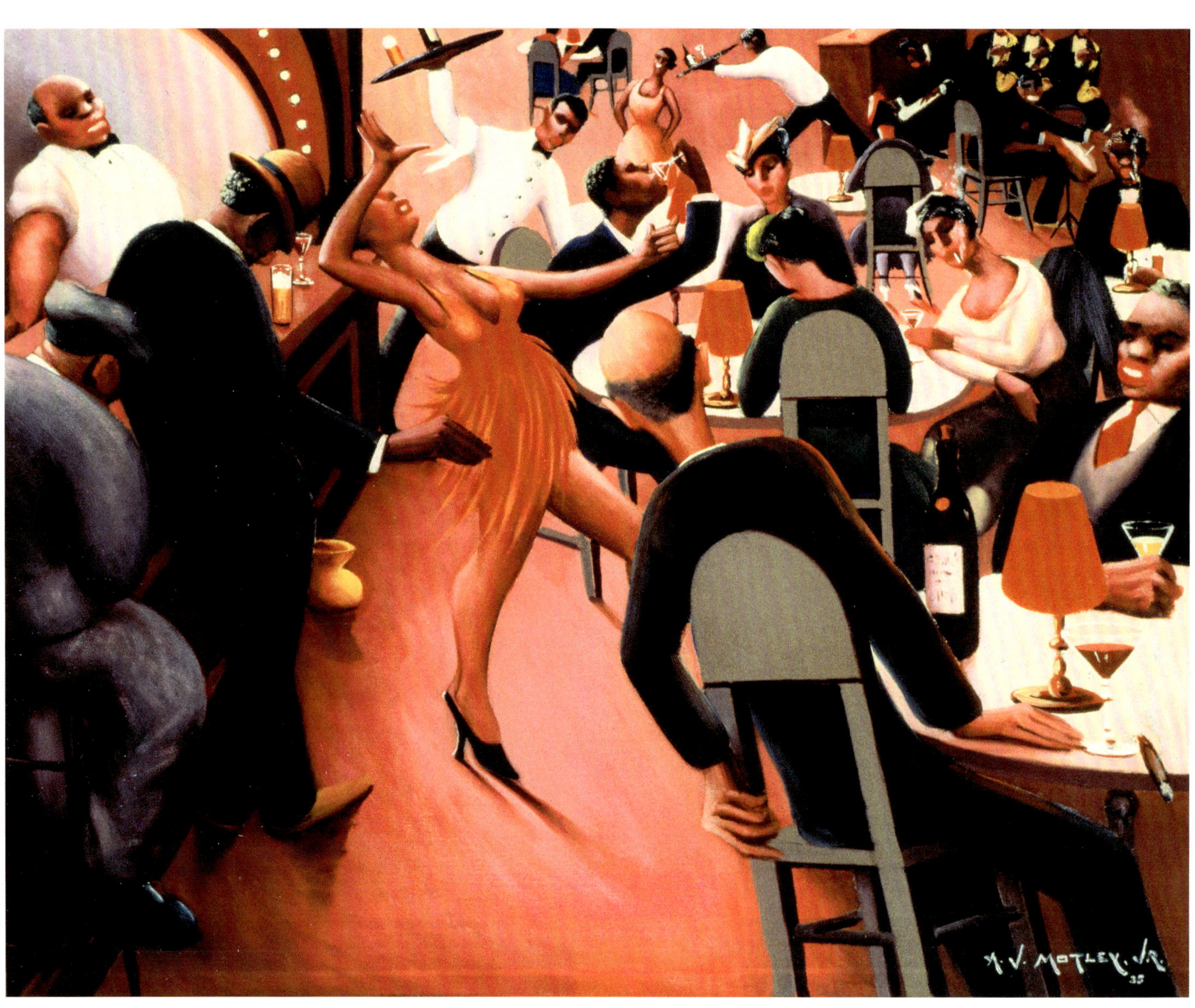

Compared to the extremes of Evergood's subject,
Archibald Motley's *Saturday Night* (fig. 10) appears extraordinarily normal in its representation of a lively nightclub populated by African Americans. Motley painted the work in 1935,
the year in which he moved from the rolls of the PWAP to the
Easel Division of the WPA's Illinois Art Project. Unlike Jones,
Neel, Cadmus, and Evergood, who were more or less politically
aligned in the selection of their 1930s subjects, Motley had
begun to test scenes of Jazz Age nightlife during a yearlong
stay in Paris, from 1929 to 1930. In works such as *Blues* (1929;
Collection of Mara Motley, MD, and Valerie Gerrard Browne),
he adopted a schematic figure style and an electric palette,
expanding upon a stylistic shift he had begun about 1926, when
he moved away from a naturalistically textured portrait style
(developed as a student at the integrated School of the Art
Institute of Chicago) in favor of a more naïve-feeling approach
to multifigure scenes. What remained constant was his focus on
African American and mixed-race subjects.

The leading Harlem Renaissance theorist and critic Alain
Locke remarked that with this aesthetic transition Motley had
become "more and more fascinated by the grotesqueries and
oddities of Negro life, which he sometimes satirically, sometimes sympathetically, depicts. His style, once curious and
restrained, is now highly imaginative, free in rhythm, riotous
in color, a combination of Dutch realism with American humor
and tempo."[37] In the Chicago subjects to which he subsequently
turned, Motley replaced the Parisian dance halls and jazz
bars—and his models from the French colonies of Martinique,
Senegal, and Haiti—with the city's vibrant Black Belt neighborhoods, nightclubs, and locals. He also heightened his new style,
adding dynamism to his compositions through the use of active
and angular figures. A number of art historians have noted that
Motley derived some of the "American humor and tempo" from
the widely published caricatures created by the Mexican artist
Miguel Covarrubias, who in 1928 published a volume of African
American "types" titled *Negro Drawings*.[38] Covarrubias's characterizations, like imagery by any number of graphic artists
who engaged with the vibrant cultural life of Harlem at the
time, adhered to many of the signal habits of racist imagery that

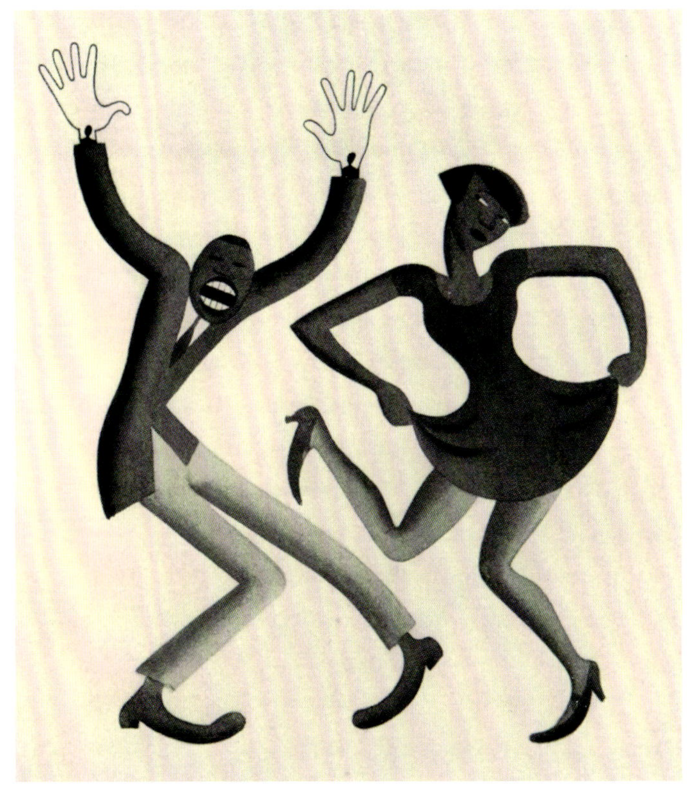

derived from the visual culture of minstrelsy. They operated
within the broader context of Jazz Age caricature that aimed
to represent liberated or even outlandish modern behavior. In
works such as *Saturday Night*, Motley similarly accepted the
risk of referencing stereotypical characterizations.

The artist did, however, achieve the then-rare feat of
describing black society independent of a white context. In
*Saturday Night*, his subject is an African American jazz bar and
the female performer at its energetic center, clad in a feathered,
hot-orange costume and in a pose—with torso tilted backwards
and limbs extended in four directions at once, à la Josephine
Baker—that signals one of the current jazz-inspired choreographies like the Black Bottom or the Chicken Shake Shuffle.
Covarrubias profiled figures in a variety of these liberated
dance poses (see fig. 11). Motley heightened the excitement
through a pattern of lively diagonals and a flickering play of
sharp contrasts across a field of hot pink. The dancer holds
the rapt attention of the five men closest to her, while the
rest of the scene buzzes with activity. Like Alice Neel, Motley

adopted a caricatured style in small-scale, multifigure narrative subjects, in part to adhere to the canvas format and subject parameters set out by the WPA program. In maintaining his goal of featuring African Americans in particular, however, he broke new ground in the address of subjects around African American community life—including neighborhood barbecues and picnics and, especially, the festive evening "stroll" through the streets of Chicago's Black Belt—unto itself, free of the white "slumming" that was so typical of the 1920s and 1930s.

No artist was better at representing Depression-era urban life than Reginald Marsh, who was a tireless consumer of the theater of New York's most crowded public venues. Raised in a family of artists and educated at Yale University, Marsh began his career in the 1920s as a staff artist for the *New York Daily News*, covering vaudeville and the subways, and for the *New Yorker*.[39] He began to paint seriously after a trip to Europe, where he first discovered the florid figure style of Baroque masters such as Rubens and the colorism of the nineteenth-century French Romantic painter Eugène Delacroix. By 1928, when Marsh inherited a steady income, he set himself up in a top-floor studio at 21 East Fourteenth Street, overlooking Union Square, where he would find endless material for his art. He began to associate with the groups of political activists that were often present in the neighborhood; he also attended classes in Communism at the Workers' School and meetings at the John Reed Club, and contributed illustrations to the Communist-leaning magazine *New Masses*. He nevertheless had little use for openly propagandistic imagery, famously saying, "Well, what should we do . . . imitate [José Clemente] Orozco, [George] Grosz, African sculpture, and draw endless pictures of gas masks, 'Cossacks,' and caricatures of J. P. Morgan with a pig-like nose?"[40]

Marsh spent every day sketching or painting, searching at once for the comic and the tragic, particularly in the immediate vicinity of his studio. As recalled by the writer and activist Alfred Kazin, Union Square in the 1930s had it all:

**The place was boiling . . . with crowds lined up at the frankfurter stands and gawking at the fur models who in a lighted corner window perched above the square walked round and round like burlesque queens. . . . [T]he usual groups in argument before the Automat, the usual thick crowd pouring round and round the park in search of something, anything, that might be in the stores. There was always a crowd in Union Square; the place itself felt like a crowd through which you had to keep pushing to get anywhere.**[41]

There could be no better illustration of the crush of people and shoppers than Marsh's *In Fourteenth Street*, of 1934 (fig. 12). The tempera medium that he had adopted in 1929 at the suggestion of Thomas Hart Benton allowed Marsh to retain the high degree of graphic detail—literally drawn in—that had characterized his lively popular illustrations; and indeed Benton's example also encouraged him to retain populist subject matter in his easel works. Here, a flood of bodies descending from the Fourteenth Street station of the El pours out onto the street in a knot of noise and confusion within which every possible type of person is conjoined. People are hawking and buying, hurrying off or pausing to watch.

Although the urgent consumer culture of Union Square might seem unlikely at the height of the Depression, consumerism was widely seen as integral to the country's economic survival. With new electric gadgets, plastic products, and up-to-the-minute fashions offered as improvements for daily life, the nation at mid-decade was described by the sociologist Robert Lynd as "a culture hypnotized by the gorged stream of new things to buy."[42] In Marsh's painting, the consumer par excellence is the young blonde deftly framed by the ladder just to the left of center. A literally bright focal point in the scene, she sports a flounced blouse and fitted skirt à la mode, as well as the obligatory bleached and permed hair topped with a small picture hat. Clearly a working girl of one sort or another, she is the very sort of female featured in movie after movie in the early 1930s—the self-reliant, unsentimental type with an appetite for the finer things in life and a determination to get them. The most notorious version was the gold-digging secretary portrayed by Barbara Stanwyck in Alfred E. Green's *Baby Face*. As Lily Powers, she escapes her impoverished circumstances by following the Friedrich Nietzsche–inspired advice offered by a poor cobbler: go to the big city, exploit yourself, and

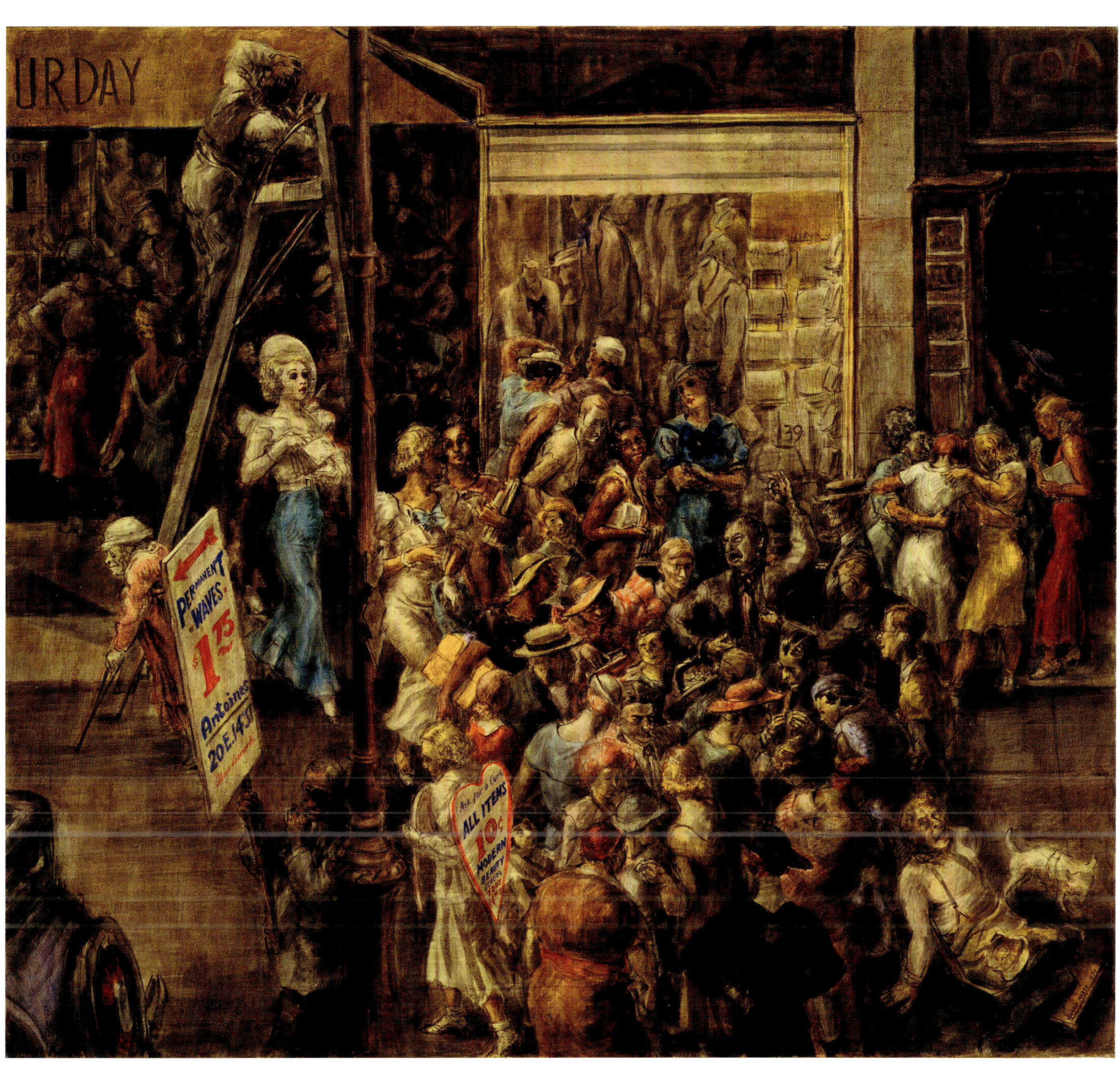
URDAY
COA
PERMANENT
WAVES
$1.75
Antoine
20 E. 14
ALL ITEMS
10¢
MODERN
BEAUTY

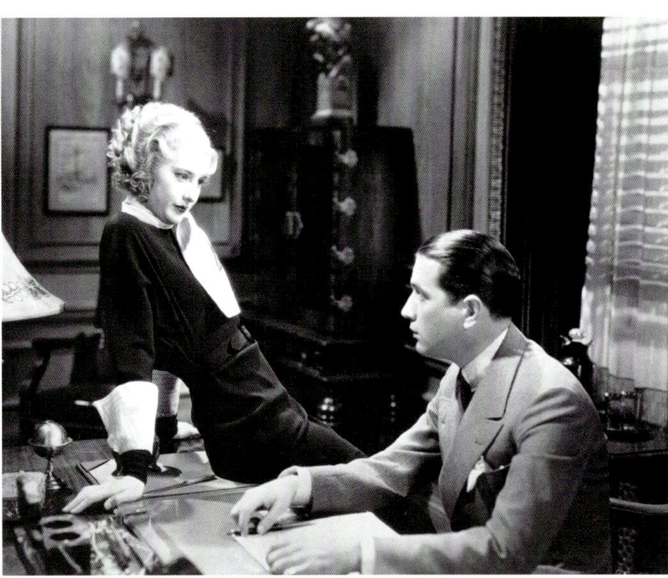

use men to get the things you want. Powers seduces her way to New York and, newly equipped with a permed, platinum hairdo and the nickname Baby Face, sleeps her way up the corporate ladder in ever more stylish clothes and apartments (see fig. 13). If film industry censors were already aware of the risk to poor young girls that "kept woman" story lines might pose in 1933, the application of the Hays Code, beginning in 1934, was more aggressive in targeting films in which girls set morals aside solely out of a desire for material luxury.[43] Marsh heightened the sexuality of the blonde in *In Fourteenth Street* through his choice of dress and demeanor and by separating her from the crowd around her, much in the way that "falling" girls in films like *Baby Face* were inevitably shown alone after an ellipsis— the cut to a neutral scene that signals the sexual encounter.[44]

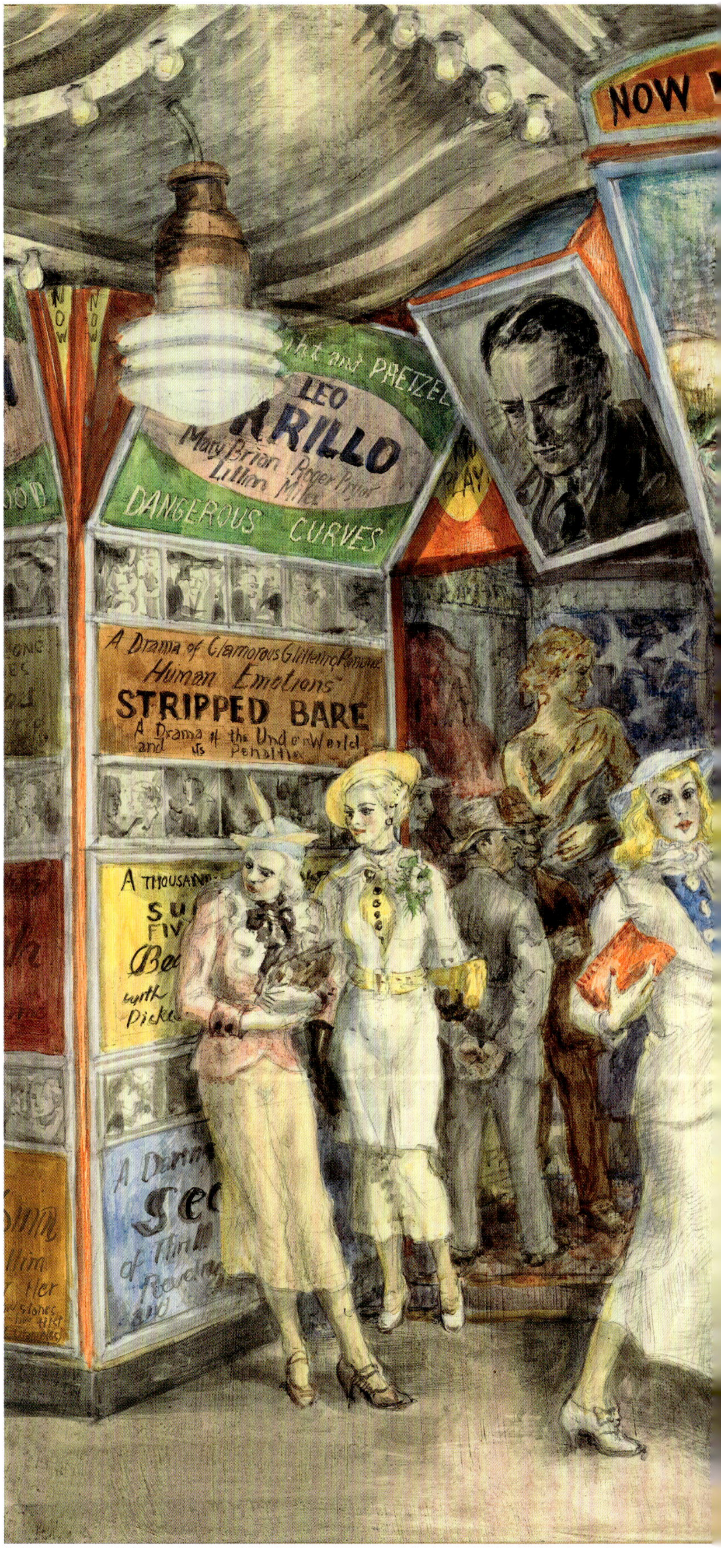

Marsh celebrated the centrality of films to Depression-era life in *Twenty Cent Movie* (1936; fig. 14), featuring people gathered—women to the left and men on the right—around the ticket booth and entrances to a bustling movie house. His preliminary drawing for the subject included full-text versions of the surrounding posters. One advertised Rouben Mamoulian's *We Live Again*, a love story set in Russia that had debuted two years before he completed his painting. Virtually every compositional detail, from the flirtatious fashions worn by the young

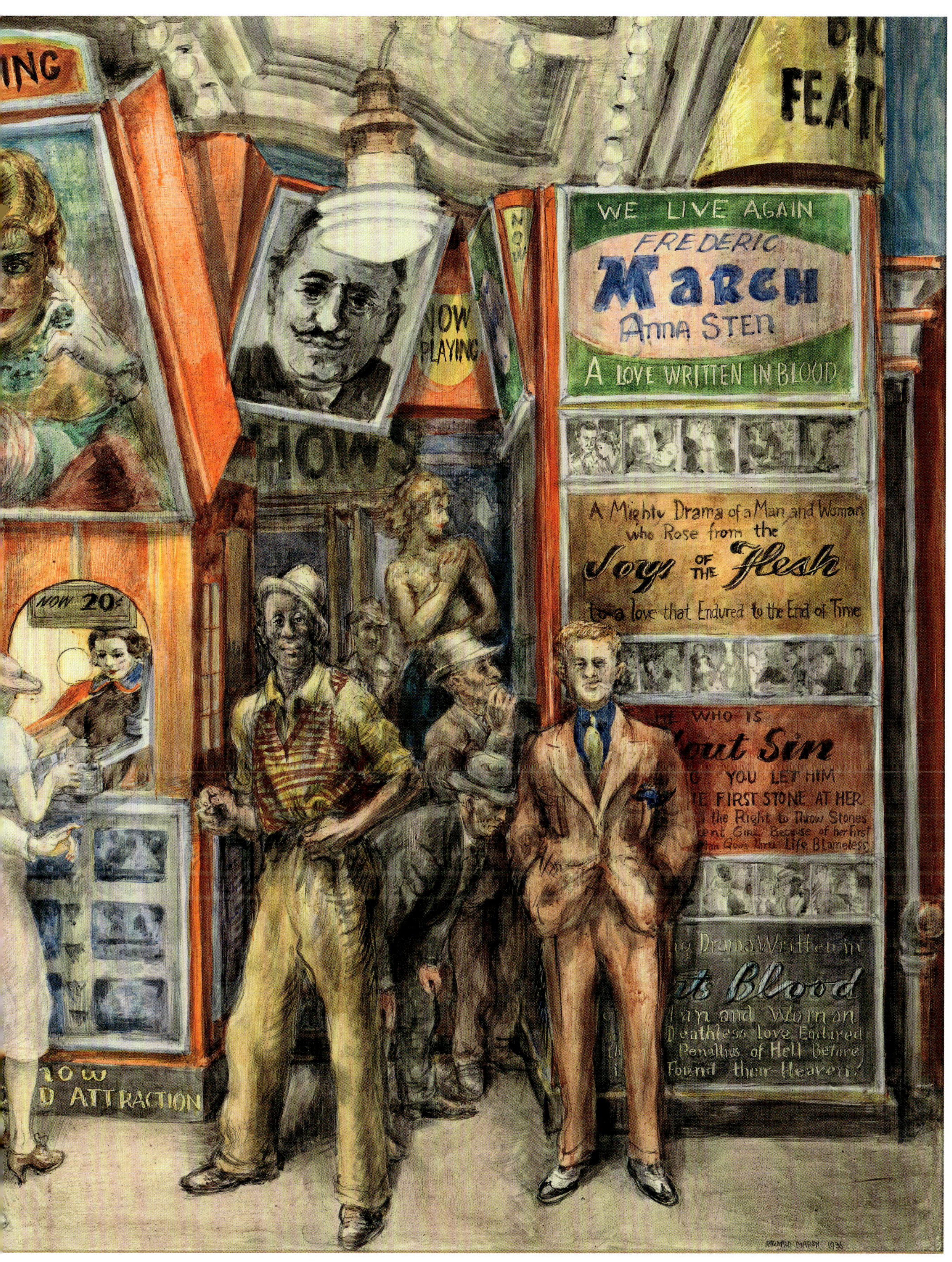
ING
FEAT
BIG
NOW PLAYING
HOWS
NOW 20¢
NOW
D ATTRACTION
WE LIVE AGAIN
FREDERIC
MARCH
Anna Sten
A LOVE WRITTEN IN BLOOD
A Mighty Drama of a Man and Woman
who Rose from the
Joys OF THE Flesh
to a love that Endured to the End of Time
HE WHO IS
out Sin
YOU LET HIM
E FIRST STONE AT HER
the Right to Throw Stones
ent Girl Because of her first
Man Goes Thru Life Blameless
Drama Written in
ts Blood
Man and Woman
Deathless Love Endured
Penalties of Hell Before
Found their Heaven!
REGINALD MARSH 1936

women to the suggestive verbiage on the other ads that paper the entry to the theater, speaks of the sexuality that infused the movies during the Depression. Just above the head of the man in the sharp, reddish suit and two-toned shoes, a sign proclaims the characters' triumph over the "Joys of the Flesh." And while the poster above the girls at left advertises a quirky 1933 musical, *Moonlight and Pretzels*, directed by Karl Freund, the sign just above their heads conjures characters "Stripped Bare." Marsh likely intended the latter phrase as a punning echo of his treatment of the two female figures, where in keeping with his technique of drawing details onto forms defined in tempera, he provided more anatomical specificity than clothed figures require (see fig. 15). Their treatment might also reference the particularly revealing fashions for which bombshells including the short-lived Jean Harlow were duly famous (see fig. 16). Hovering above all of the figures and the ticket booth is a large poster featuring a steamy and bejeweled sexpot surely intended to be Mae West (see fig. 17), who in 1936 alone starred as a seductress in Raoul Walsh's *Klondike Annie* and in Henry Hathaway's *Go West, Young Man*. Marsh remained completely engaged with theater of all sorts throughout the Depression—on the streets, the beaches, and at the movies—in spite of lackluster patronage salvaged only by a college friend who in 1935 began to purchase a picture a month.

The new stock characters of 1930s art and movies, and particularly the activist laborer and the sexy blonde, transcended the work of individual artists. A platinum-coiffed gold digger turns up in the unlikely setting of Paul Sample's wry *Church Supper* (1933; fig. 18) as a glamor girl who upsets a traditional order. The Kentucky-born Sample graduated from Dartmouth College but turned to painting during a period of recuperation from tuberculosis.[45] He continued his training in Los Angeles at the Otis Art Institute in the mid-1920s and subsequently joined the faculty of the School of Architecture at the University of Southern California. In 1931, in advance of the mandate promoted by the PWAP and WPA programs, Sample began to pursue socially relevant subject matter with canvases including *Unemployment* (1931; National Academy Museum, New York). He tempered his subjects as

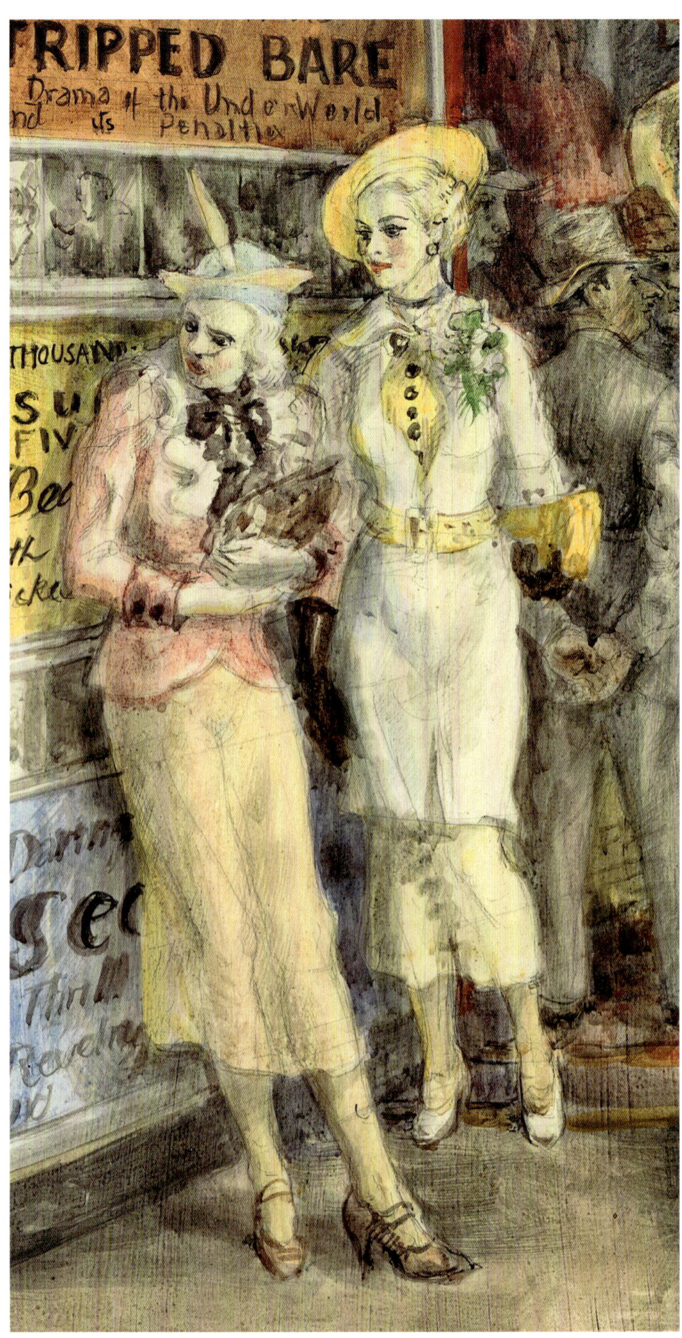

**Fig. 16** George Hurrell (American, 1904–1992). *Jean Harlow.*

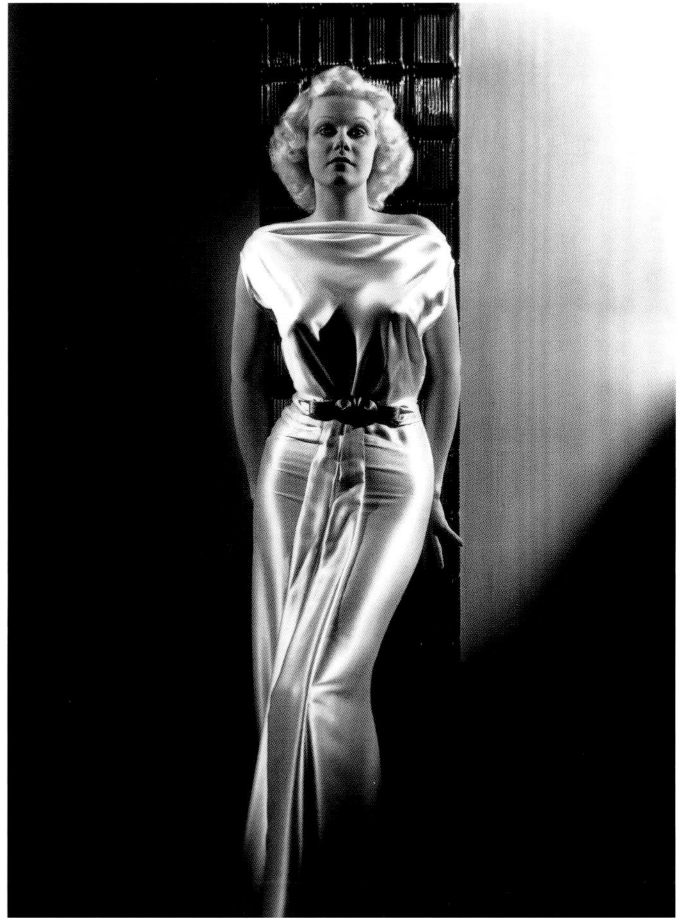

**Fig. 17** White Studio, New York. *Mae West as Diamond Lil*, 1928. The New York Public Library.

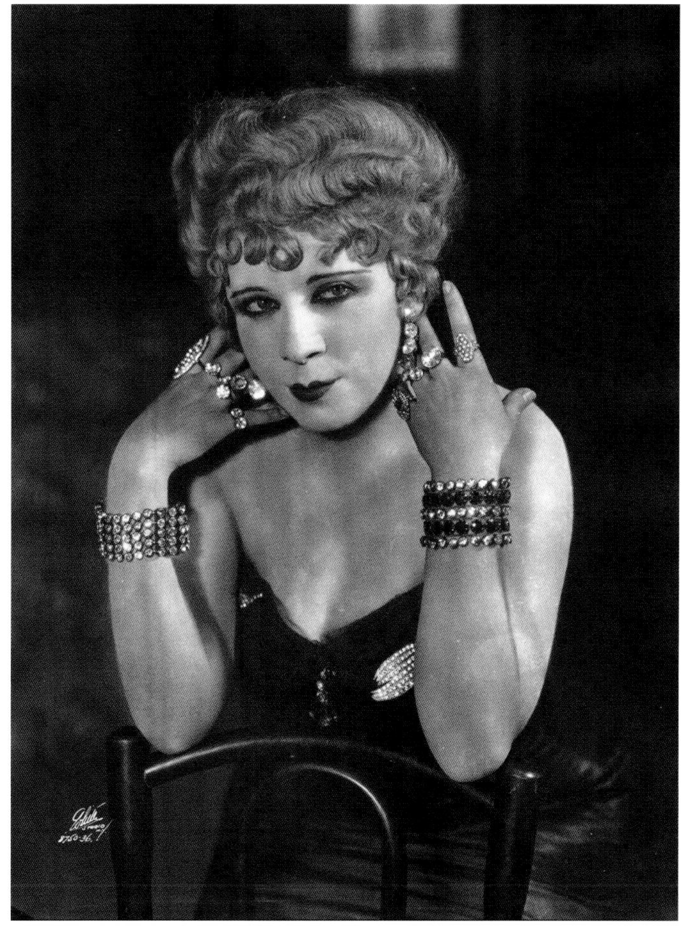

the Depression advanced, however, moving in the direction of nostalgia-based Americana under the likely influence of the increasingly popular works of the Regionalist Grant Wood.

Sample was on the WPA rolls by 1936, when he painted a number of works cast in generic New England settings and rendered with a schematic perfection more typical of the backdrops of Northern Renaissance panel paintings. In *Church Supper*, the idealized setting includes a baseball diamond, a cemetery, and precisely sown fields that together speak of unalterable American traditions. The action takes place in the foreground, however, where the blonde interloper is sending subtle shock waves into a long-established balance. While a host of stout and sour-faced matrons offer their menfolk a menu of plain fare, the majority of those men train their gazes

on the appetizing sight of the slender and shapely form that is revealed through the young woman's dress and the long leg she exposes with the lifting of her skirt. (One exception among the men is a self-absorbed figure in the foreground, who wears a telltale brown shirt and black armband and sports a Hitleresque mustache, suggesting that wantonness is not the only encroaching threat.) The leg-reveal, as coined by Claudette Colbert in Frank Capra's seminal 1934 screwball comedy *It Happened One Night*, was a signal gesture of the brazen young 1930s hottie (see fig. 19). Everything about the young blonde smacks of somewhere else—the city or the movies—and every detail, from the small hat and fox fur to the little purse, stands in contrast to the local ladies with their fallen bosoms and disappeared waists. The scene is slyly comical throughout, from

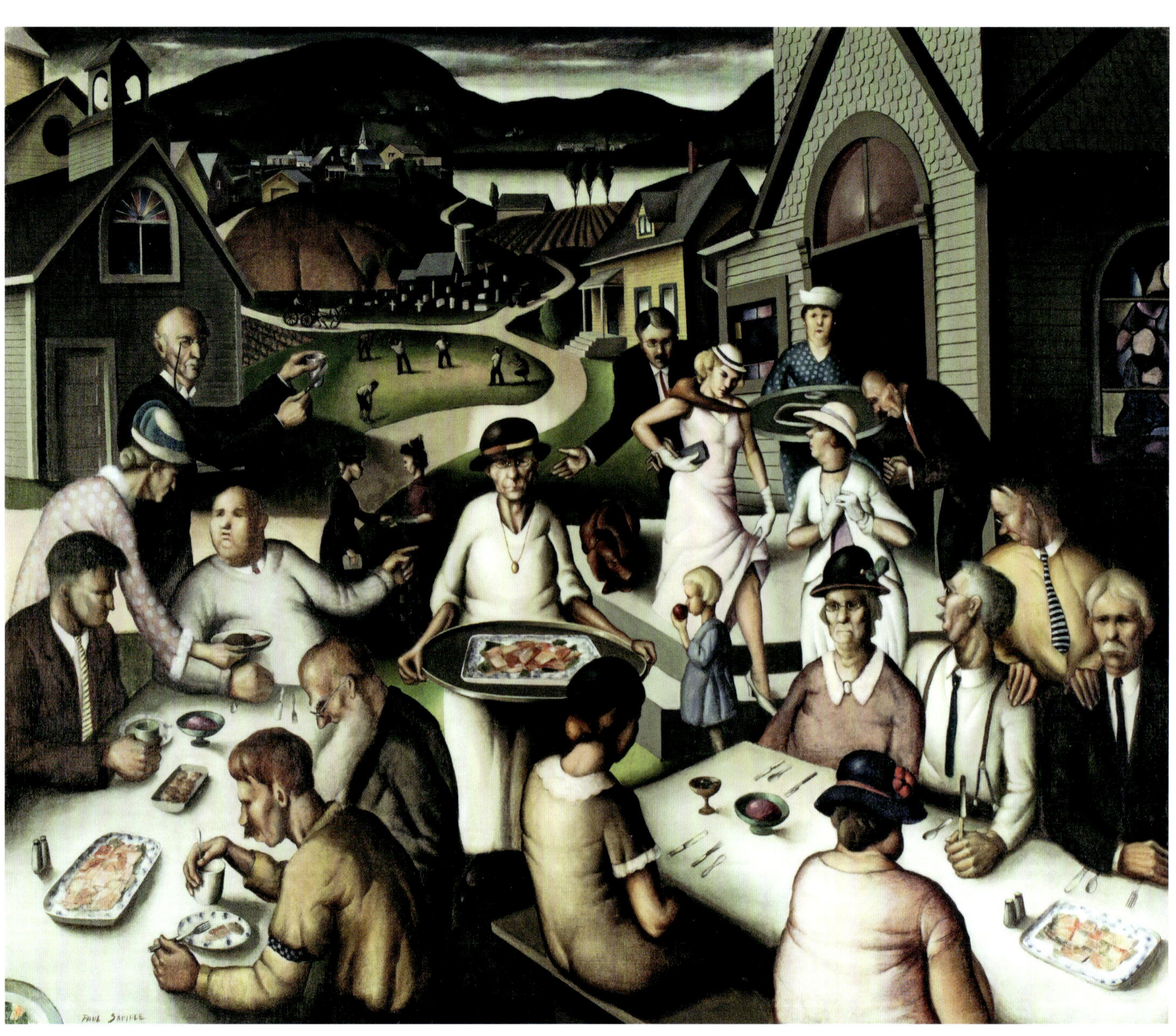

the exaggerated head-turning of the men to the dog who sniffs
something interesting and the small blonde girl who is about to
take a telling bite from an apple.

At least one artist held himself apart from the trending
developments in American figurative art during the Great
Depression. Edward Hopper continued on the trajectory he
had set in the 1920s, when his work aligned with a distilled and
quietist vision of modern America, if not completely with the
sleek figurative idealism that was equally current. In contrast
to peers such as Cadmus, Evergood, and Marsh, who sought
to convey the crush and cacophony of Depression-era lives,
Hopper held his attention away from the press of crowded
sidewalks, the contortions of the unsightly, and the intrusions
of the ill-mannered. As significant, unlike his peers, Hopper
disdained the arts programs of the FAP and WPA—as well as
the entire New Deal and Franklin Roosevelt himself—believing
their democratic approach bred mediocrity.[46]

Hopper persisted in his impulse to see and to convey
vacancy, whether in uninhabited margins or inaccessible individuals, and his adherence to his vision was rewarded with consistent and significant sales. The painter and critic Guy Pène du
Bois associated this inclination with a strain of Puritanism, one
that enabled Hopper to be "so deaf to all faddish chatter that he
can, without strain . . . remain himself." In a review of the one-
man exhibition of Hopper's work at the Museum of Modern
Art in 1933, the *Brooklyn Daily Eagle*'s Helen Appleton Read
praised the artist's tendency to "Puritan austerity and nothing
in excess, an emotional response to his native environment and
above all independence of art and spirit."[47]

In December 1938, after a protracted dry spell in his
work, Hopper undertook a subject set in a New York movie
theater that could not have been more different from Marsh's
animated *Twenty Cent Movie*. Perhaps owing to the onus of
planning a canvas after an involuntary hiatus, Hopper made
an exceptionally large number of sketches for *New York Movie*
(1939; fig. 20).[48] He began with rounds to a number of theaters,
including the Strand, Globe, and Republican, before settling
into a more extensive period of sketching at the Palace by the
middle of the month. One of the grand nineteenth-century

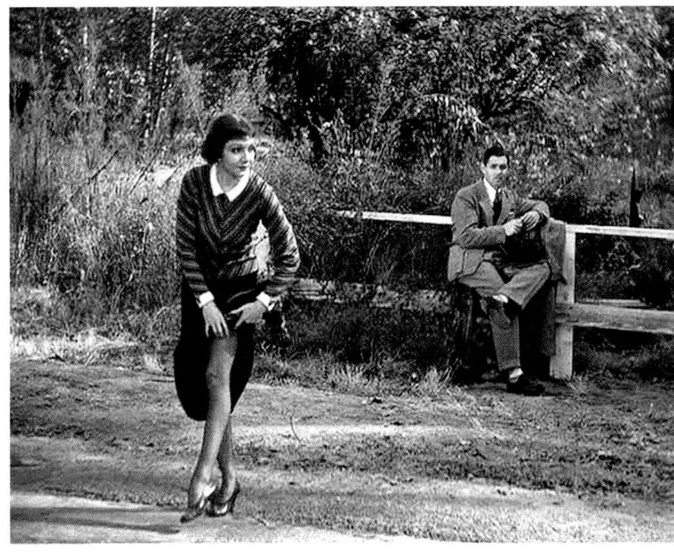

burlesque-turned-movie palaces, the Palace (now the Lunt-
Fontanne Theatre, on West Forty-Sixth Street) offered Hopper
extraordinary material in its scale and ornate architectural decorations. He found the core of his idea, however, in the marginal
feature of a curtained doorway to an upward-headed staircase.
His work on the painting is well documented. In the days after
Christmas he worked on it day and night, occasionally returning to the theaters for further details. Meanwhile, his art-
ist-wife Jo modeled in the hallway of their building repeatedly
for the figure of the usherette, wearing her own clothes rather
than the wide-legged jumpsuit featured in the finished painting
and based on the stylish costumes worn by the Palace's female
staff. Hopper's final canvas, painstakingly composed around
complex subtleties of interior light, was a supreme essay on
interiority—from the theater's inner seating on the left, to the
recesses beyond the curtained stairway, to the inward thoughts
of the young blonde featured in the brightest portion of the
composition. The signal component of Hopper's arrangement
may be the central divide—the vertical composed by the ornate
column and end of the wall separating the seating area from the
periphery—a strict enforcer of separateness.

Hopper may have conveyed separateness in this canvas
in another compelling way. Perhaps the most unexpected detail
in the painting is the grisaille vignette featured on the screen,

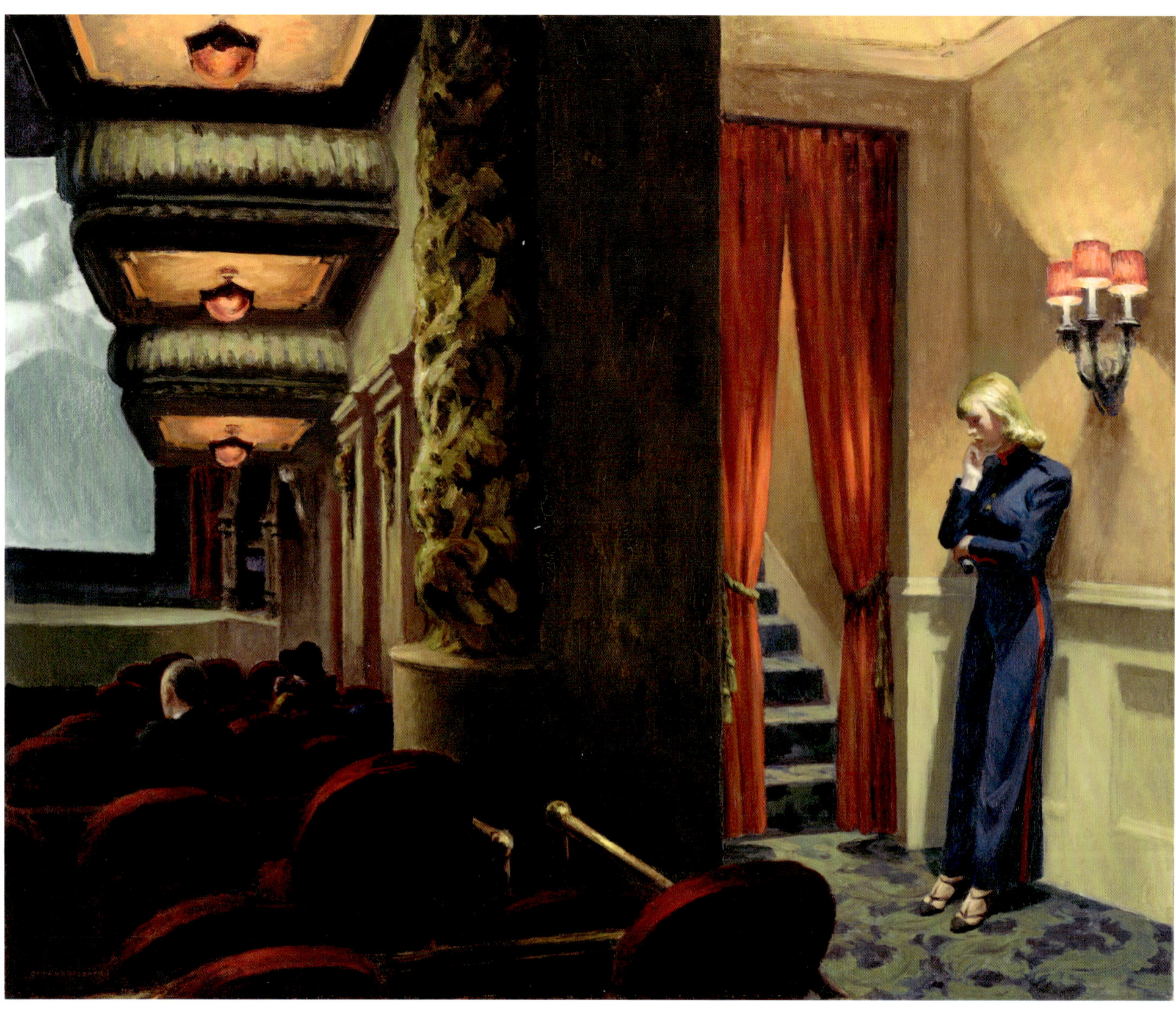

Fig. 20  Edward Hopper. *New York Movie*, 1939. Museum of Modern Art. Cat. 23.

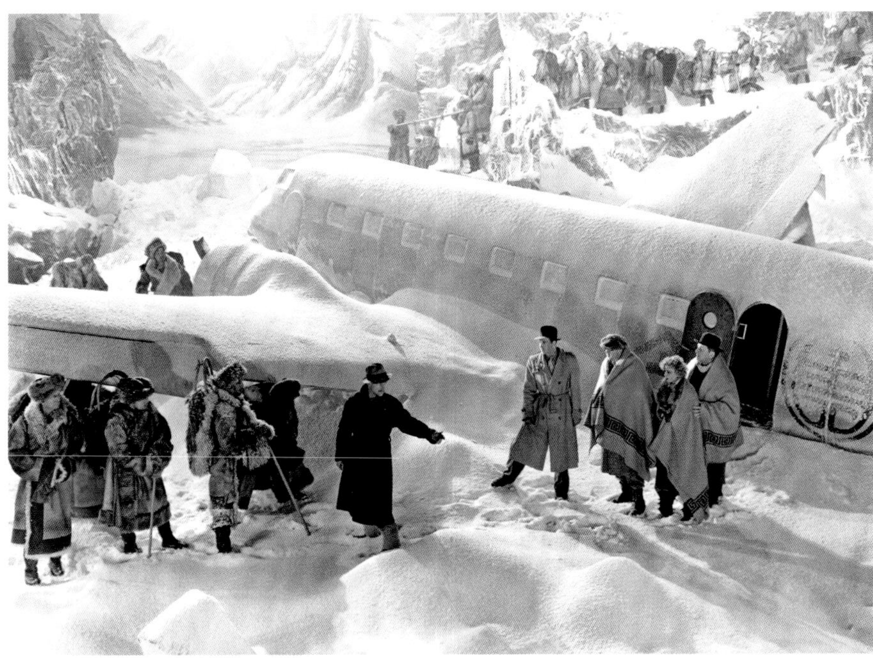

described by Hopper in his illustrated record book as "snowy
mountain tops"—the farthest thing from a flashy gold digger on
the make.[49] Hopper, like Marsh in *Twenty Cent Movie*, may have
taken some chronological liberty in quoting a film in this 1938
painting, for the likeliest candidate for the scene is a shot of the
snow-capped Himalayas featured in the hugely successful 1937
Frank Capra movie *Lost Horizon* (see fig. 21), based on a 1933
novel by British writer James Hilton. In the book and the film,
a British diplomat completing an airborne rescue mission in
India crashes with his party in the mountains near Tibet, only to
discover Shangri-La, a utopian society dedicated to inner peace
and long life and to preserving humanity from the extinction
threatened by an impending world war. In its opening titles
the film poses the question: "In these days of wars and rumors
of wars—haven't you ever dreamed of a place where there was
peace and security, where living was not a struggle but a lasting
delight?" A quote from this Capra classic would never have been
more apt than when Hopper completed the canvas early in 1939.

Hopper remained an exception among 1930s painters
in his stilled and quietist treatments of the figure. The majority tapped bold and expressive Old Master models—El Greco,
Rubens, Steen, and others—in order to convey the Depression's
upturned social order. They enlisted distorted, agitated,
unhealthy, or immodest bodies enacting uncensored or disrup-
tive behaviors that signaled failed systems and futile values.
Many painters heightened their expressionism as the decade
progressed and as the anxieties attendant to unemployment
and poverty were exacerbated by news of an armed Germany's
advance in Europe. Even in far-flung Hollywood, Nathanael
West revealed a keen awareness of these trends as he conjured
up artist Tod Hackett's final conceptualization of his master-
work, *The Burning of Los Angeles*. Hackett envisions a backdrop
depicting the burning city, "a great bonfire of architectural
styles," and before it a wild mob—an embodiment of dystopian,
Depression-era American society—pursuing a nude blonde
starlet and the artist himself, defending her.[50] As epitomized
by West's artist-antihero, artists who endeavored to record,
ameliorate, or rebel against the dire social conditions around
them—whether in images of labor activism, dance marathons,
fleet-week mischief, or a night at the movies—created unlikely
role models of survival, including fearless blondes and the artists themselves.

**1** Nathanael West, *The Day of the Locust* (1939; repr., New Directions, 2009), p. 60.

**2** For a discussion of the representation of bodies in American art of the 1920s, see Teresa A. Carbone, "Body Language: Liberation and Restraint in Twenties Figuration," in Teresa A. Carbone, ed., *Youth and Beauty: Art of the American Twenties* (Brooklyn Museum/Skira Rizzoli, 2011), pp. 15–93.

**3** "The World Crisis Expressed in Art . . . on the Theme Hunger Fascism War," *Catalogue of the John Reed Club*, December 1933, quoted in Patricia Hills, ed., *Modern Art in the USA: Issues and Controversies of the Twentieth Century* (Prentice Hall, 2000), p. 102.

**4** Andrew Hemingway, *Artists on the Left: American Artists and the Communist Movement, 1926–1956* (Yale University Press, 2002), p. 18.

**5** Opinions on the subject shifted most dramatically at mid-decade, when the Communist Party launched its Popular Front ideology and began to promote upbeat images of "normal" rather than radicalized American workers.

**6** The primary sources of biographical information on the artist are Andrew Walker and Janeen Turk, *Joe Jones: Radical Painter of the American Scene,* exh. cat. (Saint Louis Art Museum/University of Washington Press, 2010); and Hemingway, *Artists on the Left*, pp. 34–39.

**7** For a chronology of exhibitions featured at the Saint Louis Art Museum, see the museum's online exhibitions archive at http://www.slam.org/exhibitions/archive.php/.

**8** Hemingway, *Artists on the Left*, p. 35.

**9** Ibid., p. 37.

**10** For a discussion of Lange's work for the FSA, see Milton Meltzer, *Dorothea Lange: A Photographer's Life* (Farrar Straus Giroux, 1978), pp. 179–87.

**11** Hemingway, *Artists on the Left*, p. 36.

**12** Edward Alden Jewell, "Ex-House Painter in Art Show Here: Canvases by Joe Jones of St. Louis . . ." *New York Times*, May 22, 1935, p. 17.

**13** Biographical details on Neel are drawn from the chronology included in Ann Temkin, ed., *Alice Neel*, exh. cat. (Philadelphia Museum of Art, 2000), pp. 159–76. For more on Neel's interaction with the Cuban avant-garde, see Pamela Allara, *Pictures of People: Alice Neel's American Portrait Gallery* (University Press of New England, 1998), 59–63.

**14** For a detailed account of Neel's interactions with the government-funded art programs, see Phoebe Hoban, *Alice Neel: The Art of Not Sitting Pretty* (St. Martin's, 2010), pp. 104–08.

**15** Allara, *Pictures of People*, pp. 74–75.

**16** Patricia Hills, *Alice Neel* (Harry N. Abrams, 1983), p. 62.

**17** Biographical information on Whalen is drawn primarily from Daniel Hardin, "Paddy Whalen and the Midnight March of the Baltimore Brigade," *Washington Area Spark: Struggles from the Past for Today*, February 4, 2015, https://washingtonspark.word press.com/2015/02/04/paddy -whalen-the-midnight-march-of -the-baltimore-brigade/.

**18** For a consideration of the political meanings associated with the motif of workers' hands at this time, see Max Fraser, "Hands off the Machine: Workers' Hands and Revolutionary Symbolism in the Visual Culture of 1930s America," *American Art* 27, no. 2 (Summer 2013), pp. 94–117.

**19** Neel's remarks about the reception of her portraits by fellow Communists are quoted in Allara, *Pictures of People*, pp. 74–75. Shortly after sitting for Neel, Whalen went to Baltimore and embarked on a two-year effort to organize rank and file marine workers for a prolonged strike that culminated in a march on Washington in January of 1937 and the formation of the National Maritime Union. By that spring, when Neel exhibited her portrait of Whalen at the New School for Social Research in the *Waterfront Art Show*, cosponsored by An American Group (successor to the more strictly Communist Artists' Congress) and the Marine Workers Committee, it surely had more immediate relevance for union activists than the more numerous genre subjects and harbor views at hand. Bearing the title *Marine Worker*, the likeness paid tribute to Whalen's impassioned activism by embodying irrepressible roughness and militancy. Andrew Hemingway discusses the Whalen portrait in the context of the *Waterfront Art Show* in *Artists on the Left*, p. 134.

**20** Hoban, *Alice Neel*, p. 108.

**21** A concise biography of Cadmus is "Paul Cadmus: Artist Biography," http://www.dcmooregallery.com /artists/paul-cadmus/.

**22** An excellent, detailed account and contextual analysis of the entire affair is included in Richard Meyer, *Outlaw Representation: Censorship and Homosexuality in Twentieth-Century American Art* (Oxford University Press, 2002), pp. 37–56.

**23** Anthony J. Morris, "Paul Cadmus and Carnival, 1934: Representing the Comic Grotesque," *American Art* 26, no. 3 (Fall 2012), p. 94.

**24** For a thorough discussion of the references to Germany's push to rearm in 1934, see Jason Adams Ranke, "The Anglo-American Press and the 'Secret' Rearmament of Hitler's Germany," M.A. thesis, Clemson University, 2009, pp. 80–81.

**25** "Village Backs CWA Artist in Navy Row," *New York Evening Journal*, April 19, 1934, p. 4, quoted in Meyer, *Outlaw Representation*, p. 47.

**26** Meyer, *Outlaw Representation*, p. 203 n. 61.

**27** Ibid., pp. 52, 53.

**28** Ibid., pp. 53–54.

**29** For an introduction to the notion of the grotesque in cultural expression in 1930s America, see Mark Fearnow, *The American Stage and the Great Depression: A Cultural History of the Grotesque* (Cambridge University Press, 1997), pp. 6–20.

**30** After spending more than an hour in the exhibition with the First Lady, President Roosevelt remarked to the press with satisfaction that none of the works had displayed a "despondent theme"; quoted in Hemingway, *Artists on the Left*, p. 97. While FDR and Eleanor selected thirty-one works for installation in the White House, his cousin, Assistant Secretary of the Navy Henry Roosevelt, kept the Cadmus for himself and upon his death in 1936 audaciously willed it to the private Alibi Club, where it hung for more than forty years. The painting was relinquished only after art historian Philip Eliasoph urged the US government to pursue its return in 1980, armed with the threat of a civil lawsuit and the assignment of federal marshals to seize the work. In concluding the reclamation, the General Services Administration gave legal title to the painting to the navy. For a full account and documentation, see Meyer, *Outlaw Representation*, p. 56, 303–04 nn. 87–89.

**31** Philip Evergood, "Oral history interview with Philip Evergood, 1968 Dec. 3," by Forrest Selvig, Archives of American Art, Smithsonian Institution, Washington, DC, http://www.aaa .si.edu/collections/interviews /oral-history-interview-philip -evergood-12410/. Evergood had a complicated upbringing as the child of a bohemian New York artist of Polish descent and an upper-class English mother. Raised apart from both of them, he received an exclusive English education at Eton and Trinity College, Cambridge, which he left in order to pursue artistic training at London's Slade School of Art. He continued his studies in New York, at the Arts Students League and the Educational Alliance School, in the early 1920s and in several Paris ateliers at mid-decade.

**32** Evergood, "Oral history interview."

**33** Evergood's submission, *Mine Disaster* (1933), was a large and ambitious multifigure composition, arranged in a tripartite format reminiscent of Renaissance altarpieces and rendered with formal distortions, vigorous brushwork, and a discordant palette that would come to characterize his signature expressionism. If his more doctrinaire Communist colleagues were generally unappreciative of the expressionist mode until much later in the decade, they recognized the sincerity of Evergood's political views. See Hemingway, *Artists on the Left*, p. 120. For a consideration of the content of the exhibition, see pp. 60–61.

**34** Professional organizers, who traveled from place to place, brought with them professional "contestants" situated to win the prizes for which unwitting locals placed themselves in competition. For an introduction to the subject of American dance marathons, see Carol Martin, *Dance Marathons: Performing American Culture of the 1920s and 1930s* (University Press of Mississippi, 1994), pp. xvi–xxiii.

**35** Ibid., pp. 149–50.

**36** John I. H. Baur, *Philip Evergood* (Harry N. Abrams, 1975), p. 27.

**37** Alain Locke, *Negro Art: Past and Present* (J. B. Lyon, 1936), pp. 69–70, quoted in Phoebe Wolfskill, "Caricature and the New Negro in the Work of Archibald Motley Jr. and Palmer Hayden," *Art Bulletin* 91, no. 3 (September 2009), p. 348.

**38** The link to Covarrubias is discussed in both Amy Mooney, "Representing Race: Disjunctures in the Work of Archibald J. Motley, Jr.," *Art Institute of Chicago Museum Studies* 24, no. 2 (1999), p. 174; and Wolfskill, "Caricature and the New Negro," pp. 353–55.

**39** For a thorough biographical sketch of Marsh, see Barbara Haskell, "Swing Time: Reginald Marsh and the Chaos of Modern Life," in Barbara Haskell, ed., *Swing Time: Reginald Marsh and Thirties New York*, exh. cat. (New-York Historical Society/D. Giles, 2013), pp. 10–59.

**40** Reginald Marsh, "A Short Autobiography," Art and Artists of Today 1 (March 1937), p. 8, quoted in Haskell, "Swing Time," p. 67.

**41** Alfred Kazin, *Starting Out in the Thirties* (Cornell University Press, 1989), pp. 32–33.

**42** Robert Lynd, *Middletown in Transition: A Study in Cultural Conflicts* (Harcourt, Brace, 1937), p. 46, quoted in Rita Barnard, *The Great Depression and the Culture of Abundance: Kenneth Fearing, Nathanael West, and Mass Culture in the 1930s* (Cambridge University Press, 1995), p. 23.

**43** For the distinctive portrayals of "kept women" in 1930s films and their regulation by industry monitors and the Hays Commission, see Lea Jacobs, *The Wages of Sin: Censorship and the Fallen Woman Film, 1928–1942* (University of California Press, 1997), pp. 10–17.

**44** For a discussion of the nuances of plot and the use of sexually suggestive ellipses in the editing of *Baby Face*, see Jacobs, *Wages of Sin*, pp. 36, 73.

**45** Biographical information on Sample is drawn primarily from Hali Thurber, "Paul Starrett Sample (1869–1974)," http:// www .caldwellgallery.com/bios/ sample _biography.html.

**46** Gail Levin, *Edward Hopper: An Intimate Biography* (Rizzoli, 2007), p. 271.

**47** Guy Péne du Bois, *Edward Hopper* (William Edwin Rudge, 1931), p. 8; and Helen Appleton Read, "Racial Quality of Hopper's Pictures at Modern Agrees with Nationalistic Mood," *Brooklyn Daily Eagle*, November 5, 1933, p. 12 B–C, quoted in Levin, *Edward Hopper*, pp. 239, 253.

**48** For a detailed treatment of *New York Movie* centered on Hopper's numerous preparatory drawings, see Carter E. Foster, *"New York Movie,"* in Carter E. Foster, ed., *Hopper Drawing*, exh. cat. (Whitney Museum of American Art, 2013), pp. 120–49.

**49** The page from Hopper's Record Book II is reproduced in ibid., p. 122.

**50** West, *Day of the Locust*, pp. 184–85.

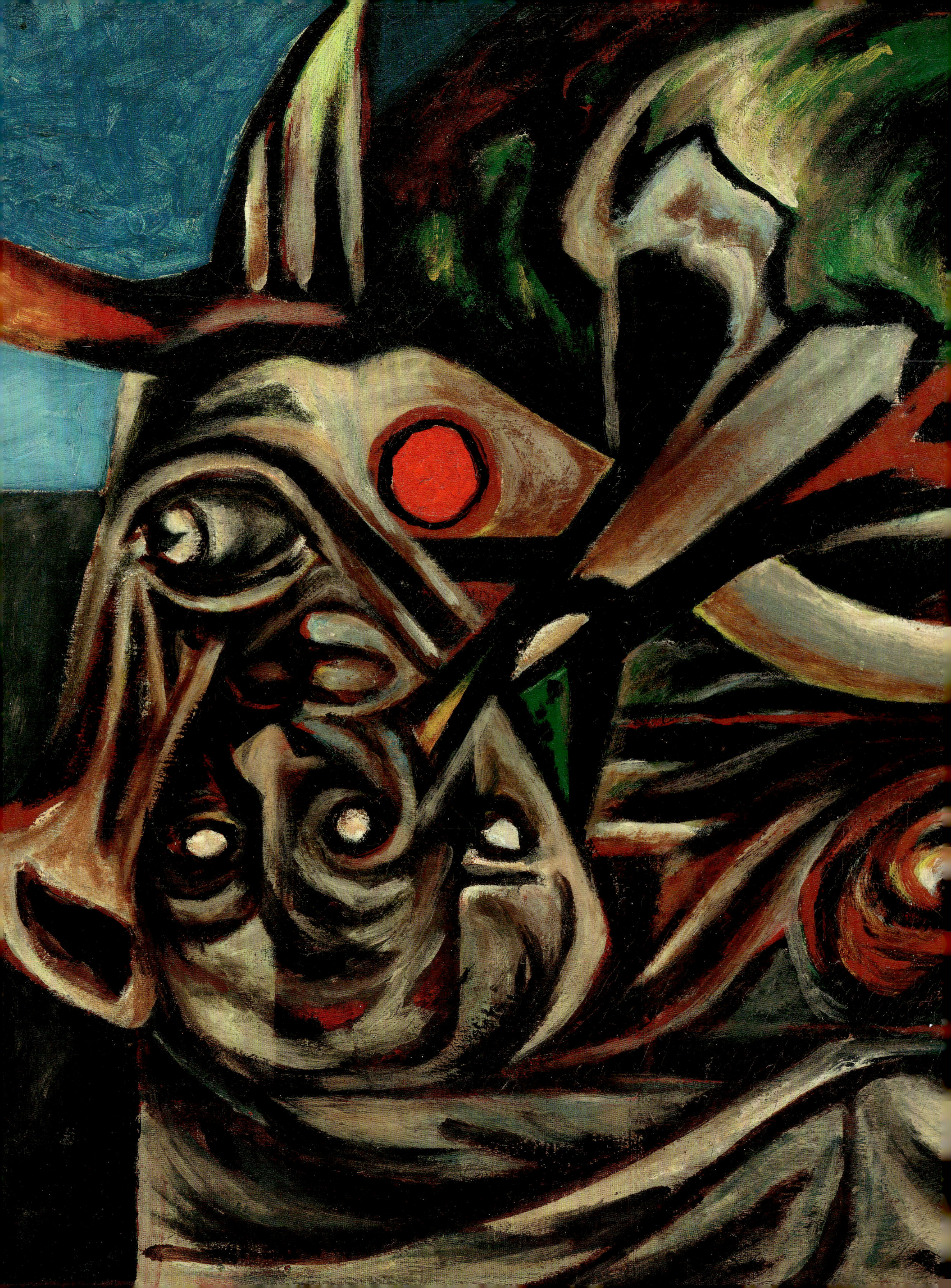

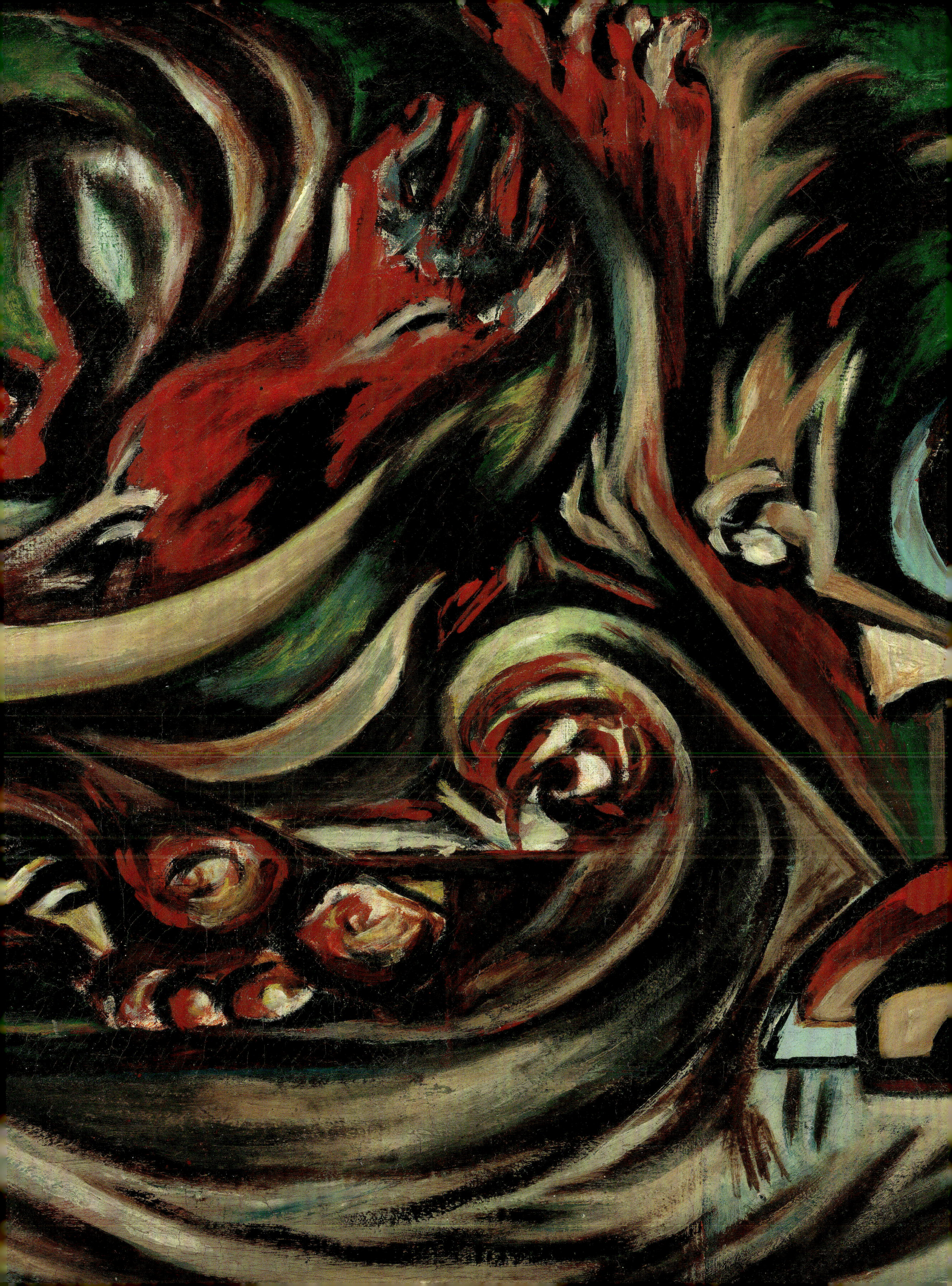

**JUDITH A. BARTER**

**W**hat was the legacy of the 1930s? What became of the American Scene subjects, the realists, the modernists, the Regionalists? What happened to the need to define American art? We can look at two pictures, Jackson Pollock's *Untitled* (1938/41; fig. 1) and Edward Hopper's *New York Movie* (1939; p. 168, fig. 20) to sort out the impact of American painting of the 1930s on the following decades.

Thomas Hart Benton was teaching at the Art Students League in New York when Pollock arrived as a student in September 1930, enrolling in his life drawing class. The two formed a close friendship, even though by most accounts Benton was not a particularly gifted teacher and Pollock not a very good draftsman.[1] Nonetheless, for the next eight years,

EPILOGUE   *Americanness after the 1930s*

Benton and his wife, Rita, formed a surrogate family for the young artist, and Pollock watched firsthand as Benton completed his famous murals for the New School.

How did Benton's twisting, turning, mannerist compositions of the 1930s become the abstractions of Jackson Pollock in the 1940s? While Benton remained in New York, his student made gloomy regionalist paintings of oil rigs, camps, pioneers moving west, and seascapes. The bitter enmity between Benton and fellow ASL faculty member Stuart Davis, whose works differed stylistically and opinions differed politically, eventually prompted him to leave New York; more broadly, he had developed a negative view of what he saw as its European-influenced, pseudointellectual elite, and he imagined his retreat to Kansas City as a return to working-class America. Pollock, who was particularly fond of Rita Benton and the couple's son, T. P., was crushed and lost in the months after their departure. In the years that followed, he maintained Benton's view that America would produce her own art, unbeholden to Parisian modernism. Indeed, by the time he had found his way and the war was over, he could say that those who were still going to Paris with the idea that one could not paint in America would soon be back.[2]

Nevertheless, Pollock abandoned Benton's baroque figuration for abstraction. In the spring of 1936, David Alfaro Siqueiros opened a workshop in New York, and Pollock signed on as a studio assistant. Siqueiros, the most militant of prominent Mexican muralists, wanted a new art to express his revolutionary ideas. He often painted on the floor in wide, sweeping strokes that he felt generated ideas. Even though Pollock did not fully experiment with these techniques until years later, he learned from Siqueiros a freedom of technique very different from the careful planning, realism, and other methods Benton used. His work, however, never conveyed the leftist political messages of the Mexican muralists any more than it did Benton's conservative aesthetic views.[3] While both Benton and Siqueiros created or re-created novel techniques in the service of their subjects and messages, Pollock used method as an end in itself.

Pollock's abstractions of the late 1930s also represent an introverted art. In these early works, he explored native American symbolism and myths, emulating the jabbing, slashing style of another Mexican muralist, José Clemente Orozco, whom he met in 1930 when both Benton and Orozco were working on their New School Murals. By 1939 Pollock explored ancient symbols just as Orozco had; he was then undergoing Jungian psychoanalysis and invented his own versions of these as he drew his interior thoughts for his therapist. In time, Pollock began to develop a style in which the physical act of painting became the subject of the work—a bodily involvement and expression that critic Harold Rosenberg would later name "action painting."

Unlike Benton, Pollock did not reject influences outside of American art. Indeed, seeing Pablo Picasso's *Guernica* (1937; Museo del Prado, Madrid) when it was on view in New York in 1939 was a life-changing experience. Pollock's wife, Lee Krasner, remarked that he admired Picasso but wanted to "go past him."[4] *Untitled* shows Pollock's debt to Cubism and Picasso's dismembered body parts. He combined this influence with the emotional expressiveness of Orozco's murals, creating twisting rhythms and a wide, mural-like format. Finally, the anthropological feeling of Pollock's unconscious symbols recalls his interest in primitive art, particularly the petroglyphs he saw in his western childhood, and his interest throughout the 1930s in ethnographic collections.[5] This particular canvas opened the door to Pollock's mature work of the 1940s. He eventually left easel painting and began to work on the floor; while this method was doubtless influenced by Siqueiros's technique, the artist also attributed it to his western experience, saying that he could "walk around" a canvas, "work from the four sides and literally be in the painting." "This," he said, "is akin to the method of the Indian sand painters of the West."[6]

Pollock, unlike Benton, considered himself apolitical. For him and other Abstract Expressionists, the WPA experience was not positive, and by 1940 many artists were fed up with the American Scene realism the program encouraged. Robert Motherwell, for example, wrote that he had no politics other than a hatred of the WPA.[7] Indeed, such painters' emphasis on the interior creative process led them to reject overt political messages and American Scene subjects. For many, their approach was about pure creativity, which was itself seen as particularly American. For this reason, Abstract Expressionist work was co-opted by business patrons in the postwar years. It was collected and hung in corporate offices, banks, and publishing houses, where it cemented and celebrated the association of abstraction with American individualism, invention, newness, and freedom.[8] Its lack of overt political content assured its safety, especially as American artists such as Social Realist painters Ben Shahn, Gregorio Prestopino, O. Louis Guglielmi, Yasuo Kuniyoshi, Karl Zerbe, and Robert Gwathmey were attacked by the press and the Senate in 1946. For members of the Senate subcommittee investigating the exhibition *Advancing American Art* (which was to be sent abroad by the

**Fig. 1** Jackson Pollock. *Untitled*, c. 1938/41. Art Institute of Chicago. Cat. 39.

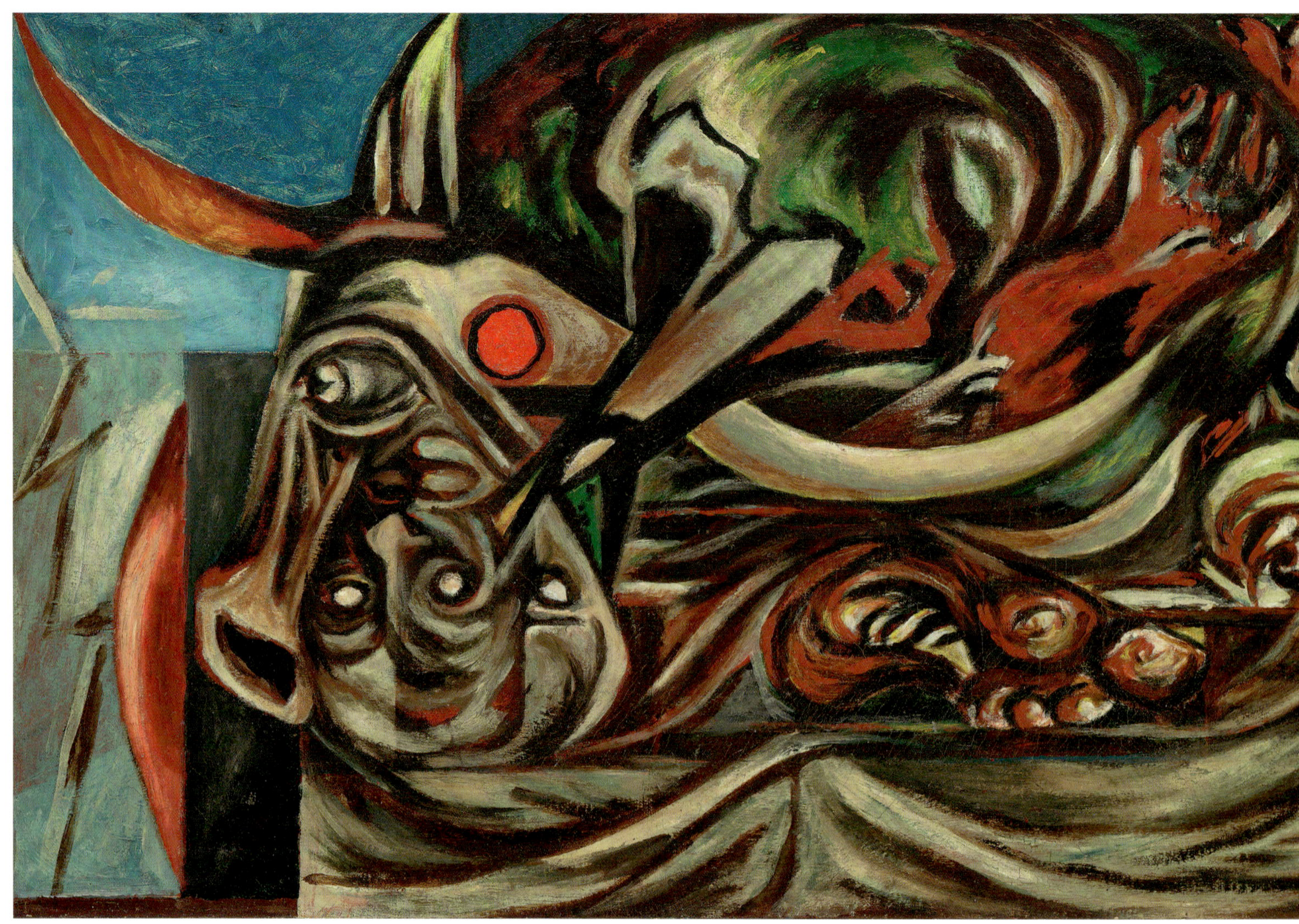

State Department), the works of these artists were the products of "alien cultures, ideas, philosophies, and [the] sickness of Europe. Those paintings . . . give the impression that America is a drab, ugly place, filled with drab, ugly people. They are definitely leftish paintings."[9] In 1959 Shahn and Philip Evergood were again singled out and identified as Communists.[10] All told, more than 350 other American artists were named by the House Un-American Activities Committee because of their supposed Communist affiliations or because of the content of their work. Abstraction became the art of the elite, and Norman Rockwell made this connection in his painting *The Connoisseur* (1961; fig. 2), in which he painstakingly re-created a Pollock "drip" painting. The Rockwell rendition became one of Willem de Kooning's favorite pictures.[11]

The influences of Surrealism, myth, and dream that informed Pollock's pictures were also present in the work of Edward Hopper, who continued to explore realism and mood over the next decades. The Surrealists who had arrived in New York, fleeing Europe in the late 1930s, admired Hopper's work. André Breton in particular identified him as one of the few American artists whose paintings possessed Surrealism's dreamlike qualities. In discussing *New York Movie*, Breton

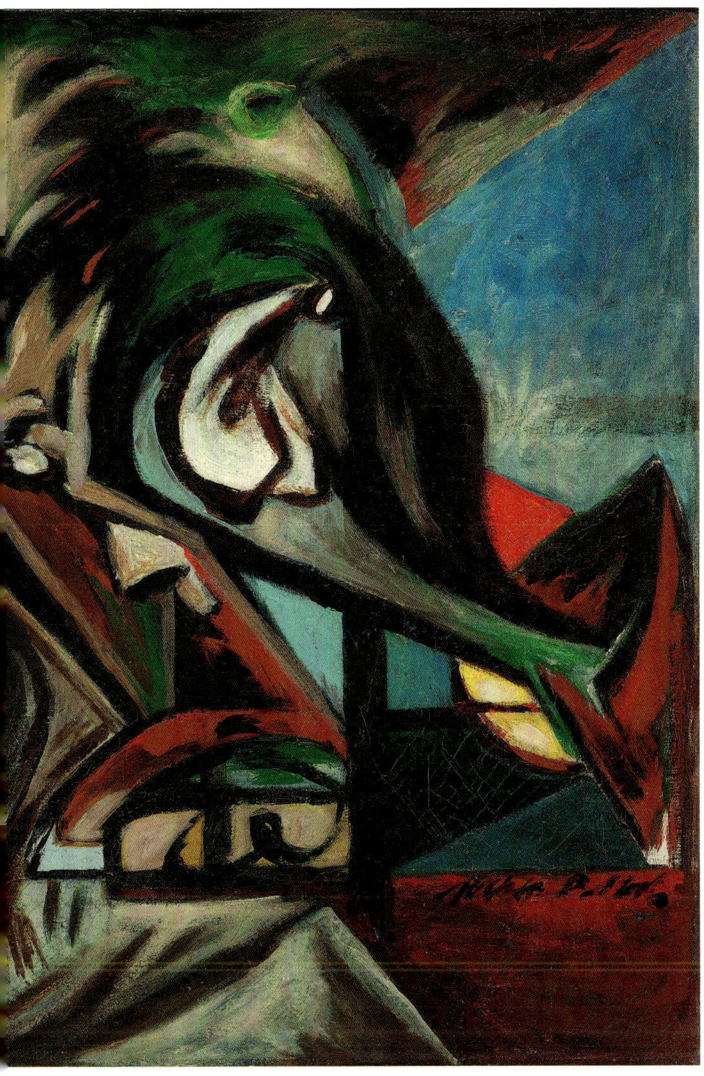

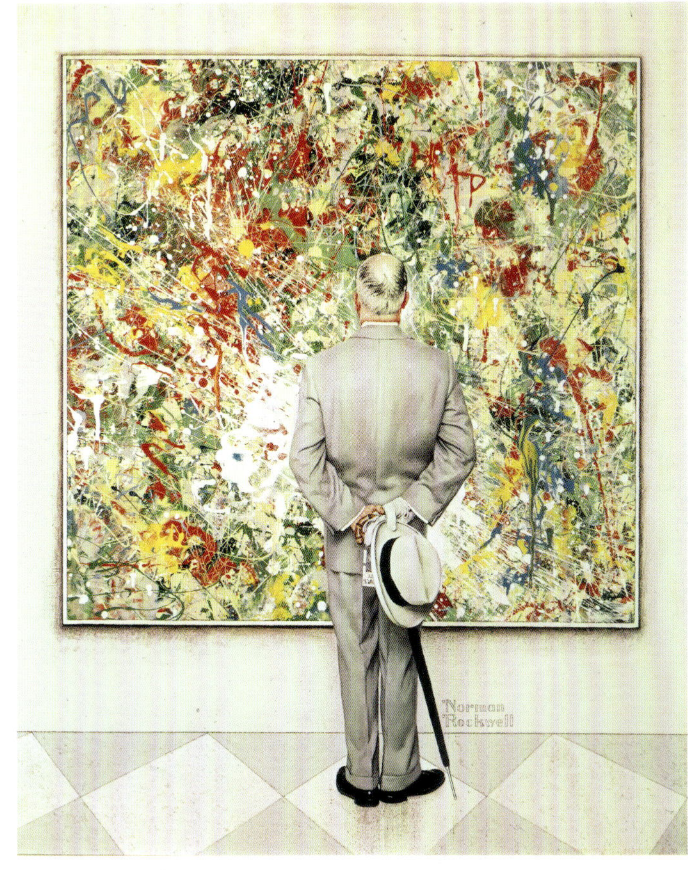



**Fig. 2**  Norman Rockwell (American, 1894–1978). *The Connoisseur*, 1961. Oil on canvas. 96 × 80 cm (37¾ × 31½ in.). Private collection.

remarked, "The beautiful young woman, lost in a dream beyond the confounding things happening to others, the heavy mythical column, the three lights . . . seem charged with a symbolical significance which seeks a way out of the curtained stairway."[12] For his part, Hopper, who had been reading the work of Sigmund Freud and Carl Jung, liked the Surrealists and thought them good artists.[13] He described his own creative process as part of every form of art: "So much . . . an expression of the subconscious, that it seems to me most all of the important qualities are put there unconsciously, and little of importance by the conscious intellect."[14] Hopper saw the works of Giorgio de Chirico

and other Surrealists at the Julien Levy Gallery in 1932 and at the Museum of Modern Art's exhibition *Fantastic Art, Dada, Surrealism* in 1936. All these influences affected his vision for his 1942 masterpiece *Nighthawks* (fig. 3), where color; lighting; pared-down, off-kilter perspective; and dreamlike interior space come together much as they do in de Chirico's work.

Hopper's landscapes, even those with figures, such as *Gas* (1940; fig. 4), transcended reality and mirrored an internal vision of the solitary just as Pollock's nonobjective paintings did. And yet, from the moment in 1943 that Peggy Guggenheim gave Pollock a solo show at her gallery, Art of this Century, the

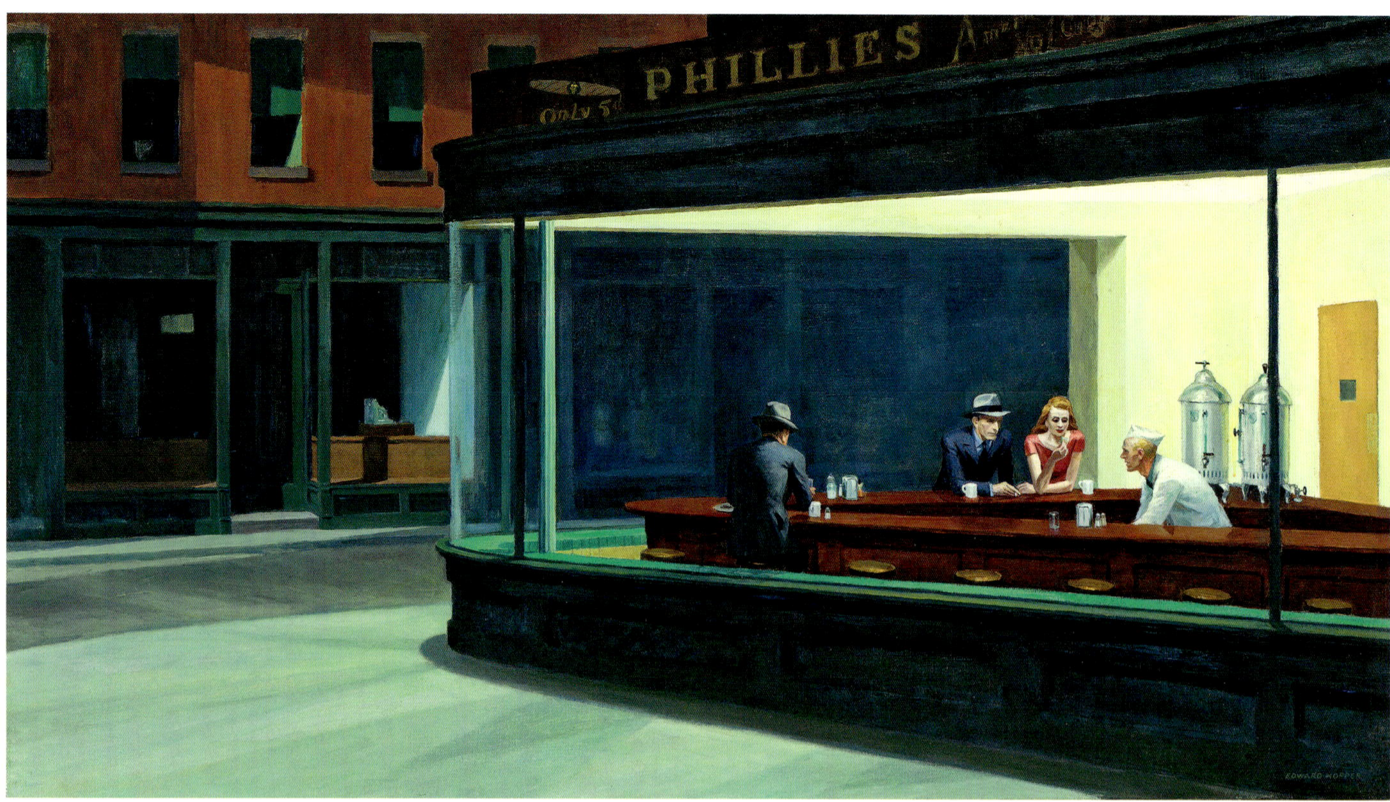


modern art scene changed. Critics of the time thought Hopper's work "photographic." Clement Greenberg, reviewing the 1946 Whitney Annual, called Hopper's work crude and academically superficial: "He is not a painter in the full sense: his means are second-hand, shabby, and impersonal.... Hopper's painting is essentially photography.... Hopper just happens to be a bad painter. But if he were a better painter, he would, most likely, not be so superior an artist."[15] Greenberg grudgingly understood that Hopper had a singular vision, but the critic disliked recognizable subject matter as a form of expression.

Realist painting continued, although it was often excluded from museum exhibitions and popular gallery shows.[16] Abstraction had so conquered New York that one critic thought Hopper "courageous" to show his work.[17] Both Greenberg and fellow critic Harold Rosenberg promoted the Abstract Expressionists, concentrating their attention on painting's capacity to produce emotion through the use of purely formal elements. In Rosenberg's words, the canvas was "an arena in which to act—rather than a space in which to reproduce, redesign, analyze or 'express' an object, actual or imagined. What was to go on the canvas was not a picture, but an event."[18] By 1950 Pollock's work represented the United States at the Venice Biennale.

In a 1957 *Art News Annual* article, Parker Tyler singled out Hopper and Pollock as the two most original painters of the era, claiming that they both explored the outermost limits of aesthetic purity and the painting of the unconscious. For Tyler, both represented the epitome of Americanness in postwar contemporary painting, capturing "the loneliness of the crowd (Hopper)" and the "loneliness of the universe (Pollock)."[19] Pollock's experiments would continue to inform the next generation of abstract painters, including Helen Frankenthaler, whose poured and stained compositions exist as quieter versions of Pollock's gestural canvases. Accidental-looking drips

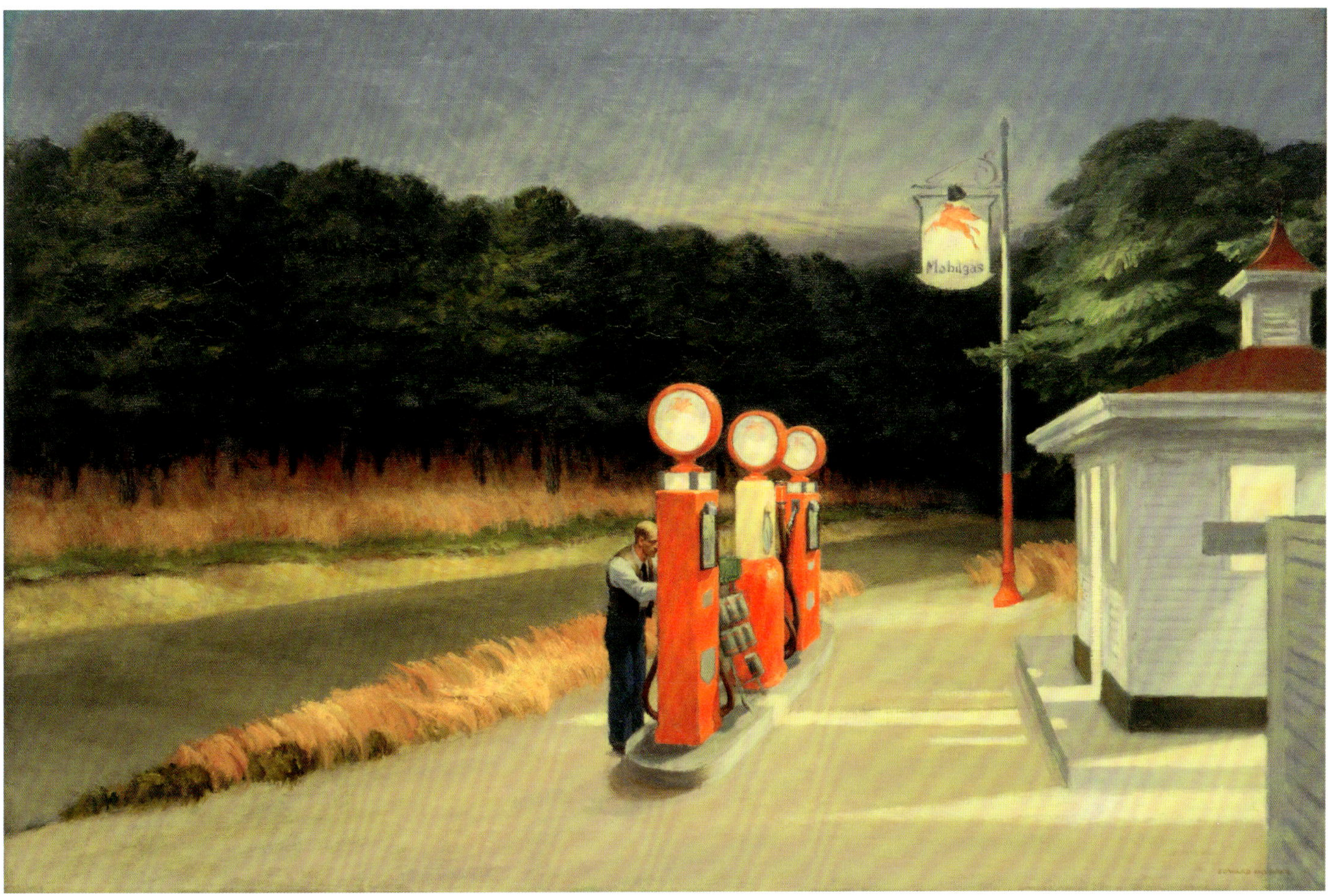


feature in Robert Rauschenberg's early works such as *Rebus* (1955; fig. 5), where they run down the canvas and through the tight grid upon which Rauschenberg places objects.[20] On a canvas like *Blue Poles [No. 11, 1952]* (1952; National Gallery of Australia, Canberra), Pollock's colors take the form of totemic if nondescriptive lines; similar lines are recognizable in the postpainterly works of Kenneth Noland.

Hopper's spare geometry, solids, voids, and celebrations of popular cultural symbols in a painting like *Gas* would influence Pop artists like Ed Ruscha, whose *Standard Station, Amarillo, Texas* (1963; fig. 6) repeats the red pumps and sharp angles of Hopper's work. The cityscapes of Richard Diebenkorn reprise the theme of light and shadows falling across gray cement roads. George Segal's sculpture *The Diner* (1964–66;

Walker Art Center, Minneapolis) emulates the coffee urns, object relationships, and mood of Hopper's *Nighthawks*.

Hopper and Pollock, representing the two poles of postwar painting, drew their seemingly opposed aesthetics from the ferment of the Depression decade, whose artists explored the tensions between self and community, nation and world in their attempt to discover what American art might be and become.

**Fig. 5** Robert Rauschenberg (American, 1925–2008). *Rebus*, 1955. Oil, synthetic polymer paint, pencil, crayon, pastel, cut-and-pasted printed and painted papers, and fabric on canvas mounted and stapled to fabric, three panels. 243.8 × 333.1 cm (96 × 131⅛ in.). The Museum of Modern Art, Partial and promised gift of Jo Carole and Ronald S. Lauder and bequest of Virginia C. Field, gift of Mr. and Mrs. Peter A. Rübel, and gift of Jay R. Braus (all by exchange), 243.205a-c.



**Fig. 6** Ed Ruscha (American, born 1937). *Standard Station, Amarillo, Texas*, 1963. 163.83 × 309.25 cm (64½ × 121¾ in.). Hood Museum of Art, Dartmouth College, Hanover, New Hampshire; gift of James Meeker, Class of 1958, in memory of Lee English, Class of 1958, scholar, poet, athlete and friend to all, P.976.281.


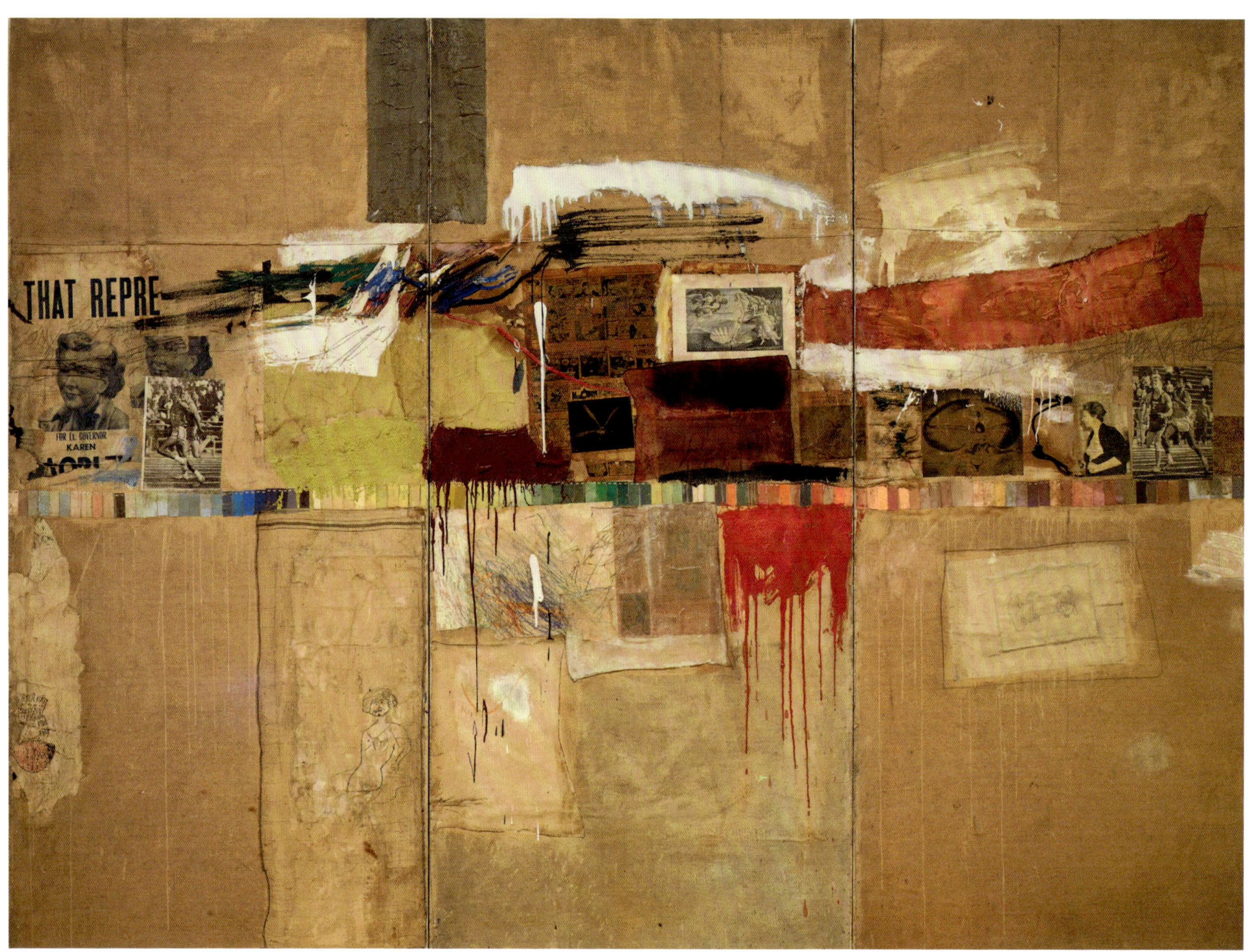

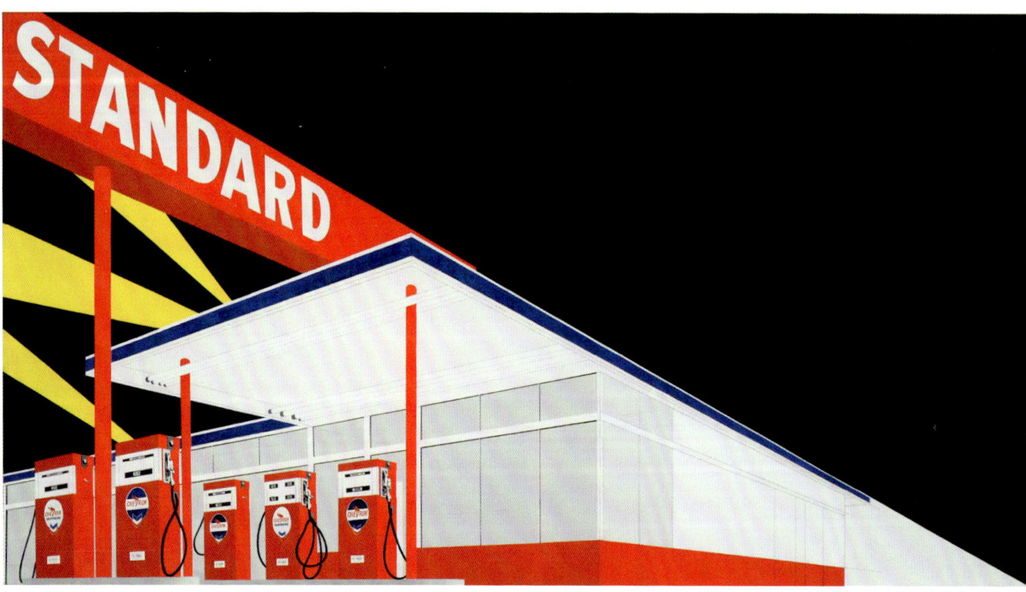

STANDARD

**1** Deborah Solomon, *Jackson Pollock: A Biography* (Simon and Schuster, 1987), pp. 49, 52.

**2** Ibid., p. 13.

**3** Claude Cernuschi, *Jackson Pollock: Meaning and Significance* (Harper Collins, 1992), p. 32.

**4** B. H. Friedman, "An Interview with Lee Krasner Pollock," in *Jackson Pollock: Black and White*, exh. cat. (Marlborough-Gerson Gallery, 1969), p. 7, quoted in Anthony White, ed., *Jackson Pollock's Blue Poles*, exh. cat. (National Gallery of Australia/University of Washington Press, 2002), p. 20.

**5** Jurgen Harten, *Siqueiros/Pollock: Pollock/Siqueiros* (Kunsthalle Düsseldorf, 1995), p. 254.

**6** Jackson Pollock, "My Painting," *Possibilities* 1, no. 1 (Winter 1947/48), p. 79, quoted in Harten, *Siqueiros/Pollock*, p. 254.

**7** Cernuschi, *Jackson Pollock,* p. 37.

**8** In particular, the Rockefeller family and Chase Manhattan Bank used abstract work as decoration in their buildings. Judith A. Barter, "The New Medici: The Rise of Corporate Collecting and the Uses of Contemporary Art (1925–1970)," Ph.D. diss., University of Massachusetts, Amherst, 1991, 156–61.

**9** "Exposing the Bunk of So-Called Modern Art," *New York Journal-American*, December 3, 1946, p. 15; *Look*, February 18, 1946, pp. 80–81.

**10** *Hearings Before the Committee on Un-American Activities, House of Representatives, Eighty-Sixth Congress, first session, July 1, 1959; The American National Exhibition, Moscow, July 1959 (The record of certain artists and an appraisal of their works selected for display)* (Government Printing Office, 1959), 941–62.

**11** Peter Schjeldahl, "A Kind Word for Norman Rockwell," *New Yorker* online, November 5, 2013, http://www.newyorker.com/books/page-turner/a-kind-word-for-norman-rockwell/.

**12** Charles Henry Ford [Nicolas Calas], "Interview with Andre Breton," *View* 1, nos. 7–8 (October–November 1941), p. 1.

**13** Gail Levin, *Edward Hopper: An Intimate Biography* (Rizzoli, 2007), p. 274.

**14** Edward Hopper to Charles Sawyer, October 29, 1939, curatorial files, Addison Gallery of American Art Archives, Andover, MA.

**15** Clement Greenberg, "Review of the Whitney Annual," *Nation* 163, no. 26 (December 28, 1946). Reprinted in John O'Brian, ed., *Clement Greenberg: The Collected Essays and Criticism* (University of Chicago Press, 1986), vol. 2, pp. 117–18.

**16** For a discussion of museum and market bias against realism in the 1940s and 1950s, see Judith A. Barter, "Travels and Travails," in Carol Troyen et al., *Edward Hopper*, exh. cat (MFA Publications, 2007), pp. 212–16.

**17** Emily Genauer, "Courageously Realistic Oils Exhibited by Edward Hopper," *New York World-Telegram*, January 6, 1948, p. 12.

**18** Harold Rosenberg, "Getting Inside the Canvas," *Art News* 51, no. 8 (December 1952), p. 22.

**19** Parker Tyler, "Hopper/Pollock: The Loneliness of the Crowd and the Loneliness of the Universe: An Antiphonal," *Art News Annual* 26 (1957), pp. 87–107.

**20** Pepe Karmel, "A Sum of Destructions," in Kirk Varnedoe and Pepe Karmel, eds., *Jackson Pollock: New Approaches*, exh. cat. (Museum of Modern Art/Harry N. Abrams, 1999), p. 94.

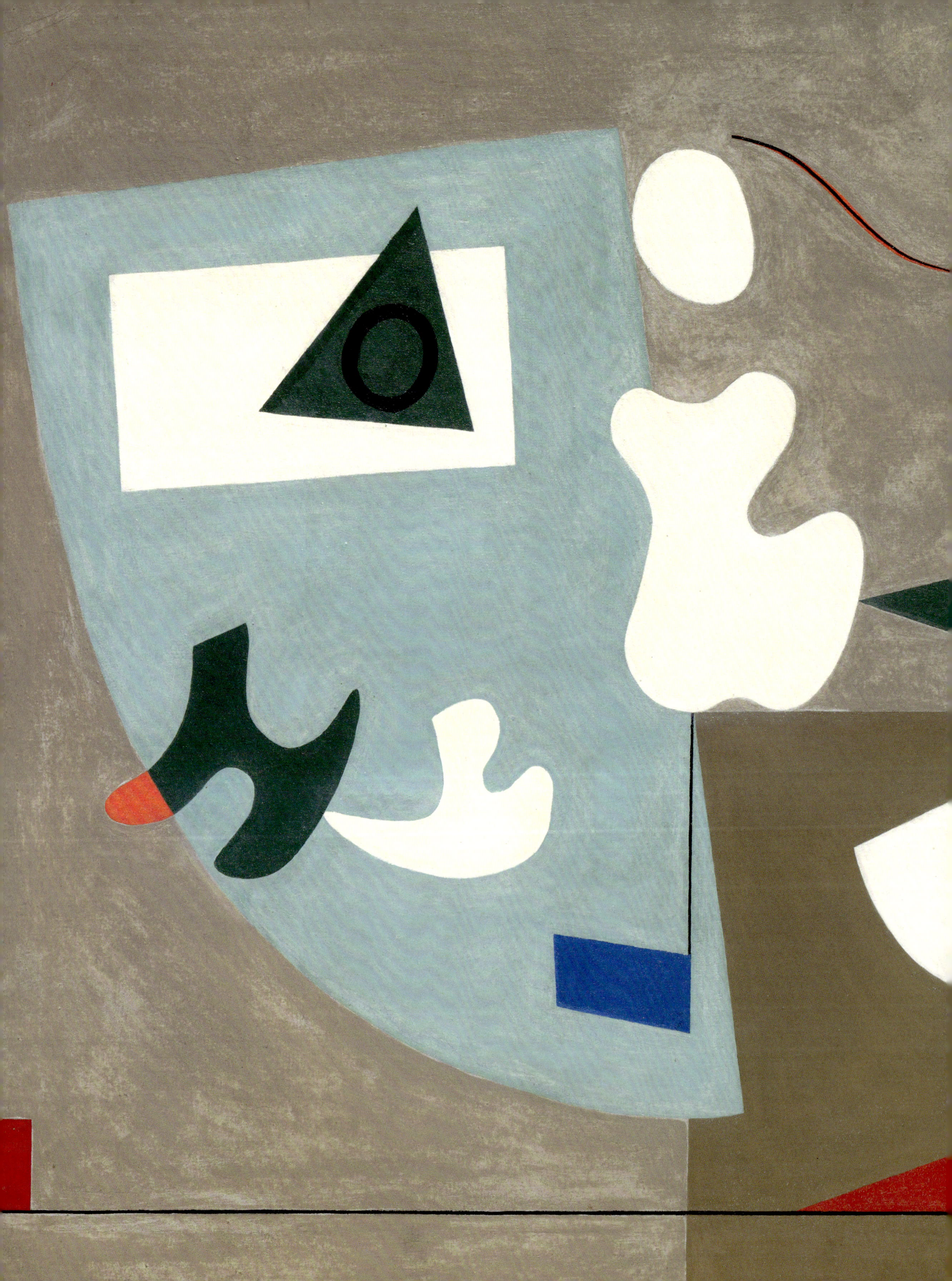

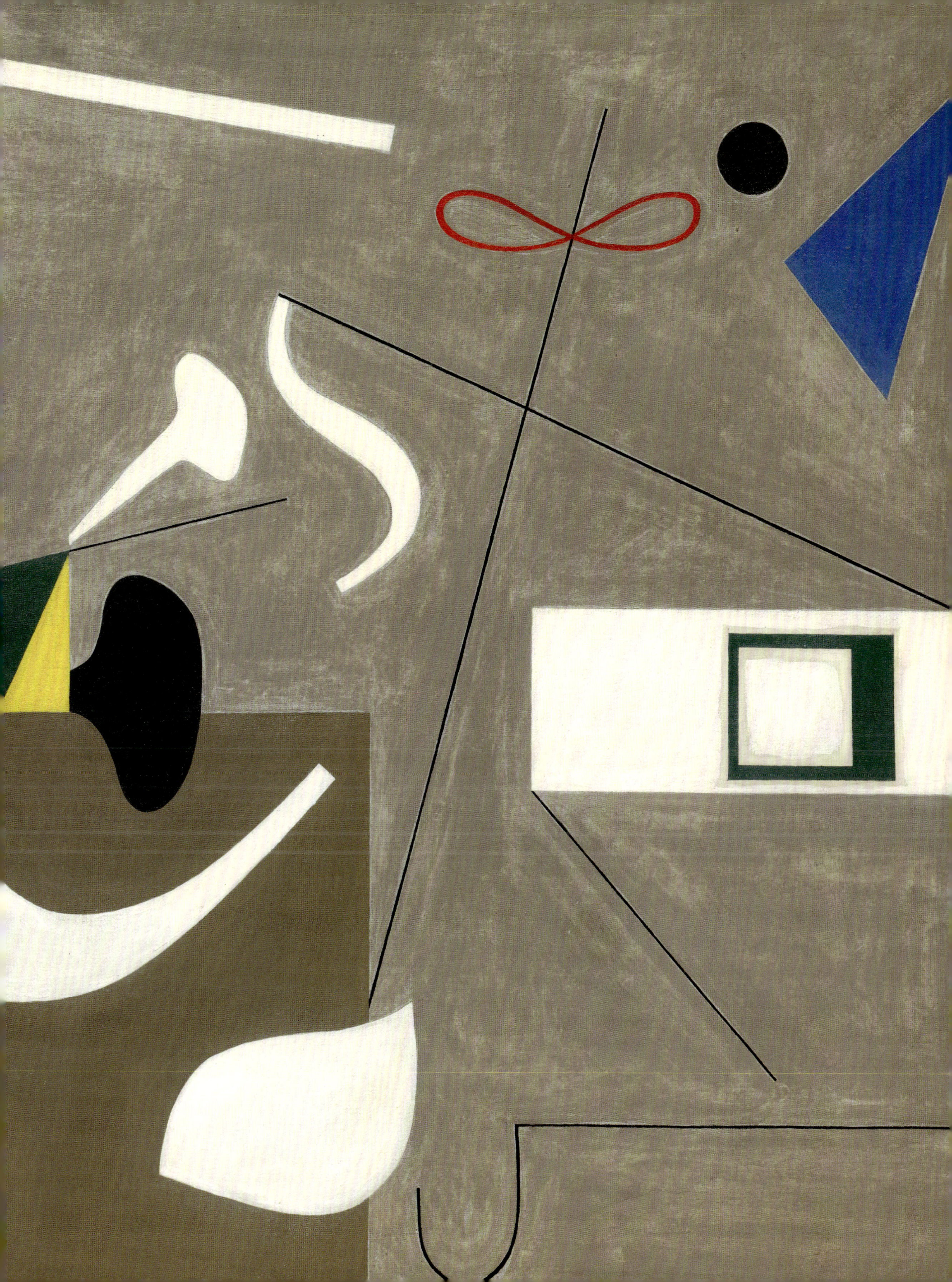

# EXHIBITION CHECKLIST

**IVAN ALBRIGHT**
American, 1897–1983

**1**

*Self-Portrait*, 1935
Oil on canvas; 77.2 × 50.5 cm
(30⅜ × 19⅞ in.)
The Art Institute of Chicago,
Mary and Earle Ludgin Collection,
1981.257

**THOMAS HART BENTON**
American, 1889–1975

**2**

*Cradling Wheat*, 1938
Tempera and oil on board;
79.5 × 100 cm (31¼ × 39¼ in.)
Saint Louis Art Museum,
Museum Purchase

**3**

*Haystack*, 1938
Tempera with oil glaze on linen,
on wood panel; 60.9 × 76.2 cm
(24 × 30 in.)
Museum of Fine Arts, Houston,
Gift of Frank J. Hevrdejs

**4**

*Cotton Pickers*, 1945
Oil on canvas; 81.3 × 121.9 cm
(32 × 48 in.)
The Art Institute of Chicago,
prior bequest of Alexander
Stewart; Centennial Major
Acquisitions Income and Wesley
M. Dixon Jr. funds; Roger and J.
Peter McCormick Endowments;
prior acquisition of the George
F. Harding Collection and Cyrus
H. McCormick Fund; Quinn E.
Delaney, American Art Sales
Proceeds, Alyce and Edwin
DeCosta and Walter E. Heller
Foundation, and Goodman funds;
prior bequest of Arthur Rubloff;
Estate of Walter Aitken; Ada

Turnbull Hertle and Mary and
Leigh Block Endowment funds;
prior acquisition of Mr. and Mrs.
Frank G. Logan Purchase Prize;
Marian and Samuel Klasstorner
and Laura T. Magnuson
Acquisition funds; prior acquisi-
tion of Friends of American Art
Collection; Wirt D. Walker Trust;
Jay W. McGreevy Endowment;
Cyrus Hall McCormick Fund;
Samuel A. Marx Purchase Fund
for Major Acquisitions; Maurice
D. Galleher Endowment; Alfred
and May Tiefenbronner Memorial,
Dr. Julian Archie, Gladys N.
Anderson, and Simeon B. Williams
funds; Capital Campaign General
Acquisitions Endowment, and
Benjamin Argile Memorial Fund,
2013.4

**PETER BLUME**
American, 1906–1992

**5**

*The Eternal City*, 1934–37
Oil on composition board;
86.5 × 121.6 cm (34 × 47⅞ in.)
The Museum of Modern Art, New
York, Mrs. Simon Guggenheim
Fund, 1942

**ILYA BOLOTOWSKY**
American, born Russia,
1907–1981

**6**

*Study for the Hall of Medical
Sciences Mural at the 1939 World's
Fair in New York*, 1938/39
Oil on canvas; 76.2 × 121.9 cm
(30 × 48 in.)
The Art Institute of Chicago,
Wilson L. Mead Fund, 1977.1

**PAUL CADMUS**
American, 1904–1999

**7**

*The Fleet's In!*, 1934
Tempera on canvas;
76.2 × 152.4 cm (30 × 60 in.)
Courtesy of the US Navy Art
Collection, Naval History and
Heritage Command

**FEDERICO CASTELLÓN**
American, 1914–1971

**8**

*The Dark Figure*, 1938
Oil on canvas; 43 × 66.5 cm
(17 × 26⅛ in.)
Whitney Museum of American Art,
New York, Purchase, 42.3

**MARVIN CONE**
American, 1891–1965

**9**

*River Bend No. 4*, 1938
Oil on canvas; 61 × 76.2 cm
(24 × 30 in.)
Private collection

**JOHN STEUART CURRY**
American, 1897–1946

**10**

*Hogs Killing a Snake*, c. 1930
Oil on canvas; 76.5 × 97.3 cm
(30⅛ × 38¼ in.)
The Art Institute of Chicago,
restricted gift of an anonymous
donor, 1947.392

**STUART DAVIS**
American, 1892–1964

**11**

*New York–Paris No. 3*, 1931
Oil on canvas; 99.1 × 132.1 cm
(39 × 52 in.)
Private collection

**CHARLES DEMUTH**
American, 1883–1935

**12**

*. . . And the Home of the Brave*, 1931
Oil and graphite on fiber board;
74.8 × 59.7 cm (29½ × 23½ in.)
The Art Institute of Chicago,
Alfred Stieglitz Collection, gift of
Georgia O'Keeffe, 1948.650

**AARON DOUGLAS**
American, 1899–1979

**13**

*Aspiration*, 1936
Oil on canvas; 152.5 × 152.5 cm
(60 × 60 in.)
Fine Arts Museums of San
Francisco, Museum purchase,
the estate of Thurlow E. Tibbs Jr.,
the Museum Society Auxiliary,
American Art Trust Fund,
Unrestricted Art Trust Fund,
partial gift of Dr. Ernest A. Bates,
Sharon Bell, Jo-Ann Beverly,
Barbara Carleton, Dr. and Mrs.
Arthur H. Coleman, Dr. and Mrs.
Coyness Ennix Jr., Nicole Y. Ennix,
Mr. and Mrs. Gary Francois,
Dennis L. Franklin, Mr. and Mrs.
Maxwell C. Gillette, Mr. and Mrs.
Richard Goodyear, Zuretti L.
Goosby, Marion E. Greene, Mrs.
Vivian S. W. Hambrick, Laurie
Gibbs Harris, Arlene Hollis, Louis
A. and Letha Jeanpierre, Daniel
and Jackie Johnson Jr., Stephen
L. Johnson, Mr. and Mrs. Arthur
Lathan, Lewis & Ribbs Mortuary
Garden Chapel, Mr. and Mrs. Gary
Love, Glenn R. Nance, Mr. and Mrs.
Harry S. Parker III, Mr. and Mrs.
Carr T. Preston, Fannie Preston,
Pamela R. Ransom, Dr. and Mrs.
Benjamin F. Reed, San Francisco
Black Chamber of Commerce,
San Francisco Chapter of Links

Inc., San Francisco Chapter of the
N.A.A.C.P., Sigma Pi Phi Fraternity,
Dr. Ella Mae Simmons, Mr. Calvin
R. Swinson, Joseph B. Williams,
Mr. and Mrs. Alfred S. Wilsey, and
the people of the Bay Area, 1997.84

**ARTHUR DOVE**
American, 1880–1946

**14**

*Tree Trunks*, 1934
Oil on canvas
46 × 63.5 cm (18 × 24 in.)
Phillips Collection, Acquired 1934.
Acc. No.: 1585

**15**

*Swing Music (Louis Armstrong)*,
1938
Emulsion, oil, and wax on canvas;
44.8 × 65.7 cm (17⅝ × 25⅞ in.)
The Art Institute of Chicago,
Alfred Stieglitz Collection,
1949.540

**PHILIP EVERGOOD**
American, 1901–1973

**16**

*Dance Marathon*, 1934
Oil on canvas; 152.6 × 101.7 cm
(60 1/16 × 40 1/16 in.)
Blanton Museum of Art, University
of Texas at Austin, Gift of Mari and
James A. Michener, 1991

**O. LOUIS GUGLIELMI**
American, born Egypt, 1906–1956

**17**

*Phoenix*, 1935
Oil on canvas; 76.2 × 63.8 cm
(30 × 25⅛ in.)
Sheldon Museum of Art,
University of Nebraska-Lincoln,
NAA-Nelle Cochrane Woods
Memorial

**18**

*Mental Geography*, 1938
Oil on Masonite; 91 × 61 cm
(35¾ × 24 in.)
Collection of Barney A. Ebsworth

**PHILIP GUSTON**
American, 1913–1980

**19**

*Bombardment*, 1937
Oil on Masonite; diam. 106.7 cm
(42 in.)
Philadelphia Museum of Art, Gift
of Musa and Tom Mayer, 2011

**MARSDEN HARTLEY**
American, 1877–1943

**20**

*Mt. Katahdin (Maine), Autumn #2*,
1939–40
Oil on canvas; 77 × 102 cm
(30¼ × 40¼ in.)
The Metropolitan Museum of
Art, Edith and Milton Lowenthal
Collection, Bequest of Edith
Abrahamson Lowenthal, 1991

**ALEXANDRE HOGUE**
American, 1898–1994

**21**

*Erosion No. 2—Mother Earth
Laid Bare*, 1936
Oil on canvas; 102 × 143 cm
(40¼ × 56¼ in.)
Loan courtesy of The Philbrook
Museum of Art, 2015

**EDWARD HOPPER**
American, 1882–1967

**22**

*Early Sunday Morning*, 1930
Oil on canvas; 89.4 × 153 cm
(35³⁄₁₆ × 60¼ in.)
Whitney Museum of American
Art, New York, Purchase, with
funds from Gertrude Vanderbilt
Whitney, 31.426

**23**

*New York Movie*, 1939
Oil on canvas; 81.9 × 101.9 cm
(32¼ × 40⅛ in.)
The Museum of Modern Art, New
York. Given anonymously, 1941

**24**

*Gas*, 1940
Oil on canvas; 66.7 × 102.2 cm
(26¼ × 40¼ in.)
The Museum of Modern Art, New
York. Mrs. Simon Guggenheim
Fund, 1943

**WILLIAM H. JOHNSON**
American, 1901–1970

**25**

*Street Life, Harlem*, 1939
Oil on plywood; 116 × 98 cm
(45⅝ × 38⅝ in.)
Smithsonian American Art
Museum, Gift of the Harmon
Foundation, 1967.59.674

**JOE JONES**
American, 1909–1963

**26**

*American Justice*, 1933
Oil on canvas; 76.2 × 91.4 cm
(30 × 36 in.)
Columbus Museum of Art, Ohio,
Museum Purchase, Derby Fund,
from the Philip J. and Suzanne
Schiller Collection of American
Social Commentary Art 1930–1970

**27**

*Roustabouts*, 1934
Oil on canvas; 63.5 × 76 cm
(25 × 30 in.)
Worcester Art Museum, Gift of
Aldus C. Higgins

**MORRIS KANTOR**
American, born Russia (now
Belarus), 1896–1974

**28**

*Haunted House*, 1930
Oil on canvas; 94.3 × 84.5 cm
(37⅛ × 33¼ in.)
The Art Institute of Chicago, Mr.
and Mrs. Frank G. Logan Purchase
Prize Fund, 1931.707

**WALT KUHN**
American, 1880–1949

**29**

*Portrait of the Artist as a Clown
(Kansas)*, 1932
Oil on canvas; 81 × 56 cm
(32 × 22 in.)
Collection of Barney A. Ebsworth

**DORIS LEE**
American, 1905–1983

**30**

*Thanksgiving*, c. 1935
Oil on canvas; 71.3 × 101.8 cm
(28⅛ × 40⅛ in.)
The Art Institute of Chicago, Mr.
and Mrs. Frank G. Logan Purchase
Prize Fund, 1935.313

**HELEN LUNDEBERG**
American, 1908–1999

**31**

*Double Portrait of the Artist in
Time*, 1935
Oil on fiberboard; 121 × 102 cm
(47¾ × 40 in.)
Smithsonian American Art
Museum, Museum purchase

**REGINALD MARSH**
American, 1898–1954

**32**

*In Fourteenth Street*, 1934
Egg tempera on board;
91.1 × 101 cm (35⅞ 39¾ in.)
The Museum of Modern Art, New
York. Gift of Mrs. Reginald Marsh

**33**

*Twenty Cent Movie*, 1936
Egg tempera on composition
board; 76.2 × 101.6 cm (30 × 40 in.)
Whitney Museum of American Art,
New York, Purchase, 37.43a-b

**GEORGE L. K. MORRIS**
American, 1905–1975

**34**

*Indian Composition No. 6*, 1938
Oil on canvas; 122 × 84 cm
(48 × 33 in.)
Brooklyn Museum, Bequest of
Laura L. Barnes and gift of Mr. and
Mrs. Allan D. Emil, by exchange
and the Dick S. Ramsey Fund,
2006.42

**ARCHIBALD J. MOTLEY**
American, 1891–1981

**35**

*Saturday Night*, 1935
Oil on canvas; 81.3 × 101.6 cm
(32 × 40 in.)
Collection of Howard University
Gallery of Art, Washington, DC

**ALICE NEEL**
American, 1900–1984

**36**

*Pat Whalen*, 1935
Oil, ink, and newspaper on canvas;
68.6 × 58.4 cm (27 × 23 in.)
Whitney Museum of American Art,
New York, Gift of Dr. Hartley Neel

**GEORGIA O'KEEFFE**
American, 1887–1986

**37**

*Cow's Skull: Red, White, and Blue*,
1931
Oil on canvas; 96 × 91 cm
(37⅞ × 35⅞ in.)
The Metropolitan Museum of Art,
Alfred Stieglitz Collection, 1952

**38**

*Cow's Skull with Calico Roses*, 1931
Oil on canvas; 91.4 × 61 cm
(36 × 24 in.)
The Art Institute of Chicago,
Alfred Stieglitz Collection, gift of
Georgia O'Keeffe, 1947.712

**JACKSON POLLOCK**
American, 1912–1956

**39**

*Untitled*, c. 1938/41
Oil on linen; 56.5 × 127.6 cm
(22¼ × 50¼ in.)
The Art Institute of Chicago, Major
Acquisitions Centennial Fund;
estate of Florene May Schoenborn;
through prior acquisitions of
Mr. and Mrs. Carter H. Harrison,
Marguerita S. Ritman, Mr. and
Mrs. Bruce Borland, and Mary L.
and Leigh B. Block, 1998.522

**PAUL SAMPLE**
American, 1896–1974

**40**

*Church Supper*, 1933
Oil on canvas; 102 × 122 cm
(40⅛ × 48 in.)
Michele and Donald D'Amour
Museum of Fine Arts, Springfield,
Massachusetts, The James Philip
Gray Collection

**BEN SHAHN**
American, 1898–1969

**41**
*The Passion of Sacco and Vanzetti*,
1931–32
Tempera on canvas; 215 × 122 cm
(84 ½ × 48 in.)
Whitney Museum of American
Art, New York, Gift of Edith and
Milton Lowenthal in memory of
Juliana Force

**CHARLES GREEN SHAW**
American, 1892–1974

**42**
*Wrigley's*, 1937
Oil on canvas; 76.2 × 114.3 cm
(30 × 45 in.)
The Art Institute of Chicago,
restricted gift of the Alsdorf
Foundation, 1978.417

**CHARLES SHEELER**
American, 1883–1965

**43**
*American Landscape*, 1930
Oil on canvas; 61 × 78.7 cm
(24 × 31 in.)
The Museum of Modern Art,
New York. Gift of Abby Aldrich
Rockefeller, 1934

**44**
*Classic Landscape*, 1931
Oil on canvas; 63.5 × 82 cm
(25 × 32 ¼ in.)
National Gallery of Art,
Washington, Collection of Barney
A. Ebsworth, 2006.39.2

**45**
*Home, Sweet Home*, 1931
Oil on canvas; 91.4 × 73.7 cm
(36 × 29 in.)
Detroit Institute of Arts, Gift of
Robert H. Tannahill

**46**
*Suspended Power*, 1939
Oil on canvas; 83.8 × 66 cm
(33 × 26 in.)
Dallas Museum of Art, Gift of
Edmund J. Kahn

**GRANT WOOD**
American, 1891–1942

**47**
*American Gothic*, 1930
Oil on Beaver board; 78 × 65.3 cm
(30 ¾ × 25 ¾ in.)
The Art Institute of Chicago,
Friends of American Art
Collection, 1930.934

**48**
*Fall Plowing*, 1931
Oil on Masonite; 62.2 × 87.6 cm
(24 ½ × 34 ½ in.)
Collection of John Deere Company

**49**
*The Midnight Ride of Paul Revere*,
1931
Oil on Masonite; 76 × 101.5 cm
(30 × 40 in.)
The Metropolitan Museum of Art,
Arthur Hoppock Hearn Fund, 1950

**50**
*Young Corn*, 1931
Oil on Masonite; 61 × 75.9 cm
(24 × 29 ⅞ in.)
Collection of Cedar Rapids
Community School District, on
loan to the Cedar Rapids Museum
of Art

**51**
*Daughters of Revolution*, 1932
Oil on Masonite; 50.8 × 101.4 cm
(20 × 39 ¹⁵⁄₁₆ in.)
Cincinnati Art Museum, The
Edwin and Virginia Irwin
Memorial

**52**
*Death on the Ridge Road*, 1935
Oil on Masonite; 99 × 117 cm
(39 × 46 ¹⁄₁₆ in.)
Williams College Museum of Art,
Gift of Cole Porter, 47.1.3

**53**
*Parson Weems' Fable*, 1939
Oil on canvas; 96.8 × 127.3 cm
(38 ⅛ × 50 ⅛ in.)
Amon Carter Museum of American
Art, Fort Worth, Texas

# BIBLIOGRAPHY

Adams, Henry. *Thomas Hart Benton: An American Original.* Knopf, 1989.

Adams, Philip Rhys. *Walt Kuhn, Painter, His Life and Work.* Ohio State University Press, 1978.

Adler, Esther. "The Problem of Our American Collection: MoMA Collects at Home." In Kathy Curry and Esther Adler, *American Modern: Hopper to O'Keeffe*, pp. 126–27. Exh. cat. Museum of Modern Art, 2013.

Allara, Pamela. *Pictures of People: Alice Neel's American Portrait Gallery.* University Press of New England, 1998.

*American Abstract Artists.* American Abstract Artists, 1938.

*American Art Today: Gallery of American Art Today, New York World's Fair.* National Art Society, 1939.

Anreus, Alejandro, et al. *Ben Shahn and the Passion of Sacco and Vanzetti.* Exh. cat. Jersey City Museum, 2001.

Apel, Dora. *Imagery of Lynching: Black Men, White Women, and the Mob.* Rutgers University Press, 2004.

*Art Digest.* "Benton Goes Home." 9 (April 15, 1935), p. 13.

——. "Guglielmi's 'First.'" 13 (November 15, 1938), p. 20.

——. "An Iowa Street." 8, no. 1 (October 1, 1933), p. 6.

——. "Mid-West Is Producing an Indigenous Art." 7, no. 2 (September 1, 1933), p. 10.

*Art Front.* Editorial. 1, no. 1 (November 1934), n. pag. (front page).

——. "On the American Scene." 1, no. 4 (April 1935), pp. 4, 8.

*The Arts of Life in America: A Series of Murals by Thomas Benton.* Exh. cat. Whitney Museum of American Art, 1932.

Ater, Renée. "Creating a 'Usable Past' and a 'Future Perfect Society': Aaron Douglas's Murals for the 1936 Texas Centennial Exposition." In Earle, *Aaron Douglas*, pp. 95–113.

Ayres, William, ed. *Picturing History: American Painting 1770–1930.* Exh. cat. Fraunces Tavern Museum/Rizzoli, 1993.

Baigell, Matthew. *Artist and Identity in Twentieth-Century America.* Cambridge University Press, 2001.

——. *Thomas Hart Benton.* Abrams, 1974.

Balken, Debra Bricker. *After Many Springs: Regionalism, Modernism, and the Midwest.* Exh. cat. Des Moines Art Center/Yale University Press, 2009.

Barnard, Rita. *The Great Depression and the Culture of Abundance: Kenneth Fearing, Nathanael West, and Mass Culture in the 1930s.* Cambridge University Press, 1995.

Barratt, Carrie Rebora, Lance Mayer, Gay Myers, Suzanne Smeaton, and Eli Wilner. "*Washington Crossing the Delaware*: Restoring an American Masterpiece." *Metropolitan Museum of Art Bulletin* 69, no. 2 (Fall 2011), pp. 11–13.

Barron Bailly, Austen. "Art for America: Race in Thomas Hart Benton's Murals, 1919–36." *Indiana Magazine of History* 105, no. 2 (June 2009), pp. 150–66.

Barter, Judith A., ed. *Art and Appetite: American Painting, Culture, and Cuisine.* Exh. cat.

Art Institute of Chicago/Yale University Press, 2013.

———. "The New Medici: The Rise of Corporate Collecting and the Uses of Contemporary Art (1925–1970)." Ph.D. diss., University of Massachusetts, Amherst, 1991.

———. "Travels and Travails." In Troyen et al., *Edward Hopper*, pp. 212–16.

Barter, Judith A., Sarah E. Kelly, Denise Mahoney, Ellen E. Roberts, and Brandon K. Ruud, with contributions by Jennifer M. Downs. *American Modernism at the Art Institute of Chicago: From World War I to 1955*. Art Institute of Chicago/Yale University Press, 2009.

Baur, John I. H. *Philip Evergood*. Harry N. Abrams, 1975.

———. *Philip Evergood*. Exh. cat. Whitney Museum of American Art/Frederick A. Praeger, 1960.

Benét, Stephen Vincent. "The Place of the Gods." *Saturday Evening Post* 210, no. 5 (July 31, 1937), p. 59.

Benton, Thomas Hart. "The Arts of Life in America." In *The Arts of Life in America: A Series of Murals by Thomas Benton*, pp. 4–13. Exh. cat. Whitney Museum of American Art, 1932.

Berman, Avis. *Rebels on Eighth Street: Juliana Force and the Whitney Museum of American Art*. Atheneum, 1990.

Berman, Greta, and Jeffrey Wechsler. *Realism and Realities: The Other Side of American Painting, 1940–1960*. Exh. cat. Rutgers University Art Gallery, 1982.

Biddle, George. *An American Artist's Story*. Little, Brown, 1939.

Bird, Paul. *Fifty Paintings by Walt Kuhn*. Studio, 1940.

Boyajian, Ani, and Mark Rutkoski, eds. *Stuart Davis: A Catalogue Raisonné*, vol. 2. Yale University Press, 2007.

Brock, Charles. *Charles Sheeler: Across Media*. Exh. cat. National Gallery of Art/University of California Press, 2006.

Brooks, Van Wyck. "On Creating a Usable Past." *Dial* 64 (April 11, 1918), pp. 337–41. Reprinted in Claire Sprague, ed., *Van Wyck Brooks: The Early Years, A Selection of His Works, 1908–1925*, pp. 219–26. Northeastern University Press, 1993. First published in 1968 by Harper.

Brown, Lorraine. "Federal Theater: Melodrama, Social Protest, and Genius." 1979. In *The New Deal Stage: Selections from the Federal Theatre Project, 1935–1939*. Washington, DC: Library of Congress, 2012, http://memory.loc.gov/ammem/fedtp/ftbrwn00.html.

Brown, Milton. "From Salon to Saloon." *Parnassus* 13 (March 1941), p. 193.

Burgard, Timothy Anglin, ed. *Masterworks of American Painting at the de Young*. Fine Arts Museums of San Francisco, 2005.

Butler, Sara A. "Reimagining the Movement: Beyond the Art of Negro Advancement at the Interior Building, 1937–1948." *American Art* 28, no. 2 (Summer 2014), pp. 70–87.

Carbone, Teresa A. "Body Language: Liberation and Restraint in Twenties Figuration." In *Youth and Beauty*, pp. 15–112.

———, ed. *Youth and Beauty: Art of the American Twenties*. Exh. cat.

Brooklyn Museum/Skira Rizzoli, 2011.

Cassidy, Donna M. "Arthur Dove's Music Paintings of the Jazz Age." *American Art Journal* 20, no. 1 (1988), pp. 5–23.

———. "Localized Glory: Marsden Hartley as New England Regionalist." In Elizabeth Mankin Kornhauser, ed., *Marsden Hartley*, pp. 175–92. Exh. cat. Wadsworth Atheneum Museum of Art/Yale University Press, 2002.

———. *Marsden Hartley: Race, Region, and Nation*. University Press of New England, 2005.

———. *Painting the Musical City: Jazz and Cultural Identity*. Smithsonian Institution Press, 1997.

Castellón, Federico. "Oral history interview with Federico Castellon, 1971 April 7–14." By Paul Cummings. Archives of American Art, Smithsonian Institution, Washington, DC, http://www.aaa.si.edu/collections/interviews/oral-history-interview-federico-castellon-5452/.

Cernuschi, Claude. *Jackson Pollock: Meaning and Significance*. Harper Collins, 1992.

Chauffier, L. Martin. "As Others See Us." *Living Age* 350 (June 1936), p. 348.

Cikovsky, Nicolai, Jr. "Notes and Footnotes on a Painting by George L. K. Morris." *Bulletin of the University of New Mexico Art Museum* 10 (1976–77), pp. 3–11.

———. "O. Louis Guglielmi (1906–1956), *Mental Geography*, 1938." In Bruce Robertson et al., *Twentieth-Century American Art: The Ebsworth Collection*, pp. 120–24. National Gallery of Art, 1999.

Clayton, Virginia Tuttle, Elizabeth Stillinger, Erika Doss, and Deborah Chotner. *Drawing on America's Past: Folk Art, Modernism, and the Index of American Design*. Exh. cat. National Gallery of Art/University of North Carolina Press, 2002.

Conn, Steven. "Henry Chapman Mercer and the Search for American History." *Pennsylvania Magazine of History and Biography* 116, no. 3 (July 1992), pp. 323–55.

Corn, Wanda M. "The Birth of a National Icon: Grant Wood's *American Gothic*." *Art Institute of Chicago Museum Studies* 10 (1983), pp. 252–75.

———. "Grant Wood (1892–1942), *Death on the Ridge* Road, 1935." In *American Dreams: American Art to 1950 in the Williams College Museum of Art*, pp. 158–61. Hudson Hills, 2001.

———. *Grant Wood: The Regionalist Vision*. Exh. cat. Minneapolis Institute of Arts/Yale University Press, 1983.

———. "Grant Wood: Uneasy Modern." In Jane C. Milosch, ed., *Grant Wood's Studio: Birthplace of American Gothic*, pp. 116–18. Exh. cat. Cedar Rapids Museum of Art/Prestel, 2005.

———. "The Great American Thing." In *The Great American Thing: Modern Art and National Identity, 1915–1935*, pp. 239–91. University of California Press, 1999.

Cortesini, Sergio. "Battling over the *Eternal City*." In Robert Cozzolino, ed., *Peter Blume: Nature and Metamorphosis*, pp. 59–83. Exh. cat. Pennsylvania Academy of Fine Arts/University of Pennsylvania Press, 2015.

Cozzolino, Robert. "Every Picture Should Be a Prayer: The Art of Ivan Albright." Ph.D. diss., University of Wisconsin–Madison, 2006.

Craven, Thomas. *Men of Art.* Simon and Schuster, 1931.

Czestochowski, Joseph S. *Marvin D. Cone: Art as Self Portrait.* Cedar Rapids Art Association, 1990.

Danieli, Fidel. "Interview of Helen Lundeberg." June 4, 1974. Los Angeles Community Group Portrait, Center for Oral History Research, UCLA Library Special Collections, http://oralhistory .library.ucla.edu/viewItem .do?ark=21198/zz0008z9qd& title=Lundeberg,%20Helen/.

Davis, Stuart. "Abstract Painting Today." In O'Connor, *Art for the Millions*, pp. 121–27.

———. "The Cube Root." *Art News* 41, no. 18 (February 1–14, 1943), p. 34.

———. Introduction to *Abstract Painting in America, February 12 to March 22, 1935*, n. pag. Exh. cat. Whitney Museum of American Art, 1935.

———. "Letter to Henry McBride." In Henry McBride, "The Palette Knife," *Creative Art* 6, no. 2 (February 1930), supplement, p. 35.

———. "The Place of Abstract Painting in America." In Diane Kelder, ed., *Stuart Davis*, pp. 109–10. Praeger, 1971.

———. "Reviews: The New York American Scene in Art." *Art Front* 1, no. 3 (Feb. 1935), p. 6.

———. "Self-Interview." *Creative Art* 9, no. 3 (September 1931), p. 211.

Delliquadri, Lyn. "A Living Tradition: The Winterbothams and Their Legacy." *Art Institute of Chicago Museum Studies* 20, no. 2 (1994), pp. 102–10.

DeLue, Rachael Z. "Arthur Dove, Painting, and Phonography." *History and Technology* 27, no. 1 (March 2011), pp. 113–21.

Denning, Michael. *The Cultural Front: The Laboring of American Culture in the Twentieth Century.* Verso, 1997.

Dennis, James M. *Grant Wood: A Study in American Art and Culture.* Viking, 1975.

———. *Renegade Regionalists: The Modern Independence of Grant Wood, Thomas Hart Benton, and John Steuart Curry.* University of Wisconsin Press, 1998.

Derleth, August, and Donald Wandrei, eds. *H. P. Lovecraft: Selected Letters*, vol. 3. Arkham House, 1971.

Dervaux, Isabelle, et al. *Surrealism U.S.A.* Exh. cat. National Academy Museum, 2005.

Donnell, Courtney Graham, Susan S. Weininger, and Robert Cozzolino. *Ivan Albright.* Exh. cat. Art Institute of Chicago/Hudson Hills, 1997.

Doss, Erika. *Benton, Pollock, and the Politics of Modernism: From Regionalism to Abstract Expressionism.* University of Chicago Press, 1991.

Dow, Eddy. "Van Wyck Brooks and Lewis Mumford: A Confluence in the 'Twenties." *American Literature* 45, no. 3. (November 1973), pp. 407–22.

Duffield, Marcus. "The Pulps: Day Dreams for the Masses." *Vanity Fair*, June 1933, p. 51.

Duncan, Michael, ed. *Post Surrealism.* Exh. cat. Pasadena Museum of California Art, 2003.

Earle, Susan, ed. *Aaron Douglas: African American Modernist.* Exh. cat. Spencer Museum of Art/Yale University Press, 2007.

———. "Harlem, Modernism, and Beyond: Aaron Douglas and His Role in Art/History." In *Aaron Douglas*, p. 5–51.

Edmonds, Walter D. *Drums along the Mohawk.* Syracuse University Press, 1997. Originally published in 1936 by Little, Brown.

Ehrlich, Susan, ed. *Pacific Dreams: Currents of Surrealism and Fantasy in California Art, 1934–1957.* Exh. cat. UCLA at the Armand Hammer Museum of Art and Cultural Center, 1995.

Eldridge, David. *American Culture in the 1930s.* Edinburgh University Press, 2008.

Evans, R. Tripp. *Grant Wood: A Life.* Alfred A. Knopf, 2010.

Evergood, Philip. "Oral history interview with Philip Evergood, 1968 Dec. 3." By Forrest Selvig. Archives of American Art, Smithsonian Institution, Washington, DC, http://www.aaa .si.edu/collections/interviews /oral-history-interview-philip -evergood-12410/.

Fahlman, Betsy. *Chimneys and Towers: Charles Demuth's Late Paintings of Lancaster.* Exh. cat. Amon Carter Museum of American Art, 2007.

Fearnow, Mark. *The American Stage and the Great Depression: A Cultural History of the Grotesque.* Cambridge University Press, 1997.

Ferreter, Ed. "Jay Sigmund and Grant Wood." *Books at Iowa* 42 (April 1985), digital.lib.uiowa.edu/ bai/books_iowa42_04.htm.

Ferris, Marc. *Star-Spangled Banner: The Unlikely Story of America's National Anthem.* Johns Hopkins University Press, 2014.

Fillin-Yeh, Susan. *Charles Sheeler: American Interiors.* Exh. cat. Yale University Art Gallery, 1987.

Fiske, John. *A History of the United States for Schools.* Houghton, Mifflin, 1899. Originally published in 1894.

Ford, Charles Henry. [Nicolas Calas.] "Interview with Andre Breton." *View* 1, nos. 7–8 (October– November 1941), pp. 1–2.

Fort, Ilene Susan. "American Social Surrealism." *Archives of American Art Journal* 22, no. 3 (1982), p. 14.

Foster, Carter E., ed. *Hopper Drawing.* Exh. cat. New York: Whitney Museum of American Art, 2013.

———. "*New York Movie.*" In *Hopper Drawing*, pp. 120–49.

Foster, Kathleen A., et al. *Thomas Hart Benton and the Indiana Murals.* Indiana University Art Museum/Indiana University Press, 2000.

Frankfurter, Felix. "The Case of Sacco and Vanzetti." *Atlantic,* March 1, 1927, pp. 409–32.

Fraser, Max. "Hands off the Machine: Workers' Hands and Revolutionary Symbolism in the Visual Culture of 1930s America," *American Art* 27, no. 2 (Summer 2013), pp. 94–117.

Furnas, Joseph Chamberlain. "—And Sudden Death." *Reader's Digest* 27, no. 160 (August 1935), pp. 21–26.

Furnas, Joseph Chamberlain, and Ernest N. Smith. *Sudden Death and How to Avoid It.* Simon and Schuster, 1935.

Gallati, Barbara Dayer. "The Williamsburg Murals: Five Monumental Works from the 1930s by Ilya Bolotowsky, Balcomb Greene, Paul Kelpe, and Albert Swinden." Brooklyn Museum, 1990.

*Gallery of Living Art: A. E. Gallatin Collection*. Gallery of Living Art, 1933.

Gellert, Hugo. "We Captured the Walls! The Museum of Modern Art Episode." *Art Front* 1, no. 1 (November 1934), p. 8.

Gibson, Campbell J., and Emily Lennon. "Historical Census Statistics on the Foreign-Born Population of the United States: 1850–1990" Washington, DC: Population Division, US Bureau of the Census, February 1999, http://www.census.gov/population/www/documentation/twps0029/twps0029.html.

Gionis, Teresa G., ed. *William H. Johnson: An American Modern.* Exh. cat. Smithsonian Institution Traveling Exhibition Service (SITES)/James E. Lewis Museum of Art, Morgan State University/University of Washington Press, 2011.

Goodrich, Lloyd. "The Circus in Paint." Exh. brochure. Whitney Studio Galleries, April 1929. Whitney Museum Library, Whitney Studio Club and Galleries, 1907–1930, http://cdm16694.contentdm.oclc.org/cdm/compoundobject/collection/p15405coll1/id/126/rec/47/.

Graham, Nan Wood, with John Zug and Julie Jensen McDonald. *My Brother, Grant Wood.* State Historical Society of Iowa, 1993.

Greenberg, Clement. "Review of the Whitney Annual." *Nation* 163, no. 26 (December 28, 1946). Reprinted in John O'Brian, ed., *Clement Greenberg: The Collected Essays and Criticism*, vol. 2, pp. 117–18. University of Chicago Press, 1986.

Greenough, Sarah, et al. *Modern Art and America: Alfred Stieglitz and His New York Galleries.* Exh. cat. National Gallery of Art, Washington/Bulfinch, 2000.

——, ed. *My Faraway One: Selected Letters of Georgia O'Keeffe and Alfred Stieglitz*, Volume 1, *1915–1933.* Beinecke Rare Book and Manuscript Library/Yale University Press, 2011.

Grieve, Victoria. *The Federal Art Project and the Creation of Middlebrow Culture.* University of Illinois Press, 2009.

Griffey, Randall R. "Reconsidering the 'Soil': The Stieglitz Circle, the Regionalists, and Cultural Eugenics in the Twenties." In Carbone, *Youth and Beauty,* pp. 245–76.

Groseclose, Barbara. "*Washington Crossing the Delaware*: The Political Context." *American Art Journal* 7, no. 2 (November 1975), pp. 70–78.

Guglielmi, O. Louis. "After the Locusts." [1939.] In O'Connor, *Art for the Millions*, pp. 113–15.

——. "I Hope to Sing Again." *Art Digest* 37 (May 1944), pp. 175–76.

Halsey, R. T. Haines, and C. O. C. "The American Wing." *Metropolitan Museum of Art Bulletin* 19, no. 11 (November 1924), pp. 251–65.

Hardin, Daniel. "Paddy Whalen and the Midnight March of the Baltimore Brigade." *Washington Area Spark: Struggles from the Past for Today*, February 4, 2015, https://washingtonspark.wordpress.com/2015/02/04/paddy-whalen-the-midnight-march-of-the-baltimore-brigade/.

Harris, Jonathan. *Federal Art and National Culture: The Politics of Identity in New Deal America.* Cambridge University Press, 1995.

Harten, Jurgen. *Siqueiros/Pollock: Pollock/Siqueiros.* Kunsthalle Düsseldorf, 1995.

Hartley, Marsden. "On the Subject of Nativeness—A Tribute to Maine." In *Marsden Hartley: Exhibition of Recent Paintings, 1936.* An American Place, 1937.

Haskell, Barbara. *Alice Neel.* Harry N. Abrams, 1983.

——. *Charles Demuth.* Exh. cat. Whitney Museum of American Art/Harry N. Abrams, 1988.

——. "Swing Time: Reginald Marsh and the Chaos of Modern Life." In Barbara Haskell, ed., *Swing Time: Reginald Marsh and Thirties New York*, pp. 10–59. New-York Historical Society/D. Giles, 2013.

Haskell, Francis. "The Sad Clown: Notes on a Nineteenth-Century Myth." In *Past and Present in Art and Taste: Selected Essays*, pp. 117–28. Yale University Press, 1987.

Havoc, June. *Early Havoc.* Hutchinson, 1960.

Haw, Richard. *The Art of the Brooklyn Bridge: A Visual History.* Routledge, 2008.

——. *The Brooklyn Bridge: A Cultural History.* Rutgers University Press, 2005.

Hawthorne, Nathaniel. *The House of the Seven Gables.* Ticknor, Reed, and Fields, 1851.

*Hearings Before the Committee on Un-American Activities, House of Representatives, Eighty-Sixth Congress, first session, July 1, 1959; The American National Exhibition, Moscow, July 1959 (The record of certain artists and an appraisal of their works selected for display).* Government Printing Office, 1959.

Hemingway, Andrew. *Artists on the Left: American Artists and the Communist Movement, 1926–1956.* Yale University Press, 2002.

——. "Realism under Duress: The 1930s." in John Davis, Jennifer A. Greenhill, and Jason D. LaFountain, *A Companion to American Art*, pp. 626–31. Wiley-Blackwell, 2015.

Hills, Patricia. *Alice Neel.* Harry N. Abrams, 1983.

——. *Painting Harlem Modern: The Art of Jacob Lawrence.* University of California Press, 2009.

——, ed. *Modern Art in the USA: Issues and Controversies of the Twentieth Century.* Prentice Hall, 2000.

Hills, Patricia, and Roberta Tarbell. *The Figurative Tradition and the Whitney Museum of American Art: Paintings and Sculpture from the Permanent Collection.* Exh. cat. Whitney Museum of American Art, 1980.

Hoban, Phoebe. *Alice Neel: The Art of Not Sitting Pretty.* St. Martin's, 2010.

Hubin, Allen J. *The Bibliography of Crime Fiction, 1749–1975.* University of California at San Diego, 1979.

Hurt, R. Douglas. "Midwestern Distinctiveness." In Andrew R. L. Cayton and Susan E. Gray, eds., *The American Midwest: Essays on Regional History*, pp. 160–79, 233–35. Indiana University Press, 2001.

*Index of American Design*, National Gallery of Art, Washington, DC, https://www.nga.gov/collection/iad/history/overview.shtm.

Indych-López, Anna. *Muralism without Walls: Rivera, Orozco, and Siqueiros in the United States, 1927–1940*. University of Pittsburgh Press, 2009.

Jack, Zachary Michael, ed. *The Plowman Sings: The Essential Fiction, Poetry, and Drama of America's Forgotten Regionalist Jay G. Sigmund*. University Press of America, 2008.

Jackson, Allen. "Art: U.S. Scene." *Time* 24, no. 26 (December 24, 1934), pp. 26–31.

Jacobs, Lea. *The Wages of Sin: Censorship and the Fallen Woman Film, 1928–1942*. University of California Press, 1997.

Janson, H. W. "Benton and Wood, Champions of Regionalism." *Magazine of Art* 39, no. 5 (May 1946), pp. 184–86, 198–200.

Jones, Alfred Haworth. "The Search for a Usable American Past in the New Deal Era." *American Quarterly* 23, no. 5 (December 1971), pp. 710–24.

Jones, Howard Mumford. "Patriotism—But How?" *Atlantic Monthly* 162, no. 5 (November 1938), pp. 585–92.

Jones, Robert Kenneth. *The Shudder Pulps: A History of the Weird Menace Magazines of the 1930s*. Plume, 1978.

Joshi, J. T. *A Dreamer and a Visionary: H. P. Lovecraft in His Time*. Liverpool University Press, 2001.

Junker, Patricia, ed. *John Steuart Curry: Inventing the Middle West*. University of Wisconsin Press, 1998.

Kachur, Lewis. *Stuart Davis: An American in Paris*. Exh. cat. Whitney Museum of American Art at Philip Morris, 1987.

Kantor, Morris. "Ends and Means." *Magazine of Art* 33, no. 3 (March 1940), pp. 138–47.

Karmel, Pepe. "A Sum of Destructions." In Kirk Varnedoe and Pepe Karmel, eds., *Jackson Pollock: New Approaches*, pp. 71–100. Exh. cat. Museum of Modern Art/Harry N. Abrams, 1999.

Kazin, Alfred. *Starting Out in the Thirties*. Cornell University Press, 1989.

Kelder, Diane, ed. *Stuart Davis*. Praeger, 1971.

Kellner, Bruce, ed. *Letters of Charles Demuth: American Artist, 1883–1935*. Temple University Press, 2000.

Kelly, Franklin. "Walt Kuhn (1877–1949), *Portrait of the Artist as a Clown (Kansas)*, 1932." In Bruce Robertson et al., *Twentieth-Century American Art: The Ebsworth Collection*, pp. 159–61. National Gallery of Art, 1999.

Kelly, Sarah E. "Charles Green Shaw (1892–1974)." In Barter et al., *American Modernism*, pp. 240–43.

——. "Doris Lee (1905–1983)." In Barter et al., *American Modernism*, pp. 183–85.

——. "Grant Wood (1891–1942)." In Barter et al., *American Modernism*, pp. 178–81.

——. "Morris Kantor (1896–1974)." In Barter et al., *American Modernism*, pp. 181–83.

Kendall, Sue M. *Rethinking Regionalism: John Steuart Curry and the Kansas Mural Controversy*. Smithsonian Institution Press, 1986.

Kennedy, David M. *Freedom from Fear: The American People in Depression and War, 1929–1945*. Oxford University Press, 1999.

Kirstein, Lincoln. "An Iowa Memling." *Art Front* 1 (July 1935), p. 8.

Kroiz, Lauren. *Creative Composites: Modernism, Race, and the Stieglitz Circle*. Exh. cat. Phillips Collection/University of California Press, 2012.

Krutch, Joseph Wood. "The Usable Past." *Nation* 130, no. 3580 (February 14, 1934), p. 191.

Kuh, Katharine. *The Artist's Voice: Talks with Seventeen Artists*. Harper and Row, 1962.

Landau, Ellen G. "Double Consciousness in Mexico: How Philip Guston and Reuben Kadish Painted a Morelian Mural." *American Art* 21, no. 1 (Spring 2007), pp. 74–97.

Lane, John R., and Susan C. Larsen, eds., *Abstract Painting and Sculpture in America, 1927–1944*. Exh. cat. Museum of Art, Carnegie Institute/Harry N. Abrams, Inc., 1983.

Lansing, Gerrit L. "'A Neurotic Mirror': The Painting of O. Louis Guglielmi, 1932–1943." Ph.D. diss., New York University, 1999.

——. "Surrealism as a Weapon." In Dervaux et al., *Surrealism U.S.A.*, pp. 30–35.

*Leading Causes of Death, 1900–1998*. United States Centers for Disease Control and Prevention, http://www.cdc.gov/nchs/data/dvs/lead1900_98.pdf.

Lears, Jackson. *Rebirth of a Nation: The Making of Modern America, 1877–1920*. Harper Collins, 2009.

Lenz, Emily. "Charles Green Shaw (1892–1974): Evolution of an Artist, 1926–1946." In Henry Adams and Emily Lenz, *Charles Green Shaw (1892–1974): The 1930s and 1940s*. Exh. cat. D. Wigmore Fine Art, 2007.

Levin, Gail. *Edward Hopper: An Intimate Biography*. Rizzoli, 2007.

Lewis, Sinclair. *It Can't Happen Here*. Sun Dial, 1936.

——. *Main Street and Babbitt*. Library of America, 1992.

*Life*. "Swing: The Hottest and Best Kind of Jazz Reaches Its Golden Age." 5, no. 6 (August 8, 1938), pp. 50–60.

[Longfellow, Henry Wadsworth.] "Paul Revere's Ride." *Atlantic Monthly* 7, no. 139 (January 1861), pp. 27–29.

Longfellow, Henry Wadsworth. *Tales of a Wayside Inn*. Ticknor and Fields, 1863.

Lorenz, Melinda. *George L. K. Morris: Artist and Critic*. UMI Research Press, 1982.

"Lynching Statistics by Year." University of Missouri-Kansas City School of Law, http://law2.umkc.edu/faculty/projects/ftrials/shipp/lynchingyear.html.

Lynes, Barbara Buhler, Lesley Poling-Kempes, and Frederick W. Turner. *Georgia O'Keeffe and New Mexico: A Sense of Place*. Exh. cat. Georgia O'Keeffe Museum/Princeton University Press, 2004.

Mahoney, Denise. "Ilya Bolotowsky (1907–1981)." In Barter et al., *American Modernism*, pp. 260–62.

Marling, Karal Ann. *George Washington Slept Here: Colonial Revivals in American Culture, 1876–1986*. Harvard University Press, 1988.

——. "Of Cherry Trees and Ladies' Teas: Grant Wood Looks at Colonial America." In Alan Axelrod, ed., *The Colonial Revival in America*, pp. 294–319. Winterthur Museum/W. W. Norton, 1985.

Maroney, James H., Jr. *Hiding in Plain Sight: Decoding the Homoerotic and Misogynistic Imagery of Grant Wood*. Gala Books, 2013. http://jamesmaroney.com/art/grant-wood/hiding-in-plain-sight.pdf.

Martin, Carol J. *Dance Marathons: Performing American Culture of the 1920s and 1930s*. University Press of Mississippi, 1994.

Mayer, Musa. *Night Studio: A Memoir of Philip Guston*. Da Capo, 1997.

McBrien, William. *Cole Porter: A Biography*. Alfred A. Knopf, 2011.

McCabe, Cynthia Jaffee. *The Golden Door: Artist-Immigrants of America, 1876–1976*. Exh. cat. Hirshhorn Museum and Sculpture Garden, Smithsonian Institution/Smithsonian Institution Press, 1976.

McCoy, Horace. *They Shoot Horses Don't They?* Serpent's Tail, 2010. Originally published in 1935 by Simon and Schuster.

Meeker, Oden and Olivia. "Screamy-weamies." *Collier's* 117 (January 12, 1947), pp. 42, 55.

Meltzer, Milton. *Dorothea Lange: A Photographer's Life*. Farrar Straus Giroux, 1978.

Mencken, H. L. "Utopia by Sterilization." *American Mercury* 41 (1937), p. 403. http://theamericanmercury.org/2010/09/utopia-by-sterilization/.

Meyer, Kate. "Broken Ground: Plowing and America's Cultural Landscape in the 1930s." Ph.D. diss., University of Kansas, 2011.

Meyer, Richard. *Outlaw Representation: Censorship and Homosexuality in Twentieth-Century American Art*. Oxford University Press, 2002.

*Modern Works of Art: Fifth Anniversary Exhibition, November 20, 1934–January 20, 1935*. Museum of Modern Art, 1934.

Mooney, Amy. "Representing Race: Disjunctures in the Work of Archibald J. Motley, Jr." *Art Institute of Chicago Museum Studies* 24, no. 2 (1999), p. 174.

Morris, Anthony J. "Paul Cadmus and Carnival, 1934: Representing the Comic Grotesque." *American Art* 26, no. 3 (Fall 2012), pp. 86–99.

Morris, George L. K. "The Quest for an Abstract Tradition." In *American Abstract Artists*, n.pag., article 3.

Mumford, Lewis. "Opening Address." In Matthew Baigell and Julia Williams, eds., *Artists against War and Fascism: Papers of the First American Artists' Congress*, p. 63. Rutgers University Press, 1986.

——. *The Brown Decades: A Study of the Arts in America 1865–1895*. New York: Harcourt, Brace, 1931.

Nash, Anedith Jo Bond. "Death on the Highway: The Automobile Wreck in American Culture, 1920–40." Ph.D. diss., University of Minnesota, 1983.

——. "*Death on the Ridge Road*: Grant Wood and Modernization in the Midwest." *Prospects: An Annual of American Cultural Studies* 8 (1983), pp. 281–301.

New Deal Art Registry. http://www.newdealartregistry.org/.

*New Republic*. "Mass Murder in America." 77, no. 993 (December 13, 1933), p. 117.

Nies, Betsy L. "Defending Jeeter: Conservative Arguments against Eugenics in the Depression Era South." In Susan Currell and Christina Cogdell, eds., *Popular Eugenics: National Efficiency and American Mass Culture in the 1930s*, pp. 120–39. Ohio University Press, 2006.

Norton, Peter D. *Fighting Traffic: The Dawn of the Motor Age in the American City*. MIT Press, 2008.

O'Connor, Francis V., ed. *Art For the Millions: Essays from the 1930s by Artists and Administrators of the WPA Federal Art Project*. New York Graphic Society, 1973.

O'Keeffe, Georgia. *Georgia O'Keeffe*. Viking, 1976.

Odum, Howard W. "Lynchings, Fears, and Folkways." *Nation* 133, no. 3469 (December 30, 1931), pp. 719–20.

Page, Max. *The City's End: Two Centuries of Fantasies, Fears, and Premonitions of New York's Destruction*. Yale University Press, 2008.

Park, Marlene, and Gerald E. Markowitz. *Democratic Vistas: Post Offices and Public Art in the New Deal*. Temple University Press, 1984.

Patterson, Jody. "Modernism and Murals at the 1939 New York World's Fair." *American Art* 24, no. 2 (Summer 2010), pp. 50–73.

"Paul Cadmus: Artist Biography." http://www.dcmooregallery.com/artists/paul-cadmus/.

Pennington, Buck. "The 'Floating World' in the Twenties: The Jazz Age and Charles Green Shaw." *Archives of American Art Journal* 20, no. 4 (1980), pp. 17–24.

Platt, Susan Noyes. "The Jersey Homesteads Mural: Ben Shahn, Bernarda Bryson, and History Painting in the 1930s." In Patricia M. Burnham and Lucretia Hoover Giese, eds., *Redefining American History Painting*, pp. 294–309. Cambridge University Press, 1995.

Pohl, Frances. *In the Eye of the Storm: An Art of Conscience, 1930–1970*. Pomegranate Artbooks, 1995.

Pollock, Jackson. "My Painting." *Possibilities* 1, no. 1 (Winter 1947/48), pp. 78–83.

Powell, Richard J. *Homecoming: The Art and Life of William H. Johnson*. Exh. cat. National Museum of American Art, Smithsonian Institution, 1991.

Ranke, Jason Adams. "The Anglo-American Press and the 'Secret' Rearmament of Hitler's Germany." M.A. thesis, Clemson University, 2009.

Ringel, Faye. "The Local Color Is Black—H. P. Lovecraft." In *New England's Gothic Literature: History and Folklore of the Supernatural from the Seventeenth through the Twentieth Centuries*, pp. 157–201. Edwin Mellen, 1996.

Roberts, Ellen E. "Arthur Dove (1880–1946)." In Barter et al., *American Modernism*, pp. 247–49.

——. "Charles Demuth (1883–1935)." In Barter et al., *American Modernism*, pp. 162–66.

——. "Georgia O'Keeffe (1887–1986)." In Barter et al., *American Modernism*, pp. 155–61.

Roosevelt, Franklin. "Back to the Land." *Review of Reviews* 84 (October 1931), pp. 63–64.

Rosenbaum, Julia B. *Visions of Belonging: New England Art and the Making of American Identity*. Cornell University Press, 2006.

Rosenberg, Harold. "Getting Inside the Canvas." *Art News* 51, no. 8 (December 1952), p. 22.

Rosenblatt, Leah. "Charles G. Shaw: Life." In *The Park Avenue Cubists: Gallatin, Morris, Frelinghuysen and Shaw*, pp. 69–73. Exh. cat. Grey Art Gallery, New York University/Ashgate, 2002.

Rosenthal, Deborah M. "Ilya Bolotowsky." In Lane and Larsen, eds., *Abstract Painting and Sculpture*, pp. 51–54.

Rourke, Constance. *Charles Sheeler: Artist in the American Tradition*. Harcourt Brace, 1938.

Rubin, Joan Shelley. "A Convergence of Vision: Constance Rourke, Charles Sheeler, and American Art." *American Quarterly* 42, no. 2 (June 1990), pp. 191–222.

Rushing, W. Jackson. *Native American Art and the New York Avant-Garde: A History of Cultural Primitivism*. University of Texas Press, 1995.

Schjeldahl, Peter. "A Kind Word for Norman Rockwell." *New Yorker* online, November 5, 2013, http://www.newyorker.com/books/page-turner/a-kind-word-for-norman-rockwell/.

Schuller, Gunther. *The Swing Era: The Development of Jazz, 1930–1945*. Oxford University Press, 1989.

Sharp, Ellen. "The Legend of John Brown and the Series by Jacob Lawrence." *Bulletin of the Detroit Institute of Arts* 67, no. 4 (1993), pp. 14–35.

Shaw, Charles G. "A Word to the Objector." In *American Abstract Artists*, n.pag, article 1.

———. "The Plastic Polygon." *Plastique* 3 (Spring 1938), pp. 28–29.

Shortridge, James R. *The Middle West: Its Meaning in American Culture*. University Press of Kansas, 1989.

Sigmund, Jay G. "Death Rides a Rubber-Shod Horse." *American Poetry* 16, no. 6 (October 1934), p. 152.

Sims, Lowery Stokes. "New York–Paris No. 3." In Lowery Stokes Sims et al., *Stuart Davis: American Painter*, pp. 206–07, cat. 91. Exh. cat. Metropolitan Museum of Art, 1991.

Skal, David J. *The Monster Show: A Cultural History of Horror*. W. W. Norton, 1993.

Smith, Shawn Michelle. "The Evidence of Lynching Photographs." In Dora Apel and Shawn Michelle Smith, *Lynching Photographs*, pp. 11–41. University of California Press, 2007.

Soby, James Thrall. "Peter Blume's 'Eternal City.'" *Bulletin of the Museum of Modern Art* 10, no. 4 (April 1943), pp. 2–6.

Solomon, Deborah. *Jackson Pollock: A Biography*. Simon and Schuster, 1987.

*Sourcebook*. "Feitelson-Lundeberg." 20, no. 4 (April 1973), p. 35.

Southworth, Herbert Rutledge. *Guernica! Guernica!: A Study of Journalism, Diplomacy, Propaganda, and History*. University of California Press, 1977.

Sprague, Claire, ed. *Van Wyck Brooks: The Early Years, A Selection of His Works, 1908–1925*. Northeastern University Press, 1993. Originally published in 1968 by Harper and Row.

Stavitsky, Gail. "A. E. Gallatin's Gallery and Museum of Living Art (1927–1943)." *American Art* 7, no. 2 (Spring 1993), pp. 46–63.

———. "A Landmark Exhibition: Five Contemporary American Concretionists, March 1936." *Archives of American Art Journal* 33, no. 2 (1993), pp. 2–10.

Stephens, Harold W. "Mask and Lash in Crenshaw." *North American Review* 225 (April 1928), p. 437.

Susman, Warren I. "The Culture of the 1930s." In *Culture as History: The Transformation of American Society in the Twentieth Century*, pp. 150–83. Smithsonian Institution Press, 2003. Originally published in 1974 by Pantheon.

Sutton, Robert P. *Heartland Utopias*. Northern Illinois University Press, 2009.

Svendsen, Louise Averill, with Mimi Poser. "Interview with Ilya Bolotowsky." In *Ilya Bolotowsky*, pp. 12–32. Exh. cat. Solomon R. Guggenheim Museum, 1974.

Sweet, Frederick A., et al. *Ivan Albright: A Retrospective Exhibition*. Exh. cat. Art Institute of Chicago/Whitney Museum of American Art, 1964.

Temkin, Ann, ed. *Alice Neel*. Exh. cat. Philadelphia Museum of Art, 2000.

Thurber, Hali. "Paul Starrett Sample (1869–1974)." http://www.caldwellgallery.com/bios/sample_biography.html.

*Time*. "Art: Benton." 17, no. 1 (January 5, 1931), p. 32.

———. "Blood and Agony." 26, no. 7 (August 12, 1935), p. 21.

———. "Housepainter." 25, no. 2 (June 3, 1935), p. 32.

———. "Lavender and Old Bottles." 38, no. 21 (November 24, 1941), p. 81.

Tompkins, Calvin. "Profiles: The Rose in the Eye Looked Pretty Fine." *New Yorker*, March 4, 1974, pp. 40–66.

Trapp, Frank. *Peter Blume*. Rizzoli, 1987.

Troyen, Carol. "'The Sacredness of Everyday Fact': Hopper's Pictures of the City." In Troyen et al., *Edward Hopper*, pp. 111–43.

Troyen, Carol, Judith A. Barter, Janet L. Comey, Elliot Bostwick Davis, and Ellen E. Roberts. *Edward Hopper*. Exh. cat. MFA Publications, 2007.

Truettner, William H., and Thomas Andrew Denenberg. "The Discreet Charm of the Colonial." In William H. Truettner and Roger B. Stein, *Picturing Old New England: Image and Memory*, pp. 105–07. Exh. cat. National Museum of American Art, Smithsonian Institution/Yale University Press, 1999.

Turner, Elizabeth Hutton. "Going Home: Geneva, 1933–1938." In Debra Bricker Balken in collaboration with William C. Agee and Elizabeth Hutton Turner, *Arthur Dove: A Retrospective*, pp. 100–03. Exh. cat. Addison Gallery of American Art, Phillips Academy/Phillips Collection/MIT Press, 1997.

Tyler, Parker. "Hopper/Pollock: The Loneliness of the Crowd and the Loneliness of the Universe: An Antiphonal." *Art News Annual* 26 (1957), pp. 87–107.

Walker, Andrew, and Janeen Turk. *Joe Jones: Radical Painter of the American Scene*. Exh. cat. Saint Louis Art Museum/University of Washington Press, 2010.

Weber, Bruce. *Stuart Davis' New York*. Exh. cat. Norton Gallery and School of Art, 1985.

Weems, M. L. *The Life of George Washington*. Sixth edition. R. Cochran, 1808. Originally published in 1800 by Joseph Allen.

West, Nathanael. *The Day of the Locust*. New Directions, 2009. Originally published in 1939 by Random House.

White, Anthony, Ed. *Jackson Pollock's Blue Poles*. Exh. cat. National Gallery of Australia/ Thames and Hudson, 2002.

Whiting, Cécile. *Antifascism in American Art*. Yale University Press, 1989.

Whiting, F. A., Jr. "Stone, Steel and Fire: Stone City Comes to Life." *American Magazine of Art* 25, no. 6 (December 1932), pp. 333–42.

Wierich, Jochen. *Grand Themes: Emanuel Leutze,* Washington Crossing the Delaware, *and American History Painting*. Pennsylvania State University Press, 2012.

Wilson, Kristina. "Ambivalence, Irony, and Americana: Charles Sheeler's 'American Interiors.'" *Winterthur Portfolio* 45, no. 4 (Winter 2011), pp. 249–76.

Wolfe, M. Melissa. "Joe Jones: Worker-Artist." In Walker and Turk, *Joe Jones*, pp. 33–54.

Wolfskill, Phoebe. "Caricature and the New Negro in the Work of Archibald Motley Jr. and Palmer Hayden." *Art Bulletin* 91, no. 3 (September 2009), p. 348.

Wood, Grant. *Revolt against the City*. Clio, 1935.

Wyld, Lionel D. "History and Humanism: A Novelist's Portrayal of the American Revolution." *North Dakota Quarterly* 51, no. 4 (Fall 1983), pp. 174–82.

# INDEX

Bartlett, Helen Birch, 58

Baum, L. Frank, 28

Benedict, Ruth, 17

Benét, Stephen Vincent, 138

Benton, Thomas Hart: *America Today* (New School murals), 31, 93, *93*, 174, 175; *The Arts of Life in America: Arts of the West*, 31–32, *33*, 52n12; *Ballad of the Jealous Lover . . .* , 52n13; *Cotton Pickers* (cat. 4), 29–30, *30*, 52n5; *Cradling Wheat* (cat. 2), 45, *48–49*, 49; Davis's feud with, 22, 24, 32, 57–58, 81, 174; Hartley's response to, 69; *Haystack* (cat. 3), 45, *47*; *Indiana* murals, 32, 33, 93; *Midwest*, 31, *31*; and modernism's place in American art, 24, 56, 58; Pollock as student of, 24, 50, 174–75; and Regionalism's decline, 49, 50; and Regionalism's objectives, 17–18, 41, 90; and tempera medium, 45, 160; *Time* article on, 33, 35

Biddle, George, 35, 111n21

Biederman, Charles, 76

Bishop Hill colony, Illinois, 41, 42, *42*

Blume, Peter: *The Eternal City* (cat. 5), 132–33, *132*, 139; as federally employed, 93; Wood contrasted with, 108–9

Bolotowsky, Ilya: and American Abstract Artists, 75; as federally employed, 35, 80, 93; as National Academy student, 85n88; *Study for the Hall of Medical Sciences Mural . . .* (cat. 6), 79–80, *79*, *80*

Bourke-White, Margaret, 20, *22*

Breton, André, 176–77

Brooks, Van Wyck, 89, 110n1, 110n5

Brown, John, 95, 111n29

Browne, Byron, 80

Bruce, Edward, 35, 148, 149, 153

Bulliet, C. J., 35

Burchfield, Charles, 58

Burlington Zephyr, 25n12

Cadmus, Paul: as federally employed, 93, 152; *The Fleet's In!* (cat. 7), 152–54, *153*, 155, 171n30; and urban scenes, 18, 167

Cahill, Holger, 18, 98, 100

Calder, Alexander, 58, 75, 76

Caldwell, Erskine, 30

California School of Fine Arts, 41

Capra, Frank, 165, 169

Carnegie International Exhibition, Pittsburgh, 92

cartoons, 118, *118*, 120, 138

Castellón, Federico: citizenship of, 142n59; *The Dark Figure* (cat. 8), *134*, 135, 139, 143n67; Wood contrasted with, 108–9

*Cat and the Canary, The* (movie), 123

Cather, Willa, 28

censorship, 111n31, 133, 153, 162

Century of Progress Exposition, Chicago, 25n12, 32, 93, 141n43

Cézanne, Paul, 57, 58, 67

Chicago: Black Belt neighborhoods, 159, 160; Century of Progress Exposition, 25n12, 32, 93, 141n43; as industrial hub, 29; Lundeberg's memories of, 123, 125. *See also* Art Institute of Chicago

Chirico, Giorgio de, 177

Church, Frederic Edwin, 67

city life. *See* urban life

Civil War, American, 106, 107, 118

Colbert, Claudette, 165, *167*

Colonial Dames of America, 39

Colonial Williamsburg, Virginia, 97

Communism: artists' alleged ties to, 15, 72, 175–76; and Artists' Congress, 170n19; artists' support for Party, 15, 25n5, 32, 72, 118, 148, 151, 155, 160; and expressionism, 171n33; and labor activism, 147, 149, 151–52; New Deal labeled Communist, 17; and Popular Front against Fascism, 72, 131, 170n5; and portraiture, 152; and Russian Revolution, 15, 142n51

Cone, Marvin: *River Bend No. 4* (cat. 9), 45, *46*, 106

Conroy, Jack, 148

consumer culture, 18, 75–77, 147, 160

Copland, Aaron, 17

Copley, John Singleton, 56

Corcoran Gallery of Art, Washington, 35, 45, 133, 153, 155, 171n30

Coronado, Francisco Vázquez de, 95

Coughlin, Charles, 17

Covarrubias, Miguel, 159, *159*

Cowley, Malcolm, 25n5

Coxey, Jacob, 52n10

Craven, Thomas, 53n23, 57, 67

Cubism: Bolotowsky's exposure to, 79; Davis's use of, 57, 61; Demuth's use of, 62; Douglas's use of, 72, 73; MoMA exhibition on, 75; Pollock's debt to, 175; Shaw's use of, 75–77; Sheeler's use of, 98; *Time* magazine's criticism of, 33, 57

Curry, John Steuart: *Baptism in Kansas*, 35–36, *36*, 38; as federally employed, 93; *Hogs Killing a Snake* (cat. 10), 36, *37*; Kansas State Capitol mural, 95; *Manhunt*, 33; and midwestern demographics, 29; photograph of, with Wood, *38*; and Regionalism's decline, 49, 50; and Regionalism's objectives, 17–18, 90; in *Time* article, 33, 35

Dada, 33, 57, 59, 76, 125, 177

Dalí, Salvador, 135

Dallas Nine, 49

dancing, 117–18, *117*, 155, *156*, 157, *158*, 159, *159*, 171n34

Daughters of the American Revolution, 39, 88, 90–93

Daumier, Honoré, 146, 147, 155

Davis, Stuart: and American-style modernism, 56–57, 58–59, 61, 80–81, 82n26; and *Art Front* magazine, 72; Benton's feud with, 22, 24, 32, 57–58, 81, 174; *Buildings, Flagpole, and Columns*, 60, *61*, 82n22; as federally employed, 35, 93; and folk art, 53n45; *History of Communication*, 80, *81*; *New York–Paris No. 3* (cat. 11), 59–61, *60*

Debs, Eugene, 52n10

Deere, John, 42

De Kooning, Willem, 176

Delacroix, Eugène, 160

Delphic Galleries, New York, 30

Demuth, Charles: and historical painting, 109; *And the Home of the Brave* (cat. 12), 61–62, *63*, 102–3; and nationalistic art, 57, 58, 61–62

Depression. *See* Great Depression

Deskey, Donald, 18

Detroit Federal Theatre, 133, 135

Diebenkorn, Richard, 179

Doolittle, Kenneth, 151

Dos Passos, John, 25n5

Douglas, Aaron: *Aspiration* (cat. 13), 72–73, *94*, 95; *Into Bondage*, 72–73, *73*; as federally employed, 72, 93, 95; and historical painting, 95, 109

Douglass, Frederick, 96

Dove, Arthur: and Stieglitz, 57, 69; *Swing Music (Louis Armstrong)* (cat. 15), 69, 71–72, *71*; *Tree Trunks* (cat. 14), 69, *70*

Downtown Gallery, New York, 53n45, 100, 135

Dreyfuss, Henry, 18

Dürer, Albrecht, 38

Dust Bowl, 42, 45, 49, *50*, *51*, 97

Dwight, Mabel, 138, *139*

Eakins, Thomas, 110n5, 127

East, the: folk art, 98, *99*, 100, *100*, 112n40; fundamentalist religion as unfamiliar to, 36; Lancaster County, Pennsylvania, scenes (Demuth), 61–62, *63*, 102–3; living history museums and displays, 97–98; and midwestern economic woes, 29; Regionalists' animosity toward, 17, 32, 41; and Washington (George), 92–93, 107, 110n14. *See also* New England; New York City

Edmonds, Walter, 18, 107

Enriquez, Carlos, 151

eugenics, 30–31

Evans, Walker, 20

Evergood, Philip: *Dance Marathon* (cat. 16), 117–18, 140n4, 140n6, 155, *156*, 157; expressionism of, 171n33; as federally employed, 93, 155; and leftist artists, 15, 176; upbringing, 171n31; and urban scenes, 18, 167

# SUPPORTERS OF THE ROYAL ACADEMY

AS OF MARCH 2016

## Major Benefactors

The President and the Trustees of the Royal Academy Trust would like to thank all those who have been exceedingly generous over a number of years in support of the galleries, the exhibitions, the conservation of the Collections, the Library, the Royal Academy Schools, the education programme and capital redevelopments projects:

HM The Queen
Her Majesty's Government
The 29th May 1961 Charitable Trust
Aldama Foundation
Lord and Lady Aldington
The Band Trust
Barclays Bank
B A T Industries plc
Sir David and Lady Bell
Big Lottery Fund (formerly New Opportunities Fund)
John Frye Bourne
William Brake Charitable Trust
British Telecom
Consuelo and Anthony Brooke
Sir Francis and Lady Brooke
Mr and Mrs John Burns
Mr Raymond M Burton CBE
The Cadogan Charity
Jeanne and William Callanan
Carew Pole Charitable Trust
The CHEAR Foundation
Sir Trevor Chinn CVO and Lady Chinn
The John S Cohen Foundation
Mr Jeremy Coller
John and Gail Coombe
The Lord Davies of Abersoch CBE
The Roger De Haan Charitable Trust
Sir Harry and Lady Djanogly
Clore Duffield Foundation
The Dulverton Trust
The John Ellerman Foundation
Mr Richard Elman
The Eranda Foundation
EY
John and Fausta Eskenazi
The Fidelity UK Foundation
The Foyle Foundation
Friends of the Royal Academy
Jacqueline and Michael Gee
J Paul Getty Jnr Charitable Trust
Mr Mark Getty
Mr Thomas Gibson
GlaxoSmithKline plc
Sir Ronald Grierson
Sir Nicholas Grimshaw CBE PPRA
Mr and Mrs Jim Grover
Diane and Guilford Glazer
The Golden Bottle Trust
Mr and Mrs Jack Goldhill
Maurice and Laurence Goldman
Horace W Goldsmith Foundation
Nicholas and Judith Goodison
HRH Princess Marie-Chantal of Greece
Mr and Mrs Charles Hale
Mrs Robin Hambro
Harold Hyam Wingate Foundation
Mr and Mrs Jocelin Harris
The Philip and Pauline Harris Charitable Trust
The Charles Hayward Foundation
Heritage Lottery Fund
Hermes GB
Mr Julian Heslop
Hiscox
Mr Damien Hirst
Holbeck Charitable Trust
Mr and Mrs Jeremy Hosking
Lord and Lady Jacobs
The J P Jacobs CharitableTrust
Mrs Gabrielle Jungels-Winkler
P Kahn
The Lillian Jean Kaplan Foundation
Daniel Katz Gallery
The Kirby Laing Foundation
The Kress Foundation
Jon and Barbara Landau
The Lankelly Foundation
The David Lean Foundation
The Lennox and Wyfold Foundation
The Leverhulme Trust
Lord Leverhulme's Charitable Trust
Christian Levett and Mougins Museum of Classical Art
Lex Service plc
The Linbury Trust
Sir Sydney Lipworth QC and Lady Lipworth
Miss Rosemary Lomax Simpson
Mr William Loschert
Mr and Mrs Mark Loveday
Ronald and Rita McAulay
McKinsey and Company Inc
Mr and Mrs Donald Main
Sir John Madejski OBE DL
Her Majesty's Government
The Manifold Trust
Mr Javad and Mrs Narmina Marandi
Marks and Spencer
Philip and Val Marsden
The Paul Mellon Estate
The Mercers' Company
The Monument Trust
The Henry Moore Foundation
The Moorgate Trust Fund
Mr and Mrs Robert Miller
The late Mr Minoru Mori HON KBE and Mrs Mori
Robin Heller Moss
Simon and Midge Palley
The Peacock Trust
P F Charitable Trust
Olive Pettit
Mr and Mrs Maurice Pinto
The Edith and Ferdinand Porjes Charitable Trust
John Porter Charitable Trust
The Porter Foundation
Mrs Tineke Pugh
Rio Tinto plc
Mr John A Roberts FRIBA
Sir Simon and Lady Robertson
The Ronson Foundation
Rothmans International plc
The Rothschild Foundation
Mr Jonathan Ruffer
Dame Jillian Sackler DBE
Mr Wafic Rida Saïd
Mrs Jean Sainsbury
The Saison Foundation
The Basil Samuel Charitable Trust
Mrs Coral Samuel CBE
The Schroder Foundation
Mr Sean Scully RA
Mrs Louisa Service OBE JP
Mr and Mrs Jake Shafran
Mr Richard S Sharp
Mrs Stella Shawzin
Miss Dasha Shenkman
William and Maureen Shenkman
The Archie Sherman Charitable Trust
The late Pauline Sitwell
Mr James C Slaughter
Mr Brian Smith
Sir Paul and Lady Smith
Oliver Stanley Charitable Trust
The Swire Charitable Trust
Sir Hugh Sykes DL
The late Sir Anthony Tennant and Lady Tennant
Baron Lorne Thyssen-Bornemisza
Tomasso Brothers Fine Art
Ware and Edythe Travelstead
Mr and Mrs Julian Treger
The Trusthouse Charitable Foundation
The Douglas Turner Trust
Unilever plc
Sir Siegmund Warburg's Voluntary Settlement
The Weldon UK Charitable Trust
The Welton Foundation
Sian and Matthew Westerman
The Weston family
Mr W. Galen Weston and the Hon Mrs Hilary M. Weston
The Garfield Weston Foundation
Mr Chris Wilkinson OBE RA
Manuela and Ivan Wirth
The Maurice Wohl Charitable Foundation
The Wolfson Foundation
The Lord Leonard and Lady Estelle Wolfson Foundation

and those who wish to remain anonymous

## Trustees

Lord Davies of Abersoch CBE (Chairman)
President of the Royal Academy (ex officio)
Treasurer of the Royal Academy (ex officio)
Secretary and Chief Executive – Charles Saumarez Smith
Petr Aven
Brooke Brown Barzun
Sir David Cannadine FBA
Sir Richard Carew-Pole Bt OBE DL
Richard Chang
Adrian Cheng
Lloyd Dorfman CBE
Stephen Fry
HRH Princess Marie-Chantal of Greece
Mrs Henry J Heinz HON DBE
Lady Suzanne Heywood
Mrs Anya Hindmarch MBE
Alistair Johnston CMG
Declan Kelly
Philip Marsden (Deputy Chairman)
Sir Keith Mills GBE DL
Mrs Minoru Mori
Christina Ong
Mrs Frances Osborne
Lord Rose of Monewden
Dame Jillian Sackler DBE
Robert Suss
Sir David Tang KBE
Sian Westerman
Peter Williams
Iwan Wirth

Honorary President
HRH The Prince of Wales

Emeritus Trustees
Lord Aldington
Susan Burns
Sir James Butler CBE DL
The Rt Hon the Lord Carrington KG GCMC CH MC
Sir Trevor Chinn CVO
John Coombe
Ambassador Edward E Elson
John Entwistle OBE
Michael Gee
The Rt Hon the Earl of Gowrie
Reverend C. Hugh Hildesley
Susan Ho
Lady Judge CBE
Gabrielle Jungels-Winkler
Lady Lever
Sir Sydney Lipworth QC
The Rt Hon Lord Luce GCVO DL
Lady Myners
Eddy Pirard
John Raisman CBE
John Roberts FRIBA
Sir Simon Robertson
Sir Evelyn de Rothschild
Mrs Maryam Sachs
Richard Sharp

## Patrons

The Royal Academy is extremely grateful to all its Patrons, who generously support every aspect of its work.

Chair
Robert Suss

Platinum
Celia and Edward Atkin CBE
Mr and Mrs Christopher Bake
Alex Beard and Emma Vernetti
Mr Stephen Gosztony
Mr Jim Grover
Charles and Kaaren Hale
Mr Yan Huo
Mr Maurice Pinto
Mr and Mrs Jake Shafran
David and Sophie Shalit
Sir Alan and Lady Yarrow

Gold
Molly Lowell Borthwick
Sir Francis Brooke Bt
Gaurav and Karima Burman
Christopher and Alex Courage
Mrs Robin Hambro
Ted Hirst
Mrs Elizabeth Hosking
Mr Michael Jacobson
Miss Joanna Kaye
William and Lavina Lim
Sir Sydney Lipworth QC and Lady Lipworth CBE
Mr Nicholas Maclean
Sir Keith and Lady Mills
Lady Rayne Lacey
Jean and Geoffrey Redman-Brown
The Lady Renwick of Clifton
Richard Sharp
Jane Spack
David Stileman
Mr Robert John Yerbury

Silver
Ms Susanna Abu Zalaf
Lady Agnew
Mrs Anna Albertini
Miss H J C Anstruther
Mrs Jane Barker
Catherine Baxendale
The Duke of Beaufort
Mrs J K M Bentley, Liveinart
Eleanor E Brass
Mr and Mrs Richard Briggs OBE
Mrs Marcia Brocklebank
Jeremy Brown
Mrs Rosamond Brown
Mr and Mrs Zak Brown
Lord Browne of Madingley
Mr F. A. A. Carnwath CBE
Sir Roger and Lady Carr
Mrs Ann Chapman-Daniel
Mr Matthew Charlton
Sir Trevor and Lady Chinn
Mr and Mrs George Coelho
Denise Cohen Charitable Trust
Sir Ronald and Lady Cohen
Ms Linda Cooper
Mark and Cathy Corbett
Mr and Mrs Ken Costa
Julian Darley and Helga Sands
Gwendoline, Countess of Dartmouth
Mr Daniel Davies
Peter and Andrea De Haan
The de Laszlo Foundation
Dr Anne Dornhorst
Mr and Mrs Jim Downing
Thomas A Doyle
Ms Noreen Doyle
Mrs Janet Dwek
Lord and Lady Egremont
Bryan Ferry
Benita and Gerald Fogel
Mr Sam Fogg
Mrs Jocelyn Fox
Arnold Fulton
Mrs Jill Garcia
The Robert Gavron Charitable Trust
Mrs Mina Gerowin Herrmann
Caroline and Alan Gillespie
Mr Mark Glatman
Lady Gosling
Piers Gough RA
HRH Princess Marie-Chantal of Greece
Mrs Margaret Guitar
Mrs Jennifer Hall
Mr James Hambro
Sir John Hegarty and Miss Philippa Crane
Sir Michael and Lady Heller
Mrs Katrin Henkel
Ms Margarita Hernandez
Lady Heseltine
Mary Hobart
Anne Holmes-Drewry
Mr Philip Hudson
Mr and Mrs Jon Hunt
S Isern-Feliu
Mrs Caroline Jackson
Sir Martin and Lady Jacomb
Mrs Raymonde Jay
Mr Alistair DK Johnston CMG and Ms Christina M Nijman
Fiona Johnstone
Mrs Ghislaine Kane
Dr Elisabeth Kehoe
Princess Jeet Khemka
Mr D H Killick
Mrs Aboudi Kosta
Mr and Mrs Herbert Kretzmer
Kathryn Langridge
Mr George Lengvari and Mrs Inez Lengvari
Lady Lever of Manchester
Miss R Lomax-Simpson
The Hon Mrs Virginia Lovell
Mr and Mrs Henry Lumley
Gillian McIntosh
Sir John Mactaggart
Madeline and Donald Main
Scott and Laura Malkin
Mr and Mrs Richard C Martin
Andrew and Judith McKinna
Zvi & Ofra Meitar Family Fund
Mrs Elizabeth Mellows
Mr Daniel Mitchell
Mrs Susan Moehlmann
Dr Ann Naylor
Mr Richard Orders
Mr Michael Palin
John Pattisson
Nicholas B Paumgarten
Mr and Mrs D J Peacock
David Pike
Mr and Mrs Anthony Pitt-Rivers
Mr Basil Postan
Mrs Becky Quintavalle
Mr Pinto Rai Dhir
John and Anne Raisman
Serena Reeve
Rothschild Foundation
Miss Elaine Rowley
Sir Paul and Lady Ruddock
Mrs Janice Sacher
Mr Adrian Sassoon
Christina Countess of Shaftesbury
Mr Robert N Shapiro
Mr Richard Simmons CBE
Alan and Marianna Simpson
Roberta Downs Stewart Sandeman
The Lady Henrietta St George
Anne Elizabeth Tasca
Lady Tennant
Nick Thexton
Anthony Thornton
Mr Anthony J Todd
Mrs Carolyn Townsend
Miss M L Ulfane
John and Carol Wates
Mrs Anja Weiss
Edna and Willard Weiss
The Duke and Duchess of Wellington
Anthony and Rachel Williams
Mrs Adriana Winters
Alex Zadah

Patron Donors
Stephen Barry Charitable Settlement
William Brake Charitable Trust
Jean Cass MBE and Eric Cass MBE
Peter and Elizabeth Goulds, L.A. Louver
Jacqueline and Marc Leland
Mrs Josephine Lumley
The Michael H Sacher Charitable Trust
H M Sassoon Charitable Trust
Mrs Patricia Yunghanns

and those who wish to remain anonymous

## Architecture Patrons

Gold
Mr Bruce Roe
Mr Peter Williams

Silver
Jacqueline and Jonathan Gestetner
Lifschutz Davidson Sandilands
Mr and Mrs Robin Lough
Ms Rebecca Early Marques
Mr Simon Mills
Stephen Musgrave
Mrs Noreen L Poulson
Christopher J Viney

and those who wish to remain anonymous

## Benjamin West Group Patrons

Chair
Lady Judge CBE

Platinum
David Giampaolo

Gold
Mr Steve Cardell
Lady Barbara Judge CBE
Mr Christian Levett
Ms Alessandra Morra
Afsaneh Moshiri
Mrs Deborah Scott

Silver
Lady J Lloyd Adamson
Mr and Mrs Amir Adnani
Mr Dimitry Afanasiev
Mrs Spindrift Al Swaidi
Poppy Allonby
Ms Sol Anitua
Ms Ruth Anderson
Mr Andy Ash
Marco and Francesca Assetto
Mrs Leslie Bacon
Mr Sam Bagot
Mr and Mrs Benjelloun
Mr Mark Bergman
Naomi and Ted Berk
Jean and John Botts
Ms Pauline Cacucciolo
Mrs Sophie Cahu
Brian and Melinda Carroll
Mrs Caroline Cartellieri Karlsen
Damian and Anastasia Chunilal
Andrew and Stefanie Clarke
Mr and Mrs Paul Collins
Vanessa Colomar de Enserro
Ms Ruth Crabbe
Christophe de Taurines
Cathy Dishner
Mr and Mrs Jeff Eldredge
Mr David Fawkes
Mrs Stroma Finston
Cyril and Christine Freedman
Ronald and Helen Freeman
Ms Nicola Green
Mr and Mrs Jan Hagemeier
Mr Christopher Harrison
Katie Jackson
Syrie Johnson
Suzanne and Michael Johnson
Miss Rebecca Kemsley
Suzanne Leguel
Lord and Lady Leitch
Mrs Stephanie Léouzon
Ms Ida Levine
Mr Guido Lombardo
Charles G Lubar
Mrs Victoria Mills
Neil Osborn and Holly Smith
Lady Purves
Ms Elena Shchukina
Mr Stuart Southall
Sir Hugh and Lady Sykes
Mr Ian Taylor
Miss Lori Tedesco
Frederick and Kathryn Uhde
Debra Valentine
Mrs Neena Vaswani
Mr Craig D Weaver
Professor Peter Whiteman QC
Mr and Mrs John Winter

and those who wish to remain anonymous

## Contemporary Circle Patrons

Chair
Susan Elliott

Gold
Joan and Robin Alvarez
Mr and Mrs Thomas Berger
Ms Ilaria Bulgari
Mr Jeremy Coller
Ms Miel de Botton
Mr and Mrs Eric Dusansky
Shareen Khattar
Mr and Mrs Scott Mead
Simon and Sabi North
Yana and Stephen Peel
Francoise Sarre
Mr Kevin Sneader and Ms Amy Muntner
Robert and Simone Suss
Manuela and Iwan Wirth

Silver
Mrs Susie Allen-Huxley
Mrs Charlotte Artus
Mr Timothy Attias
Mrs Niloufar Bakhtiar-Bakhtiari
Ms Martina Batovic
Mr David Baty
Charles Dib & Aurore Belkin
Ms Sara Berman
Valeria Bertoli
Viscountess Bridgeman
Simon Morris and Annalisa Burello
Ms Debra Burt
Mr Steven Chambers
Jenny Christensson
Nadia Crandall
Mrs Caroline Cullinan
Mrs Georgina David
Helen and Colin David
Patrick and Benedicte de Nonneville
Mollie Dent-Brocklehurst
Mr Paul Doyle
Mrs Jennifer Duke
Susan Elliott
Mr Timothy Ellis
Maria Almudena Garcia Cano
Mr Stephen Garrett
Stephen and Margarita Grant
Jed and Allison Hart
Mrs Susan Hayden
Tristan and Michele Hillgarth
Mr and Mrs Urs Hodler
Mr Gerald Kidd
Mr Matthew Langton
Mr Jeff Lowe
Nozha Khader
Mrs Julie Lee
Mrs Sophie Mirman
Victoria Miro
Mrs Joanna Nicholls
Mr and Mrs Jeremy Nicholson
Mrs Tessa Nicholson
Dr Carolina Minio Paluello
Roderick and Maria Peacock
Mr Malcolm Poynton
Mrs Tineke Pugh
Mr Paul Price
Mrs Yosmarvi Rivas Rangel
Mrs Catherine Rees
Miss Harriet Ruffer
Edwina Sassoon
Ms Elke Seebauer
Mr Eric Shen
Richard and Susan Shoylekov
Mrs Veronica Simmons
Karen Smith
Jeffery C Sugarman and Alan D H Newham
Mrs Arabella Tullo
Anna Watkins
Mrs Debora Wingate
Mr and Mrs Maurice Wolridge

Patron Donor
Ms Cynthia Wu

and those who wish to remain anonymous

## International Patrons

Mr Howard Bilton
Lady Alison Deighton
Jacques and Valentina Drouin
Mr and Mrs Stephen Fitzgerald
Mr Alexis Habib
Joanna Kalmer
Nelson Leong
Mrs Fatima Maleki
Mr Hideyuki Osawa
Frances Reynolds
Mr Thaddaeus Ropac
Mrs Sabine Sarikhani
Mr and Mrs Julian Treger
Mr Bruno Wang
Sian and Matthew Westerman
Mr and Mrs Basil Zirinis

Patron Donors
Mr Richard Chang

and those who wish to remain anonymous

## RA Schools Patrons

Chair
Mr Keir McGuinness

Platinum
Mr Mark Hix
Lance and Lisa West

Gold
Sam and Rosie Berwick
Mrs Sarah Chenevix-Trench
Ms Cynthia Corbett
Rosalyn and Hugo Henderson
Mr Charles Irving
Christopher Kneale
Mr William Loschert
Mr Keir McGuinness
Janet and Andrew Newman
Carol Sellars

Silver
Lord and Lady Aldington
Mrs Elizabeth Alston
Sarah Barker and Daniel Freeman
Mr and Mrs Jonathan and Sarah Bayliss
Mr Paul Beatson
Joanna Bird
Alex Haidas and Thalia Chryssikou
Rosalind Clayton
Mr Richard Clothier
Marian Cramer
Ms Davina Dickson
Mrs Dominic Dowley
Nigel and Christine Evans
Miss Roxanna Farboud
Mrs Catherine Farquharson
Catherine Ferguson
Adam Gahlin
Gaye and Kent Gardner
Mr Mark Garthwaite

Mrs Michael Green
Mr and Mrs G Halamish
Mr Lindsay Hamilton
Mrs Lesley Haynes
Mr Philip Hodgkinson
Professor and Mrs Ken Howard RA
Mark and Fiona Hutchinson
Mrs Marcelle Joseph
Mr and Mrs S Kahan
Mr Paul Kempe
Mrs Alkistis Koukouliou
Nicolette Kwok
Mrs Anna Lee
Mr and Mrs Mark Loveday
Philip and Val Marsden
Itxaso Mediavilla-Murray
The Lord and Lady Myners
Mr William Ramsay
Ms Mouna Rebeiz
Peter Rice Esq
Anthony and Sally Salz
Brian D Smith
Lisa Stocker
Miss Sarah Straight
Mr Ray Treen
Mrs Diana Wilkinson
Marek and Penny Wojciechowski

and those who wish to remain
anonymous

Young Patrons

Chair
May Calil

Gold
Mr Alexander Green

Silver
Ms Léonie Achammer
Kalita al Swaidi
Ms Ingrid Anid
Ms Katharine Arnold
Miss Henrietta Ash
Sophie Ashby
Ms Vanessa Aubry
Mr Gergely Battha-Pajor
Ms Elif Bayoglu
Lucinda Bellm
Mr Alexander Bradford
May Calil
Mr Alessandro Conti
Mr Alexander Flint
Ms Emily Fraser
Mr Rollo Gabb
Flora Goodwin
Miss Amelia Hunton
Ms Dalya Islam
Mrs Fernanda Jess
Ms Huma Kabakci
Miss Min Kemp
Miss Tiggi Kempe
Mr Callum Kempe
Alexandra Ames Kornman
Benjamin Lockwood
Wei-Lyn Loh
Tessa Lord
Christina Makris
Mr Jean-David Malat
Ignacio Marinho
Isabella Marinho
Florence Mather
Mr Oliver Morris-Jones
Ziba Sarikhani
Ms Jane Singer
Mr Amar Singh
Mr Mandeep Singh
Emily Skeppner
Mr Henry Thorogood
Mr Milan Tomic
Sydney Townsend
Mr Vassili Tsarenkov
Miss Navann Ty
Ms Zeynep Uzuner
Alexandra Warder
Mark Whitcroft
Ms India Williamson
Miss Eugenie York
Miss Burcu Yuksel

and those who wish to remain
anonymous

Trusts, Foundations
and Charitable Giving

Artists Collecting Society
The Atlas Fund
The Albert Van den Bergh
    Charitable Trust
The Nicholas Bacon Charitable Trust
The Bomonty Charitable Trust
The Charlotte Bonham-Carter
    Charitable Trust
William Brake Charitable Trust R M
    Burton 1998 Charitable Trust
P H G Cadbury Charitable Trust
The Carew Pole Charitable Trust
C H K Charities Limited
The Clore Duffield Foundation
John S Cohen Foundation
The Sidney and Elizabeth Corob
    Charitable Trust
The Dovehouse Trust
The Gilbert and Eileen Edgar
    Foundation
The John Ellerman Foundation
Lucy Mary Ewing Charitable Trust
JM Finn and Co.
The Margery Fish Charity
The Flow Foundation
The Garfield Weston Foundation
Gatsby Charitable Foundation
The Golden Bottle Trust

Sue Hammerson Charitable Trust
The Charles Hayward Foundation
Heritage Lottery Fund
Hiscox plc
Holbeck Charitable Trust
The Harold Hyam Wingate Foundation
Intrinsic Value Investors
The Ironmongers' Company
The Emmanuel Kaye Foundation
The Kindersley Foundation
The de Laszlo Foundation
The Leche Trust
The Maccabeans
The McCorquodale Charitable Trust
The Machin Foundation
The Paul Mellon Centre
The Paul Mellon Estate
The Mercers' Company
Margaret and Richard Merrell
    Foundation
The Millichope Foundation
The Mondriaan Foundation
The Monument Trust
The Henry Moore Foundation
The Mulberry Trust
The J Y Nelson Charitable Trust
The Old Broad Street Charity Trust
The Peacock Charitable Trust
The Pennycress Trust
PF Charitable Trust
The Stanley Picker Charitable Trust
The Pidem Fund
The Edith and Ferdinand Porjes
    Charitable Trust
Mr and Mrs J A Pye's
    Charitable Settlement
Rayne Foundation
T Rippon & Sons (Holdings) Ltd
Rootstein Hopkins Foundation
The Rose Foundation
Schroder Charity Trust
The Sellars Charitable Trust
The Archie Sherman Charitable Trust
The Alfred Teddy Smith and Zsuzsi
    Roboz Art Fund
Paul Smith and Pauline Denyer-Smith
The South Square Trust
Spencer Charitable Trust
Oliver Stanley Charitable Trust
Peter Storrs Trust
Strand Parishes Trust
The Joseph Strong Frazer Trust
The Swan Trust
Taylor Family Foundation
Thaw Charitable Trust
Sir Jules Thorn Charitable Trust
The Bruce Wake Charity
Celia Walker Art Foundation
Weinstock Fund
Wilkinson Eyre Architects
The Spencer Wills Trust
The Maurice Wohl Charitable
    Foundation
The Wolfson Foundation

Royal Academy America

Honorary Patron
HRH Princess Alexandra,
    The Hon Lady Ogilvy KG GCVO

Board Members
Professor Sir David Cannadine FBA
Jim Clerkin
The Hon Anne Collins
Elizabeth Crain
C Hugh Hildesley
David Hockney OM CH RA
Brian Kelley
Declan Kelly, Chairman
Mr Kenneth Jay Lane
Marc Lasry
Andrew Liveris
Monika McLennan
Sir David Manning GCMG CVO
Richard J Miller, Jr, Esq
Mr David Remfry MBE RA
Dame Jillian Sackler DBE
Ms Joan N Stern, Esq
Raymond Svider
Frederick B Whittemore

Chairmen Emeriti
James Benson
Ambassador Philip Lader
President Emerita
Kathrine (Kitty) Ockenden OBE

Honorary Trustees
Christopher Le Brun PRA
Sir Nicholas Grimshaw CBE PPRA
Professor Phillip King CBE PPRA

Royal Academy America Supporters
Mr and Mrs Charles N Atkins
Mr and Mrs Steven
    and Anne Marie Ausnit
John Berggruen
Mr Donald Best
Mrs CeCe Black
Mr Constantin R Boden
Mrs Deborah Loeb Brice
Mr and Mrs Calvin Cafritz
Ms Patrice Clareman
Ms Alyce Faye Cleese
The Hon Anne Collins
Zita Davisson
Edward Field and Jennifer Kyner
Katherine Findlay
Mr Lawrence S Friedland
Mr and Mrs Ellis Goodman
Mrs Helen Groves
Ms Harriet Heyman and
    Mr Michael Moritz

C Hugh Hildesley
David Hockney OM CH RA
Ms Jo Hannah Hoehn
Dr Bruce C Horten and Mr Aaron Lieber
Ellen E. Howe
Mr and Mrs Philip Keevil
The Hon General Samuel K Lessey, Jr
Leon Levy Foundation
Arthur L Loeb
Mr Henry S Lynn, Jr
The Hon and Mrs Earle Mack
Ms Clare E McKeon
Ms Christine Mainwaring-Samwell
J Maxwell Moran
Mr and Mrs Wilson Nolen
Mrs Charles W Olson III
Cynthia Hazen Polsky and
    Leon B Polsky
Mrs Eileen Powers
Mr Paul K Rooney
Mr and Mrs Elihu Rose
Dame Jillian Sackler DBE
Mrs Louisa Stude Sarofim
Mrs Sylvia Scheuer
Mr and Mrs Stanley De Forest Scott
Mrs Georgia Shreve
Sylvia Slifka
Mr and Mrs Morton I Sosland
Mrs Frederick M Stafford
Mr and Mrs Robert K Steel
Joan N Stern, Esq
Martin J Sullivan OBE
Mr Peter Trippi
Christopher Tsai
Frederick B Whittemore
Ms Margaret Williamson

Corporate and Foundation Support
Henry C Beck Jr Charitable Trust
British Airways plc
Crankstart Foundation
Sunny and Frederick Dupree Children's
    Trust
The Charles and Carmen de Mora
    Hale Foundation
Leon Levy Foundation
Andrew W Mellon Foundation
Morris and McVeigh LLP
Siezen Foundation
Smart Family Foundation
Starr Foundation

Corporate Members of
the Royal Academy

Launched in 1988, the Royal Academy's
Corporate Membership Scheme has
proved highly successful. Corporate
membership offers benefits for staff,
clients and community partners and
access to the Academy's facilities and
resources. The outstanding support we
receive from companies via the scheme
is vital to the continuing success of the
Academy and we thank all members for
their valuable support and continued
enthusiasm.

Premier Level Members
American Express®
The Arts Club
Bird & Bird LLP
BNY Mellon
Cazenove Capital Management
Chestertons
Christie's
Deutsche Bank AG London
FTI Consulting
HS1
Insight Investment Management
JLL
JM Finn & Co.
JTI
KPMG LLP
Linklaters
Newton Investment Management
Sanlam
Smith & Williamson
Sotheby's
Turkish Ceramics
XL Catlin

Corporate Members
Bloomberg LP
BMO Global Asset Management
The Boston Consulting Group UK LLP
Capital Group
Clifford Chance
Dechert
GAM London Ltd
Generation Investment Management
    LLP
GlaxoSmithKline plc
Hansteen Holdings
John Lewis Partnership
Lindsell Train
Marie Curie Cancer Care
Moelis & Company
Morgan Stanley
Native Land
Quilter Cheviot
Rathbones
Ridgeway Partners
The Royal Society of Chemistry
Slaughter and May
Trowers & Hamlins LLP
UBS Wealth Managment
Vitol SA
Weil, Gotshal & Manges

Associate Members
Bank of America Merrill Lynch
BNP Paribas
Bonhams 1793 Ltd

British American Tobacco
The Cultivist
EY
Heidrick & Struggles
Imperial College Healthcare Charity
Jones Day
Lazard
Lubbock Fine
Momart
Pentland Group plc

Supporters of Past Exhibitions

The President and Council of the Royal
Academy would like to thank the
following supporters for their generous
contributions towards major exhibitions
in the last ten years:

2015

In the Age of Giorgione
2009–2016 Season supported by JTI
Maserati
Royal Academy International Patrons

Painting the Modern Garden: Monet to
Matisse
BNY Mellon, Partner of the Royal
    Academy of Arts

Jean-Etienne Liotard
2009–2016 Season supported by JTI
The Pictet Group
Cockayne Grants for the Arts, a donor
    advised fund of London Community
    Foundation
Mr and Mrs Bart T. Tiernan
The Jean-Etienne Liotard Supporters'
    Group

Joseph Cornell: Wanderlust
2009–2016 Season supported by JTI
The Terra Foundation for American Art
The Cornell Leadership Circle

Premiums, RA Schools Annual Dinner
and Auction and RA Schools Show 2015
Newton Investment Management

247th Summer Exhibition
Insight Investment

Richard Diebenkorn
2009–2016 Season supported by JTI
The Terra Foundation for American Art

Rubens and His Legacy
BNY Mellon, Partner of the Royal
    Academy of Arts

2015 Architecture Programme
Lead supporter Turkishceramics

2014

Allen Jones RA
Lead Series Supporter JTI

Giovanni Battista Moroni
2009–2016 Season supported by JTI
UBI Banca

Anselm Kiefer
BNP Paribas
White Cube

Radical Geometry: Modern Art of South
America from the Patricia Phelps de
Cisneros Collection
2009–2016 Season supported by JTI
Christie's

Dennis Hopper: The Lost Album
Lead Series Supporter JTI
Nikon UK

Premiums, RA Schools Annual Dinner
and Auction and RA Schools Show 2014
Newton Investment Management

246th Summer Exhibition
Insight Investment

Dream, Draw, Work: Architectural
Drawings by Norman Shaw RA
Lowell Libson Ltd
Collections and Library Supporters
    Circle

Renaissance Impressions: Chiaroscuro
Woodcuts from the Collections of Georg
Baselitz and the Albertina, Vienna
JTI
Edwards Wildman

Sensing Spaces: Architecture Reimagined
Scott and Laura Malkin
AKT II
Arauco

2013

Bill Woodrow RA
Lead Series Supporter JTI
The Henry Moore Foundation

Daumier
2009–2016 Season supported by JTI

Australia
National Gallery of Australia
Qantas Airways
The Woolmark Company

Richard Rogers RA: Inside Out
Ferrovial Agroman
Heathrow Airport
Laing O'Rourke

Mexico: A Revolution in Art, 1910–1940
2009–2016 Season supported by JTI
Art Mentor Foundation Lucerne
Conaculta

Mexican Agency for International
    Development Cooperation
Sectur
Visit Mexico

245th Summer Exhibition
Insight Investment

George Bellows
2009–2016 Season supported by JTI
Edwards Wildman

Premiums, RA Schools Annual Dinner
and Auction and RA Schools Show 2013
Newton Investment Management

Manet: Portraying Life
BNY Mellon, Partner of the Royal
    Academy of Arts

2012

Mariko Mori
JTI

RA Now
JTI

Bronze
Christian Levett and Mougins Museum
    of Classical Art
Daniel Katz Gallery
Baron Lorne Thyssen-Bornemisza
John and Fausta Eskenazi
The Ruddock Foundation for the Arts
Tomasso Brothers Fine Art
Jon and Barbara Landau
Janine and J. Tomilson Hill
Embassy of the Kingdom of the
    Netherlands
Eskenazi Limited
Lisson Gallery
Alexis Gregory
Alan and Mary Hobart
Richard de Unger and Adeela Qureshi
Rossi & Rossi Ltd
Embassy of Israel

244th Summer Exhibition
Insight Investment

From Paris: A Taste for Impressionism –
Paintings from the Clark
2009–2016 Season supported by JTI
Edwards Wildman
The Annenberg Foundation

Premiums, RA Schools Annual Dinner
and Auction and RA Schools Show 2012
Newton Investment Management

Johan Zoffany RA: Society Observed
2009–2016 Season supported by JTI
Cox & Kings

Building the Revolution: Soviet Art and
Architecture 1915–1935
2009–2016 Season supported by JTI
The Ove Arup Foundation
The Norman Foster Foundation
Richard and Ruth Rogers

David Hockney RA: A Bigger Picture
BNP Paribas
Welcome to Yorkshire: Tourism Partner
Visit Hull & East Yorkshire: Supporting
    Tourism Partner
NEC

2011

Degas and the Ballet:
Picturing Movement
BNY Mellon, Partner of the Royal
    Academy of Arts
Region Holdings
Blavatnik Family Foundation

Eyewitness: Hungarian Photography in
the Twentieth Century. Brassaï, Capa,
Kertész, Moholy-Nagy, Munkácsi
2009–2016 Season supported by JTI
Hungarofest
OTP Bank

243rd Summer Exhibition
Insight Investment

Premiums, RA Schools Annual Dinner
and Auction and RA Schools Show 2011
Newton Investment Management

Watteau: The Drawings
2009–2016 Season supported by JTI
Region Holdings

Modern British Sculpture
American Express Foundation
The Henry Moore Foundation
Hauser & Wirth
Art Mentor Foundation Lucerne
Sotheby's
Blain Southern
Welcome to Yorkshire: Tourism Partner

2010

GSK Contemporary – Aware: Art
Fashion Identity
GlaxoSmithKline

Pioneering Painters: The Glasgow Boys
1880–1900
2009–2016 Season supported by JTI
Glasgow Museums

Treasures from Budapest: European
Masterpieces from Leonardo to Schiele
OTP Bank
Villa Budapest
Daniel Katz Gallery, London
Cox & Kings: Travel Partner

Sargent and the Sea
2009–2016 Season supported by JTI

242nd Summer Exhibition
Insight Investment

Paul Sandby RA: Picturing Britain,
A Bicentenary Exhibition
2009–2016 Season supported by JTI

The Real Van Gogh: The Artist and
His Letters
BNY Mellon, Partner of the Royal
    Academy of Arts
Hiscox plc
Heath Lambert
Cox & Kings: Travel Partner

RA Outreach Programme
Deutsche Bank AG

2009

GSK Contemporary
GlaxoSmithKline

Wild Thing: Epstein, Gaudier-Brzeska,
Gill
2009–2016 Season supported by JTI
BNP Paribas
The Henry Moore Foundation

Anish Kapoor
JTI
Richard Chang
Richard and Victoria Sharp
Louis Vuitton
The Henry Moore Foundation

J W Waterhouse: The Modern
Pre-Raphaelite
2009–2016 Season supported by JTI
Champagne Perrier-Jouët
GasTerra
Gasunie

241st Summer Exhibition
Insight Investment

Kuniyoshi. From the Arthur R. Miller
Collection
2009–2016 Season supported by JTI
Canon
Cox & Kings: Travel Partner

Premiums and RA Schools Show
Mizuho International plc

RA Outreach Programme
Deutsche Bank AG

2008

GSK Contemporary
GlaxoSmithKline

Byzantium 330–1453
J F Costopoulos Foundation
A G Leventis Foundation
Stavros Niarchos Foundation
Cox & Kings: Travel Partner

Miró, Calder, Giacometti, Braque:
Aimé Maeght and His Artists
BNP Paribas

Vilhelm Hammershøi: The Poetry of
Silence
OAK Foundation Denmark
Novo Nordisk

240th Summer Exhibition
Insight Investment

Premiums and RA Schools Show
Mizuho International plc

RA Outreach Programme
Deutsche Bank AG

From Russia: French and Russian
Master Paintings 1870–1925 from
Moscow and St Petersburg
E.ON
2008 Season supported by Sotheby's

2007

Paul Mellon's Legacy: A Passion for
British Art
The Bank of New York Mellon
Georg Baselitz
Eurohypo AG

239th Summer Exhibition
Insight Investment

Impressionists by the Sea
Farrow & Ball

Premiums and RA Schools Show
Mizuho International plc

RA Outreach Programme
Deutsche Bank AG

The Unknown Monet
Bank of America